KNOW YOUR BIBLE

Commentary for our times on the Hebrew Prophets and Holy Writings (NaKh)

I0154111

by

Rabbi Avraham Greenbaum

Edited by Nachum Shaw

Promised Land

JERUSALEM   LONDON   NEW YORK

For further information:

Promised Land Publishers

Apt. 8, 5 Gimmel Alroyi St.

Jerusalem 9210808

ISRAEL

or

Promised Land Publishers

8 Woodville Road

London NW11 9TN

ENGLAND

or

Promised Land Publishers

67 Wood Hollow Lane

New Rochelle

NY 10804

USA

Email: promisedland920@gmail.com

www.promisedlandpublishers.com

Volume One

JOSHUA

JUDGES

SAMUEL

KINGS

KNOW YOUR BIBLE

*On Simchat Torah, we conclude the annual reading of the Five Books of Moses and immediately start over with Bereishit (Genesis 1). Likewise on Simchat Torah we read Joshua 1 as the Haftarah – the supplementary reading from the prophets – thereby taking the first step in studying the NaKh (Nevi'im, The Prophets and Ketuvim, The Writings).***

Although KNOW YOUR BIBLE can be studied at whatever pace you choose, you should know that by reading two chapters every day, you can complete the world's greatest Book of Wisdom in one year!

The practice of studying two chapters of NaKh every day starting immediately after Simchat Torah is recommended in "Yesod VeShoresh Ha-Avodah" (Foundation and Root of Service") by Rabbi Alexander Ziskind of Horodna (d. 1794), a guide to devotion endorsed by all streams of Torah Jewry (see Gate 6 Chapter 2, The Order of Study).

Just as we commence our study of NaKh, so may we pursue it until we complete it with G-d's help. "Let no error befall us and let us not stumble in any matter of law. Let us not call that which is impure pure or that which is forbidden permitted. Let none of us stumble: For HaShem will give wisdom: from His mouth are knowledge and understanding. Open our eyes and let us behold wonders from Your Torah!"

"Try to go through all our holy books in the course of a lifetime so that you will have visited every place in the Torah. Wealthy people constantly travel from place to place, spending enormous sums in order to boast about where they have been. In the same way in this life you should visit all the holy places in the Torah. Then in the future life you will be able to take pride in having visited every place in our holy literature. For in the world to come you will remember everything you have ever learned."

RABBI NACHMAN

CONTENTS

יהושע

JOSHUA

CHAPTER 1

"MOSES MY SERVANT IS DEAD"

The Book of Joshua is the direct continuation from the end of Deuteronomy which narrates the death of Moses. Prior to his death, Moses had already said to Israel: "For I know that after my death you will surely go to ruin and depart from the path that I have commanded you, and evil will befall you at the end of days because you have done evil in the eyes of HaShem to anger Him with the work of your hands" (Deut. 31:29).

The entire NaKh will narrate the story and draw out the moral of this departure from the path with its terrible consequences, tracing the history of Israel in their time of glory (the conquest of the land and the building of Solomon's Temple) and their time of decline (destruction of the Temple and exile).

Our rabbis taught that "the face of Moses was like the face of the sun, while the face of Joshua was like the face of the moon" (Bava Batra 75a). Now that the sun had gone down with the death of Moses, it was time for the moon to shine. As long as the moon is aligned with the sun, the entire face of the moon is lit up and perfectly reflects the light of the sun. As long as Joshua reflected Moses' Torah, the people succeeded. Joshua was from the tribe of Ephraim (son of Joseph, son of Rachel, Jacob's beloved). The task of Ephraim is to actualize the keeping of the Torah in this real, material world (and thus Rachel signifies the Shechinah, the Indwelling Presence in this world). Keeping the Torah to perfection in this world had to be accomplished in God's chosen land, the Land of Israel, and thus Joshua's task was to lead the people in and conquer the land. But when the moon is not aligned with the sun, its face becomes successively darkened. Thus, it was Ephraim under the leadership of Jeraboam - Yeravam ben Nevat - who led the people away from the path, which brought about the exile, as we will see later. The people of Israel today must study and ponder the story of the NaKh and its moral in order to gain possession of the Land of Israel forever and shine its light to the whole world.

Joshua ch 1 vv 3-4 reiterates the boundaries of the Promised Land as already laid down in Numbers 34:1-15. Here in verse 4 we simply have a brief depiction of the "breadth" of the land (from the Wilderness of Zin up to the Euphrates), and its "length" (from those two points until the Great Sea, the Mediterranean). From verse 3 we learn that **after** Israel have conquered the entire Promised Land, then "any place where the sole of your footsteps I will give to you", thereby incorporating other territories (see Rashi on vv 3-4).

The condition upon which Israel is able to conquer and retain the Land is made completely clear here at the beginning of the Prophets: "Be strong and very firm to guard and practice according to all the Torah that Moses my servant commanded you..." (v 7). "And the book of this Torah shall not depart from your mouth..." (v 8). Everything depends on **keeping the Torah**, and this depends upon **constant study of the Torah by day and by night**. For then HaShem your God will be with you.

CHRONOLOGY OF THE ENTRY INTO THE LAND

Rashi proves from the text that it was on the 7th of Nissan that Joshua gave orders to prepare the people to cross the Jordan "in another three days" (v 11). The 7th of Nissan was the conclusion of the 30-day period of mourning for Moses, who died on the 7th of Adar (just as he had been born on that day, 3 months exactly before the 7th of Sivan, the day he was cast into the river and the date of the giving of the Torah 80 years later). The 10th of Nissan would be an appropriate day for the supernatural miracle of the parting of the Jordan, as it was the anniversary of the day when the Children of Israel took the

Paschal Lamb in Egypt just prior to the Exodus. Taking the lamb for sacrifice indicates submitting the power of nature, symbolized in the constellation of Aries, the "Ram", to the higher power of God. God controls nature and can bend it at will. God has the power to give a tiny nation dominion. If the people of Israel would keep to God's covenant they would always be above nature.

Joshua reminds the tribes of Reuven, Gad and the half of Menasheh who had taken their territories east of the Jordan of their commitment to help their brothers conquer the land of Canaan (v 14). Today this can be taken as a message to the Jews living in the Diaspora of their responsibility to identify with and help their brothers and sisters living in Israel in their struggle to settle the land in the proper way.

CHAPTER 2

Rashi proves from the text that Joshua sent the two spies to Jericho two days before he commanded the people to prepare to cross the Jordan. According to tradition the spies were Caleb (Joshua's only faithful companion among the 12 Spies sent by Moses) and Pinchas. Thus Joshua (Ephraim) works together with Caleb (the royal tribe of Judah) and Pinchas (the Priest). Why were they sent to Jericho specifically? Because Jericho "was as hard as all the rest of the country put together because it was on the border" (Rashi v 1) - it was the "lock" of the land of Israel (which was why in the days of Oslo the slogan was " Jericho first").

RAHAV- A GREAT HEROINE

Rahav is celebrated as one of the outstanding converts of all time (together with Hagar, Asnat, Tzipora, Shifra, Puah, Pharaoh's daughter Batya, Ruth and Yael). This is because Rahav acknowledged that "Hashem your God is God in heaven above and on the earth below" - she alone among the Canaanites was willing to join Israel instead of fighting them, because she recognized the divine hand in their Exodus from Egypt, the crossing of the Red Sea and their complete victory over the kings of the Emorites (vv 9-11). Her above-quoted declaration of faith is incorporated in the first paragraph of the Aleinu prayer recited at the end of each of the 3 daily prayer services.

Why did Rahav alone draw the right concluson? Was it because she was lowly and therefore humble? According to Targum Yonatan, Rahav was an innkeeper, but the Midrash Mechilta is less delicate. "She was 10 when the Children of Israel went out of Egypt and practiced prostitution for all of the forty years that they were in the wilderness. There was not a minister or dignitary that had not been with Rahab". That was how she knew so intimately that "no more spirit stands up in any man in face of you".

Rahav was obviously a woman of profound understanding as she drew the right conclusion. More than that, she showed the trait that is the hallmark of Israel: **chessed**, kindness. She did not **have** to save the two spies - she could quite easily have handed them over to the authorities. It was because she showed them pure **chessed** by saving them without expecting a reward that she felt able to ask them for pure **chessed** when the children of Israel would conquer Jericho: that they should save her life and that of her family. There was a great **tikkun** (repair) in her letting the spies out through her window in the city wall and later using the sign of the scarlet thread: her clients used to use a rope to climb in and out of her window unseen. According to the rabbis, Rahav prayed that the three elements of the wall, the window and the thread should atone for her neglect of the 3 commandments incumbent upon an Israelite woman: lighting the Shabbat lights, separating Challah and observing the laws of Niddah (family purity). The rabbis said that no less than eight prophets and priests were descended from Rahav, including Jeremiah and Hilkiah and the prophetess Hulda.

In their later history, Israel was frequently compared to a whore. Rahav is the outstanding example of such a woman who repented with all her heart and attained the greatest heights.

* Joshua 2:1-24 is read as the Haftarah of Parshat **Shelach Lecha**, Numbers 13:1-15:41 *

CHAPTERS 3

THE CROSSING OF THE JORDAN

"The sea saw and fled, the Jordan turned backwards" (Psalm 114:3).

Psalm 114 compares the greatness of the miracle of the splitting of the Jordan, enabling the Children of Israel to cross easily on dry land into their homeland, to the greatness of the splitting of the Red Sea, whereby they had been saved from their Egyptian enslavers. Likewise, Joshua, who presided over the splitting of the Jordan, is specifically compared in today's text to Moses, who raised his staff to split the sea (Joshua 4:14). However, it was not his staff that Joshua raised. Instead he instructed the Children of Israel to follow the Ark of the Covenant of the Lord of all the Earth.

The Midrash on Psalms 114 asks what it was that the sea saw to make it flee. It answers that the sea "saw" the Ark (coffin) of Joseph being carried up from Egypt. Through the merit of Joseph, who bent and controlled his physical passions in order to serve his Maker, God bent nature and caused the sea to part for the Children of Israel. Now Joseph's descendant, Joshua, who had learned the Torah from Moses, sent the Ark of the Covenant ahead of his people to teach that God is stronger than nature and can bend it to his will. In the Ark were the Tablets of Stone and Moses' Sefer Torah.

It was necessary for the people to purify themselves to experience this miracle (ch 3 v 5) because they were about to enter a new path through which their observance of God's Covenant -- His Torah -- would enable them to transcend natural law. This was one of only three occasions when the Ark was carried not by the Levites but by the Cohanim (priests) - the other two occasions were in the siege of Jericho and when the Ark was returned from the Philistines.

To impress the lesson of this great day upon everyone, in verse 9 Joshua says to the people: "Draw close to me over here!" Our rabbis taught that "Joshua assembled the entire nation **between the two poles of the Ark**, and this was one of the places where the little held the great".

Skeptics will wonder how this was possible. Even those who sincerely want to believe often find it hard if not impossible to understand and accept the sometimes apparently quite outlandish and rationality-defying statements found in rabbinic Midrash ("exposition, searching out"). Since this series of study notes on NaKh will rely heavily on teachings of the Talmud and Midrash illumining our biblical texts, let me say at the very outset of the series that the Hebrew Bible is the Word of the Living God, revealed to us through His prophets and sages. As soon as you scratch beneath the surface of the biblical words, you see that they are far from what they appear - "deep, deep, who can find it?" The Bible teaches about the spiritual dimension of this material world in which we live. Since this spiritual dimension is often quite unapparent to those sunk in materialism, the sages of the Midrash and Talmud - who lovingly counted every single word and letter of the Hebrew text and who were alert to its every subtle nuance and allusion - developed a unique poetry of allegories and riddles in order to encourage us to jump out of our pre-existing misconceptions about the nature and purpose of the world and rethink everything we thought we knew.

Johsua's bringing the entire nation "between the poles of the Ark" may be understood as his having succeeded in bringing everyone within the bounds of a totally new level of consciousness emanating out of the Ark and what it represented, in which they all perceived that God alone rules over everything. "The Living God" (v 10) alludes kabbalistically to the Sefirah of Yesod, the Covenant. It is precisely this quality of moral purity, embodied in Joseph the Tzaddik, that would drive out the Seven Canaanite Nations, who were the physical, mental and ideological **kelipah** (husk) over the Covenant (corresponding to the 7 days prior to circumcision, during which the Orlah-foreskin still hides the holy crown).

The greatness of the miracle of the splitting of the Jordan was enhanced because it was Nissan, springtime, when the melting snows of winter made the river so full that it was bursting its banks. It was in the merit of the Israelites having taken and slaughtered the Paschal Lamb (alluding to Aries, head of the constellations) on the 10th of Nissan 40 years earlier, bending the constellations under the will of God, that the new generation witnessed this new, unheard of miracle of the splitting of a flowing river.

The Talmudic discussion of the splitting of the Jordan is contained in Sotah 35a ff. Just to further irritate the skeptics, the Talmud states that according to Rabbi Yehuda, when the river split and the flow from the north backed up, it caused a huge cubic pillar of water 12 by 12 miles large corresponding to the size of the Israelite camp. Rabbi Elazar ben Shimon (bar Yochai) objected, saying that the pillar was more than 300 miles high so that all the kings of the east and the west saw it, as it says, "When the kings of the Emorites heard." Just to increase the mystery, the rabbis said of the city of "Adam" mentioned in verse 16, "Did you ever in your life hear of a city called Adam? No, this alludes to Abraham, 'the great man (Adam) among giants' (Joshua 14:15). It was in Abraham's merit that this miracle took place" - because he was the first to bend nature to his will when he circumcised himself.

CHAPTER 4

WRITING THE TORAH ON STONE

According to the Talmudic account in Sotah, the essential gist of which is quoted with characteristic brevity in Rashi's commentary on our text, the day of the crossing of the Jordan was one of superhuman activity by the twelve representatives of the tribes who took up stones from the Jordan to set up in Gilgal, and indeed superhuman activity by the entire people. This was a day to remember for ever.

Altogether there were three sets of 12 stones. The first had been set up by Moses in the land of Moab (Deut 1:5 and 27:8), and on them he wrote the entire Torah. Then Joshua set up a second set of stones in the Jordan itself (Joshua 4, verse 9), while a third set of stones was taken from the Jordan and set up in Gilgal (v 8). The Torah was likewise written on these stones.

However, the third set of stones was not merely taken directly from the Jordan to Gilgal. According to the Talmud, on the very day of the crossing of the Jordan the entire people journeyed to Mount Gerizim and Mount Eival, built an altar, coated it with lime and wrote the entire Torah on it, offered burnt offerings and peace offerings, ate and drank, recited the blessings and the curses, all in accordance with Moses' instructions (Deuteronomy ch 27). It was only after this that they took the stones **that same day** and carried them to Gilgal, where they were set up to educate the future generations.

Thus, on the very day of their entry into the Land, the Children of Israel wrote the Torah not merely on parchment but onto the very rocks and boulders of their new Land. The whole purpose of this was to teach their children and descendants in all the generations to come a profound lesson about how God works through history (ch 4 vv 6-7). It was through the power of God's Covenant, inscribed in His holy Torah, that the Children of Israel entered their land. Using the stones to stimulate the children's curiosity and give them a lesson in history is reminiscent of the annual Seder Night recalling the Exodus. (The ancient idolaters, including the Canaanites, were wont to set up stone circles as part of their highly-sophisticated systems of worship of the stars. The twelve stones of the twelve tribes, corresponding to the twelve signs of the Zodiac, were the ultimate **tikun** (repair) for this idolatry.

MORE MIRACLES

Ch 4 vv 10 & 15-19 go back to narrate further miracles relating to the splitting of the Jordan. It was only when the priests carrying the Ark first dipped their feet into in the water by the east bank of the river that the main miracle - the splitting of the river -- occurred, enabling the entire people to cross on dry land. Rashi, reflecting the Talmudic discussion, which is based on hints in our text, explains that after the people crossed the river to the west bank of the Jordan, the priests returned with the Ark to the **east** bank. The moment the priests stepped out of the water, the river returned to its normal flow, after which the priests crossed the river **over the flowing water, carried by the Ark** - thus graphically showing the entire nation that **the Ark carries those who carry it** and not vice versa (see Rashi on vv. 16 and 18.). The Torah may seem like a heavy yoke, but in fact it carries those who practice it - it carries them above and beyond nature!!!

The lesson of this unforgettable day in the history of the Children of Israel is summed up in the concluding verse of our text (ch 4 v 24): "In order for all the peoples of the land to know that the hand of HaShem is mighty, in order that you should fear HaShem your God all your days."

CHAPTER 5

THE CIRCUMCISION

It was through the power of the Ark of the Covenant that the River Jordan had split to enable the Children of Israel to walk into their home country on dry land. Immediately after their entry into the Land, it was necessary to inscribe the mark of the Covenant on the very flesh of all the males as laid down in the Torah (Genesis 17:1-14, Leviticus 12:3) as a sign that observance of the Covenant is the absolute condition for possession of the Land.

The circumcision was urgent as they had entered the Land on the 10th of Nissan and four days later everyone would have to offer and eat of the Pesach lamb, which was only permitted to the circumcised since partaking of the Paschal lamb is an intrinsic part of the Covenant. Our rabbis teach that immediately following their entry into the Land, during those four days before Pesach the people also went through purification from defilement from the dead using the ashes of the Red Heifer so as to be able to bring the Pesach sacrifice in a state of complete purity.

At the time of the Exodus from Egypt all the Israelite males had been circumcised as part of their "conversion" to the faith of Israel. But according to the simple meaning of our text (**p'shat**), the new generation that had been born during the 40 years of wandering in the wilderness had not been circumcised. The rabbis explain that since the people were journeying in the wilderness by the word of God and might at any time be called upon to break camp and travel, it was impossible to circumcise the baby boys. Furthermore, they teach that the north wind, which has curative powers, did not blow throughout the forty years in the wilderness so as not to disperse the Cloud that led the people (see RaDaK on Joshua 5:2). [That beneficial north wind is the same wind of divine power that would blow through the strings of King David's harp and awaken him at midnight, Berachot 3b.]

On the other hand, Tanna Devei Eliyahu (the Midrash of Elijah the prophet) states that it is not possible that the people who received the Torah at Sinai could have neglected the mitzvah of circumcision in the wilderness. Rather, they had only performed the first part of it - the actual **milah**, cutting off the foreskin - but had failed to perform the second part, **periyah**, the peeling back of the membrane, which is an intrinsic part of the mitzvah ("if one cuts off the foreskin but does not perform **periyah**, it is as if he has not circumcised"). This was why God told Joshua to circumcise them "a second time" (v 2) - i.e. to complete the mitzvah.

The circumcision was performed in the location of the Israelites' first encampment in their land, which to mark this mass demonstration of recommitment to the Covenant was named **Gilgal** for the reason explained in our text (v 9): "I have **rolled off** (**gal**oti) the shame of Egypt from upon you" -- for the Egyptian astrologers saw blood on the Israelites and thought it was a sign they would be defeated, not knowing that it was the blood of the circumcision, through which they would be victorious (Rashi). **Gilgal** is also related to the Hebrew word **gilgul** which has the connotation of recycling - reincarnation. Each and every generation must rededicate itself to the Covenant because history goes in cycles.

Eating of the "produce of the land" from the day after Pesach (v 11) brought the Children of Israel to a new mode of being. For 40 years in the Wilderness their food had been the miraculous, spiritual Manna. It was because they were now going to be living in a real, actual country making a living using natural methods, agriculture etc. that they first had to rededicate themselves to the Covenant, through which we cut the flesh to indicate that our task is to bring this material world under the law of God. The Covenant enables the material world (**Malchut**) to receive spiritual blessing, and thus ARI (Rabbi Yitzchak Luria, outstanding 16th century Kabbalist) points out that in our verse (v 11) the Hebrew word for produce, **eebur**, is made up of **bor** (a "pit", signifying the inherently "empty" receiving Sefirah of Malchut) together with the letter **ayin** (=70), signifying the flow of all the seven Sefirot of Building, each of them containing all 10 Sefirot - 7 x 10 - into Malchut.

The 16th of Nissan, when they started to eat the produce of the Land, is the day of the Omer offering in the Temple: it is only after this offering that it is permitted to eat from the new harvest (Leviticus 23:14).

THE ANGEL

Now that the people were purified, God's Angel - a being so fearsome that even Joshua was uncertain if he was for us or against - appeared to protect the people. "**Now** I have come" (v 14) - in the time of Joshua, but not before! For Moses had insisted that God Himself lead the people into the Land and not through a mere angel (Exodus 33:15). But now that Moses had departed, only a trace or residue of the exalted providence of his time remained in the form of this angel - Michael, Israel's protective angel (see Likutey Moharan II, 5). The angel impresses on Joshua that the Land of Israel is not like any other: "Take off your shoe from your foot, for the place upon which you are standing is holy". Similarly, the priests went barefoot in the Temple. (Zohar Chadash 59a indicates that the removal of the shoe alludes to Joshua's having to separate from his wife in order to be ready to receive prophecy at any time just as Moses had been.)

JERICHO

"And Jericho was closed up..." (Ch 6 v 2). The Hebrew word for "closed up" is doubled, indicating that they wouldn't let anyone in or anyone out. Targum Yonatan says they had gates of iron with bars of bronze. ARI explains that Jericho (**Yereicho**) alludes to the Moon (**Yareiach**) which signifies **Malchut**, the receiver - this world, which must receive the spiritual flow from above. But under the Canaanites, Jericho was completely closed up - i.e. surrounded by walls and barriers - **kelipah**, the evil husk - preventing the divine flow from entering and manifesting in this world.

Now that the Children of Israel were in the Land, they could not expect that all their affairs would be run miraculously by God as in the wilderness without their having to take any action here on earth. They had to act in some way in the material world in order to conquer Jericho (Radak). While their daily encirclement of the city can be seen as an exercise to demoralize the enemy, its significance goes far deeper. Our rabbis teach that the seven days of encirclement started on a Sunday, culminating with seven circuits on the Shabbat. This was not coincidental: the entire exercise came to prove that Israel's conquest and possession of the Land depend upon observance of Shabbat - the weekly Shabbat, the seven-year Sabbatical cycle of six years of agricultural work and then rest -- Shemittah - in the seventh year, and then the seven cycles of seven years culminating in the 50th "Jubilee" year, called after the **yovel** - the ram's horn of freedom sounded in that year.

Sounding the Shofar - signifying man's wordless cry to God from the very depths of the heart - was an integral part of the ritual that led to the capture of Jericho. The entire ritual was built around sevens. It came to undermine the idolatrous Canaanites, whose religions were built around the worship of the 7 planets. The Israelite processions must have been a most awesome spectacle, with the men of the tribes of Reuven and Gad leading, followed by the Shofar-blasting priests and the Ark, followed by Dan at the rear gathering up any stragglers (Rashi on v 9). The entire camp of Israel was involved in this Shabbat demonstration!

The Talmud Yerushalmi in Shabbat explains why Joshua declared Jericho and all its plunder **cherem** - - completely dedicated to God. This was because the city fell on Shabbat and it is forbidden to benefit from labor performed on Shabbat. The first conquest in the Land of Israel came about not through the agency of man but essentially through God's miracle. Nobody was allowed to have material benefit from God's miracle as this would detract from His glory. Joshua gave the city the status of **ir hanidachat** - an idolatrous city, all of whose property must be destroyed (Deut. 13:3-19).

The ethics of the commandment to destroy the Canaanites completely will be addressed in a future installment. Suffice it to say here that had they been willing to accept the One God they could have saved themselves, as Rahav did. The rabbis taught that Joshua himself took Rahav as his wife and their descendants included prophets and priests.

Joshua's grim oath (v 26) that anyone who tried to rebuild Jericho would pay with the lives of all his sons was actually fulfilled many generations later in the time of King Achav, as we will learn when we reach the Book of I Kings ch 16. The TaNaKh is first and foremost a moral teaching on a grand scale. God is very patient with His creatures but He always fulfills His word in the end.

* * *Joshua 3:5-7, 5:2-6:1 and 6:27 are read as the Haftarah on the First Day of Pesach* * *

AYAYAY!!!

The heady mood of self-confidence engendered among the Israelites by the spectacular collapse of the walls of Jericho was quickly punctured by the disaster at the city of Ai, caused by the sin of Achan ben Karmi in embezzling from the treasures of Jericho that Joshua had dedicated to God. "And Israel sinned with the devoted treasure…." A single individual's sin is the sin of the whole people, for we are all responsible for one another! The Hebrew root of the word sin in v 1 is ma'al. While referring generically to sin, this word specifically indicates stealing from **hekdesh**, property dedicated to God, such as Temple property, for one's own personal benefit. This sin leads to the corruption of religion when people use what belongs to God for their own personal pleasure and enrichment.

"Pride comes before a fall": heady after the capture of Jericho, the spies sent by Joshua to check out Ai (mentioned in Genesis 12:8 as one of Abraham's first stopping places in the Land and site of his second altar there) returned and advised that only a small force was needed to take the city "for they are few" (v 3). In saying this they showed that they did not yet understand that for God, victory in the Land of Israel depends not on numerical advantage but only upon our loyalty to Him. It was the fatal flaw in loyalty expressed in Achan's embezzlement that caused the reverse at Ai. "And they smote **about** thirty-six men" (v 5). Rabbi Yehuda said literally 36 men were lost, but Rabbi Nehemiah pointed out that the verse says, "**like** thirty-six men" (the **kaf** of **kishloshim** is comparative). The one man who was lost in the battle was **like** (the equivalent of) thirty-six men (36=a majority of the 71-member Sanhedrin): this was Yair ben Menasheh (Numbers 32:41; Bava Batra 121b) - it was a national disaster for even a single Israelite to be lost.

Our text shows the proper reaction of a true Israelite leader when even a single man loses his life in war. "And Joshua tore his garments and fell on his face on the ground..." (v 6). Unlike contemporary leaders, who appoint commissions of inquiry into their failures in order to blame someone else, Joshua took personal responsibility. Indeed, God told him that it was his own fault because he had stayed back in the camp instead of going out to battle against Ai in front of his men. Moreover, it was he who declared Jericho **cherem** (dedicated/destroyed) on his own initiative without being so commanded by God. Therefore, Israel would be **cherem** until the sinner was punished (Rashi on v 10).

THE LOTTERY

God could have simply **told** Joshua directly who the guilty man was, but instead He revealed his identity indirectly through a series of lotteries that were held publicly to establish from which tribe the sinner was, from which clan of that tribe and from which family. There was an ulterior purpose in turning the exposure of Achan into a national spectacle using the lottery (**goral**): this was because the Land was destined to be divided up among the tribes and families using the very same method of **lottery**, as Moses had been commanded (Numbers 33:54). Having seen how holy spirit governed the lottery in a capital case like Achan's, the people would accept its validity in matters of property (Rashi on v 19; Yerushalmi Sanhedrin 86).

Rashi (on v. 20) explains that before Achan's confession the situation was explosive. Achan was in denial and the members of his tribe (Judah) were getting ready to make war against Joshua (Ephraim) for accusing their leader of a crime. It was only when Achan realized his continuing silence would cause the death of many Israelites that he confessed. Joshua's messengers **ran** to Achan's tent to find the booty (v 22) in order to prevent men from the tribe of Judah getting there first to hide it.

"And I saw in the booty a robe of Shin'ar..." (v 21). Shin'ar is Babylon (Genesis 10:10). Explaining what a Babylonian robe was doing in Jericho, Rashi (v 21) says that every foreign power wanted a foothold in Israel and no king felt content until he established his influence there. Thus, the king of Babylon had a palace in Jericho, and left special robes there for him to wear when he visited. The presence of foreign kings explains why the tiny country of Israel had no less than **thirty-one** of them, as we will see in the continuation of the book of Joshua. Likewise, today every self-respecting nation demands a say in what happens in Israel!

It was through his confession that Achan redeemed himself, becoming the archetype of the sinner that confesses (following in the footsteps of his tribal ancestor, Judah, who was the first to confess - Genesis 38:26). "Everyone who confesses has a share in the world to come" (Sanhedrin 43b). The law that a condemned man confesses before his execution and that this brings him atonement is derived from our text. Thus, Joshua said to Achan, "As for your having sullied us, God will sully you **on this day**" - i.e. in **this world** but not in the World to Come, because confession brings atonement. Achan's atonement before Joshua is one of the main foundations of Rabbi Nachman's teaching on confession of one's sins before a Torah sage (see Likutey Moharan Vol. 1 Discourse 4).

CHAPTER 8

Achan's confession and punishment cleansed the Israelites of the flaw that led to their defeat at Ai. At God's command, they now used a brilliant military ruse against Ai, engaging the men of the city in battle and then feigning retreat in order to lure them out of the city so that a waiting ambush could enter unopposed and set the whole place on fire (Joshua 8:1-29). Sometimes the best way to advance and make gains is by first retreating a little.

After the capture of Ai, the text gives an account of the ceremonies that took place at Mount Gerizim and Mount Eival after the entry of the Children of Israel into the Land. Rashi (chapter 8 v 30) comments that the narrative is not written in order, because Joshua's building of the Altar on Mount Eival, the writing of the Torah on the stones and the solemn ceremony of reciting the Blessings and Curses before the entire nation in fact all took place on the very same day that they crossed the Jordan (see **Know Your Bible** on Joshua ch 3). The description of the sacrifices and the ceremony in today's text relates back to the commandment given by Moses in Deuteronomy ch. 27, where he says all this was to be done "on the day that you cross the Jordan" (v 2).

Since the ensuing chapters of Joshua will recount the conquest of the Land in detail, the positioning of the account of the recital of the Blessings and Curses right here underlines yet again that Israel's conquest and possession of the Land are conditional upon our observance of God's Torah.

CHAPTER 9

All the Canaanite kings throughout the land "gathered together to fight with Joshua and with Israel **with one mouth**" (ch 9 v 2).

This was all out war not only against Israel but against the One God who had promised them the Land. "In three places, we find the people of the world rebelling against the Holy One blessed be He: at the Tower of Babel (Genesis 11:1), in the war of Gog and Magog (Psalms 2:2) and in the days of Joshua. Why does it say, 'with **one** mouth'? Because they went against God, of whom it is said, 'Hear, O Israel, HaShem is **one**!'" (Tanchuma). Since many today are convinced that the world is in the throes of the war of Gog and Magog, this Midrash underlines the connection between many aspects of our present text about the war in the days of Joshua and the times we are living in now.

For Israel in the time of Joshua, the war for the conquest of the Land was a holy war. The decadent Canaanite star-worshippers, suddenly threatened with being driven out of their lovely homeland, doubtless saw the Israelites as a new breed of religious fanatics waging a dangerous Jihad that had to be thwarted at all costs. Yet after witnessing God's miracles on behalf of the Israelites, many of the Canaanites were already demoralized and fearful, and felt that "if you can't beat 'em, join 'em".

However, in the Torah God had strictly forbidden the Israelites to make any covenant with the Cananites and their gods or permit them to dwell in their Land "lest they make you sin against Me when you serve their gods, for they will be a snare for you" (Exodus 23:32-3).

The classic biblical commentator RaDaK (Rabbi David Kimche 1160-1235) in a lengthy comment on our text v. 7 explains exactly what the Israelite warriors were demanding of the Canaanites. They were not intending to kill them no matter what. The commandment to destroy the Canaanites applied only if "they make you sin". However, if they would agree to uproot idolatry from among them and accept the 7 Universal Commandments of the Children of Noah, they would be allowed to remain in the Land on condition that they agreed to serve and pay taxes to the Israelites - i.e. subordinate themselves to the Israelite national agenda of building God's Temple and spreading His light to the nations. Only if they refused these conditions and refused to evacuate would they be killed. The one difference between the Canaanites and any other nations against whom Israel made war was that if other nations refused to make peace and insisted on waging war, the Israelites would on defeating them kill only their males but keep their wives and children as slaves. However, if the Canaanites made war, the Israelites were commanded by God to kill them all, men, women and children.

For some this may raise agonizing ethical issues, which I cannot address except by saying that the biblical commandment to exterminate these nations is evidently founded on the premise that they were a thoroughly evil influence that had to be nullified completely for the sake of God's plan to reveal Himself to the entire world by replacing ancient idolatry with faith in the one God. It must be emphasized that nowhere in Judaism is there any justification whatever for the wholesale extermination of any nation excepting the Amalekites and the Canaanites, both of whom have now completely disappeared. If today some evil criminals and terrorists **behave** like Canaanites and Amalekites, then the individuals or gangs exhibiting such behavior should be brought to justice by the legitimate forces of law and order in order to neutralize their destructive influence.

Yerushalmi Shevuot 6:5 states that on entry to the Land, Joshua sent three written proclamations to the Canaanites. "Whoever wants to make peace can make peace; whoever wants to make war may make war, and whoever wants to evacuate may leave."

Some of the Canaanites departed voluntarily and went to N. Africa (Carthage) where they received a land as prosperous as the one they left. Some sources state that some of the Canaanites went to Europe (Germany).

Since the Gibeonites knew that they could save themselves without leaving if they agreed to the Israelite conditions, RaDaK (ibid.) asks why they resorted to the ruse described in our chapter, and answers that having seen how the Israelites had destroyed Jericho and Ai, they were afraid that the Israelites might not adhere to their conditions.

THE BITE OF THE SERPENT

The Gibeonites were actually Hivites (v 7). Their deception of Joshua and the Children of Israel was a deep historical irony, as the Hivites had tried to "convert" and intermarry with Israel in the time of

Jacob (Genesis ch 34) when Shechem son of Hamor the Hivite raped Dinah. Jacob's sons tricked the men of Shechem into circumcising, but "on the third day" when they were in great pain, Shimon and Levi entered the town and killed them all (for having failed to protest the rape of Dinah, which flouted the Noahide code.) Thus, in our chapter, we read that "they **also** acted with cunning" (v 4). This was the cunning of the serpent - in Aramaic, a serpent is **hivia**, from the same root as the Hivites.

Students of Kabbalah will note that the fake old provisions, clothes and shoes the Gibeonites used included "crumbs" (**nekudim**) alluding to the Kabbalistic World of Chaos, Nekudim, the root of evil. RaDaK, noting that moldy bread is covered in red, green and black spots, also relates **nekudim** to Laban's **spotted** flock (Genesis 30:32ff), likewise bound up with the mystery of the world of Nekudim.

Midrash Tanchuma shows the parallel between how the serpent tricked Adam and Eve into sinning in the hope of killing Adam and marrying Eve, and how the Gibeonites tricked the Israelites into making a forbidden covenant with them: "If they kill us they will violate their oath, while if they keep us alive they will violate God's commandment: either way they will be punished and will not inherit the land."

The Gibeonites were not true converts since they converted not because they wanted to serve the One God but out of fear (verse 24). It was "at the end of **three days**" that the Israelites found out that they had been deceived: this is a hark-back to Shimon and Levi's deception of the men of Shechem "on the third day…." Despite the Gibeonites' deception, the Israelites, having publicly sworn to protect them, could not violate their oath as this would have been a **Chillul Hashem**, desecration of God's Name (Gittin 46a).

Joshua therefore gave the Gibeonites the status of a caste of Temple laborers who were not permitted to intermarry with Israelites (in this respect they were similar to a **mamzer**, a child born of an incestuous union). They appear on the stage of history again in the time of King Saul and King David, and after the destruction of the First Temple they went into exile to Babylon with the tribe of Judah, returning to Israel with Ezra. The Gibeonites are unknown today.

CHAPTER 10

"And when Adoni-Tzedek king of Jerusalem heard…" (ch 10 v 1). The Midrash comments on his name: "This place (Jerusalem) makes its inhabitants righteous - Malki-Tzedek (Genesis 14:18), Adoni-Tzedek. 'Righteousness (**Tzedek**) will dwell in it' (Isaiah 1:21; Bereishit Rabbah 23).

Since Jerusalem was to be the place of God's Temple, it is significant that the main war of the Canaanites against the Israelites was initiated by the king of that city. However, Adoni-Tzedek's "righteousness" was for the sake of appearances. Instead of confronting the Israelites directly, he devised a roundabout way to provoke them by following the classic Middle East method of staging an attack on the pro-Israeli "collaborators", the Gibeonites.

The Israelites were honor-bound to come to their aid, and God fought for Israel, raining down from heaven stones of **algavish** on the backs of their fleeing enemies (**al gavish** -- "on a man's back"). The giant stones littering the area of Beit Choron (ch 10 v 11) were visible in Talmudic times and are mentioned in Berachot 54b as a spectacle over which one should make a blessing for the miracles performed for our ancestors.

The truly outstanding miracle in our chapter is how Joshua caused the sun and the moon to stop in their tracks in order to give the Israelites more time to chase after and destroy their enemies (verses 12-14). "Then Joshua **spoke**…" - his words were a prayer and a song (see RaDaK ad loc.). The Talmud states that the battle took place on a Friday, the eve of Shabbat, and Joshua was afraid lest the Israelites would come to violate the Shabbat (Avoda Zara 25a). Midrash Tanchuma states that from the time the sun rises until the time it sets, it sings a song of praise to God. Joshua commanded the sun to "**be silent in Giv'on**" - for if the sun were to cease to sing, it would immediately stop in its tracks. The sun asked Joshua why it should stop singing since it was created on the fourth day while Joshua, a man, was created only on the sixth. Joshua replied that God had given Abraham possession of the heavens (Genesis 14:19), and moreover, the sun had bowed down to Joseph, Joshua's ancestor (Genesis 37:9). The sun said, 'If I don't sing to God, who will?' "**then Joshua spoke**", as if to say, "**I will!!!**" The "Book of Righteousness" (Joshua 10:13) in which this was already prophesied is the Torah, in which it is written that Jacob promised Joseph that the fame of the seed of Ephraim would "fill the nations" (Genesis 48:19; see Rashi on Joshua 10 v 13).

No human can explain or understand how exactly Joshua succeeded in "bending time" to his will and extending the day by as much as 36 hours according to some rabbinic opinions. Pirkey d'Rabbi Eliezer states that Joshua saw that the Canaanite astrologers were planning an attack on the Israelites on the rapidly approaching Shabbat and this was why he prayed to extend the Friday. That God "listened to the voice of a man" (v 14) indicates that the power of holy prayer is greater even than the influence of the stars and planets, which govern time, while prayer can elevate us beyond time.

CHAPTER 11

The book of Joshua recounts the conquest of the Land in six not particularly lengthy chapters (6-11), yet at the end of the account it says, "Joshua made war with all these kings for **many days**" (ch 11 v 18). Thus, we see that our text presents only the highlights and main contours of what was in fact a lengthy process: the NaKh is in essence God's moral teaching, not a detailed military history.

Nevertheless, the strategy of the conquest is clear. It began with Jericho, which our sages call the "lock" of Eretz Israel. Jericho is the only good gateway between the south west of the Land of Israel and the territories east of the Jordan, which had been conquered in the days of Moses and had been given to the tribes of Reuven, Gad and half of Menasheh. The conquest of Jericho thus ensured the link between the Israelite populations on both sides of the Jordan as well as cutting off the Canaanite nations from possible help from elements east of the Jordan hostile to the Israelites.

We may understand the significance of the conquest of Ai (chs 7-8) and the subjugation of Givon (chs 9-10), both in the hills of Shomron north of Jerusalem, when we take into account that in the times of Joshua much of the center of the Land was covered by extensive forests (see Joshua ch 17 vv 14-18). The conquest of these two cities thus brought the entire central region of the country, which was relatively uninhabited, under Israelite control. (Shechem, the largest city in the area, was inhabited by Hivites, and evidently submitted to Israelite dominion at the same time as their clansmen the Hivite Giveonites.) Israelite control of the center of the country cut off the Canaanite city states of the north (Chatzor etc.) from those of the south, and they were thus unable to unite to fight all together against the Israelites.

After the defeat of the five Emorite kings in the south, as described in the previous chapter (10 vv 1-11) Joshua did not immediately destroy their cities but instead turned against Makedah, Livnah, Lachish and Eglon (ibid 28-35), these being the key cities guarding the approach to the mountains of Judah dominating the south of the country. The mountain region was thus cut off from the coastal plain, thereby isolating Mount Chevron from all possible assistance from the west, north and south. Joshua then went up to conquer Mount Chevron and the rest of the southern regions of the country, which meant that the entire south and center of the Land were now under Israelite control.

The hardest part of the conquest was that of the north, as described in our present text, Chapter 11, because the city-state of Chatzor, under King Yavin, was the most powerful influence in the region, possessing great wealth as well as "a very great number of horses and chariots" (11, 4), of which the Israelites had none.

Kabbalistically, we must look at the Land of Israel not through the spectacles of modern geography, where every map is aligned along the north-south axis. Instead, we must bear in mind that, Kabbalistically, the all-important axis is the center column, corresponding to the daily journey of the sun from east (Tiferet) to west (Malchut). When you face east, the south is to your right, corresponding to Chessed, Kindness, while the north is to your left, corresponding to Gevurah, Strength. South and north are thus the two arms. The Israelites entered the Land from the east (Tiferet) and first conquered the center (Ai, Giv'on), then the south (Chessed) and then the north (Gevurah). Thus, the king of Hatzor, the major power of the north, was Yavin (Heb.="he will understand"), alluding to the left column root sefirah of Binah.

God commanded Joshua to break the ankles of all their enemies' horses and burn all their chariots (v 6) even though the prohibition of Bal Tashchit ("do not destroy" Deut. 20:19) forbids wanton destruction. RaDaK (v 9) explains that the Canaanites had put their trust in the power of their horses and chariots, and God did not want the Israelites to plunder them in order to ensure that they would not also come to put their faith in military might. It was not necessary to kill the horses. All that was needed was to cut their hooves so that they would not be of any use in battle.

"MANY DAYS"

As we have seen, our text gives a brief account of what was in fact a long process of conquest and subjugation. Joshua was criticized for taking "many days" to conquer all the kings of Canaan. God had promised him that "as I was with Moses, so shall I be with you" (ch 1 v 5), which indicates that Joshua should have lived to the age of 120 like Moses. However, the Midrash tells us that Joshua feared he would be taken from the world as soon as he completed the conquest, and was therefore inclined to tarry. God said to him: "Moses your teacher did not act like that when I told him to exact vengeance from the Midianites and then die (Numbers 31:1) - he made war on them immediately. Since you think this way, I shall **subtract** from your years (Joshua - like his ancestor Joseph - died at the age of 110.) 'Many are the thoughts in a man's heart, but it is God's counsel that will stand'" (Bamidbar Rabbah 22:7). Sometimes the stratagems we devise to stave off perceived dangers actually bring those very dangers nearer.

"IT WAS FROM GOD TO HARDEN THEIR HEARTS"

The Canaanites themselves caused their own destruction by refusing to submit to the Israelite conditions for remaining in the Land - giving up their idolatry. As v 20 states, their recalcitrance was sent by heaven. RaDaK explains that God hardened their hearts similarly to the way He hardened the heart of Pharaoh, in order to punish them for their sins, and secondly, in order to enable the Israelites to destroy them as God had commanded Moses so that they would not cause the Israelites to sin.

The recalcitrance of the Canaanites has been mirrored in modern times by that of the Arabs who have systematically resisted the return of the people of Israel to resettle their ancestral lands. Many Jews find it impossible to understand the unrelenting opposition of the Arabs to Jewish settlement of the Land - and indeed, it is impossible to understand it in rational terms. It might appear that the Arabs would have a lot to gain from peaceful cooperation with a people who have time and time again manifested their God-given blessing of being able to turn a tiny strip of land in the dry, backward

Middle East into a flourishing, prosperous jewel of a country. Those Arabs who agree to help the people of Israel in our national mission as laid down in God's road map in the Bible will indeed have a place and a role in the future order as foretold by the prophets. But those who refuse will one day discover that their trust in bombs, missiles and machine guns is entirely misplaced.

"AND THE LAND RESTED FROM WAR"

"This means that the Canaanites did not rise up again and gather to make war against the Israelites because they saw they had been defeated in all the wars. Likewise, the Israelites remained in the territories they had conquered but did not conquer more land. When Joshua was old, God told him to urge on Israel to conquer the remaining territories and He ordered him to divide up the Land in his life time. Joshua began with the tribes of Judah and Joseph, because he was told prophetically that they were the heads of Israel and would stand on the boundaries of Israel, Judah to the south [Chessed] and Ephraim to the north [Gevurah], with the other seven tribes between them. Once the territories were allotted to each tribe by the lottery, they considered the whole land to have been conquered as all the boundaries were in their hands and any remaining Canaanites were locked in between. (RaDaK on v 23).

CHAPTER 12

THE THIRTY-ONE KINGS OF CANAAN

In Hebrew, the number 31 is written with the letters Lamed (=30) and Aleph (=1). The two possible permutations of these two letters make up two Hebrew words. The first is **El** (literally, "power" but also "God" - as such it is pronounced **Kel** except in prayer since this is one of the seven names of God that may not be erased). The second is **lo** (="no"). The 31 kings all said "No" to Israel, and paid for their intransigence with their very lives in order to show that "it is God's counsel that will stand".

When the Five Books of Moses are written on a parchment scroll for the public reading of the Torah in the Synagogue, the scribe must observe detailed rules and conventions in writing the text. In the same way, there are specific rules governing the writing of the Prophets and Holy Writings on a parchment scroll (some communities read the weekly Haftarah and the Megillot from valid scrolls). Yerushalmi Megillah ch 4 tells us that in the parchment scroll of Joshua, the names of the 31 kings of Canaan must be written similarly to the way the names of the 10 Sons of Haman hanged on the tree are written in Megillat Esther. The 31 kings are written each on a separate line with the name at the beginning of the line and the repeated word **"one"** (vv. 9-23) at the end. Perhaps the repetition of the word **one** comes to emphasize that although Israel were faced with a multiplicity of enemies, they were all sent by the One God who ultimately destroyed them all.

With the completion of the summary of the conquest of the Land in Chapter 12, we are ready for the account of its allocation by lottery to the Tribes of Israel as narrated in the coming chapters.

CHAPTER 13

SOME HISTORY

"And Joshua was old, advanced in days..." (Joshua 13:1). The deeper meaning of this verse is illumined by Rabbi Nachman's teaching that the true elder constantly advances in holiness and wisdom with every single day and every hour and minute.

In terms of the literal chronology of our text, God's command to Joshua to divide the land even though it was not yet fully subdued came after seven years of conquest following the Children of Israel's entry. This is learned from this text Chapter 14 v 10 where Calev ben Yefuneh - Joshua's fellow spy among the twelve sent by Moses from the wilderness at the start of what became 40 years of wandering - says, "God has given me life this **forty-five** years" (i.e. it was 45 years since God's promise to give Calev the land he trod upon in his visit to Israel, since he was the only faithful spy out of the twelve besides Joshua). Rashi on this verse says that it is from here that we learn that the conquest took seven years, because Moses sent the spies in the second year in the wilderness, and the remaining 38 years of wandering with another seven for the conquest make a total of 45.

According to the dating system of the rabbinic historical Midrash **Seder Olam** ("Order of thc World") followed in this series (which puts the Destruction of the Second Temple in the year 3828=68 of the Common Era), the Exodus from Egypt took place in 2448 (1312 B.C.E.), with the death of Moses and Joshua's subsequent entry into the Land in 2488 (1272 B.C.E.).

Joshua had been 44 at the time of the sending of the spies, and was 82 when he entered the Land. Thereafter he ruled over Israel for 28 years until his death at the age of 110, and was thus 89 at the time of the commencement of the division of the Land.

SOME GEOGRAPHY

This text and the following texts are filled with the names of various peoples and tribes and very many place-names. These are chapters filled with the love of God's holy Promised Land and its every mountain, hill, plain and river. Many profound secrets are woven into these subtle texts. By way of introduction to the coming chapters of the book of Joshua, let us establish some basic principles relating to the Land God has given to Israel.

In the "Covenant between the Parts" God promised Abraham "this Land from the river of Egypt until the great river, the River Euphrates. The Keinite, the Kenizzite and the Kadmoni. And the Hitite, the Perrizite and the Refa'im. And the Emorite and the Canaanite and the Girgashite and the Jebusite". (Genesis 15:18-20). This is the "Promised Land".

As noted by Rashi (ad loc.), ten peoples are listed here - whereas in the time of the conquest of Joshua, the Israelites were commanded only to take possession of the lands of the seven Canaanite nations. The three other peoples listed in God's promise to Abraham, the Keinite, Kenizzite and Kadmoni, refer to Edom, Moab and Ammon, which are destined to come under the rule of Israel in time to come.

The geographical definition of the Holy Land promised to Abraham is "from the river to the river" - the entire Mediterranean arm of the "Fertile Crescent" from the western point of the Euphrates all the way to the eastern arm of the Nile delta (this is the usual interpretation of "the River of Egypt" though some identify it with Wadi Arish).

A similar definition of the Promised Land is in God's Covenant with Israel at Sinai, where the territory is "from the Red Sea to the sea of the Philistines (Mediterranean) and from the wilderness until the River (Euphrates)" (Exodus 23:31).

King David conquered most of this area, and under King Solomon the entire area was indeed under the sway of Israel: "And Solomon was the ruler over all the principalities from the River (Euphrates) to the land of the Philistines and the border of Egypt" (I Kings 5:1-5). After Solomon, the Israelite influence waned but in the later history of the kingdom of Israel, King Jeraboam ben Joash restored most of the lands over which Solomon had held sway. Thereafter, however, the Israelite grip on the land was lost when first the Ten Tribes went into exile and subsequently Judah.

The period from the conquest of the Land by Joshua until the destruction of the First Temple in 3338 (422 B.C.E.) is one of 850 years, in which the people of Israel practiced the laws and customs of their fathers with varying levels of fidelity, following the agricultural and other laws of the Torah. After Ezra's return from exile in Babylon, with the rebuilding of the Second Temple, there followed another period of more than 700 years of continuous Jewish residence in the Land of Israel until several centuries after the destruction of the Second Temple.

Knowledge of the exact boundaries and divisions of the Land is important in order to know how the various agricultural laws of the Torah apply in different regions. (For example, in Temple times the Omer barley offering could not be brought from east of the Jordan; certain details of the laws of tithing of produce are different in Ammon and Moab from Israel west of the Jordan, etc.)

THE EAST AND WEST BANKS OF THE JORDAN

Most of Chapter 13 of our text today deals not with the allocation of the lands of the Seven Canaanite nations but with the territories **east** of the River Jordan which had been taken in the time of Moses and given by him to the tribes of Reuven, Gad and half of Menasheh, as related in the Torah in the later chapters of Numbers (chs 21 ff) and again in the early chapters of Deuteronomy. The conquest and division of these territories are recounted in detail in our present chapter, Joshua 13. Their topography is given in detail - from the territories to the south taken from the Emorite (Canaanite) king Sichon comprising areas of Moab and Ammon (current day Jordan) through the fertile Gil'ad (also in Jordan) up to the Bashan taken from King Og, a remnant of the (Canaanite) Refa'im (Bashan includes parts of the present-day Golan heights and other parts of Syria and Jordan).

From Biblical times until well after the destruction of the Second Temple, the Israelite population thus spread both in the "Land of Israel", **west** of the Jordan and also in the ancestral territories given to them by Moses, **east** of the Jordan (**mey-eyver la-Yarden**). Their respective populations were in constant communication (thus Mishnah Rosh HaShanah describes how the news of the Sanctification of the New Moon was signaled by torches from mountain to mountain across vast swathes of territory until everyone knew it.)

The political geography of the Middle East since 1948 has concealed the intimate bond that exists for Israel between the east and west banks of the Jordan. Prior to 1948, Palestine was a generic term for territories that are now divided up between present day Egypt, Jordan, Syria, Lebanon and Israel. The name Palestine was given by the Romans after the destruction of Jewish sovereignty in the Land, and was originally intended as an insult to the Jews by calling their ancestral homeland by the Latinized name of their traditional national enemies, the Philistines. [The Philistines were not a clan of the Canaanites but a powerful sea-faring invader people who came in waves from earlier habitations in the Mediterranean area from the times of Abraham and thereafter.] When in 1917 Britain assumed the mandate over "Palestine" and made the "Balfour Declaration" stating that its government "viewed with favour the establishment in **Palestine** of a national home for the Jewish people", the term Palestine still referred to territories stretching from east of the Nile through present day Israel, Jordan, Syria and Lebanon.

It was only in the years after 1917 that sprawling "Palestine" was successively trimmed, cut down and redefined until the State of Israel was left with territory that is only a small part of the Promised Land given by God to Abraham. It is deeply significant that the extensive areas that did not come under Israelite possession in the times of Joshua are still beyond the borders of the State of Israel.

CHAPTER 14

The allocation of the Land amongst the Children of Israel in the time of Joshua was determined by the **goral** or "lottery" involving the High Priest (Elazar son of Aharon) and the "King" (Joshua student of Moses) using the Urim VeTumim - holy spirit channeled through the High Priest's breastplate inscribed with the luminescent Hebrew letters of the names of the Tribes, which would flash one after another to reveal divine messages.

The main narrative of Chapter 14 concerns the request of Calev to receive the territory where he alone had trod as a Spy, 45 years earlier. Numbers 13:21 hints through the use of the Hebrew singular "and **he** came to Hebron" that Calev alone out of the spies had the courage to risk the perilous journey to Hebron, the burial place of Adam and the three Patriarchs, in order to pray (see Rashi ad loc.).

Here at the very beginning of the chapters dealing with the allocation of the Land of Israel among the tribes, the prominent positioning of Calev's request to receive Mount Hebron as the very heart of the royal tribe of Judah's portion shows the supreme importance of Hebron to Israel and the Jewish people. King David (Judah) reigned in Hebron for seven years before he reigned in Jerusalem - he had to bind himself to the Three Fathers in Hebron before taking his position as the "fourth leg of the Throne". Joshua Chapter 14 shows the antiquity of Judah's bond with Hebron, which will never be broken.

CHAPTER 15

"AND THE LOT FOR THE TRIBE OF JUDAH..." (Joshua 15:1)

The royal tribe of Judah took their share in the Land first. We learn in Talmud Bava Kama 122a: "Rabbi Yehuda said, One measure of land in Judah is worth five in the Galilee, and the Land was divided by the **goral** (="lottery", "destiny"), as it says (Numbers 26:55) 'Through the **goral** shall the Land be divided'. It was divided through the Urim Ve-Tumim. How? Eliezer would wear the Urim Ve-Tumim (the High Priest's breastplate) and Joshua and all Israel stood before him. Placed in front of him was the urn of the lots with details of the boundaries of each of the different portions of the land lying in it. He would concentrate with holy spirit and say, If Zevulun comes up, the region of Acco will come up for him. He would shake the urn containing the names of the tribes and Zevulun would come up. Then he would shake the urn with the boundaries and up in his hand would come Acco. And so with Naftali, and so on." [i.e. Everyone saw that the Land was divided through Holy Spirit and this way everyone knew it was the Will of God and accepted their portions joyously.]

The Talmud continues: "Not like the division in this world (i.e. in the time of Joshua) shall be the division in time to come. In this world, a man who has a fruit grove doesn't have a field, or if he has a field he doesn't have a fruit grove. But in the division of the world to come, there is not a single Israelite who does not have a share in the lowlands, the mountains and the south, and the Holy One blessed be He will divide it among them Himself, as it says (in the account of the future division, Ezekiel 48:29): 'And these are their allotments says HaShem'".

NAMES, NAMES, NAMES

These texts and the following texts are full of many names and topographical details. It can be taxing to try to focus on so many details, but we can fortify ourselves with Rabbi Nachman's teaching that in Torah study, it is sufficient simply to read the words one by one, even without understanding.

For these chapters about the boundaries, towns and villages of the Land of Israel are the national treasures of our nation, proving the antiquity of our link with that contested strip of land on the eastern Mediterranean seaboard. The Canaanites and Philistines of old have disappeared without trace together with their cultures and languages, and the Jewish people's link with the Land is far older than that of any of the other peoples who have laid claim to the land. Those who preserve and study the Torah and this book of Joshua possess the true deed of title to the Land.

Difficult though they may be to read and study, these chapters are far more than mere lists of names. Those familiar with present-day Israel will recognize many of the names of the towns and locations in the text. The names have their own poetry, whose beauty is particularly discernible to those with a broad acquaintance with the Hebrew of the Bible and the connotations of different words and roots. Some towns were called after their founder-builders or conquerors, some after an associated event, some after some striking and important environmental feature, a hill, valley, plain, rock, well, spring, a tree or trees, animals etc. Some names relate to the occupations of the original inhabitants, notably in the fields of agriculture, vine-culture, and the like.

Besides their simple **p'shat** meaning, these lists of the boundaries and towns and villages of the Land are woven of holy names and letters containing a wealth of wisdom for those who would dig amidst these treasures. Rabbi Nathan of Breslov writes in his introduction to **Sefer HaMiddot** ("The Aleph Beit Book") by his master, Rabbi Nachman, that the Rebbe said he learned **all the remedies in the world** from these chapters in the book of Joshua detailing the boundaries of the Land of Israel (chs 15-19). He explained that the names of all the cities in each tribe's portion are ciphers denoting the names of all the remedies in the world in all languages. The reason is that the Land of Israel corresponds to the human form and the division of the land corresponds to the divisions of the body. One tribe's portion is the "head", another's the "right arm" etc., and the biblical passage describing each tribe's portion contains the remedies relating to the corresponding body part.

It is noteworthy that Jerusalem appears both directly and indirectly several times in Chapter 15, even though Jerusalem itself was not part of Judah's tribal inheritance but in Benjamin's. Nevertheless, Jerusalem is alluded to in the account of Judah 's boundaries, because, as Rashi (v 3) notes, "Wherever the text speaks about the boundary "going up" (**oleh**) from the south, it means going up to Jerusalem, and where it speaks about from Jerusalem and beyond it speaks of how it goes down. From here we learn that Jerusalem is higher than all of Eretz Israel".

Verse 8 (see Rashi) explicitly teaches that while Judah's northern boundary touched the southern tip of Jerusalem, it did not include the city, which Jacob had promised to Benjamin, the youngest of his twelve sons, and son of his beloved Rachel. In fact, Judah's boundary came right inside the Temple, touching the south-east corner of the Altar, which for this reason had no **yesod** (foundation) in that corner, so that no part of the Altar should stand anywhere except in the territory of Benjamin.

KIRYAT SEFER & OTNIEL BEN KENAZ

An intriguing part of Chapter 15 is Calev's challenge for someone to capture D'vir-Kiryat Sefer in return for marrying his daughter Achsa. His half-brother Otniel son of Kenaz stepped forward and took the town, after which Achsa asked her father for "springs of water... the upper springs and the lower springs" (vv 15-19). This is one of those deep, deep sections that can only begin to be grasped with the help of rabbinic Midrash. Here we have the first appearance of he who was to become the first of the Judges after Joshua. "'And the sun rises, and the sun goes down' (Ecclesiastes 1:5): Said R. Abba bar Kahana, 'Don't we know that the sun rises and the sun sets?' What this verse means is that before the Holy One blessed be He causes the sun of one Tzaddik to set, He already causes the sun of another one to rise. Even before Joshua's sun set, the sun of Otniel ben Kenaz rose, as it says, 'And Otniel ben Kenaz captured [Dvir]'" (Bereishit Rabbah, Noah).

The mystery of the capture of D'vir whose name was formerly Kiryat Sefer (City of the Book) is, as the Talmud (Temurah 16a) states, that during the thirty days of mourning for Moses, one thousand seven hundred detailed laws were forgotten, but even so, Otniel ben Kenaz was able to bring them back through the power of his **pilpul** (Talmudic logical reasoning). It is his recovery of all this lost Torah that is alluded to in v 17: "And he captured". Of Achsa (relating to the Hebrew root **ka'as**, anger) the rabbis said cryptically that "any man who saw her got angry with his wife" (ibid.) - presumably because she showed other women up badly??? Not that her head was only in the clouds. Rashi v 19 notes that her complaint that the portion she received with her new husband was "dry" means "dried up from all good, a man who has nothing in him except Torah". "And Calev gave her the upper springs and the lower springs" (v 19). The Hebrew for "springs" is **goolot**, from the root **galah**, to "reveal". Otniel was one "to whom the secrets of the upper realms and the lower realms were revealed". Otniel is also identified with Ya'abetz, an archetypal Torah teacher in Israel.

We should derive encouragement from the example of Otniel, because it means that even if some of the Torah has been forgotten, it can be recovered through the power of logic.

AND THE SONS OF JUDAH COULD NOT DRIVE OUT
THE JEBUSITES, DWELLERS OF JERUSALEM (v 63).

Rashi on this verse notes that these Jebusites dwelling in Jerusalem were not from the Canaanite tribe of the Jebusites but Philistines descended from Avimelech, to whom Abraham, in return for purchasing the burial cave in Hebron, had to swear that he would not harm his grandson or great-grandson.

While the **kri** (pronunciation of the text as handed down by the Rabbis), means "they could not", the **ktiv** (the word as written by tradition in the parchment manuscript) means "they will not be able to". Many **drashot** come out of such divergences between the **kri** and the **ktiv**. Here it indicates that Judah did not drive out the Jebusites not because they were not physically able to but because they were not allowed to. This was because Abraham's oath still stood because Avimelech's great-grandson was still alive. It was only King David who took Jerusalem after the elapsing of the oath, when the appointed time came, and thus it was called David's city as destined by God. David purchased the site of the Temple from Aravna, the last king of the Jebusite Philistines. Everything comes at its proper time, especially when it comes to the possession of the Holy Land.

CHAPTER 16

THE PORTION OF EPHRAIM

Second among the tribes to receive their portion was the tribe of Ephraim, blessed by Jacob to be the more prominent, although the younger, of Joseph's two sons. While Judah's share of the Land was south of Jerusalem and much of it arid, Ephraim's share included the rich, fertile territories to the north of Jerusalem (Shomron), with Benjamin nestling in between the two, and a number of other tribes having certain portions within those of Judah and Ephraim.

The concluding verse of Chapter 16 does not say that the children of Ephraim "could not" drive out the Canaanites from certain parts of their territory as in the case of Judah (ch 15:63). Rather it says that they **did not** drive them out, indicating that they could and should have done so. It is not until we reach the book of Judges that we begin to feel the increasingly heavy **reproof** that the Prophets who wrote the Bible directed at the Children of Israel for their sins and failures in the Land. There we shall see that was precisely their failure to drive out the Canaanites as they had been commanded in the Torah that caused all of their subsequent problems in the land, leading eventually to the destruction of the Temple and exile. Here in Joshua the text simply notes that they did not drive out the Canaanites.

Each one of us has the task of driving out the Canaanite from within ourselves - that "merchant" who is constantly trying to sell us the fake goods of This World. Today the conquest of the Land must be first and foremost on the spiritual plane: we must reclaim the Land for God by spreading His Torah among all the people and spreading His word to the whole world. By keeping firm in this mission, we will welcome Melech HaMashiach quickly in our times.

CHAPTER 17

Following the delineation of Ephraim's inheritance in the previous chapter (16), our text continues with the account of the division of the Land of Israel among the other Tribes, giving the boundaries of Menasheh, Joseph's firstborn, in chapter 17. While part of the tribe of Menasheh had already taken their inheritance in the territories captured in the time of Moses east of the Jordan (see Joshua ch 13:29-31), the majority of this populous tribe took their share in the Land of Israel proper, to the north of the portion of Ephraim.

THE DAUGHTERS OF TZELAFCHAD

When God commanded Moses to divide the Land among the tribes (Numbers 26:52-56), the daughters of Tzelafchad (from the tribe of Menasheh) immediately stepped forward to press their claim for their share since their father had no sons (Numbers 27:1-11; see also Numbers 36:1-13). Under Torah law, daughters inherit their father's estate only when there is no surviving son: if there is a son or sons, the males inherit the entire estate and from it they have to pay to support and marry off their sisters.

Now that Joshua was actually dividing the Land, the irrepressible daughters of Tzelafchad again stand up before Elazar the High Priest and Joshua the king to demand their share. Not only are the daughters of Tzelafchad archetypes of the Israelite women that show even greater love and yearning for the Land than the men. They were also very wise (see Rashi on Numbers 27:4) and their insistence on their rights to the Land brought about the revelation of several portions relating to the Torah laws of inheritance.

An interesting, if somewhat subtle, point relating to these laws comes out of our text today, ch 17 v 5: "**Ten** shares fell to Menasheh besides the territories of the land of Gil'ad and Bashan east of the Jordan". Rashi (ad loc.) explains that out of these ten, the daughters of Tzelafchad took **four**: (1) Tzelafchad's own share as one of those who went out of Egypt, because the Land was divided among those who left Egypt; (2) The share that Tzelafchad took with his brothers in the possessions of his father Heifer, who was also one of those who went out of Egypt; (3) Tzelafchad's "double" share in his father's estate as a firstborn; (4) The share belonging to Tzelafchad's brother, who had died in the wilderness without children.

Rashi concludes: "The verse did not need to tell us about the shares of the daughters except to teach us that they took the share of the firstborn and also to inform us that their share in the Land of Israel was already under their ownership [**muchzeket**] from the time of their fathers, for if not, there is a legal principle that the first-born does not take a share in property that is not yet part of the estate and merely **due** (**ro-ouiy**) to come later. The firstborn takes his double share only from property that has already come into the estate (**muchzak**)." [E.g. the first born would **not** take a share of a debt owing the estate that was uncollected at the time of death of the deceased but only of lands and goods that were already part of the estate.]

To those unfamiliar with the intricacies of Torah law, the above may be somewhat confusing, but what it means is that even before the Land of Israel was actually conquered and occupied by the generation of Joshua, it was already in the **possession** (**muchzak** - under the **Chazakah**, "ownership") of the Children of Israel as an ancestral inheritance from those to whom its ownership had been given by God - the generation that actually left Egypt in the Exodus. The same would apply today. Even though the Children of Israel do not as yet control by any means all of the Promised Land, it is all still their property and belongs to them as an ancestral inheritance.

AND THE CHILDREN OF JOSEPH SPOKE TO JOSHUA (v 14)

They were asking for more land because of their numbers. The commentators tell us that these were the Children of Menasheh, who were particularly populous (see Rashi on 17:4), as we learn from the substantial increase in their numbers - by **twenty thousand five hundred** -- between the first count of the Children of Israel in the wilderness and the second (Numbers chs 1:35 and 26:34). This was in fulfillment of God's promise to Abraham "Thus - KoH - shall be your seed" (Gen. 15:5). KoH is made up of Kaf (=20) and Heh (=5) alluding to the **twenty thousand** and the **five hundred** (Midrash).

Ephraim was less populous. One reason is that according to the Midrash, many of the Bney Ephraim were killed prior to the Exodus from Egypt when they tried to calculate the time of the redemption but erred. They went up to Israel before the proper time and when they came to Gat to take possession of the Land, the Philistine inhabitants, who had been born there and were therefore familiar with it, overwhelmed and killed them. It was their bones that Ezekiel saw in his vision of the Valley of the Dry Bones. The sources for this fascinating and very suggestive Midrash are I Chronicles 7:21: "The sons of Gat who were born in the land killed them (the sons of Ephraim), for they went down to take their possessions, and Ephraim their father mourned them many days and his brothers came to comfort him" (see Metzudat commentary on this verse). See also Sanhedrin 92b and see RaDaK on Ezekiel 37:1.

CHAPTER 18

SHILO

"And all the assembly of the Children of Israel gathered to Shilo and set up there the Tent of Meeting" (Joshua 18:1).

This was fourteen years after their entry into the Land (RaDaK). The fourteen years consisted of seven years of conquest and seven more dividing up the Land. All this time the Tent of Meeting made by Moses in the wilderness had stood in Gilgal, their first encampment after crossing the Jordan.

Establishing the Sanctuary in Shilo signified more settled times: "...and the Land was conquered before them" (ch 18 v 1): Comments Rashi: "From the time the Sanctuary was established, the Land became easy for them to conquer".

The Sanctuary remained in Shilo for a total of 369 years - until the time of Eli the High Priest, when the Philistines sacked it and took the Ark. Shilo was in the territory of Joseph. It was predestined that the Sanctuary and the Two Temples should stand only in the territories of Rachel's two sons, Joseph and Benjamin. (This is why in Genesis 45:14 it says that on their reconciliation in Egypt, Joseph fell on the **necks** of Benjamin - the Hebrew plural signifies the **two** Temples - while Benjamin wept on Joseph's **neck** - the singular alludes to the Sanctuary in Shilo.)

With the conquest of the Land still in progress, the enterprise of turning the Land of Israel into the light of the Nations was still incomplete, and this was signified in the structure of the Sanctuary in Shilo. Our text here calls it a **tent** - because the "roof" was made of skins, as in the case of the wilderness Sanctuary. However, the walls of Shilo were stone, unlike those of the wilderness Sanctuary, which were made of gold-coated wood. It would only be in Jerusalem - the place of the Temple forever - that the roof of the Temple would also be of stone.

The Sanctuary in Shilo will figure in several important passages in the Book of Judges and particularly in the early part of Samuel dealing with Eli and Hannah. The reference in our text today to Shilo makes a fitting start to the chapter delineating the tribal inheritance of Benjamin, youngest son of Jacob's beloved wife Rachel, nestling as it did between the two great tribes of Judah to the south and Ephraim to the north.

We see from this text and subsequent chapters that the territories of the different tribes sometimes entered into one another. Similarly, in the human body, the different limbs and organs are closely interconnected and enter into one another.

CHAPTER 19

"AND THE SECOND PORTION WENT TO SHIMON..." (Joshua 19:1)

As Rashi notes on this verse, the tribe of Shimon was "second" after Benjamin, the first of the **seven** tribes that only received their portions **after** Reuven, Gad and half Menasheh took theirs east of the Jordan and **after** the royal tribe of Judah and the first-born Joseph (Ephraim and Menasheh) took theirs to the west of the Jordan. Only after these leading tribes had already taken their portions did Joshua command the remaining seven tribes to send a team of three envoys each to make a survey of the rest of the Land in order to receive their portions (see ch 18 v 7).

After Benjamin (son of Jacob's beloved Rachel), the remaining tribes out of these seven were - in the order given in our present chapter - Shimon, Zebulun and Issachar (the three other sons of Leah besides Reuven, Levi - who did not receive a portion, and the royal tribe of Judah) followed by Asher (son of Leah's handmaiden Zilpah, as was Gad, who had already taken his portion east of the Jordan), then Naftali and finally Dan (these last two being the sons of Rachel's handmaiden Bilhah).

The kabbalistic Sefirot corresponding to the tribes are: Judah-Malchut; Issachar-Netzach of Malchut; Zevulun-Hod of Malchut; Reuven-Chessed of Malchut; Shimon-Gevurah of Malchut; Gad-Hod of Malchut; Ephraim-Ateret-Yesod of Zeir Anpin; Menasheh-Yesod; Binyamin-Nekudat Tzion; Dan-lowest limb of Hod of Malchut; Asher-heel of Netzach of Malchut; Naftali-lowest limb of Netzach of Malchut.

SHIMON

The tribe of Shimon received their portion from part of Judah's territory (verse 9) since Judah had taken more territory than required for their population (Rashi ad loc.) This is bound up with the fact that Shimon was something of a maverick tribe - Shimon had gone with Levi to kill the men of Shechem (Genesis 34:25) and while both were criticized by Jacob when he blessed his sons ("accursed is their anger. I shall divide them in Jacob and scatter them in Israel" Genesis 49:7), Levi was "divided" and "scattered" in an honorable way in the Levitical cities, while Shimon was "divided" and "scattered" amidst the territory of Judah. (This is also bound up with the fact that Zimri ben Saloo Prince of the Tribe of Shimon had flouted Moses in taking the Midianite woman - Numbers 25:6 & 14 -- as a result of which Moses did not give Shimon a blessing.) Nevertheless, Shimon did receive Be'er Sheva, one of the outstanding features of the land since the time of Abraham and now one of present-day Israel's most important cities.

ZEVULUN, ISSACHAR, ASHER AND NAFTALI

These four tribes took their portions in some of the most fertile and beautiful territories of northern Israel. Although many of the locations mentioned in our text cannot be identified conclusively today, there are many that can be identified (including some whose names survive in the present-day Arab names of the associated villages), and the general areas in which each tribe took their portions can be discerned until today.

Yissachar and Zevulun took their portions around the Valley of Yizre'el and the Lower Galilee respectively, while Asher and Naftali took theirs in the Upper Galilee, with Asher to the west alongside the Mediterranean coast and Naftali to the east running all the way to the upper Jordan valley. After the time of Joshua, a contingent from the tribe of Dan took a portion in between Asher and Naftali around the sources of the River Jordan (Tel Dan, Banyas), although Dan's main portion was in the center of Israel (Tel Aviv-Jaffo etc. - see below). Dan's joining Asher and Naftali in the Galilee is bound up with their having been neighbors in the Israelite camp in the Wilderness (Numbers 2:25-31).

The locations in which the tribes were to take their portions had already been indicated allusively in Jacob's blessings to his sons and in Moses' blessings to the tribes.

Zevulun's portion was around Yokne'am (mentioned explicitly in this text) including present-day Zichron Yaakov. Although the coastal region from Mount Carmel and northwards was in the territory of Asher, Zevulun also jutted into Asher's portion in order to take a share in the coastal region in fulfillment of Jacob's blessing that "he shall be by the coast and his flank shall reach to Sidon" (Genesis 49:13).

Our text indicates that the territories of the three tribes of Zevulun, Issachar and Naftali all met at Mount Tabor. In the light of Rabbi Nachman's teaching that all of the names in our chapters allude to parts of the human body (as discussed in the commentary on Joshua ch 15) it is interesting to examine Rashi's comment on our text, Joshua 19:12, speaking about where Zevulun's portion touched Mount Tabor. "And it turned from Sarid eastward toward the sunrising unto the border of **Chislot-Tabor**". In the words of Rashi, "I say that **Chislot** has the connotation of **chesalim**, the flanks - it was not on the peak of the mountain or at its foot but on the slope near the middle towards the back and away from the front in the same way as the flanks stand in an animal. And where it says **Aznot-Tabor** [in verse 34, speaking of where Naftali's portion touched Mount. Tabor] it means near the head in the place of the ears - **oznayim**." Note how many anatomical terms Rashi introduces here in speaking about the topography of the Holy Land!!!

Yissachar's territory, as mentioned, included the fertile region of the Yizre'el Valley.

Asher's territory was in the western part of the Upper Galilee including the coastal strip, and extended way up into present-day Lebanon up to Sidon. The portion of Naftali (the letters of whose name, when rearranged, spell out **Tefilin**) was in the eastern Upper Galilee in one of the areas of Israel that is most conducive to spiritual ascent, including the beautiful mountain region around Safed and Meiron, the Kinneret (v 35) and the lush valley of the upper Jordan (v 34).

THE TRIBE OF DAN

The well-known phrase "from Dan to Be'er Sheva" seems to indicate that Dan's portion was located in the **north** of Israel at the opposite end from Be'er Sheva in the south. However, in fact our text indicates that Dan's main portion was in the **center** of present-day Israel including the locations of present-day Tel Aviv and Bney Brak - still known as the Dan Region - as well as areas further into the interior as far east as Beit Shemesh, Eshta'ol and Zor'ah, near which the grave of Dan ben Yaakov can be visited until today. (Some may wonder whether Dan's role in the wilderness as the tribe marching at the very rear, gathering in the stragglers, has some relationship to the presence of latter-day Tel Aviv in his portion???)

Dan's additional territory located in the north of Israel around the sources of the River Jordan is mentioned briefly in our text in verse 47. Dan's capture of this territory actually took place after the death of Joshua in the time of Otniel ben Kenaz and is described in more detail in Judges ch 18.

CHAPTER 20

With the division of the Land among the tribes complete, it was now left to Joshua to establish the foundations of a society governed by the Torah that he had received from his teacher Moses. The first foundation of a civilized society is the protection of its citizens from violence and particularly from murder. Human beings all have their own interests, which often conflict with those of others, and strife is inevitable in human society. A successful society is one that can keep this inevitable strife under control without its being allowed to get out of hand. This is why the first institution that Joshua laid down after the division of the land was that of the Cities of Refuge for unwitting killers. This was in fulfillment of God's commandment to Moses that three cities of refuge were to be established in Israel proper - the territories west of the Jordan -- and another three in the territories east of the Jordan (Exodus 21:12; Numbers 35:13f; Deuteronomy 4:41-3 & 19:2).

Accidents do occur, and in any society where people are active and busy it can always happen that one person may cause another person's death quite unintentionally. The purpose of the Cities of Refuge is to ensure that the accidental killing of one person does not escalate into a bloody cycle in which that person's relatives seek to avenge the death by killing the killer. Torah law provides that intentional murder must be punished with the death penalty, but the unintentional killer can take refuge in one of the Cities of Refuge in order to live securely while repenting for the unintended tragedy that came about because of what may have been some element of negligence on his part.

In the words of Rambam (Maimonides, Mishneh Torah, Laws of Murder 4:9): "While there are sins that are more serious than bloodshed, they do not destroy civilization in the same way that bloodshed destroys it." It is profoundly ironic that of the three cities of refuge mentioned in today's text in the Land of Israel proper west of the Jordan, two - Hebron and Shechem ("Nablus") - have been turned into cities of refuge not for unwitting killers but for willful killers and terrorists. Whether the third of the cities of refuge - Kedesh in the north - can be identified with present-day Safed is a moot point, though it was certainly in the near vicinity.

Let us pray that the tranquil spirit of Safed will spread to all the inhabitants of the Holy Land, and that sanity will return so that willful killers and terrorists are duly punished and unwitting killers sent into exile in order that ordinary law-abiding citizens may once again live securely without fear in a state of true peace.

CHAPTER 21

CITIES OF THE PRIESTS AND LEVITES

Following the establishment of the cities of refuge for unwitting killers (Joshua ch 20), the next step in laying the foundations for a truly Godly society in the Holy Land was to set aside special cities up and down the country for the Levites and the Priests, as God had commanded Moses (Numbers 35:1-8).

Under Torah law, those who had a special responsibility for maintaining the spiritual bond of the people as a whole with God were not a group of democratically-elected or self-selecting religious leaders. Rather they were a hereditary caste consisting of the entire tribe of the Levites, of whom one family in particular - the descendants of Aaron - were set aside as Cohanim, the priests.

The Torah had provided a unique system of tithes of produce and other vital necessities to be given by all the people in order to provide the Cohanim and Levites with their livelihood so as to leave them free from the need to earn a living in order not only to serve in the Temple but also to be able to teach the people Torah and minister to their spiritual needs. The Cohanim were to receive Terumah (about 2% of a farmer's crops) together with the first-fruits and first of the dough (**Challah**), gifts of wool for their clothing, choice parts of animals slaughtered for regular consumption, portions of sacrificial animals and certain other gifts. The Levites were to receive Ma'aser (10% of the crops) for their livelihood, out of which they were to contribute one tenth as their own **Terumat Ma'aser** to the priests.

Our present chapter (Joshua 21) gives an account of the cities set aside from the territorial portions of the other tribes in order to provide the Levites and Priests places for their residence and for their livestock and other needs. (It was not forbidden for the Levites and Priests to work the land, but their main task was to serve in the Temple and to teach and minister to the people.) The account in our chapter parallels the account of the cities of the Priests and Levites given with their genealogies in I Chronicles 6:39-66.

Altogether the Priests and Levites received 42 cities of their own together with the 6 cities of refuge for unwitting killers (who needed the presence of spiritual ministers to help them in their repentance) making a total of 48 cities, corresponding to the 48 ways in which the Torah is acquired (Avot 6:6). Of these 13 were for the Cohanim-Priests and the remaining 35 for the Levites.

From the accounts here in Joshua and in Chronicles it emerges that the different tribes did not contribute equal numbers of cities. Judah contributed the most - 8 cities - while Shimon gave only one. Naftali gave 3 and all the other tribes gave four, "each according to his inheritance" (Numbers 35:8).

The Cohanim were all concentrated in the territories of Judah (9 cities including that given by Shimon, who lived in Judah) and Benjamin (4). This made sense since the Cohanim were required to serve regularly in the Sanctuary / Temple -- in Shilo, Nob, Giv'on and finally Yerushalayim - all of which were in or adjacent to the territories of Benjamin and Judah.

The giving of Hebron - the outstanding jewel in the crown of Judah - to Aaron and his sons - signifies the close alliance between the tribe of Judah and the priesthood ever since Aaron the Priest had taken for his wife Elisheva, sister of Nachshon, Prince of the Tribe of Judah (Exodus 6:23). The royal tribe of Judah took particular responsibility for the establishment of the Temple, which was built through the efforts of David - from the tribe of Judah -- and his son Solomon. It would be David's songs that were sung by the Levites in the Temple as the Cohanim offered the sacrifices.

The dispersal of the Priests and Levites in cities up and down the Land served a vital function in bringing the Torah and its spiritual message to the people. The Torah's unique method of giving the Priests and Levites their livelihood ensured that they were in constant contact with the Israelite population of independent farmers, who could never separate their business affairs from their religious obligations because the Priests and Levites would come to their very barns and threshing floors in order to collect their tithes and gifts. This was how the Torah to which the Priests and Levites were particularly devoted percolated to the entire nation.

Today the majority of Jews do not live in agricultural societies and in any case, cannot give **Terumah** to the Priests, since it may only be eaten in a state of ritual purity which today's Cohanim are unable to attain in the absence of the ashes of the Red Heifer to purify them from defilement from the dead. Unless a Levite can **prove** his pedigree, there is no obligation to give him **Ma'aser**. Thus, although there is still today an obligation to separate **Terumah** and **Ma'asrot** from the produce of Eretz Yisrael, the separation is largely symbolic as we cannot give the gifts to their intended recipients.

The contemporary equivalent of tithes for the Priests and Levites is the charity money given to **Torah scholars** to enable them to pursue their profession of studying and teaching the Torah. Rambam (Maimonides) was strongly opposed to the scholars' relying on charity rather than working to make their living and supporting themselves to study Torah (Laws of Torah Study 3:10-11). However, in Rambam's time it was possible to earn sufficient to live off in about three hours work a day (ibid. 1:12). This would probably still be possible today were it not for the extravagances of contemporary "civilization", whose obscene military budgets and many other excesses result in heavy taxation and all kinds of other expenses that eat away at people's income, leaving the majority enslaved to their work for many hours every day. Without the generosity of the brave few who provide financial support for Torah scholars, the Torah would be in danger of being entirely forgotten by the people. Charity support for Torah scholarship is intended not to allow lazy layabouts to smoke and drink coffee all day in front of an open **sefer**. It is intended to enable truly sincere and devout seekers to discover and internalize God's Torah and prepare themselves to practice it and teach it to others. In our times of spiritual darkness and confusion there is no worthier charitable cause than that of the Torah institutions that are genuinely and seriously pursuing the study of the Torah as it applies practically in our time and spreading that knowledge among the wider population. Let us pray that as more and more **ba'aley batim** (working householders) make their way to the true Torah scholars to study, the overall level of Torah knowledge among the people will increase to the point where we will be ready to return to the Temple system with its Priests and Levites speedily in our time. Amen.

CHAPTER 22

With the Cities of Refuge and those of the Priests and Levites established, the people were ready to settle down to their intended life of Torah, Mitzvot and devotion to God in the Holy Land, "each under his vine and each under his fig tree". The Canaanites had been largely subdued, though not completely defeated, and with the entire Land apportioned to the Tribes, the period of conquest had come to an end. Thus, the tribes of Reuven, Gad and half of Menasheh that had taken their territories east of the Jordan were ready to return to their homes, having fulfilled their undertaking to Moses not to do so until they had fought with their brothers for the conquest of the Land west of the Jordan (Numbers ch 32).

The building of an Altar by the tribes of Reuven, Gad and Menasheh close to the Jordan river near the boundary between the Land of Israel west of the Jordan and their territories to the east set off a confrontation with the other tribes of Israel that was an ominous precursor of what was to come in the times of the Judges and almost led to a terrible internecine war.

With the building of the Sanctuary at Shilo, it was strictly forbidden to offer sacrifices anywhere else (see Rashi on Joshua 22:12). Torah law explicitly prohibited offering sacrifices on a "private" altar (**bamah**, "high place") once the Sanctuary was at rest in the Holy Land (Deuteronomy 12:6; 12:11). The penalty for violating the prohibition is **karet** (spiritual excision), the most severe punishment in the Torah (Leviticus 17:4). The unity of God was to be affirmed through the choice of one and only one place in the whole world for the offering of animal sacrifices by the Cohanim. It was forbidden for each individual to set up his own personal Temple ritual, which could lead to the development of weird and alien cults that would quickly turn into the very opposite of what the Torah intended.

This was why the 10 Tribes in Israel proper sent Pinchas the Priest with a delegation of tribal representatives ready to make war against Reuven, Gad and half Menasheh. (Pinchas had shown himself the nation's outstanding "zealot" in the time of Moses, thereby earning the priesthood for himself, Numbers 25:7-13.)

When the three tribes answered and defended themselves against all misconceptions, they invoked three names of God twice over: **Kel Elokim HaShem**. (v 22). The Midrash (Shocher Tov 3) comments: "What did the children of Gad and Reuven see to invoke these three names twice over? For through them He created the world (see Psalms 50:1) and through them He gave Israel the Torah ("for I am the Lord - **HaShem** - your God - **Elokim** - a jealous God - **Kel**"). These three names correspond to the three attributes through which the world was created, with Wisdom (**Kel**, column of **Chessed**, kindness), Understanding (**Elokim**, column of **Gevurah**, might) and Knowledge (**HaShem**, center column, **Tiferet**, beauty and harmony) - (see Proverbs 3:19).

The reason why they built the Altar was not to sacrifice on it but as a sign that they too were Israelites like their brothers east of the Jordan, so that nobody should come along in the future and say they had nothing to do with the people of Israel. They were appealing to their brothers not to drive them away.

This is a message that could today be addressed to those who consider themselves to be the "mainstream" of Jewry: Do not push away those who are earnestly and sincerely seeking God's true Torah, even if at times they do things that are not comprehensible to you and even seem like verging on the forbidden. A similar message could be addressed to those in Israel to keep their arms open to their brothers and sisters in the Diaspora. Before you jump to conclusions, first ask, enquire and listen carefully.

Pinchas' mission was a successful exercise in conflict resolution and the Talmud comments, "And Pinchas **the priest**... heard..." (ch 22 v 30) - "Pinchas was not inaugurated as a Kohen until he made peace among the tribes" (Zevachim 101b). May Pinchas in his incarnation as Eliyahu HaNavi come soon to make peace among us all! Amen.

CHAPTERS 23-24

THE SUMMATION

Joshua's address to the nation and its elders, heads, judges and officers, points to the lessons that were to be drawn from the conquest of the Land of Israel, one of the most decisive events in the people's history. Having witnessed how God had miraculously defeated the Canaanite nations on their own territory, the people of Israel were to internalize the message that their entire future in the Land depended on keeping God's Torah as a whole, and specifically upon not intermarrying or in any way becoming culturally integrated with the remaining Canaanites, whose pluralistic religions and cultures were the very antithesis of the monotheism of the Torah.

Joshua warns of the existential danger of Israelite intermarriage with the Canaanites, which would result in God's not driving the latter from the Land, leaving them as "a trap and a stumbling block, whips at your sides and thorns in your eyes until you are destroyed from upon the good land that the Lord your God has given you" (ch 23 v 13). This would occur if the Children of Israel made any compromise with the idolatry of the surrounding nations: just as God had showed His faithfulness in bestowing all His promised good upon the Israelites, so He would show His faith in wreaking vengeance upon them if they betrayed His Covenant.

THE FINAL ASSEMBLY IN SHECHEM

Rashi (ch 24 v 26) notes that Joshua had the Ark of the Covenant brought to Shechem to add to the great solemnity of his final reproof to the nation before his death. Our Rabbis cite numerous examples of the outstanding Tzaddikim of the Bible (Abraham, Isaac, Jacob, Moses, Samuel, David) who only delivered their reproofs immediately prior to their deaths so as not to have to repeat them over and over, causing the recipients embarrassment and bad feelings (Sifri on Deut. 1:1; see Likutey Moharan II:8).

In his address, Joshua reviews the key events in the formation of the nation and its identity, tracing their roots back to their idolatrous forefathers who dwelled "on the other side of the river (Euphrates)", i.e. in Babylon. The opening words of this passage (vv 2-4) will be familiar to many since our sages quoted them at the beginning of the Seder night Haggadah, when every Israelite father is commanded to relate our national history starting with shame and ending in glory.

Joshua emphasizes that the victory of Israel over their enemies was "not through your sword and not through your bow" (v 12) but only through God, Who controls the entire universe and every tiny detail in it (see Rashi on v 7). Israel's mission is to serve the One God and Him alone, and to shine the light of His unity to the entire world. This is why their national mission in the Land of Israel was to eliminate completely all trace of the idolatrous Canaanites - representing the antithesis of God's unity. The commentary Metzudat David (on verse 14) points out that in essence the task of removing idolatry is internal to each person: "Remove the gods that your fathers served on the other side of the river and in Egypt" - "entirely remove any thought of idolatry from your **heart**".

Rashi (on v 22) comments that Joshua's reason for needling the people until they reaffirmed their staunch commitment not to mingle and assimilate with the nations was that he saw (through holy spirit) that in time to come they would rebel and say, "Let us be like the nations" (Ezekiel 20:32). Reflecting on the ravages caused to the Jewish people by the mass assimilations of the past few hundred years should also needle us into mentally and spiritually separating ourselves from contemporary alien influences that can weaken our devotion to the Torah.

MYSTERIES OF TANAKH

The TaNaKh is a unique work that transcends time and applies to all the generations. As we study our national heritage, we must have the humility to accept that the apparent simplicity of the beautiful weave of stories through which our prophets taught us God's Torah is deceptive. Buried within and behind the prophetic words and letters of the Hebrew text are layers upon layers of meaning, with multiple hints and allusions flying off in every direction. The rabbis and sages who cherished and revered this literature and knew it forwards and backwards by heart have through their Midrashim and other comments opened tiny chinks in the thick veil concealing the infinite light that shines from the words of these texts.

Thus, we cannot always take the stories of NaKh as simple consecutive historical narratives. For example, some readers ask why ch 24 v 32 on the burial of Joseph's bones in Shechem comes **after** the account of the burial of Joshua - is it possible that the people have waited **thirty-eight** years after their entry into the Land before burying Joseph's bones, which they had brought up with them from Egypt??? But the truth is that it is not necessary to infer from our text that they did not bury Joseph until after they had buried Joshua. One of the most important hermeneutic principles of the Torah is that "there is no **before** and **after** in the Torah". Events are often juxtaposed in the verses not because of their temporal contiguity but because of their thematic interconnection.

With Joshua's death and burial in his tribal inheritance in Timnat-Serach in Mount Ephraim next to Shechem, a whole cycle of history was complete. It was from Shechem that Joseph, Jacob's chosen "first-born", had been stolen by his brothers in accordance with God's deep plan (Genesis 37:14; see Rashi there) and it was to Shechem that he was returned by his brothers, the Children of Israel, in the end. Shechem had been the first place in the Holy Land that Jacob had acquired - he paid good money for it (Genesis 33:19) - and he had given it to Joseph as the "double portion" of the "firstborn" (ibid. 48:22). Joseph's mission (**Yesod**) was to cause the Divine Presence to dwell in the very Land itself, the material world. The conquest of the Land by Israel under the leadership of Joshua, Joseph's direct descendant, was a crucial stage in the fulfillment of this mission. Now that Joshua had completed his own life's work, it was fitting that he should be laid to rest in Shechem, the very place from which Joseph had been stolen, because Joshua, who like Joseph lived 110 years, was in fact his incarnation. Joshua's burial in Shechem - thereby acquiring his burial place as his eternal possession - was the completion of the cycle that began with Joseph's sale, concluding now with Israel's possession of the Land. Thus, the **atzmot Yosef** (literally the "bones" of Joseph, but allusively his very "essence"= **etzem**), were now absorbed into the Land itself. It may be that the physical burial of Joseph's bones actually took place in the early days of the conquest, but it is mentioned here in order to point up the perfection of God's deep plan, through which the cycle always swings around to the end.

JOSHUA

"If Israel had not sinned they would have received only the Five Books of Moses and the Book of Joshua, which is the Registry of the Land of Israel (i.e. of its tribal portions)" (Nedarim 22b). The whole of the rest of the narrative and prophetic portions of the NaKh tells the story of how the Israelites failed to drive out the Canaanites and the terrible consequences to which this led. Some say that the only lesson we learn from history is that nobody ever learns anything from history. It may be true that many fail to draw and implement the lessons of history, but we do not have to be like them. In Joshua's final discourse he emphasizes that we are **free** to choose our own path (ch 24 vv 14-15). Let us choose the path of life and learn the lessons of our national history now in order not to repeat the mistakes of the past in future.

שופטים

JUDGES

CHAPTER 1

THE BOOK OF JUDGES

The Book of Judges narrates the inner, spiritual history of Israel from after the death of Joshua until the very threshold of the establishment of the kingship by the prophet Samuel - a span of some four hundred years, in which the nation was largely without a single, unifying leader except at times when outstanding "Judges" - spiritual leaders of exceptional stature - arose to save them from their plight in face of their enemies. According to our rabbis, the Book of Judges was written by Samuel on the basis of "kabbalah" - i.e. the prophetic tradition handed down from generation to generation until it came to his teacher, Eli the High Priest (Bava Batra 14b; see RaDaK on Judges 1:21). The entire book can be seen as an intimate study of the developing moral sickness of the Israelites in their land that necessitated the establishment of the messianic kingship by Samuel.

NO BEFORE AND AFTER IN THE TORAH

The principle that "there is no before and after in the Torah" was already discussed in our comments on Joshua 23-24. We need this principle now in order to resolve possible confusion caused by the "time-line" of Judges chs 1-2, which zig-zags quite sharply back and forth. Chapter 1 verse 1 of Judges seems to pick up the historical narrative where the book of Joshua left off, but as it begins to describe the tribe of Judah's conquest of their territories, the narrative seamlessly slips back to events that apparently took place in Joshua's lifetime and were already described in the book of Joshua - the conquest of Hebron and that of Dvir by Otniel ben Knaz, (see Joshua chapter 15).

Similarly, Chapter 2 of Judges opens with the appearance of God's messenger from Gilgal to reprove the people, which would seem to have taken place after Joshua's death. Whether or not it did, the text of Chapter 2 then interjects with the retelling of Joshua's death and burial (ch 2 vv 6-10) even though the whole book of Judges 1:1 has already started **after** Joshua's death. (Likewise, Numbers 1:1 starts in the **second** month of the second year after the Exodus, while a later chapter, Numbers 9:1 tells what happened in the **first** month of the second year!) As stated in the last installment, it is not necessarily the temporal contiguity of events that determines their juxtaposition in the text, but rather their thematic interconnection. Thus, we shall find that the two striking episodes described at the end of the book of Judges (chs 17-21) - Michah's idol and the Concubine of Giv'on - actually occurred in the very beginning of the period of the Judges.

"WHO WILL GO UP FOR US" (Judges 1:1)

Although it appears that the people consulted the Urim Ve-Tumim of the High Priest in order to ask which **tribe** should "go up" first against the Canaanites, our rabbis taught that God's answer - "Yehudah shall go up" (ch 1 v 2) specifically referred to **Otniel ben Knaz**, the hero of the capture of Dvir, whose name was in fact "Yehudah brother of Shimon". He was called **Otniel** because it contains the letters of the Hebrew word **anita**, "You have answered" - because God answered his prayers (see Temura 16a).

Otniel ben Knaz (also called **Yaabetz** see I Chronicles 2:55) was the second Judge of Israel after Joshua, and the account of his capture of **Kiryat Sefer-Dvir** refers allegorically to his conquest of the Torah (particularly those portions that were forgotten after the death of Moses.)

PURIFYING THE WORLD OF EVIL

A few hints of the profound allegory that underlies the book of Judges are contained in **Sefer HaLikutim** of the ARI (R. Yitzhak Luria, outstanding 16th century kabbalist). Following the account of the capture of Dvir, we are told that "the children of **Kayni**, Moses' father in law (=Jethro) went up from the city of dates (=Jericho) to be with the children of Judah in the wilderness of Judah." (1:16).

Rashi (ad loc.) explains that the fat, lush territory around Jericho was given to Jethro's offspring (who as converts did not have a share in the land) but only temporarily, as it would later be given in "compensation" to the Tribe in whose territory the Temple was to be built (Benjamin) as the place of the Temple would no longer be theirs but would belong to all Israel. However, Jethro's offspring, the **Kaynites**, had more sense than to attach themselves to a temporary material plot of land. Instead, since they lived in tents anyway, they went to the wilderness of Judah - a territory with no material benefits - in order to learn Torah from **Yaabetz=Otniel ben Knaz** and thereby gain an eternal spiritual acquisition. The **Kaynites** were later adduced by Jeremiah as the prime exemplar of the righteous convert who chooses the Torah itself as his inheritance (Jer. ch 35).

The **Kaynites** will reappear in our narrative in Judges ch 4 where Yael wife of **Hever HaKayni** distinguished herself by killing Sisera. In chapter 4 it says that "Hever HaKayni **separated** himself from Kayin (=Adam's son)" (Judges 4:11). They also appear in Samuel, when Saul asks them to move away from the Amalekites, where they were then encamped, in order to facilitate his attack.

ARI explains that Jethro was from the root of Kayin (**Gevurot**, severe judgment) and Hever was from the seed of Jethro. This is why he is called **HaKayni** from the root Kayin. Kayin was a mixture of good and evil, and in Jethro the "food" was sifted out from the "waste" and thereby rectified. This was when the good was **separated** from the evil, as alluded to in the above-quoted verse. The evil descended into the husks (Amalek, Goliath) while the good was left in Jethro. **Kayni** succeeded in bringing the husk "inside", into the realm of the holy, and thus, "In the place where penitents stand, even complete Tzaddikim cannot stand", because, as ARI explains, the penitents bring the husk inside and sweeten it.

Within the context of these notes it is impossible to condense the ARI's elaborate teachings about the various incarnations alluded to in these stories of **Rahav**, **Yael** and **Eli** (the last two have the same Hebrew letters), **Kayin**, **Yitro** (Jethro) and others. I am mentioning them only to underline how profoundly deep are these chapters of NaKh that we have the privilege of studying.

THE MYSTERY OF LUZ

The above secrets relating to these souls are revealed in an extensive Drush of ARI relating to the entire first section of Judges and centering in particular on Deborah (chs 4-5).

In the course of this Drush ARI reveals that the town of Beit El mentioned in our present text, Judges 1:23 (and is first mentioned in Genesis 12:8 as having been visited by Abraham and later, in Genesis 28:19, as the site of Jacob's dream of the Ladder) alludes to the Partzuf of Leah in the world of Beriyah, while Luz - the "name of the town before" - alludes to the Partzuf of Leah in the world of Atzilut. (Lamed Zayin=37=gematria of Leah). In the Form of Man, this corresponds to the place of the knot of the strap (**Retzu'ach**) of the Tefilin of the Head. As explained in Shulchan Aruch (Code of Torah Law) the knot must be placed at the bottom of the skull (**oref**), just above where the neck (**tzavar**) begins. According to our rabbis, it is from this bone that the body of man will develop in time to come, at the time of the resurrection, and this bone is called **luz**. (Many Jews know the tradition that this bone is nourished only by the food we eat at the **Melaveh Malka** feast accompanying out the departing Shabbat each week.)

ARI's introductions may open a tiny chink in the veil to help us appreciate the awesome depths of the very beautiful Midrashim about Luz brought in the "revealed" Torah as opposed to the esoteric Torah of ARI. Thus Rashi (on v 24) tells us that the only way into this mysterious city of Luz was through a cave, at the entrance to which stood a **luz** (= almond? nut?) tree. (Was there a hidden door in the tree?) The man who showed the Israelites how to get in did not even say a word. He merely gestured with his finger. Further details of the story are given in Sota 46b, where we learn that in return for this great favor, the Israelites spared the man, who went off to found a city likewise named Luz in the Land of the Hitim (Asia Minor) that became prosperous from the Techeilet (blue die) industry, survived even the ravages of Sennacheriv and Nebuchadnezzar, and which even the Angel of Death was not authorized to enter. When the elders of the city, after living on and on, reached the limits of knowledge, they would go outside the city walls and die. All this was the man's reward for having **accompanied** the Israelites and pointing them in the right direction (just as we accompany out the Shabbat). This Midrash suggests that the mystery of Luz is bound up with the mystery of drawing the timeless world to come (Leah in Atzilut) down towards this world (which derives from Beriyah).

CHAPTER 2

English translations of the Bible say that an **angel** of the Lord came up from Gilgal to Bochim (Judges 2:1). What is an **angel**? Our rabbis taught that this "angel" was none other than Pinchas the Priest, of whom the rabbis said that "when holy spirit would rest upon him, his face would burn like fiery torches" (Midrash Tanchuma).

Those who imagine angels as radiant winged beings from other realms may have been looking at medieval artists' reconstructions of events that are based on complete ignorance of the Hebrew language and the true meaning of the Bible. The Hebrew world **Mal'ach**, which is frequently translated as "angel", simply means an **agent** or **messenger**. Indeed, this exactly is the meaning of the ancient Greek word **angelos** from which our word **angel** derives.

A **Mal'ach** from God is definitely not an ordinary, animalistic human being that eats and drinks like a glutton and is three quarters asleep most of the time. This does not mean that God may not at times choose outstanding Tzaddikim who have completely transcended the physical to be His **Mal'achim**, as in the case of Moses, who is referred to both in the Chumash and in Psalms as a **Mal'ach**.

THE CYCLE OF WEEPING

The message of the **Mal'ach** who came up "from **Gilgal**" (=reincarnation, recycling) to **Bochim** ("the weepers") gives the very essence of the moral of the Book of Judges as a whole: The cyclical problem with which Judges deals is that the Israelites failed to drive out all of the Canaanites, instead permitting them to continue to dwell among them. This alone and in itself was not the fatal flaw. The flaw was that as a result, the Israelites mixed with and **learned from** the Canaanites, and adopted the religions and idolatrous practices of the nations around them.

Chapter 2 suddenly interjects the death and burial of Joshua into the reproof that traces the failure of the Children of Israel to live up to God's Covenant (vv 6-10). We read once again, as already told at the end of Joshua, that Joshua was buried in **Timnat Cheres** to the north of **Har Ga'ash**. **Timnat Cheres** means "picture of the sun" - for an image of the sun was placed over Joshua's grave (see Rashi on v 9). This in itself does not have anything to do with idolatry: the allusion to the sun was fitting since it was Joshua who had stopped the sun in its tracks at Giv'on - Joshua **transcended nature**. **Har Ga'ash** is the **volcano**. The rabbis taught that the people failed to eulogize Joshua properly after his death, and as a result God almost destroyed them all under a flood of lava (Rashi on Joshua 30. We note that our texts never refer to thirty days of mourning for Joshua as they do in the case of Moses, Jacob, etc. This is presumably the textual hint that Joshua was not properly eulogized.)

In other words, after Joshua's final address to the people in Shechem (Joshua ch 24), they all went home to attend to their own vineyards and fig trees without "eulogizing Joshua" i.e. without seeking to **internalize** the lessons that Joshua had imbibed from **his** teacher, Moses (who **was** eulogized for thirty days). This rupture in the tradition is the key to the subsequent tragic history of the Israelites in the Land. They did not draw close to and internalize the messages of their spiritual leaders except when they were direly threatened by their enemies, whereas they should have continued to keep their departed leaders' Torah near to their hearts all the time. (Perhaps this indicates that attaining the true Chassidic relationship between Chassid and Tzaddik would be the remedy and thus one of the main keys to our future redemption???)

Chapter 2 verse 13 tells us that "they abandoned HaShem and served the Baal and the Ashtarot". Since these terms for idolatrous deities will recur frequently in our texts, it is worth noting that RaDaK (ad loc.) comments that Baal is a generic term for graven images and idols, "since they are like a **lord** (Adon=Baal) to those that serve them". (Today also, we see that much of the world is under the spell of the images daily spun by the communications media, which are the latter-day purveyors of idolatry.)

While **Ashtarot** are literally images of female sheep, they also allude to the idolatry of wealth (the Hebrew letters of the word **osher**, "wealth" are contained in the name **Ashtarot**.)

CHAPTER 3

The opening verses of our text paint a picture that is depressingly familiar to the modern Israeli. The generation that witnessed the heroic days of the miraculous conquest of the Land had passed, and a new generation arose that had not seen God's great work and they rebelled against Him (see Rashi on v 1). Instead of enjoying peace and prosperity in the Land pursuing the Torah, they were forced to learn the art of warfare, just as in contemporary Israel, where the very flower of the country's youth are sacrificed on the altar of war.

Significantly the locations in the Promised Land over which the Israelites lost their hold as told in our present text (v 3) correspond exactly to those that are the sorest trial for Israel until today. The "five officers of the Philistines" ruled over the "big five" Philistine cities, Ashdod, Gaza, Gat, Ashkelon and Ekron in the Mediterranean coastal region. The Sidonians and Hivites were dwelling in present-day Lebanon, southern Syria and the Golan Heights.

Were it not for the hostility of the Arab population to the Jews, it is very likely that much of today's secular Israeli population would have intermarried with the surrounding peoples just as the Israelites did after the death of Joshua (v 6). Verse 7 adds a new element to the idolatry which the ancient Israelites adopted from their neighbors: the **Asherot** (not to be confused with the **Ash-t-erot** in Judges ch 3). The **Ashera** is a tree worshiped as a god: tree veneration is mentioned in the Torah (Deut. 16:21) as one of the idolatries practiced by the Canaanites. The prohibition of anything that comes from an Ashera tree recurs throughout the Shas and Poskim (Talmud and Codifiers). Significantly, the Kabbalah sees all worlds, revealed and concealed, as parts of the Tree of Life, the Tree of the Sefirot, yet the sages typify any kind of theology that splits off divine powers from one another as "uprooting saplings" (Chagigah 14b).

KUSHAN RISHATAYIM

Kushan Rishatayim king of Mesopotamia, whom God sent to try Israel (v 8), was an ideological as well as a physical enemy. The Talmud (Sanhedrin 105b) states that this was none other than Bilaam-Laban (**Rishatayim** means a **double** wickedness) - i.e. the treacherous spirit of Laban the Aramean and his sorcerer offspring Bilaam reared its head and ruled again in the world. That Otniel ben Knaz had the power to overcome this attests to his great power. It is said that Otniel noted that God had said to Moses "I have surely seen (**ra'oh ra-iti**, the verb is doubled) the misery of My people" (Ex. 3:7). Otniel learned out from the doubling of the verb that God had already seen that the people would sin with the Golden Calf, yet He still had compassion on them. Otniel said, "Whether they are worthy or guilty, He is obliged to save them" (Rashi on v 10). Let us turn this into our prayer today for contemporary Israel!

EGLON KING OF MOAB

After the death of Otniel, the people's sins caused Eglon king of Moab to gain ascendancy. Just as the Arameans of Kushan Rishatayim were relatives of the Israelites - being from the family of Abraham's brother Nachor - so too were the Moabites, who were descended from Abraham's nephew Lot, through his incestuous relation with his oldest daughter. Moab corresponds to the southern region of present-day Jordan east of the "Dead" Sea.

The capture by Moses of the territories of the Emorites east of the Jordan (who had previously taken over parts of Moab) had driven a wedge between Moab and her sister nation to the north, Ammon (=Amman, capital of Jordan), severely weakening Moab. Eglon took advantage of the moral deterioration of the Israelites to reassert Moabite sovereignty over the territories of Reuven, Gad and Menasheh east of the Jordan, thereby joining up with Ammon again and also with Israel's implacable enemy Amalek (who dwelled in the wilderness areas south east and south west of the "Dead" Sea). Eglon even conquered Jericho, the "lock" of the Holy Land.

Given the choice of going right or left by Abraham, Lot had opted to go to the left (Genesis 13:9 ff). It is therefore significant that Ehud ben Gera used a "sinister" ploy to kill Eglon through the power of his **left hand**. Although from the tribe of Benjamin (**bin-yamin**, "son of the **right**"), Ehud, like many other members of his tribe was **left-handed** (cf. Judges 20:16. Rabbi Nachman, who discusses left-handedness in a number of places, notes that Benjamin corresponds to the Tefilin, and the Tefilin of the arm are worn on the **left** arm - Likutey Moharan II, 77; see Rabbi Nachman's Wisdom p.293).

The small "sword that had two mouths" (v 16) which Ehud made and hid on his right thigh under his clothes for surprise use against Eglon with his **left** hand was none other than the Torah, which is called "a sword of mouths" (Psalm 149) because those who engage in its study eat in this world and in the world to come (Tanchuma).

RUTH

Our rabbis note that when Ehud told Eglon "I have the word of God for you" (Judges 3:20), Eglon arose from his throne out of respect. "Said the Holy One, blessed be He, 'You accorded Me honor and rose from your throne for the sake of My glory. By your life, I will raise up a descendant from you whom I shall seat upon My throne, as it is said, And Solomon sat upon the throne of God as king'" (Ruth Rabbah 2:9). Eglon had two daughters: While Orpah was the mother of Goliath, Ruth became one of the most celebrated converts of all time and was the great-grandmother of King David, father of Solomon.

It is noteworthy that in this roundabout way Ruth's conversion came about through Ehud, who was from the tribe of Benjamin, from which came Saul, the first king of Israel. Saul persecuted David, who was said to be not even Jewish since the Torah explicitly forbids a Moabite to enter the Assembly (Deut. 23:4). Only when the sages of the generation revived Samuel's Midrash that this does not apply to a Moabit**ess** was David accepted. Evidently left-handed, roundabout courses of events are part of the coming of Mashiach!!!

Just as Benjamin contributed Ehud ben Gera to the illustrious history of Israel's judges, so every one of the tribes of Israel contributed at least one judge, including Levi (Eli and Samuel), with the sole exception of Shimon, whose history of rebellion under Zimri ben Saloo in the time of Moses precluded the possibility of their producing a judge.

CHAPTER 4

A certain "confusion" between right-handedness and left-handedness continues in Chapter 4: even Rabbi Chaim Vital, who wrote down the teachings of the ARI, states that he cannot remember if his master said that Yavin king of Canaan who ruled in Chatzor (Judges 4:2) was from the **left** side, Imma-Binah (Yavin, "he will understand") or from the **right** side, Abba-Chochmah (YaVIN=72=Chochmah; see Sefer HaLikutim, Shoftim). In any event, ARI reveals that the root of **Kayin** (Adam's first son), which derives from the **Gevurot** of **Binah**, descended into the unholy realm of the husks to manifest as the unholy **Da'at** ("knowledge").

For this reason, Yavin's general was called **Sisera**: The two middle letters of his name are Samech (60)-Reish (200) = 260 = 26 x 10 = i.e. ten Havayot (Each HaVaYaH is one Tetragrammaton, in gematria = 26; HaVaYaH is Da'at, here spreading through all ten Sefirot). The remaining letters of **Sisera** are Samech (60), Yud (10) Aleph (1) making a total of 71, which is the sum of MaH (the "Milui" - filling of the letters -- of HaVaYaH, corresponding to Zeir Anpin=45) plus Kaf-Vav (26=HaVaYaH). ARI states that Sisera alludes to the mystery of Da'at of Zeir Anpin on the side of the Kelipot-husks (ibid).

The Midrash attributes enormous military resources to Sisera. Besides the 900 chariots of iron mentioned in our text (v 13), "he brought 40,000 commanding officers each of whom had one hundred thousand men. Sisera was thirty years old and conquered the whole world. There was not a city whose wall he did not cause to fall through his roar. Even a wild animal that he roared at in the field would stand unable to move from its place. When he went to bathe in the River Kishon, he would come out of the water with his beard full of enough fish to feed many, many people." (Yalkut). All of this seems to be alluding allegorically to what the ARI expresses Kabbalistically through the use of Gematrias.

Given that, as ARI explains, this was on one level a war of spirit and ideology, it is interesting to note that the war actually took place in areas of Israel that many today find to be the most spiritual - the lower and upper Galilee. Yavin's Hatzor had been destroyed together with its king, also called Yavin, in the time of Joshua (ch 11). Now, however, the new Yavin reasserted the Canaanite power, threatening the entire north and center of the Land: the territories of Ephraim, Zevulun and Naftali. With all the other tribes now settled in their respective inheritances, they were so preoccupied with their lives, farms etc. that they did not unite as in former times to help their threatened brothers.

The leader of the hour was the prophetess **Deborah** of the tribe of Ephraim. The Midrash states that she was exceptionally wealthy (Targum on Judges 4:5 teaches that the topography in this verse alludes not to places but to her sources of wealth, see Rashi ad loc.). ARI explains the topography spiritually: Devorah is rooted in **Malchut**, her "husband" **Lapidot** (=flashing torches=**Barak**=flash of lightning) is **Yesod**. The **Tomer** under which she modestly sits so as not to have **yichud** with the Israelites who come to consult her on Torah law also alludes to **Yesod**. It was "between **Ramah** and **Beit El**" because **Beit El** is Leah who is **ramah**, "high up", the concealed world of **Binah**. Thus, we begin to see how it is that Devorah was part of the repair of the faulty world of Yavin-Daat of Kelipah.

"What was Devorah doing there judging Israel - wasn't Pinchas ben Elazar still alive? **I bring Heaven and Earth to witness: be it a Gentile or Israelite, a man or a woman, a slave or maidservant, according to a person's deeds, so Holy Spirit dwells upon them.** In the academy of Elijah, it was taught that Devorah's husband was an ignoramus, but Devorah said to him, 'Go and make wicks for the lamp in the Sanctuary in Shilo and then your share will be among the righteous among them and you will come to the life of the world to come.' Thus, he would make the wicks and he had three names: Lapidot, Barak and Michael." (Midrash Tanchuma). The concept of the wick of the lamp is bound up with Binah (see Likutey Moharan I:60 etc.).

The ten thousand men of Naftali and Zevulun that Barak brought against Sisera were nothing but small farmers - how were they to stand up against Sisera's hosts and his 900 iron chariots? Barak went to Mount Tabor to lure Sisera out against him, but Sisera was a wily general and knew that his chariots would be useless in the rocky terrain of the mountain. It was springtime, and he stayed down below in the valley of the upper Kishon, where he expected that his chariots would easily overcome the Israelites. (The River Kishon starts in the eastern Galilee and runs all the way through the Jezreel valley down to the Mediterranean Sea by Haifa).

In the Song of Deborah (ch 5) we learn that "from heaven they fought -- the very stars fought from their tracks with Sisera" (v 20). (The initial letters of **Hakochavim Mimeslotam Nilchamu** make up HaMaN, for the Divine victory over Sisera was the victory over the husk of Amalek, with which he was bound up. Amalek touts the Law of Nature, but God transcends nature.) How exactly did the very stars miraculously transcend the normal laws of nature to bring about the defeat the Canaanites? It is thought that the miracle consisted in a sudden, totally unexpected tornado sweeping in from the region stretching from the Rift Valley (**Arava**) to the Kinneret east of the Lower Galilee, bringing torrents of pelting rain that turned the Kishon Valley into a treacherous muddy bog that totally incapacitated the iron chariots of the Canaanites and swept them into the river, forcing Sisera to flee ignominiously. The miracle is not that there was a tornado - these occur periodically in this region - but that the tornado came exactly when it did (see Baal Shem Tov al HaTorah, Beshalach).

The other heroine of this story is **Yael**, another of the outstanding converts of all time. The wife of the itinerant **Keini**, she could have saved Sisera, let him lie with her in the tent and risen to "greatness". Instead she remained faithful to her husband, cleverly giving Sisera not the thirst-quenching waters of kindness but soporific milk, which caused him to doze off exhausted from the battle. She then took the tent peg and smashed his head. It was fitting that it should have been his brain that she dashed, since, as revealed by ARI, Sisera's hold was in the brain and mind (**Da'at**).

With the destruction of the unholy husk, the holy spark was released, and thus Rabbi Akiva ben Yosef came forth from the descendants of Sisera, just as Rav Shmuel bar Shilat came from those of Haman (ARI). Rabbi Chaim Vital concludes the ARI's Drash on Devorah by saying: "And my master told me that my soul was there too."

*** The story of the destruction of Sisera's forces and Devorah's song, Judges 4:4-24 and 5:1-31, is read as the Haftarah of Parshat **Beshalach**, Exodus 13:17-17:16 ***

CHAPTER 5

THE SONG OF DEVORAH

It was fitting that Devorah should sing the song of victory over Sisera. **Devorah** is from the root **davar**, "word", as in **dibur**, "speech" (=Malchut, through which Godliness is revealed.) When speech rises to the level of song, speech is perfected through the musical notes of the melody (**Ta'amey HaMikra**), which come from a higher level. Speech is from the Nefesh ego-soul (Malchut) while song is from the Neshamah-soul (Binah, Understanding). Understanding elevates speech.

Devorah's song is the sixth of the ten great songs of history. They are listed in Targum on Shir HaShirim 1:1: Song of the Sabbath day at creation, Song at the Red Sea, Song over the well in wilderness (Numbers 21:17), Moses' song of Ha'azinu, "Hear O heavens…"; Joshua's song that stopped the sun at Giv'on, Deborah's song, Hannah's song over the birth of Samuel, David's song over his victory over all his enemies, Solomon's Song of Songs and the Song of the future redemption. The Hebrew word for song is **shir**, linked to the root **sheir**, a "chain". A song is a chain of words and notes that give **ta'am** -- deeper **meaning** - to events and experiences that would otherwise seem disconnected. The song links everything together as part of God's symphony of creation: the melody is the song of His **hashgachah**, His "providence" over every detail.

Deborah's song was sung with Holy Spirit. It is highly allusive, and we are in need of the commentators if we are to trace the multiple hints it contains. First among the commentators we need on any such a flighty, eloquent passage is the Aramaic Targum, which in translating simple narrative portions of NaKh is normally terse and direct, but which expands considerably on the meaning of many prophetic passages in order to explain them in greater depth. While the best-known Aramaic Targum on the Five Books of Moses is that of Onkelos the Ger (Convert) our Aramaic Targum on the Prophets and Holy Writings was written by R. Yonatan ben Uzziel (who also wrote a Targum on Chumash, somewhat lengthier and with more midrash than that of Onkelos). R. Yonatan was the greatest of the students of Hillel - while Rabban Yochanan ben Zakai, who went on to lead the Jewish people during and after the destruction of the Second Temple, is described by the Talmud as Hillel's "smallest" pupil. Given that Raban Yochanan knew all the secrets of the universe and even the "conversations of trees", it boggles the imagination to try to understand the level of R. Yonatan ben Uzziel, who was so devoted to the Torah that he never even married.

The Targum of Yonatan brings out various allusions in Deborah's song to past and future events in Israel's history, including the Crossing of the Red Sea and the Giving of the Torah. The miracle that Deborah's generation witnessed whereby the overwhelming forces of Sisera and his allies were swept away by the River Kishon was seen as a miracle on the soil of the Holy Land that bore comparison with that of the splitting of the Red Sea in its significance for the nation and its survival. The Targum and Midrash state that at the time of the Giving of the Torah, Mount Tabor and Mount Carmel had come asking for the Torah to be given on them, but God decreed that it was to be given on the humble Mount Sinai in the Wilderness. Nevertheless, Tabor and Carmel were rewarded: Elijah performed the miracle of the consumption of his offering by heavenly fire on Mount Carmel, while Mount Tabor was the scene of the "Giving of the Torah" in the time of Deborah.

The song of Deborah (as explained by Targum, Rashi and the other commentators) portrays the dire state of Israel prior to the victory over Sisera. It had become impossible to travel the roads because of danger from the enemies; it was impossible even for the girls to go out to draw water from the wells; it was impossible to live in open, unfortified settlements - the Israelites had to take refuge behind walls! (See Targum and Rashi on vv 6-7, v 11.) The Israelites were faced with an "Intifada" from the Canaanites that made life impossible in the country, not unlike today.

The song also hints at the cracks of disunity among the tribes. Reuven in particular comes in for criticism (vv 15-16) for sitting on the east of the Jordan telling Barak "we are on your side" and Sisera "we are on your side", waiting to see who would win (Targum). The tribe of Dan is also criticized for loading their possessions into boats on the River Jordan in order to escape (v 17), and **Meiroz** is severely cursed (v 23) although there are different opinions as to whether this was a city, a prominent individual, or perhaps a star (Mo'ed Katan 16a).

The greatest praise goes to **Yael**, who became a Judge in her own right (Rashi on v 6). "She is blessed more than women in the tent" (v 24). This implies that she is compared favorably to the matriarchs Sarah, Rivkah, Rachel and Leah, all of whom are described in the texts as being "in the tent".

How did Yael have the strength to kill a mighty warrior like Sisera. The Talmud states that her greatness lay in carrying out a sin for the sake of God (**lishmah**), which is greater than carrying out a mitzvah not for the sake of God (**shelo lishmah**). The Talmud infers from v 27 that Sisera had relations with her seven times, thereby exhausting all his strength and thus enabling her to kill him (Nazir 23b).

"Thus, let all your enemies be destroyed... and those who love Him are like the sun coming out in its strength" (v 31). On the latter part of the verse, the Talmud comments, "This verse refers to those who allow themselves to be insulted and do not insult back, who hear themselves abused and do not answer, who do what they do out of love and rejoice in suffering" (Yoma 23a). In time to come the light will be seven times seven the light of the seven days of creation - i.e. 343 times greater (7 x 7 x 7; see Rashi on this verse).

CHAPTER 6

The victory over Sisera brought relief to the Israelites but they did not take advantage of the victory to drive out the Canaanites and consolidate their hold on the Land. This gave the Midianites their opportunity to make ever more destructive predatory incursions. The Midianites, who were descended from Abraham's son from the "concubine" Keturah (Genesis 25:2), were a group of five clans, some shepherds, some traders and some of them marauding bandits, who lived as nomads across the vast stretch of desert east of Ammon and Moab (present day eastern Jordan and north west Saudi Arabia). They were sworn enemies of Israel (Numbers 25:18). The Israelite failure to drive out the Canaanites from their strongholds in the Jezreel valley enabled the Midianites to cross the Jordan river fords into the Land and establish a footing in the Beit She'an valley, from which they began attacking the tribes of the Galilee and advancing into the center of the country into the tribal areas of Ephraim and Menasheh.

"And Israel became very low" (vayi**dal**, **dal**=poor, wretched) (v 6). "They were poor without good deeds. And they didn't even have the resources to bring a **Minchah** offering" (Tanchuma, Behar).

The prophet who came to reprove the people (verse 8) was according to tradition Pinchas ben Elazar.

Gideon was from the tribe of Menasheh, from that half of the tribe that had settled in the Land itself. The town of "Ofra" in which he lived is not to be confused with Ofra north of Jerusalem in the territory of Benjamin, an important settlement until today. RaDaK on verse 11 states that Gideon's Ofra was a town of the same name further to the north: it was probably a little to the south west of Shechem (Nablus).

The Zohar (I, 254) states that Gideon was not a tzaddik, nor the son of a tzaddik, but that he merited his role as savior because he spoke in defense of Israel (see Rashi on v 13).

The depiction of Gideon helping his father to beat and sift wheat in a wine vat out of fear of the Midianites shows the dire state of affairs in Israel. According to the Midrash, Gideon said he would do all the work so that his father could go to hide from the Midianites, and it was for this act of filial piety that he was worthy of the visit from the angel (v 11).

Our commentators make no effort to identify the angel with any human. It is clear from the text that this was a spiritual messenger from God who appeared to Gideon when he was in a state of prophecy (see RaDaK on v 9).

From Gideon's sacrifice of **matzot** before the angel, we learn that it was Pesach (Rashi on v 19). According to tradition, Gideon had heard his father recounting the miracles of the Exodus at the Pesach Seder and said to God, "If our ancestors were Tzaddikim, then save us in our merit, and if they were wicked, then just like You did wonders for them for free, so too perform wonders for us – **where are all His wonders that our fathers told us???**

Gideon's smashing of the Baal-idol is reminiscent of Abraham's smashing the idols of his father Terach as told in the famous midrash. His father Joash's challenge to the men of the city that Baal himself should avenge those who broke his statue is somewhat reminiscent of Abraham's mocking answer to Terach when asked how the idols were smashed and he said that the biggest idol smashed all the others.

When Gideon sacrificed to God on an altar built from the stones of the altar to Baal and with vessels and fuel taken from the Ashera tree, eight Torah prohibitions were temporarily suspended to enable him to do so: (1) sacrificing outside the sanctuary (2) at night (3) by a non-Kohen (4) using vessels of an Ashera, which is forbidden for benefit even for a mitzvah (5) using the stones of an idolatrous altar (6) using the wood of the Ashera for fuel; (7) sacrificing an animal set aside as an offering to an idol - the fattened ox (8) sacrificing an animal that had been worshipped - the other ox (Temura 28b). "It is time to do for the Lord, they have broken (**heifeiroo**="you should break") Your Torah" (Psalms 119:126).

Even though Gideon was obliged to perform his revolutionary, iconoclastic mission at nighttime because of fear of repercussions from the local bastions of political correctness, his heroic act was the beginning of a sweeping movement of repentance from idolatry that led to victory over the Midianites. As soon as one simple Israelite was willing to get up and shatter the gods of political correctness, the redemption could take place.

If Gideon believed in God, why did he ask for a **second** sign after God had already performed a patent miracle in drenching the fleece with dew when everything around was dry (vv 36-40)? RaDaK (on v 39) points out that "You shall not try the Lord" (Deut 6:16) but answers in the name of R. Saadia Gaon that it was not that Gideon had any doubt about God's **ability** to save Israel. To test God would be to say, "Prove that you can do it". But what Gideon wanted was reassurance about whether he himself was worthy to be the channel for such a great miracle.

We can learn from Gideon that even a simple person can merit God's communicating with him directly and using him as the instrument of His redemption, all through the power of simple mitzvot, good deeds and love of the people of Israel.

CHAPTER 7

The magnitude of the challenge facing Gideon must be reconstructed from hints scattered through our text. The marauding Midianites with their Amalekite and other allies, the "Children of the East" (ch 7 v 12), numbered one hundred and thirty-five thousand warriors (ch 8 v 10) -- over four times as many as Gideon's 32,000 - the great majority of whom proved to be too afraid to go out to battle (ch 7 v 3). The Midianites were encamped in the western corner of the Beit She'an valley between the protruding spurs of Giv'at HaMoreh with Mount Tabor behind it to their north and Mount Gilboa to the south. They had watchmen posted on the hills (ch 7:2 see Targum/RaDaK). Gideon had rallied Naftali and Asher, the tribes of the Galilee, to Mount Tabor, intending that they should attack the Midianites on their northern flank, while he himself was waiting for reinforcements to come up from his own tribe of Menasheh in the south in order to advance northwards from Gilboa to attack the Midianites on their southern flank. However, the plan for a pincer attack failed because the hoped-for reinforcements from Menasheh did not arrive in time, and from ch 8 vv 18-19 we learn that the Midianites succeeded in routing the northern tribes on Mount Tabor under the leadership of Gideon's brother, whom they killed.

Thus, Gideon was left with no more than ten thousand men to stand against the vast army of invading hordes from the east. Yet even Gideon's 10,000 were far too many for God, Who wanted to teach that Israel does not need great numbers in order to accomplish His purpose, "lest Israel boast against Me saying 'my own hand saved me'" (verse 2). God does not need numerical advantage for His victories. For "not because of your multitude out of all the peoples did the Lord desire you and chose you, for you are the small minority out of all the peoples" (Deut. 7:7).

What counts for God is true devotion and righteousness. Gideon showed outstanding faith and courage in sending away all but the 300 Tzaddikim who, rather than fall down on their knees like Baal-worshippers in order to plunge their faces into the stream to slake their desperate thirst, preferred to draw up the water with their hands and bring it up to their mouths with dignity. **Derekh Eretz** ("the way of the land", "good manners") comes even before the Torah. "And his **hand** was **faith**" (Exodus 17:12). Instead of greedily bending down and swallowing what they needed to take from the world, they drew it to themselves through the hand of **faith** and **prayer**.

Why was kneeling down by the water the sign of an idolater? RaDaK (on v 4) brings an illuminating midrash that says that the people of that generation used to kneel down and bow down **to their reflections** - i.e. they were filled with narcissistic pride. (Do we too look too much in the mirror?) Self-love with the accompanying craving for kudos were the fatal flaws that subsequently led to so much strife between Gideon and Ephraim, the men of Succot and Penu-el (ch 8) and eventually to the downfall of Gideon's own dynasty (ch 9).

THE CAKE OF BARLEY

Man's egotistical pride is precisely what the Omer barley offering brought in the Temple on the second day of Pesach, the 16th of Nissan, comes to rectify. We have already seen (ch 6 v 19) that Gideon's smashing of the idols took place on the first day of Pesach. He "rose early in the morning" (ch 7 v 1) and advanced all day, dispatching all who were unworthy to take part in the miracle. It was thus on the eve of the 16th of Nissan that God told him to go down to spy on the Midianite camp, and they were routed that night.

The Midianite man's dream about the coal-baked cake of barley that rolled through and overturned the Midianite camp alludes to the merit of the small Omer-measure of Barley offered by Israel (Rashi on v 13). The Omer offering, which initiates the harvest season, is a kind of national Sotah (unfaithful wife) offering to propitiate God for apparent disloyalty. The only two grain offerings in the Temple that had to be of barley and not wheat were the Omer and Sotah woman's offerings. Barley is normally for animal consumption. Offering barley on the Altar signifies man's repentance for having succumbed to his animal instincts. RaDaK relates the unusual word **tzlil** referring to the barley cake (**tzlil** is the **kri**, the way the word is to be **read**), **tzlil** meaning a "noise", alluding to the tumult in the camp that the barley-cake brought in its wake. However, the Midrash darshens the **ktiv** - the word as **written** in the parchment scroll, **tzalool** - as indicating that the generation was **tzalool**, "strained off" of all Tzaddikim (see Rashi on v 13 and Vayikra Rabbah 28:6). Practically no-one was left except Gideon's tiny band. Even so, they saw victory through their humble faith and their confidence that even in their degradation and smallness, their repentance could bring God to perform miracles for them.

The Shofars and Torches that were their only military "equipment" came to arouse the merit of the Giving of the Torah, which was accompanied by the blast of the shofar, thunder and lightning (Rashi on v 16). From the point of view of psychological warfare, the idea was to surround the Midianites and make them think that they were in the middle of a surprise night-time ambush on all sides by a vast Israelite army.

Thus, God showed that one man's dream could throw an entire army into a state of such demoralization that an ingenious display of night-time fireworks with accompanying Shofar-blowing could send them all into flight. The defeat of the Midianites came about not through numbers but all through the power of the spirit.

The Midianites fled southwards along the western bank of the River Jordan, hoping to cross over the river fords into Ammon in order to escape eastwards to their home territories in the Arabian desert.

CHAPTER 8

God's miraculous defeat of the Midianites and their allies is celebrated in Psalm 83 (particularly vv 10-12). The lesson that comes forth from the narrative in our text in Judges is that the vital flaw of pride and arrogance, together with the internecine rivalry to which it leads, still prevented the Israelites from uniting under a messianic king whose goal would be not his own personal glorification and that of his dynasty but only the sanctification of God's great Name. It would take generations before the nation was ready for a true king of Israel.

Gideon himself showed himself largely free of this pride: he eloquently dissipated a potential conflict with the Ephraimites by humbly offering them the kudos, but he was faced with excessive mean-mindedness from the men of Succot and Penu-el, whose refusal to assist him in his efforts against the common enemy is reminiscent of Naval's later refusal to help David. Succot and Penu-el are east of the River Jordan near the Adam Bridge in the valley of the River Yabok. Penu-el had been the site of Jacob's encounter with the angel prior to his confrontation with Esau (Genesis 32:31) while Succot was where Jacob subsequently built a house for himself and "tabernacles" for his animals (ibid. 33:16). Perhaps the severe reprisals which Gideon the Judge meted out against the men of Succot and Penu-el were intended to eradicate the animalistic Esau-trait that their meanness betrayed.

The remaining forces of Midian and their allies succeeded in reaching **Karkoor**, which is about 200 km. **east** of the River Jordan. There they thought they would be safe from Gideon, yet he succeeded in capturing their kings and routing the entire camp.

The final destruction of the Midianites by a scion of the tribe of Menasheh was fitting since it was the Midianites who had purchased Menasheh's father Joseph from his brothers and sold him to the Egyptians (Genesis 37:28 & 36). Gideon refused the Israelite offer to be their king with a dynasty of his own offspring as kings after him: he understood that Israel was not yet ready for a king. Instead he took a rich share of the booty captured from the Midianites, who in v 24 are referred to as Ishmaelites since as a son of Keturah (=Hagar) Midian was Ishmael's brother and came under his wing. The splendid gold necklaces and ornaments of the Midianite hosts indicate pride. Gideon's receiving the Midianite booty was perhaps a "repayment" for the sale of Joseph, his ancestor, but could he rectify the pride?

Why did Gideon make himself an **Ephod**? The **Ephod** is one of the eight garments of the High Priest (Exodus 28:6 ff). Gideon had indeed, although not a **Kohen**, served as "High Priest" when he broke down the altar of Baal and sacrificed to HaShem. However, the Midrash (Bereishit Rabbah 45) explains that he had a particular motive in making an **Ephod** for himself. On the **Choshen Mishpat**, the breast-plate of the High Priest worn with the **Ephod**, there were twelve stones corresponding to the Twelve Tribes of Israel. But because one of the stones was for Levi, it was impossible to have more than one stone for the tribe of Joseph even though it had become two, with Ephraim and Menasheh. Since Ephraim was the natural leader of Joseph there was apparently no stone in the High Priest's breastplate for Gideon's tribe of Menasheh. Since the twelve stones correspond to the twelve constellations (**Mazalot**), it was as if Menasheh had no **Mazal**, and this was why Gideon made the **Ephod**. If **Mazal** means "luck" (well, kind of), Gideon's **Ephod** proved to be very luckless, for although he intended it for the sake of heaven, this symbol of "his" victory over the Midianites became a stumbling-block for Israel as they turned it into a cult object, and although Gideon himself enjoyed a good old age, his success in weaning the Israelites from idolatry was thus short-lived.

May God save us from pride and unholy rivalry and bring us to the humility that will enable us to be worthy of His victory over our enemies despite our tiny numbers and their overwhelming force.

<h1 style="text-align:center">CHAPTER 9</h1>

BETRAYAL

At the end of Judges Chapter 8 we learned that after the death of Gideon (=Yeruba'al, "he who strives with Baal") the Children of Israel reverted "and they went astray after the Baalim and they put **Baal Brit** as god over them" (v 33). It is unnecessary to try to imagine the ancient Israelites falling down and mindlessly prostrating to sticks and stones. The Talmud (Berachot 12b) interprets the word **ve-zonu**, "they went astray", lit. "they whored after", as implying that they entertained **thoughts** of idolatry, which suggests that many may not have openly practiced idolatrous rituals but were ideologically alienated from their ancestral faith. In fact, the ideology underlying certain kinds of idolatry can be seemingly highly profound and indeed very attractive to the enquiring mind.

What exactly the ideology of **Baal Brit** was is hard to say. The Talmud (Shabbat 83) says that **Baal Brit** (lit. "master of the covenant") was identical with **Zvuv**, the god of the Philistines of Ekron. A **zvuv** is a "fly". It may seem weird that anyone would worship a fly, though in fact flies have been even more successful than humanity in populating the world with their kind and can usually move a lot faster than even the best swatters. Whether this god was actually represented as a fly of some kind is open to question. The rabbis encouraged mispronouncing the names of idols in order to deride them. What is significant is that the Israelites, who were sworn to God's Covenant (**Brit**), had now allowed the very concept of the Covenant, with the loyalty it demands, to become degraded. Thus, the story of **Avimelech** - who burned up the people of Shechem who followed this idolatry - is essentially one of betrayal and its bloody consequences.

I WANT TO BE KING

We also learned at the end of Chapter 8 that Gideon had seventy legitimate sons and one son from his **pilegesh** in Shechem. Under Torah law a **pilegesh** is a woman that a man designates for himself as a concubine but without the ceremony of **Kiddushin** (sanctifying a woman to oneself as a wife, the first stage of marriage) and without the protection of a **Ketubah** (the "marriage contract" guaranteeing the woman financial security even in widowhood or after divorce). The **pilegesh** thus does not have the status of a wife and is considered somewhat disreputable: thus, RaDaK on Judges 11:1 equates **pilegesh** with **zonah**, "whore".

Did Gideon call this son **Avimelech** - or did the boy that was born of this not-so-proper relationship take the name for himself? From Judges 8:31, a careful reading of the Hebrew suggests that he himself gave himself the name of **Avimelech**, which literally means "My father is king": thus, he tried to cover over his disreputable origin using the **kudos** of Gideon. However, **Avimelech** also has the connotation of **I want to be king**: **avi** is thus from the same root as **ava**, I want, as in **eviyon**, the "poor one", who "wants" (see Likutey Moharan I, 10:4).

Midrash Tanchuma contrasts this **Avimelech** unfavorably with **Avimelech** king of the Philistines in the time of Abraham (Genesis ch 20 etc.). "'Better is a near neighbor than a distant brother' (Proverbs 27:10). Better was Avimelech king of the Philistines who gave great honor to Abraham, saying 'Here, my land is before you' (Gen. 20:15) than Avimelech son of Yerubaal who killed his brothers. Said the Holy One blessed be He to Avimelech: 'You wicked man. You killed **seventy men on one stone** (Judges 9:5) - You will be punished': 'And a certain woman cast down the **millstone**' (ibid. v 53). 'He who digs a trap will fall into it and he that rolls a stone will have it come back against him' (Proverbs 26:27)."

AND AVIMELECH WENT TO SHECHEM (v 1)

The city of Shechem was designated for punishments from long before. It was there that Jacob's daughter Dinah had been raped, sullying the purity of his family and leading to the slaughter of the men of Shechem by Levi and Shimon (Gen. ch 34). It was to Shechem that Joseph's brothers went to graze and devise their plan to destroy him. The solemn ceremony of the Blessings and Curses (Deut. 11:29 ff; ibid. 27:11; Joshua ch 8) had been carried out on Mount Gerizim and Mount Eival overlooking Shechem. Joseph's bones had been finally buried in Shechem, but since the death of Joshua there had been a steady decline in the Israelites that was expressed now in the corruption of the leadership. Faith and trust in God were replaced with mob appeal.

In Shechem, Avimelech used his mother's family's influence to build a political base for himself founded not on loyalty but on popular resentment against the splendid dynasty of 70 princes that Gideon had established. Avimelech won over the **Baaley Shechem** - the "owners", "masters" or "bosses" of the place with all the Mafiosi connotations that the term has. With money taken from the Temple of **Baal Brit** (was this the local bank?) Avimelech hired a gang of ruffians to form a private militia to carry out the bloody killing of his seventy paternal brothers.

Only **Yotam** was saved. The name implies "God (**Yo**) is perfect/pure (**tam**)" and is also an anagram of **yatom** (="orphan"). To put his curse upon the murderer Avimelech, Yotam went up Mount Gerizim. In the ceremony of Blessings and Curses, the blessings had been delivered from Mount Gerizim and the curses from Mount Eival. Yotam reasoned that if so, the blessings went in the direction of Mount Eival and the curses to Mount Gerizim, and thus the latter was a suitable location from which to send curses in the direction of the Bosses of Shechem. (In later time, after the exile of the Ten Tribes, Sennacheriv under his policy of population exchange settled the **Kootim**, who came to be known also as the **Shomronim** - Samaritans - in Shechem. They semi-converted to Torah practice but later fell into idolatry and placed an image of a dove on the ill-fated Mount Gerizim, after which they were proscribed by the rabbis as idolaters. In many Talmudic editions, the term **Kooti** is used synonymously with **Nachri** or **Akum** - oveid avodah zarah, "idolater".)

Yotam's eloquent parable about the trees turning successively to the Olive Tree, the Fig Tree and the Vine to rule over them alludes to the growing degeneracy of the Israelite leadership. The Olive Tree alludes to Otniel ben Knaz (Judah is compared to an olive tree -- Jeremiah 11:16). The Fig Tree alludes to Devorah, who gave the people sweet nourishment with her Song, while the Vine refers to Gideon. That Avimelech could be compared only with the prickly thorn bush which hurts anyone who touches it and affords scarcely any shade is symptomatic of the decline of the leadership.

Our text (ch 9 v 22) states that Avimelech ruled over Israel for three years, implying that he was more than merely a local tyrant, although no heroic acts of national service are attributed to him. He was merely power-hungry. Nevertheless, he is considered the Seventh Judge of Israel, and was the first to actually be called **Melech** ("king"; ch 9 v 6). He had about as much staying power as the succession of rickety governments with which contemporary Israel has been plagued in recent years: Avimelech ruled for only three years.

The **ru'ach ra'ah** ("bad spirit") that God sent between Avimelech and the bosses of Shechem is also reminiscent of the break-up of so many latter-day Israeli political coalitions with all the accompanying betrayal and acrimony. Opportunism and shifting loyalty were the order of the day. "And all the bosses of Shechem. went and made Avimelech king" (v 6). "And the bosses of Shechem **betrayed** Avimelech" (v 23). "And Ga'al ben Eved moved into Shechem, and the bosses of Shechem **trusted in him**" (v 26). Verse 25 illustrates the anarchy that prevailed: this verse is cited in Talmud Bava Kama 72b as the paradigm case of blatant robbery.

Rashi states that **Ga'al ben Eved** "was from another people" (Rashi on v 26). **Ga'al** has the connotation of vomiting, and **eved** is a slave. His influence over the bosses of Shechem illustrates the extent of the

Israelite assimilation with the surrounding peoples. They listen when Ga'al tells them they would be better off serving **Hamor, father of Schechem** (the Hivite, the archetypal serpent) than serving Avimelech (v 28).

Avimelech is the embodiment of degenerate **Malchut** (kingship). **Malchut** is identified with **fire** (see Likutey Moharan I, 4) - and Avimelech takes vengeance on the people of Shechem for their rebellion against him by going on a rampage of bloodshed and burning, moving from town to town to chase after and destroy his enemies.

This was a horrible civil war the like of which had not been known among the Israelites. It was stopped only through the quick thinking and resourcefulness of the anonymous woman who rolled a heavy millstone down from the fortress tower of the city of Tebetz, smashing Avimelech's skull just in time to prevent him setting fire to it. The moral of the whole sorry story seems to be that secular politics is a dirty business.

CHAPTER 10

Our sources contain scant information about the exploits of Tola ben Pu'ah of the tribe of Issachar who judged Israel after Avimelech, and very little about Ya'ir Ha-Gil'adi, who seems to have established a splendid dynastic empire with his thirty sons on their thirty foals and their thirty cities. Rashi on verse 6 states that even he was numbered among those who abandoned HaShem and did not serve Him.

The deepening idolatry of the people now encompassed the cults of no less than **seven** of the surrounding nations, despite the fact that God had saved Israel from **seven** enemies (v 6 &v 11, see Rashi). This led to a terrible retribution in which the Israelites became subject to yet another "existential threat", this time from the Philistines and the Ammonites.

The Ammonites, who not only gained sway over the territories of Reuven, Gad and half-Menasheh east of the River Jordan but were now attacking the very heartland of Judah, Benjamin and Ephraim (vv 8-9) were the offspring of Lot's incestuous relationship with his younger daughter (Genesis 19:38). Their territory was in what is today northern Jordan, whose capital, Amman, is named after them. The Ammonites' frightening successes against the Israelites left the distraught leaders of Gil'ad asking the same question that so many are asking today. "Who is the man who will start to fight for us?" There is a vacancy for Mashiach: who is going to fill it?

CHAPTER 11

* * * Judges 11:1-33 is the Haftarah of Parshat **Chukat**, Leviticus 19:1-22:1 * * *

GOOD INTENTIONS

Like Avimelech, Yiftach (Jephthah) son of Gil'ad, the Tenth Judge of Israel, was also the son of a **pilegesh** (concubine). However, despite being rejected by his half-brothers, the sons of Gil'ad's full wife, Yiftach did not follow the example of his blood-thirsty predecessor Avimelech, but instead fled from the more "respectable" members of his family and "dwelled in the land of **Tov**" (="good", ch 11 v 3). The commentators (Metzudat, RaDaK), explaining **p'shat**, the simple, direct meaning of the text, say that Tov was the name of a man, the baron of that region (cf. Ruth 3:13, where Tov may also indicate a man's name). Yet it is clear that our allusive Bible is here teaching us something deeper. Yiftach was not a **Rasha** (wicked man) like Avimelech. He was a Tzaddik - a "good guy" with truly good intentions. The flaw lay in the fact that his righteousness was not combined with clear understanding of Torah. Yiftach wanted to do the right thing, but not being a scholar, he did what he **imagined** to be right and brought about a terrible tragedy. "Because he was not a **Ben Torah** he lost his daughter. Even if a man is a tzaddik, if he does not study the Torah he is left with nothing in his hand" (Tanchuma).

A LESSON IN HISTORY

The Ammonite "existential threat" to Israel was described at the end of Chapter 10. The Ammonites were encamped by the town of Gil'ad, which is east of the River Jordan, south of the River Yabok about 30 kilometres north of present day Amman. The broader region of Gil'ad stretches along the entire east bank of the Jordan from the northern tip of the "Dead" Sea up to the Kinneret. This region was part of the huge swathe of territories east of the Jordan which the Children of Israel captured from the Emorite king Sichon and Og king of Bashan as described in the later sections of the book of Numbers (chs 21 and 32). They were given to the tribes of Reuven, Gad and half Menasheh, who took their portions east of the Jordan.

Prior to the time of King Sichon this entire swathe of territories was under the influence of the sister nations of Moab and Ammon. Their lands had been promised by God to Abraham together with that of Edom as part of the "greater" Promised Land (Genesis 15:19-20, see Rashi), but they were only to come under the full possession of Israel in the "final settlement" at the end of days. Until then Moses was enjoined not to take from the lands of Edom (Deut. 2:5) or Moab (Deut. 2:9) or Ammon (Deut. 2:19). Deuteronomy ch 2 describes the primeval tribes of "giants" etc. who dwelled in these territories before their conquest by Edom, Ammon and Moab, and also describes the conquest by Moses of the territories which Sichon had conquered from Moab and Ammon.

The reason why it was permitted for Israel to take possession of those areas previously occupied by Moab and Ammon that Sichon had conquered was because Sichon's conquest "purified" those lands of their association with the children of Lot (Gittin 38a).

LAND FOR PEACE

The Israelite presence in the areas of Gil'ad taken from Sichon drove a wedge between Ammon, who had been driven into the hinterland east of present-day Amman, and their sister nation Moab, who were left only with their territories south east of the River Arnon, (which meets the tongue-shaped "Dead" Sea approximately in the middle).

This gave the Ammonites strong motivation to seek a **Casus Belli** against Israel, and when Yiftach sent messengers to the king of Ammon protesting their aggressions, the Ammonite king replied with an argument that has been repeated endlessly by Israel's enemies until this very day: "Because Israel **took my land**" (v 13). Moreover, the king promised exactly the same as Israel's enemies until this very day. "And now, return them..." (note how "my land" has seamlessly turned into the **plural**) "…in **peace**". In other words, the Ammonite king proposed exactly the same formula as Israel's present day Arab friends: **Land for Peace**.

The messengers whom Yiftach sent back to the king of Ammon gave him a detailed history lesson the purpose of which was to explain precisely the above-mentioned point: the territories which Israel took east of the Jordan no longer belonged to Ammon or Moab since they had been conquered by Sichon king of the Emorites. This refutation of the Ammonite claim is based on the principle that "the whole world belongs to the Holy One blessed be He: He created it and He gave it to whoever it was right in His eyes to give it. Through His will, He gave it to them and through His will He took it from them and gave it to us" (see Rashi on Genesis 1:1).

YIFTACH'S VOW

The Ammonite intransigence in spite of Yiftach's arguments (reminiscent of years of Arab **"No! No! No!"**) left him with no alternative but to go to war to prevent them penetrating the very heartland of Israel (see Judges 10:9). The Spirit of God was on Yiftach, who advanced from the northern Gil'ad towards the Ammonite camp.

The practice of vowing to make a dedication to God if He grants one's request goes back to Jacob, "head of those who take vows". After his dream of the Ladder during his flight from the wrath of Esau,

Jacob had vowed to give God a tithe of everything if He would bring him home safely (Genesis 28:20ff). Likewise, in the wilderness, when Israel was attacked by "the Canaanite" king of Arad (=Amalek, see Rashi on Numbers 21:1), "And Israel vowed a vow to God..." (Numbers 21:2). Likewise, as we shall see when we begin the book of I Samuel, Hannah vowed that if she would be granted a child she would dedicate him to God.

"Two vowed and were rewarded; two vowed and lost. Israel vowed and they won. Hannah vowed and she was rewarded. But Jacob vowed and lost, because his wife Rachel died, while Yiftach vowed - and lost his daughter" (Bereishit Rabbah 70).

The fatal flaw that vitiated Yiftach's vow was that it was imprecisely formulated. The mark of the wise man is that "he sees what will develop" (Avot ch 2). Yiftach lacked the wisdom to see the hidden pitfall contained in the vow that he uttered at the height of his inspiration and enthusiasm. The vow was insufficiently articulated, and because its implications were not perceived by Yiftach at the time that he made it, he caused a terrible tragedy.

It is hard when we enthusiastically make some commitment to stop for a moment to ask whether we will really be able to stand up to it. Sometimes people make wild offers and some **Mazal** enables them to get out clean, but if the person lacks **Mazal** it can lead to disaster. "Four asked improperly; to three He gave properly, but to one He gave improperly" (Ta'anit 4a). The four were Eliezer, servant of Abraham, Calev, Saul and Yiftach. Eliezer said that the first girl who offered to water his camels would be Isaac's wife - how did he know that she wouldn't be some lowly waif who was not fit for him? When Calev offered his daughter to whoever would capture Kiryat Sefer, how did he know that the man would not be disreputable. The same applies to King Saul's offer of his daughter to whoever would kill Goliath. Eliezer, Calev and Saul all had some **Mazal** that ensured that despite their imprecise wording, they were not answered improperly. However, Yiftach apparently lacked something. He **imagined** that the one who would first come out of the doors of his house to greet him on his safe return from the war would be some **fat ox** or **fat lamb** that would make a fitting thanksgiving sacrifice to God, and it did not occur to him that perhaps it would be his own **daughter**.

WHY DIDN'T YIFTACH ANNUL HIS VOW?

The laws of vows and oaths and their proper formulation is the subject of three entire tractates of the Talmud - **Nedarim**, **Nazir** and **Shevuot**. Had Yiftach been more of a **Talmid Chacham** (Torah scholar), he would have known that in fact he was under no obligation to offer his daughter as a sacrifice. The Midrash (Bereishit Rabbah 60) presents an intricate discussion between Rabbi Yochanan and his student-chaver Reish Lakish (Rabbi Shimon ben Lakish) whose meaning is readily comprehensible to those with some background in the above laws. Rabbi Yochanan maintains that Yiftach could have redeemed his daughter for money which he would then have dedicated to the purchase of a sacrificial animal, while Reish Lakish maintains that even this was unnecessary since "One who says of an impure animal or of an animal with a blemish that it is a burnt offering has not said anything" since these animals are not eligible as a sacrifice anyway. The same applies to Yiftach's daughter.

Yiftach is an example of the many people who have very high principles but lack the detailed knowledge of the Torah to know how properly to apply them in practice. Yiftach **imagined** he was bound by his vow, and his high-minded determination to carry out what he thought was his obligation brought him to an unparalleled perversity. Even Abraham was not commanded to **kill** Isaac, and indeed according to the commentators, Yiftach did not actually **kill** his daughter. Rather, she was condemned to remain unmarried in a state of permanent **hitbodedut** (isolation) and divine service except for the few days of the year when her maiden friends would come to comfort her (see Metzudat David on v 37 and RaDaK on v 40).

The Midrash brings out the absurdity and criminality of Yiftach's condemning his only child to a life of celibacy, thereby destroying the continuity of his own line. Not only was Yiftach criticized but so too were all the rabbis and scholars of his time and even Pinchas the High Priest (who according to tradition was still alive despite the passage of over 300 years since he entered the Land with Joshua).

Through a mixture of high principles and pride, Yiftach would not go to Pinchas to nullify his vow, although the **Halachah** specifically permits this. Likewise, Pinchas would not go to Yiftach to nullify the vow, reasoning that his own status as Priest required that Yiftach should come to him. Between the two of them, the poor girl "died". Pinchas was punished with the withdrawal from him of holy spirit (I Chronicles 9:20 - "HaShem was with him **previously**"). Yiftach was punished with an illness akin to leprosy in the modern sense of the term, which caused his limbs to drop off one by one while he was still alive. For this reason, "he was buried **in the cities** of Gil'ad" (ch 12 v 7) i.e. in several different places.

Yiftach's daughter said to him: "Leave me for two months and I will go **and I shall descend upon the mountains**" (ch 11 v 37). Since when do you **descend** upon a mountain - first you have to **go up???** These were not regular mountains. What she was really saying was, Let me go down to the elders of the Sanhedrin (who are called Mountains) in case they can find some release clause (**petach**, an "opening") from your vow.

The Tanna de'Vei Eliyahu puts the responsibility for the tragedy squarely on the shoulders of the Sanhedrin. "Anyone who has the power to protest and does not do so, carries responsibility for all the blood shed in Israel. The great Sanhedrin that Moses left behind him should have girded their loins with metal chains and lifted their garments above their knees and gone around to all the cities of Israel, one day in Lachish, one day in Eglon, one day in Hebron, one day in Beit El, one day in Jerusalem... and that way they could have taught them the proper way of doing things (**Derech Eretz**) in one, two, three, four or maximum five years until the land would have been properly settled. Instead, after Israel entered the Land, each one ran to his vineyard and olive tree and said, Peace be upon my soul - let me not have to make too much effort."

CHAPTER 12

The ruffled pride of the Ephraimites who felt that Yiftach had not involved them in the war against the Ammonites led more to bloody consequences. There is a suggestion in the above-quoted passage from Tanna de'Vei Eliahu that the Ephraimites that were killed if they could not pronounce **shibbolet** properly were involved in some kind of idolatry, because "**sibolet**" is an idolatrous term, as when a man says "**Sa Beil**" ("Exalt **Beil**", this being the name of a Babylonian god, as in Belshazzar in the book of Daniel.)

Little is known of the succession of Judges enumerated in the latter part of Chapter 12, except for **Ivtzan** from Beit Lechem (verse 8), whom the rabbis identified with **Bo'az**, known to us from the Book of Ruth. The Midrash tells that Bo'az lost all his thirty sons and thirty daughters because he did not show hospitality to Manoah, father of Shimshon, and thus he was childless when he married Ruth, who conceived Oveid, father of Yishai, the father of King David. As we thus approach the threshold of the dawn of David's kingship, the Bible steadily delineates the national crisis into which Israel had sunk, from which David would come to save them.

CHAPTERS 13-14

* * * The story of the birth of Samson, who was a Nazirite, Judges 13:2-25, is read as the Haftarah of Parshat **Naso**, Numbers 4:21-7:89, which includes the commandment of the Nazirite * * *

AND GOD GAVE THEM INTO THE HAND OF THE PHILISTINES.

From the time of Shimshon (=Samson) until that of David, the Philistines were foremost among the oppressors of Israel (just as the "Palestinians" who have adopted the Latinized version of their name are today). The Philistines originated from the descendants of Ham, whose son Mitzrayim gave birth among others to the Patrusim and Kasluchim (Genesis 10:13). It was from between the two of them that the Philistines "emerged" (i.e. they were a "bastard" people, see Rashi ad loc.). A sea-faring nation, they spread to Crete and throughout the Greek islands into Greece proper, where they lived until the Dorian Greeks invaded and began to oppress them, causing many to migrate eastwards to the coastal regions of the eastern Mediterranean. They were no match for the powerful Egyptians, who fought against them, but they were able to settle in the Land of Canaan and became particularly strongly entrenched along the entire coastal strip all the way from present-day Ashdod to the eastern arm of the Nile delta.

The Philistines were new immigrants to the Land in the time of Abraham, who was also a new-comer. The fact that both had come to live in a new country might help explain why relations between Abraham and Avimelech, the Philistine king of Gerar, were cordial to the point that Abraham swore an oath not to harm Avimelech or his descendants to the fourth generation (Genesis 21:23ff). However, with increasing pressure on the Philistine communities in mainland Greece and the Greek islands, more and more were moving in waves into Canaan. Many came in the period of the Israelite exile in Egypt, and more entered during the early period of the Judges. They were fierce fighters and far more powerful than the Israelite settlers, who were mainly farmers without a centralized government or regular army. Through the sins of the Israelites the Philistines were able to gain power over them and dominate them.

Kabbalistically, the "bastard" nation of the Philistines is emblematic of the most severe concealment of God's light. The Hebrew letters of their name, **Philishtim**, are Peh (80) + Lamed (30) + Shin (300) + Tav (400) + Yud (10) + Mem (40) = 860 = 10 x 86. 86 is the gematria of the divine name **Elokim** expressing the attribute of **Gevurot**, "mighty powers", restraint, severe judgment. In the Philistines, this attribute dominates in all their 10 Sefirot.

It could be that Abraham, as the embodiment of **Chessed**, kindness, knew that his offspring would have to be tested by and would have to overcome the husk of the Philistines and for that reason swore the oath allowing them to remain in the Land for the necessary period of time. By the time of Shimshon, the time had elapsed. As the Angel tells Manoah's wife, "For the lad shall be separated to God from the womb, and **he will begin (yachel) to save Israel from the hand of the Philistines**" (ch 13 v 5). "Said Rabbi Hama ben Hanina: The oath of Avimelech was annulled (**huchal**), as it written, Do not betray me, my grandson and my great-grandson" (Sotah 9b).

Those who imagine Shimshon as a muscled superman out of a wham-bam cartoon animation will be greatly disappointed on trying to penetrate the deeply-veiled allegory in our text with the help of our rabbis. The first surprise is that Rabbi Yochanan states that while Bilaam was lame only in one leg, Shimshon was lame in both! (Sotah 10). Who ever heard of a lame Superman? We may begin to unlock the mystery if we ponder the verse R. Yochanan cites as proof. While of Bilaam it is said "And he went **shefi** (has connotation of lame)" (Numbers 23:3), it says of Dan, "a serpent (**shefifon**) by the path" (Genesis 49:17) - it is the doubled form of **shefifon** that is the hint that Shimshon - the outstanding Judge from the tribe of Dan - was "lame".

"Dan will judge his people like one of the tribes of Israel" (ibid. v 16) - this refers to Shimshon, the only judge contributed by that tribe. He is described as "biting the heels of the horse, his rider will fall backwards" (ibid. v 17). In the wilderness, the tribe of Dan marched last, gathering in all the weak remnants and saving them from the Amalekite "serpent". It was now Shimshon's task to bite back - to use the bite of the serpent against the serpent itself in order to redeem Israel - except that he failed in his lifetime and succeeded only in his death.

Shimshon's lameness has the deepest roots, as revealed by the ARI (in Likutey Torah on Judges), who explains that Shimshon was the **Gilgul** (incarnation) of **Adam HaRishon**, the first man. Shimshon had the power to rectify Adam's sin, which came about through the eyes ("and the woman **saw**" Gen. 3:6), but he failed, because "Shimson rebelled with his eyes, as it says, 'And Shimshon said to his father, take **her** for me because she is right in my **eyes**' (Judges 14:3)". Accordingly, Shimshon was punished by having his eyes gouged out. After his capture by the Philistines, he was taken in "chains of copper" (**nechushtayim**, related to the root **Nachash**=serpent) and placed in the House of the Bound=Domain of the Kelipot, the "husks" (ch 16 v 21). Just as the serpent was condemned to crawl with no legs, so was Shimshon "lame".

Just as Adam sinned and allowed his power to fall into the Kelipot, so did Shimshon. It was only with his death that he was able to take vengeance on the Philistines, the husks, and by pushing the **pillars** of their Temple - the **legs** that supported the entire structure - thereby redeem his own sin.

Shimshon was a **Nazir** although the rabbis are divided about the exact nature of his particular form of Nazirite status, which diverges somewhat from the normal Nazirite status as set forth in Numbers ch 6. Shimshon was forbidden to cut his hair at all, while a normal **Nazir** would make his vow only for a specified period, usually 30 days, after which he was at liberty to cut his hair. Shimshon, like a regular Nazir was forbidden wine or anything deriving from the grape, but he was evidently permitted to defile himself with the dead, which is strictly forbidden to a Nazir who takes the vow himself. But since Shimshon was dedicated from the womb, he was subject only to the restrictions explicitly stated in our text, and we find him defiling himself with the dead by stripping Philistine corpses of their clothes etc. (ch 14 v 19; see RaDaK on Judges 13:4 for a detailed discussion of Shimshon's status).

Zohar (Parshat Naso) explains that the **Nazir** alludes to the divine **Partzuf** of **Arich Anpin**, the "long face", which stands as **Keter**, the crown over **Zeir Anpin**, which is the "small face" whereby God is revealed to the world. The sweetness of **Arich Anpin** rectifies the harsh judgments of **Zeir**. Thus, the attributes of the Partzuf of Arich Anpin include long white hair, which is bound up with the concept of the long hair of the **Nazir** (each hair – **se'ar** - is a **sha'ar** or gateway - a channel of divine light. These revelations of kindness must not be "cut").

Because of the **Nazir's** association with this exalted level, he is forbidden to drink wine or indeed even partake of any part of the grape left after the juice is squeezed out, the lees. Adam's wife Eve "squeezed wine" from the primordial grapes but gave Adam the lees and husks - harsh judgments. It was through this unpurified wine that Adam fell, and Shimshon was to make the repair by being separated from wine.

Shimshon was to go down into the very lair of the husks - the Philistines - and take out any remaining divine sparks in order to then destroy the remaining husks and waste. This is why our text repeatedly speaks of Shimshon "going down" (ch 14:1 & 5 etc.). However, he "went after his eyes" and fell, revealing his own secrets to his Philistine wives and thereby falling into the net of the Kelipot. It may seem strange that Shimshon the Judge took Philistine wives - yet he is not criticized for this in our text, whereas if he had done anything sinful he would have been criticized (see RaDaK on ch 13 v 4). Shimshon's sin was that he was drawn after the "beauty" of his Philistine wives and instead of drawing out the holy sparks, he revealed all his holy secrets to them, causing more holiness to fall into the clutches of the Kelipot.

Shimshon's tragic end should not be allowed to overshadow his tremendous power, which was not that of a Superman in the modern entertainment sense but literally that of **Adam**. The rabbis stated that the fruit that Eve gave to Adam was wheat, figs or grapes. (In fact, because of the mysterious way in which midrash "works", it was all three!) The mystery of the **fig** enters into the deep allegory of these chapters in ch 14 v 4: "And his father and his mother did not know, for it was from God, for he (He?) sought a **pretext (to-a-nah)** against the Philistines". The word **to-a-nah** has exactly the same Hebrew letters as **te-enah**, a "fig".

The fruit caused Adam to fall to the realm of the husks - for one hundred and thirty-years he had relations with demons, chief among them "Lilith". This was why Shimshon had to take **Delilah**, who was the embodiment of Lilith. Had he accomplished the Tikkun and not revealed his secret to her, he would have rectified everything and been the Redeemer. But the time was not yet ripe. "He will **begin** to save Israel from the hand of the Philistines" (ch 13 v 5), but he was not able to complete the task. However, he "sought a **pretext**" - he initiated Israel's war of liberation against the Philistines and showed the Israelites that they could become free.

He was called **Shimshon** from the root **Shemesh**, the Sun=**Da'at**, Godly knowledge. The Rabbis said that Adam's very heel darkened the sun - i.e. through his sin, he darkened the light of **Da'at**. Abraham began the repair - "Abraham had a jewel which he hung on the sphere of the sun" - but the repair was still not complete. Shimshon had the power to finish it but he failed because the time was not ripe. Melech HaMashiach will complete the **Tikkun** "and his name will continue **as long as the Sun**" (Psalms 72:17).

CHAPTERS 15-16

It must be understood that Shimshon's life came at the very end of the period of the Judges on the very threshold of the institution of the kingship under the prophet Samuel, the cycle of whose stories is told in I Samuel. After today's text a sizeable portion of the book of Judges still lies ahead of us before we reach the Book of Samuel, but the two episodes related in the last five chapters of Judges - Michah's idol (chs 17-18) and the Concubine in Giv'ah (chs 19-21) - in fact occurred early in the period of the Judges, as noted by the commentators. They are placed at the end of the book in order to characterize the deep national malady that prevailed throughout the period of the Judges in order to explain the need for the kingship.

The narrative in our present text, with all its many riddles and deep allegories, reflects the situation prevailing immediately before the institution of the kingship. The Israelites had practically turned into a subject nation living in constant fear of their Philistine rulers. As the men of Judah complained to Shimshon, whom they saw as a dangerous provocateur: "Don't you know that the Philistines rule over us?" (ch 15 v 11).

RaDaK in his lengthy introduction to the story of Shimshon (ch 13 v 4) notes that the Israelites were not fighting the Philistines at this time: Shimshon alone was engaged in a single-handed campaign against them. RaDaK states that it is unthinkable that Shimshon simply married idolatrous Philistine women without converting them, for if he had, he would have been criticized for violating the prohibition against intermarriage with other peoples (Deut. 7:3-4). Likewise, Rambam (Maimonides) in the Laws of Forbidden Relationships (Issurey Bi'ah 13:14) states categorically that one should not imagine that Shimshon married unconverted women. As in the case of King Solomon, who also took foreign wives, Rambam and RaDaK state that Shimshon converted them first. If Shimshon could be criticized, it is because he "went after his eyes" - he strayed from his original holy intentions because of some kind of "material desire" (on his exalted level). This showed that he did not convert them entirely **lishmah** (in the name of true conversion). Nevertheless, "it was from God" (ch 14 v 4) that he took Philistine wives. This was because "He sought a **pretext** against the Philistines" (ibid.) in order to take revenge against them, and this is why God was with Shimshon and gave him such success.

RaDaK states that the Israelites in that period were not sufficiently God-fearing to be worthy of God's sending them complete salvation from the Philistines. Shimshon kept the Philistines in check through using the various "pretexts" that God arranged (the honey in the lion's carcass, the giving of Shimshon's wife from Timnah to another man, etc.) in order to terrorize and wreak havoc among them.

Shimshon's heroism in single-handedly struggling against those seeking to deny the people of Israel their right to live at peace in their ancestral land is reminiscent of the courageous few who are today willing to defy the contemporary "political correctness" of latter-day Israel's so-called "peace camp", endorsed by its mainstream media and high court etc., which is essentially a policy of appeasement and capitulation to Arab terror. Just as the men of Judah tied up Shimshon and handed him over to the Philistines, so too Israel's latter-day appeasers have had no scruples about doing everything in their power to gag, strap, tie up and inhibit those who would defend the actual people of Israel from their worst enemies in the absence of any concerted government campaign against them.

The subtle weave of riddles and allegories in our text makes for a colorful story replete with word-play and other mysteries leading up to the heart-rending conclusion in which Shimshon reveals his secret and falls prey to his barbaric enemies. "If I am shaved, my power will depart from me and I will become weak (**ve- choliti** - I will be **chol**, profane) and I will be **like every man (ke-chol ha-adam)**". It is here that the deep inner truth of the allegory stares us right in the face. "If I fail, I will be like **Adam**". Shimshon was the **gilgul** (incarnation) of **Adam**. His mission was to rectify Adam's sin, but he was unable to do so in his lifetime and could only take vengeance on the Philistines with his death.

We see that Shimshon constantly called out to God and prayed for all that he needed. He was a **Chatzot Jew** - he was awake and active from midnight (=**Chatzot**), thus escaping the wiles of the Philistines who plotted to kill him in the morning (ch 17 v 3). Similarly, every Jew can escape the wiles of the **Yetzer Ra**, the evil urge that lurks in wait to kill him each morning - by getting up long before the dawn in order to pray and study Torah thereby outwitting the **Yetzer**, destroying its power.

There was no end to Shimshon's ambition: he wanted to take all the sparks of holiness from the Philistines and thereby destroy them. But their **Gevurot** (mighty powers) proved too much for him, because Israel was not yet ready for salvation. The five "captains" of the Philistines who offered Delilah money to extract Shimshon's secret are called "**sarney** Philishtim". The gematria of **sarney** is 320, alluding to the **ShaCh** Dinim (320 severe judgments) that hide Godliness from the world. The rabbis taught that Delilah tormented Shimshon by pulling out from under him immediately before he could climax. Embodiment of the evil demon Lilith, she thereby succeeded in steadily wearing him down until he came closer and closer to revealing his secret and finally did: his power came from his uncut locks. As discussed in yesterday's commentary, Shimshon the Nazirite's hair alludes to the hairs of the head of the Partzuf of Arich Anpin, source of all the sweetening mercies in the world. Once these were cut, the Shechinah departed from Shimshon without his even knowing it.

The Talmud comments on the verse "and the lad grew, and God blessed him" (ch 13:24) that He blessed him in his organ, because it was like that of a regular man, but his seed was like a flowing river (Sotah 10a). All this creative power was captured by the forces of evil. "And he was grinding in the house of the prisoners" (Judges ch 16 v 21). "Said Rabbi Yochanan, 'grinding' is an expression having the connotation of sin. This teaches that each and every Philistine would bring his wife to the prison house to be impregnated by him" (Sotah 10a).

The Philistine celebration of the capture of their most feared enemy and their praise of their idols for the victory was a terrible **Chilul HaShem**, desecration of God's Name. We shed tears as we read Shimshon's last prayer to God (ch 16 v 28). "Let my soul die with the Philistines" (v 30): Shimshon was the true archetype suicide martyr, who gave his life to bring about an eternal **Kiddush HaShem** (Sanctification of God's Name). He sacrificed the merit of one of his gouged eyes in order to take vengeance on his enemies in this world. The merit of his second eye is stored up in the World to Come (Yerushalmi Sotah). There the truth of the mystery of Shimshon is known and revealed.

CHAPTERS 17-18

Rashi on Judges 17:1 writes: "Even though these two portions about Michah (chs 17-18) and the Concubine in Giv'ah (chs 19-21) are written at the **end** of the Book of Judges, these episodes actually took place at the **beginning** of the period of the Judges in the days of Otniel ben Knaz". Rashi's opinion follows that of **Seder Olam** (the ancient rabbinic historical Midrash giving the dates of all the main biblical events based on calculations of the years mentioned in the text and other hints). RaDaK, however, characteristically seeks to follow the simple **p'shat** of the narrative, arguing in great detail that these episodes could equally well have taken place at the **end** of the period of Judges, between the time of Shimshon and that of Eli the High Priest. (See RaDaK on ch 17 v 1 & ch 18 v 1.)

Nevertheless, the very heavily-veiled tale of Michah and his idol has a timelessness that makes the question of when exactly it took place almost incidental. The NaKh is teaching us lessons that go beyond any specific time and place: The recurrent motif is: "In those days, there was no king in Israel; each man would do what was right in his eyes" (ch 17 v 6). The text presents the narrative without moralizing, leaving the student to seek to deduce and understand the subtle lesson and reproof.

MICHAH

Michah is unidentified in our text except for his location in Mount Ephraim, but this does not necessarily mean he was from that tribe (cf. Rashi on Judges 17:7). The rabbis taught that he was called **Michah** because he was **squashed** (nis**mach-mech**) in a building (Sanhedrin 101b) - alluding to the ancient Aggadah (tale, midrash) as brought by Rashi (ad loc.): "This was in Egypt. They placed him in a building instead of a brick. Moses said to the Holy One blessed be He, 'You have done evil to this people' -- Now, if they don't have bricks, they put the Israelite babies in the walls. The Holy One blessed be He replied: 'They are merely destroying thorns, for it is revealed before Me that if they were to live they would be complete villains. If you want, try and take one of them. Moses went and took out Michah."

According to the rabbis, Michah should have been numbered with those who have no share in the world to come, but he was not for one reason: because his bread was available for passersby (Sanhedrin 103a): thus, we see that Michah showed hospitality to Yehonatan ben Gershom in his travels.

THE IDOL

The rabbis stated that all of the divine names in the chapter about Michah are **chol** - they possess no holiness - with the exception of ch 18 v 31 (Shevuot 35b). What this means is that the prohibition against erasing one of the seven principal names of God does not apply to the divine names written in these two chapters, because the names had been taken and applied to idolatrous gods.

Our text does not give any indication as to when the mysterious incident of Michah's confession to his mother of his theft of silver and her dedication to idolatry took place. The rabbis have handed down the tradition that Michah's idol came with the Children of Israel out of Egypt and indeed that at the very moment they were miraculously crossing the sea on dry land, the idol was going with them (Tanchuma). This idolatry was like an alien germ hidden and deeply embedded - "bricked up", as it were -- within the unconscious mind of Israel, ready to rise to the fore and test the people in later times. It is bound up with the mystery of the idolatry of the Mixed Multitude who went up with Israel out of Egypt. The disease engendered by this germ manifested in various ways in the later history of the people - such as in the idols that Jeraboam set up in Ephraim and Dan (the two key locations in our present text), and those which king Menasheh (son of Hezekiah) set up in the Holy Temple in Jerusalem.

In chapter 17 v 5 we are told that "Michah had a house of god and he made an **Ephod** and **Teraphim**." As discussed in the commentary on the story of Gideon, the Ephod was the apron-like garment of the High Priest to which the breast-plate, with its jewels inscribed with the names of the Twelve Tribes, were attached. Michah's **Ephod** was clearly intended as a replica of that of the High Priest (it would have to be a good one to con the intelligent Israelites into believing, or at least half-believing in it). In Genesis 31:19 the **Teraphim** are Laban's gods - i.e. some kind of statuettes used for divination. Whereas Holy Spirit that spoke through the High Priest's breastplate was channeled through the **Urim Ve-Tumim**, it was through the **Teraphim** that the fake spirit spoke to Michah's priest.

RaDaK on ch 18 v 5 offers two explanations of what the **Teraphim** actually were. "Some say this was a copper instrument showing the divisions of the hours whereby astrologers could determine the path of the stars. Others say that the astrologers have the power to produce at known times a certain form (**tzura**) that actually speaks. And the sage R. Abraham Ibn Ezra has written that the most likely explanation in his opinion is that the **Teraphim** were in the form of a human made to receive the power of the supreme beings, and the proof is that the **Teraphim** placed by Michal (when Saul's soldiers came searching for David) caused the guards think it was David."

YEHONATAN BEN GERSHOM BEN MENASHEH

The mystery of the veiled allegory in our text is immeasurably deepened when we learn from our rabbis that the opportunistic Levite who went up from Bethlehem and found himself a fat livelihood as Michah's private Priest was none other than the grandson of **Moses**, although this is only hinted at allusively in the text. In ch 18 v 30 his **yichus** (pedigree) is given as **Yehonatan ben Gershom ben Menasheh**. In the Hebrew written text on parchment, it is traditional to write the **Nun** of **Menasheh** "hanging" (**tolui**) above the line. If you remove this **Nun** from **Menasheh** you are left with the letters of the name **Mosheh**. Rashi states on this verse that it is out of honor for **Mosheh** that the **Nun** was inserted to change the name (and thus somewhat obscure the connection between Yehonatan and his most illustrious grandfather). The Yerushalmi Talmud Berachot ch 9 indicates that **Menasheh** alludes to king Menasheh son of Hezekiah (as mentioned above) who placed an idol in the very Temple. In other words, the same underlying disease was manifested in a variety of forms in the history of the nation.

When the men of Dan pass through Mount Ephraim on their search for new territory, they come to Michah's house, "**and they recognized the voice of the lad, the Levite.**" (ch 18 v 3). Once again, the Midrash of the rabbis opens a tiny chink to hint at the profound depth that lies behind this mysterious allegory. "They said to him, 'Aren't you a descendant of Moses?' He replied, 'I have a tradition from the house of my father that a person should even hire himself out to **Avodah Zarah** rather than become dependent on others.' [The Talmud comments:] He thought this meant literal **Avodah Zara**, idolatry, whereas the real intention was that one should even take on a demeaning job like flaying animal carcasses - a work (**avodah**) that is **strange**, **zarah**, to oneself -- rather than depend on others. Later on, when King David saw that he was very fond of money he appointed him over the Treasuries, as it is written, 'and Shevu-el son of Gershom son of Menasheh was officer over the treasuries' (I Chronicles ch. 26). Was his name Shevu-el then? No, it was Yehonatan, but this teaches that he **returned to G-d (shav le-El)** with all his heart." (Bava Batra 110a).

So Yehonatan was a Levite for whom the intended system of supporting the nation's spiritual teachers through tithes (the Levitical **Ma'aser**) was evidently not working in Bethlehem, forcing him to go off in search of opportunities for **parnassah**, livelihood, wherever he could find them!

This in itself is a reproof against the people of whatever time it was that this story occurred: by failing to support their teachers by the Torah system of tithes, they forced them to demean themselves and base their ministry on money, with all the attendant evils.

THE TRIBAL PORTION OF DAN

In the commentary on Joshua ch 19 we have already discussed the fact that Dan took tribal portions both in the center of the Land and in the north. (See Joshua 19:47). Dan's main portion was in the center, in what is today the Tel Aviv-Dan region of Israel. This is where all the events in the story of Shimshon took place (Judges 13-16). The place names that recur both in the story of Shimshon and in that of Michah and the **Bney Dan** - Tzor'ah and Eshta'ol - will be particularly familiar to present-day residents of Israel who know the road connecting the Jerusalem-Tel Aviv highway with the town of Beit Shemesh, "**between Tzor'ah and Eshta'ol**".

It was population pressure and the limitations caused by the Philistine presence in the south and center that led the **Bney Dan** to search for more territory. The peaceful, idyllic Sidonian town of **Layish** which their team of five surveyors found, as described in Chapter 18, was located in the region of **Tel Dan** ("the mound of Dan") in the north of present-day Israel amidst the sources of the River Jordan (Banyas etc.) The Sidonians were one of the Canaanite nations. The settlement of the western Galilee by the tribe of Asher and the eastern Galilee by Naftali had left the Sidonians of Layish isolated from their fellow Canaanites on the coast of present-day Lebanon, and this is why there was no-one to come to their aid when the **Bney Dan** attacked them.

Rashi (on ch 18 v 27) states that **Layish** is the same as **Leshem** mentioned in Joshua 19:47. **Leshem** is the name of the Jacinth-stone in the High Priest's breast-plate - this was the stone of the Tribe of Dan! When they came to this town they discovered a **Leshem** stone, and they took this as proof that the location was destined for them from heaven.

However, our narrative makes it clear that the **Bney Dan** conquered their new territory not through divine miracles of the kind we read about in Joshua but through overwhelming military might against a people whose idyllic life had left them totally ignorant of the art of war. We also find that the Bney Dan exhibited an extraordinarily overbearing, threat-laden attitude to both Yehonatan the Priest and his boss-manager Michah. To Yehonatan their attitude was basically, "Shut up and come with us", whereas they told Michah that if he made his voice heard he would be killed.

Here we see how the enterprise of settling the Holy Land in order to live the life of Torah had been corrupted into territorial expansionism based on brute force, and legitimized with the veneer of religion through a "high priest" who was for sale to the highest bidder. Religion had thus been hijacked for mundane goals and purposes, posing very perplexing issues for lovers of Moses' Torah.

RaDaK and Metzudat David (on ch 18 v 30) both argue that Yehonatan and his sons served as "priests" to the tribe of Dan only until the Ark was captured by the Philistines from Shiloh in the days of Eli, and that this is the meaning of the phrase "until the day of the exile of the land". However, Rashi maintains that this fake religion continued until the days of Sennacheriv, who exiled the Ten Tribes. Rashi's view would link the idolatry delineated in our present text with the idolatry that eventually led to the exile of Israel.

The Talmud states that the location of Michah's temple was only **three miles** from Shilo and that the smoke of the Altar of the Sanctuary would mingle with the smoke of Michah's idolatrous altar. The Ministering Angels wanted to drive Michah out, but the Holy One blessed be He said, "Leave him: his bread is available for all passers-by" (Sanhedrin 103a). The mingling of the two columns of smoke indicates how very fine indeed can be the dividing line between true and fake religion.

CHAPTERS 19-20

The sorry tale of **Pilegesh Be-Giv'ah**, "the Concubine in Giv'ah" and the civil war to which it gave rise is one of the most shocking and gruesome in the whole Bible.

THE NEGATIVE CONSEQUENCES OF ANGER IN THE HOME

A careful reading of our narrative makes it clear that the Children of Israel were considered justified in wreaking a terrible vengeance on the "left-handed" Benjaminites - almost wiping out the entire tribe -- for refusing to hand over the perpetrators of a barbaric gang-rape for punishment. Gevurah (force) was requited with Gevurah. However, the rabbis indicate that the entire affair came about only through an excess of Gevurah on the part of the mysterious Levite man that lived on the edge of Mount Ephraim. In Talmud Gittin (6b) there is a discussion about the cause of the domestic altercation that led to his concubine walking out on him. One opinion is that he chastised her when he found a fly in his soup; another is that he found a hair in "that place", and "these and these are the words of the Living God". When he found the fly, which is merely disgusting, he was not that upset, because it was not necessarily her fault, but a hair in "that place" could cause him injury and this was clear negligence on her part. Nevertheless, the Talmud concludes, "A man should never make the members of his household excessively afraid of him, because the husband of the Concubine in Giv'ah made her excessively afraid and caused the death of tens of thousands of Israel ".

HOSPITALITY AND ITS OPPOSITE

In the previous story about Michah and his idol, we see that Michah was saved from complete obliteration from the world to come because of his trait of hospitality. Hospitality like that which Abraham showed to the three angels that he took for idolatrous Arabs (Genesis ch 18) was intended to be one of the distinguishing traits of his progeny: bringing strangers under the shelter of one's home is tantamount to bringing them under the wings of the Shechinah! However, the horrible tragedy of **Pilegesh Be-Giv'ah** came about through the very opposite of hospitality. The Levite's Judean father-in-law from Beit Lechem - presumably anxious to re-endear his daughter to the Levite - detained him more than necessary to the point that he felt the need to break away and leave hurriedly even though it was too late in the day for him to complete the journey before him.

The Levite refused to seek lodging for the night by turning into Jebus (=Jerusalem, then occupied by the Canaanite Jebusites), because, as he said to his attendant, "We shall not turn aside to a city of an alien people that are not from the Children of Israel" (ch 19 v 12). Yet it was precisely the kind of abominable behavior he **expected** from the Canaanites that he **actually encountered** among the Benjaminite-Israelite inhabitants of Giv'ah, despite the fact that he was a **pilgrim**, no less, on his way to Shilo (see RaDaK on ch 19v 18)! He was not even asking for full hospitality, i.e. food and drink, since he had plenty of bread, wine and animal feed with him (v 19). The one old man from Giv'ah who was willing to open the doors of his home to this party of wayfarers knew all too well the actual nature of his Benjaminite fellow-townsmen. The conversation between the Levite and the old man (vv 16-20) is reminiscent of the conversation between Lot and the angels who came to visit him in Sodom (Genesis 19:1-3). The old man knew that the men of Giv'ah were already suffering from the Israelite vice of mingling with and imitating the Canaanites. The threatening demand of the Giv'ites that he hand over his guest for them to use for their perverse pleasure is exactly parallel to the Sodomites' demand for Lot to hand over his guests (Genesis 19:4).

BRUTE FORCE

The men of Giv'ah are called **Baaley Giv'ah** (ch 20 v 5) - the Mafiosi **bosses** of the town. This appellation is reminiscent of the Baaley Shechem in the time of Avimelech the Judge (Judges ch 9 v 2), but whereas the Bosses of Shechem were primarily interested in political power, those of Giv'ah were after perverse sexual gratification of the kind that is the very opposite of the Covenant of Sinai. "...And according to the deeds of the Land of Canaan to which I am bringing you, you shall not do, and you shall not go in their statutes" (Lev. 18:3).

That the Levite man could have thrown his **pilegesh** "to the dogs" to save himself and his host is in its way quite as repugnant as the Giv'ites' treatment of her as nothing but a sex object to be tossed aside and abandoned after brutal abuse. (Repugnant as all this is, the fact is that today, with very little ingenuity, anyone can use the Internet underbelly to gain instant access to literally thousands of websites devoted to gang rape fantasies and worse: all this obviously continues to fascinate and excite a significant portion of the population until today.)

The horrible fate of the **Pilegesh Be-Giv'ah** alludes perhaps to the "rape" of the Shechinah by the forces of evil. The Levite man saw that it was fit to cut her body into twelve parts and send them to each of the tribes to **shock** them into action. Indeed, the gang-rape murder in Giv'ah was a national scandal for the Israelites, who immediately gathered in Mitzpah to take counsel. The Torah itself provides that if a city of Israel turns aside to idolatry (as an **Ir Hanidachat**, the "cast-aside city"), the people are to make a careful enquiry into the affair and kill all the guilty inhabitants, destroy their property and burn the entire city (Deut. 13-19). The national gathering at Mitzpah was a most solemn affair judging a case that was quite as serious for the people as **Ir Hanichadat**.

THE ASSEMBLY AT MITZPAH

The site of **Giv'ah** itself is on a **tel** (mound) north of Jerusalem between present-day French Hill and Nevey Yaakov. The site of Mitzpah is somewhat further north, just a little south of present day Ramallah. Mitzpah was an appropriate place for a national gathering as this was where Joshua was victorious over the northern kings of Canaan (Joshua 11:3) and, as RaDaK explains (ad loc.), Joshua probably set up an altar there and inaugurated it as a place of national assembly and prayer (Judges 11:11; 20:1; I Samuel 7:5).

So great was the unity of the tribes that the verse describing their armed forces' advance on Giv'ah "**as one man, friends**" (ch 20 v 11) was taken by the sages as the foundation for their teaching that on the pilgrim festivals in Jerusalem the usual stringencies of those who strictly observed all the laws of tithing were somewhat relaxed to allow them to give credibility even to an **am haaretz** ("ignoramus") who claimed to have separated Terumah, because **kol Yisrael chaverim**, "all Israel are friends" (Chagigah 26a).

The founder of the tribe of Benjamin had ten sons all of whom had families. Benjamin's ten sons together with Joseph's two (Ephraim and Menasheh) made up a total of twelve, giving their mother Rachel twelve "tribes" corresponding to the Twelve Tribes of Israel. The Levites did not take part in the Israelite assault on the tribe of Benjamin, and of course the latter were on the other side. Thus, there were Ten Tribes of Israel against ten "tribes" of Benjamin (see Rashi on ch 20 v 12).

Unlike Michah, who made a fake **Ephod** and fake **Teraphim** which were used by the **Bney Dan** for divination, the Tribes of Israel in their campaign against Benjamin turned to the legitimate High Priest wearing the authentic priestly Breastplate for true divine guidance from the **Urim Ve-Tumim**. (That Pinchas the High Priest was still alive at the time of **Pilegesh Be-Giv'ah** is proof that this episode took place before the time of Shimshon.) There is a deep irony in the fact that Judah was told to lead the campaign against Benjamin since in Egypt in the time of Joseph Judah had taken personal responsibility for Benjamin's welfare (Genesis 43:9, 44:32-3).

We see from our present narrative that the Children of Israel were indeed in anguish about whether to make war against "the children of Benjamin my brother" (ch 20 v 23) for refusing to hand over the perpetrators of the crime for appropriate punishment. The Children of Israel did not go to war lightly and repeatedly consulted the **Urim Ve-Tumim** to make sure that God approved of their path.

If God was with them, why did they lose so many of their own in abortive battles before finally overcoming Benjamin? "God said to them: You have shown zealousness against immorality, but you did not show zealousness when it came to Michah's idol (an affront to the glory of God)! It was because they did not show zealousness with respect to Michah's idol, which they made no effort to uproot, that the Benjaminites succeeded in killing so many of them in their first, second and third assaults, until the Israelites fell before the Ark of the Covenant of HaShem seeking to repent and begging for an answer, and then He was reconciled with them" (Pirkey d'Rabbi Eliezer).

THE MISSING BENJAMINITES

The commentators discuss the apparent discrepancy between the numbers of male Benjaminites who went out to battle (=26,700, verses 16-17), the number of men they lost (25,000, v 46) and the number that fled to Sela Rimon and survived (600, v 47. N.B. **All** the Benjaminite women were killed v 48, leaving only these 600 men alive). RaDaK (on ch 20 v 15) suggests that of the missing 1,100 about a thousand may have fallen in the earlier battles, but also refers to a most fascinating Midrash that appears in some editions of Rashi (on v 45): "Eliyahu revealed to the author of **Megaleh Amukot** that the other one hundred went and settled in Rome and Ashkenaz (=Germany), and this is why Elijah (said by some to be from Benjamin) was from among the inhabitants of Gil'ad (as in Eliyahu **Ha-Gil'adi**), because they alone did not leave their land but stayed in their place." This Midrash would tend to support the theories of those who maintain that from the earliest times and afterwards some Israelites mingled with the populations of Europe, creating a pool of Israelite souls exiled among the other peoples of the world.

CHAPTER 21

The Book of Judges concludes with a heartening story of national reconciliation and healing which brought the Tribe of Benjamin back within the fold of the Twelve Tribes, and indeed Benjamin went on to provide the first king of Israel - Saul -- as well as Mordechai many generations later.

The behavior of the tribe of Benjamin in trying to protect the perpetrators of the brutal rape-murder of the Concubine in Giv'ah showed that they had strayed way outside the boundaries of the Torah code of civilized behavior. At their national gathering in Mitzpah the other tribes thus put the Benjaminites into **Niddui**, which like **Cherem** is the state of being "driven out," excommunicated from the **Kahal**, the Assembly of Israel, just like **Mamzerim** (illegitimate children), Moabites, Ammonites and Gibeonites etc. who are not allowed to marry Israelite women (see Radak on Judges 21:1). Since all the Benjamin-ite women had been killed, there was nobody for the surviving 600 Benjaminites who had fled to Sela HaRimon (ch. 20:47) to marry.

Yet the very severity of this sanction, which threatened to wipe out an entire tribe from Israel, aroused a spirit of profound national soul-searching and collective repentance in the whole nation who now gathered at the Sanctuary in Shilo (=Beit El, Metzudat David on v 2).

"If you want to know the power of the sanction of **Cherem**, come and see it in operation in the tribes that avenged the immorality of the tribe of Benjamin. They took a solemn oath that **all Israel** must follow them in prohibiting intermarriage with Benjamin, as it says, 'For the **oath** was great' (v 5). This oath was the **Cherem**, and since the men of Yaveish Gil'ad were not with them at the Assembly, they were liable to the death penalty" (Pirkey d'Rabbi Eliezer).

The town of Yaveish Gil'ad, whose inhabitants failed to attend the national Assembly, was east of the River Jordan about 30 km south east of Beit She'an, presumably in the territory of Menasheh. The punitive slaughter of all its male inhabitants and all females who were not virgins may seem very shocking, but its practical outcome was to leave 400 girls for the surviving Benjaminites to marry. (The subsequent connection between Benjamin and Yaveish Gil'ad became of crucial importance in the time of King Saul, who with the Prophet Samuel mobilized the whole of Israel to come to the town's rescue when threatened by the Ammonites - Samuel ch 12). Since there were 600 Benjaminite survivors, after 400 married, 200 were left without wives, leaving the Children of Israel in a quandary since they had sworn not to intermarry with the Benjaminites (Judges 21:16-18).

THE MYSTERY OF TU BE'AV

The resolution of this national crisis came about through the mystery of **Tu Be'Av**, the 15th day of the month of Av, which enters allusively into our text (vv 19-23). This is the "festival of HaShem in Shilo from year to year." (verse 19; Talmud Ta'anit 30b). **Tu Be'Av**, whose sanctity the rabbis compared to that of Yom Kippur (Ta'anit ibid.) had become a national festival since the 40th year of wandering in the Wilderness. All the men who accepted the slander of the spies about the Land had been condemned to die in the Wilderness, and for that reason throughout the forty years of wandering, the entire nation used to dig graves and sleep in them on the night of the anniversary of the sin, **Tisha Be'Av** (the 9th of Av). Each year some of the condemned generation would die while everyone else would climb out of their graves in the morning and go on living for at least another year. In the fortieth year of wandering they all slept in graves as usual, but nobody died. They thought they might have miscalculated the date and slept in graves the following night, and the next. However, by the 15th of Av, the full moon showed that they had certainly passed the 9th of Av and no-one had died, indicating that the decree was at an end.

This was why **Tu Be'Av** became a national festival celebrating God's reconciliation with Israel and signifying that His favor was with the new generation. God wants Israel to multiply, and thus **Tu Be'Av** is particularly propitious for **Zivug** - the pairing of male and female soul-mates together. **Tu Be'Av** is exactly 40 days before the 25th of Elul, the day when Creation began (for man was created on Rosh HaShanah, the 1st of Tishri, which is the sixth day of Creation). Since "forty days before a child is born, a heavenly voice goes out proclaiming **Ploni** ("so-and-so") is matched with **Plonit**", we may infer that forty days before the start of creation (on **Tu Be'Av**) all the souls are matched with one another.

This is why **Tu Be'Av** was a most propitious time for the remaining 200 Benjaminites to wait in the vineyards around Shilo as the maidens came out to dance, and for each to "snatch" his bride (for "Benjamin is a wolf that snatches..." Genesis 49:27, Tanchuma). This way none of the men of Israel violated their oath not to **give** their daughters to the Benjaminites, for the latter **took** them for themselves. The rabbis taught that it was **Tu Be'Av** when the Israelites revoked the **Cherem** on Benjamin from that time on, darshening the wording of the original oath, "not a man **of us** shall give his daughter as a wife to Benjamin" to refer only to those who were actually present but not to their descendants. On the same occasion, they also darshened from the verse in Numbers 36:6, "**This** is the matter that God commanded regarding the daughters of Tzelaphchad" that the prohibition of a woman marrying a man from a different tribe to avoid land inherited by women passing from tribe to tribe applied only to that generation (Ta'anit 30b).

The relaxation of both decrees signified national integration and unity among the Twelve Tribes, and the fact that the girls' dance circle at Shilo could take place safely out in the open in the vineyards around the town without fear of rape despite the absence of the strict separation between males and females that we normally require showed that this was truly a "festival of HaShem" (v 19), a celebration **Lishmah** in holiness and purity at which the new generation of pure, young Israelite men and women could find and link up with their **Basheirt** (destined soul-mate). The gross violation of this norm of purity that had occurred in Giv'ah was thus atoned, and the Book of Judges ends on a note of national reconciliation and healing, with all Israel going to their tribes, families and inheritances.

"In those days, there was not a king in Israel and each man would do what was right in his eyes" (Judges 21:25). Through his weave of stories and allegories in this book, the Prophet has left it to us to draw the moral of his reproof and understand why, without a king and without anyone of sufficient stature and authority to tell the people what was truly right instead of what each one **thought** to be right, Israel was in need of a prophet on the level of Moses - Samuel - to bring them to a state of repentance and unity fit for the inauguration of their age of national glory.

שמואל

SAMUEL

The beautiful and evocative tale of Hannah and God's answer to her prayer and vow with the birth of the prophet Samuel is familiar as the Haftarah of the first day of Rosh HaShanah (Gevurah, "might"), anniversary of the birth of Isaac (Gevurah) and Shmuel the Levite (Gevurah). It was Shmuel - Samuel - whose Gevurah brought about the appointment of Israel's messianic king.

Like the story of **Pilegesh Be-Giv'ah**, the story of the birth of Samuel begins with a Levite from Mount Ephraim, but whereas the Levite husband of the Pilegesh brought great suffering to Israel, Elkanah brought great **tikkun** (repair). It is said that "the sons of Korach did not die" (Numbers 26:11), from which we learn that "when Korach descended into hell, a place was formed for them where they stood and sang" (Megillah 14a). Elkanah was a grandson of a grandson of Korach. At a time when the Israelites were neglecting to go up to Shilo for the thrice-yearly pilgrim festivals, our rabbis teach that Elkanah made it his personal mission to go from town to town - each year to new towns - encouraging the people to go up with him to the Sanctuary, thus reviving the national consciousness of the divine plan for a Temple "in the place that He will choose". It was in this merit that Elkanah, himself a prophet, was worthy of his son Samuel. Hannah was one of the seven outstanding prophetesses of Israel.

Kabbalistically, Elkanah is the partzuf of **Abba** ("Father", Chochmah, wisdom) and Hannah is **Imma** ("Mother", Binah, understanding, as alluded to by the Gematria of her name, Chet 8 + Nun 50 + Heh 5 =63=the second Milui of HaVaYaH -- SaG corresponding to Imma/Binah). Elkanah and Hannah had to come together in **Zivug** to bring Shmuel – **Zeir Anpin** (Gevurah in relation to Abba) - into the world. (ARI, Likutey Torah Shmuel). Thus, it was Shmuel who played the key role in establishing the kingdom, **Malchut**, by appointing Saul and then David as the first kings of Israel. In the reign of David and his son Solomon, God's kingship was completely revealed in the world (**Gadlut** of Zeir Anpin) through the successful establishment of the earthly kingship which perfectly reflected and served the Kingship of God.

Samuel - Shmuel - was the last of the Judges and first of the Prophets who led Israel. Thus, in her prayer Hannah invoked "the Lord of Hosts", **HaShem Tzevakot** (I Samuel 1:11), being the first in Israel to use this appellation. The kabbalistic writings teach that this name signifies the attributes of **Netzach** and **Hod**, the "breasts" from which the prophets suckle. Thus, the later prophets from the time of Shmuel onwards repeatedly invoke this Name.

Hannah's magnificent and profoundly allusive prayer was elicited through the constant taunting of her rival, Peninah, who appears as the villain of the piece yet is said by our rabbis to have acted purely **Lishmah** in order to stir Hannah to prayer. Hannah's whispered prayer is the very archetype of silent prayer and is darshened in great detail in Talmud Berachot 31b as a lesson in many of the most fundamental **halachot** (laws) of prayer, in particular those relating to the daily **Amidah** prayer.

As discussed in the commentary on Yiftach (Jephthah), Hannah is one of the examples of those who vowed successfully. Her son Shmuel proved to be the "seed of men" that she requested. Eli had been appointed judge on the very day that Hannah came to the Sanctuary to pray ("And Eli the Priest **yosheiv**, was sitting, on the chair." v 9, i.e. now but not before), and on that same day God granted Hannah's prayer for a son - a son who was to come to prophesy the doom of Eli's house. While Eli was a true Tzaddik who had received the tradition from the Beit Din (court) of Pinchas and of Shimshon, he nevertheless showed that he was lacking in **Ru'ach HaKodesh** - he mistook Hannah for a drunken woman, causing her to say, "**lo adnoni**" (v 15), as if to say, "You are not my master!".

When the young Shmuel was brought to the Sanctuary as a two-year old boy, he already showed his child-prodigy Torah genius by darshening that the ox did not need to be slaughtered by a Kohen specifically, unlike the ensuing sacrificial rituals, which could only be performed by a Kohen - thereby incurring Eli's wrath for "ruling in front of his teacher". Eli wanted to curse the boy to death, and when Hannah protested, said he would give her a better son. Until Hannah cried out, "It was for **this** lad that I prayed" (v 27; see Rashi on v 25).

"This lad" was to become the towering leader of Israel at a time of searing national crisis within and from external enemies like the Ammonites and Philistines etc. - a prophet who is mentioned in the same breath as Moses and Aaron: "Moses and Aaron among His priests and **Shmuel** among those who call upon His Name" (Psalms 99:6).

* * * I Samuel 1:1-2:10 is read as the Haftarah on the First Day of Rosh HaShanah * * *

CHAPTERS 2-3

HANNAH'S SONG

As mentioned in the commentary on the Song of Devorah (Judges ch 5), Hannah's song is the seventh of the ten outstanding prophetic songs of all times. The tenth, which we are now awaiting: will be sung when those in exile will come out of their exile (Targum Yonatan on Shir HaShirim 1:1).

Hannah is counted as one of seven outstanding prophetesses (with Sarah, Miriam, Devorah, Avigail, Huldah and Esther) enumerated with the 48 male prophets who (besides the millions of other men and women who prophesied in Israel) delivered prophecies that were relevant to all the generations (Megillah 14a).

As discussed in the commentary on the Song of Devorah, **song** connects together and gives deeper meaning to the apparently disconnected happenings in this world. Hannah turned her personal triumph over the taunts of her rival, Peninah, into a song of triumph over God's victory over the enemies of Israel. The theme is how He brings down those who are arrogant and raises those who lowly. Targum Yonatan in his characteristically expansive rendering of a prophetic passage of this kind specifies the enemies of Israel alluded to in these verses: the Philistines in the time of Samuel (v 1); Sennacherib king of Assyria in the time of king Hezekiah (v 2); Nebucadnezzar of Babylon, who destroyed the First Temple (v 3); Greece (Macedonia) overcome by the Hasmoneans (v 4); Haman and his sons (v 5); Rome, whose destruction will inaugurate the consolation of Jerusalem (v 6); The hordes of Magog at the end of days.

So important is Hannah's song with its many proverbial expressions that in some communities it is customary to recite this passage as one of the preliminary preparations for the daily prayer service.

MEASURE FOR MEASURE

Hannah's song was over the birth of a son descended from Korach. In the Wilderness, Korach (intense **Gevurah**) had challenged Moses for apparently putting his own family interests over the national interest by appointing his brother Aharon as High Priest and founder of the line of Kohanim. Korach demanded that **all** the Levites should have a share in the priesthood (Numbers ch 16). It was God's rejection of Korach's rebellious challenge through the earth's opening her mouth to swallow him and his band alive (Numbers ch 17) that led to the subsequent reaffirmation of the priestly privileges in the Torah portion enumerating the various gifts they received, including specified portions of sacrificial animals, Terumah (the priestly tithe) etc. (Numbers ch 18). Yet while Korach went down to hell, "the sons of Korach lived" and his descendants were later to sing on the **Duchan** (platform) in the Temple. There is deep irony in the fact that now, in the generation of Eli, it was Korach's descendants - Elkanah and Shmuel - who were sent to reprove Eli's own sons, the descendants of Aharon, for abusing their priestly privileges. Indeed, in the time of David, Shmuel reorganized the entire basis of the priestly and Levitical service in the Temple, establishing the rota-system whereby the various priestly and Levitical families took turns to serve there week after week throughout the year.

Eli's sons had become examples of precisely the kind of prosperous, fat, arrogant workers of evil that Hannah in her song had praised God for bringing down and humbling. "They did not know the Lord" (ch 2 v 12): "They had cast the yoke of Heaven from upon them - they said, 'There is no kingdom in Heaven'" (Torat Kohanim, Tzav). "And Yeshurun became fat and he kicked" (Deut. 32:15). Eli's sons were abusing their priestly privileges for their own pleasure and self-aggrandizement.

The service of the priests was intended to atone for Israel through the ritual consumption by the priests of specified sacrificial portions. However, Eli's sons were eating the meat for their own gratification, thereby shamefully exploiting the people. The Midrash (Torat Kohanim, ibid.) delineates their exact sin: (1) They took more than their fair assigned share of the **Shelamim** (peace) sacrifices, the meat of which was supposed to be shared between the priest who offered it on the Altar and the Israelite who brought it; (2) They took their priestly share by force even before the **Cheilev**-fat of the animal and the **Kometz**-handful of the grain offerings had been burned on the Altar - they consumed their own shares while leaving the **Kometz** to the flies and the **Cheilev** to get spoiled out in the hot sun!

In addition, our text tells us "that they would sleep with the women assembled at the entry to the Tent of Meeting" (verse 22). On this the Talmud states that anyone who thinks they did so literally is mistaken. The Talmud explains that their sin was to delay sacrificing the sacrificial birds brought by women who had either given birth or who needed atonement for a morbid non-menstrual flow of blood (**Zavah**). This delay forced these women to stay overnight in the vicinity of the Sanctuary, thus being unable to return home and be with their husbands that night. The sons of Eli thus impeded their ability to "be fruitful and multiply", which was considered as if they had adulterously slept with other men's wives (Yoma 9a; Shabbat 55b).

Eli's sons were thus guilty of "immorality" and despising the very Sanctuary ritual and sacrifices over which they were appointed as priests. It was thus "measure for measure" that God rejected them from the priesthood. Pinchas, the previous High Priest and son of Aharon's third son, Elazar, had himself been rejected in favor of Eli, who was from the descendants of Aharon's fourth son, Itamar. The rejection of Pinchas came about because he had failed to go from city to city to reprove the people, with the result that in the days of the Concubine in Giv'ah they abandoned most of the commandments (see commentary on Judges 12). After Eli rose to be High Priest instead of Pinchas, we see from our text that he did indeed reprove his sons for their misdemeanors. However, he was at fault for not being more forceful. Eli had shown himself capable of severely cursing the little boy Samuel for ruling in front of his teacher (see commentary on I Samuel 1), yet when it came to his own sons he merely chided them when he should have dismissed them from the priesthood. This was why Eli was considered guilty of putting his own family dignity before the honor of Heaven and for this reason his descendants were fated to die young and to be in the humiliating position of having to practically beg for a small coin and a loaf of bread. (v 36). In the time of King Solomon, Eli's descendant Eviatar was rejected from the priesthood in favor of Pinchas' descendant Tzadok.

SHMUEL RISES TO PROPHECY

According to rabbinic tradition, the "man of God" who came to reprove Eli (I Samuel ch 2 vv 27-36) was none other than Shmuel's father Elkanah. In the meantime, Shmuel was growing. We must remember that Shmuel was a boy of only two years old when he first came to Shilo. Our text goes into precise details about his clothing. First, we are told that he went in a linen **Ephod** (ch 2 v 18); immediately afterwards we learn that his mother would bring him a "small coat" (small because it was to fit a small boy) each time she came to Shilo for the fesivals (v 19 - the boy was growing fast).

Shmuel's **Ephod** was somewhat different from the **Ephod** of the High Priest, which had been imitated by Gideon in his time and by Michah, maker of the idol. RaDaK (on v 18) provides a detailed explanation of the different kinds of garment to which the word **Ephod** refers in various different contexts in NaKh. Shmuel's **Ephod** was **not** an imitation of the High Priest's (Shmuel was a Levite). Shmuel's **Ephod** was a simple linen robe that was typically worn by those truly given over to divine service regardless of their pedigree (cf. I Samuel 22:18; II Samuel 6:14).

The account of Shmuel's growth and his childhood clothing is bound up with the mystery of the **Katnut** ("smallness" or "childhood") of the divine Partzuf of **Zeir Anpin**, who is nurtured and bedecked by **Imma** (=Binah, "understanding"), and thus Shmuel wears a succession of garments corresponding to his spiritual growth.

THE GATHERING STORM

In those days, the word of God was "precious" (**yakar**, ch 3 v. 1) because it was so rare. The ascent of Shmuel signified the revelation of a new level of prophecy out of the "womb" of Imma -- a birth accompanied by great pangs of travail.

The commentators are at pains to point out that despite the apparent simple meaning of the text (ch 3 v 3), Shmuel **was not sleeping in the Sanctuary** when the call to prophecy first came to him. Those familiar with the cantillation notes (trope) will readily see that there is an **Etnachta** ("resting note") under the word **shocheiv**, "was lying", separating it from the next words "in the Sanctuary of the Lord", which begin a new phrase. It was strictly forbidden for a Levite even to enter the Sanctuary itself, let alone lie down to sleep there. Shmuel was lying **outside** the Sanctuary Courtyard by the gate, performing his Levitical guard duty. The prophetic voice did indeed come forth from the Sanctuary, and **reached** Shmuel in the very place where he lay despite the fact that it by-passed Eli. God is perfectly capable of making His voice heard to one and not to another, regardless of where they are situated (see Rashi on v 3).

It is very noteworthy that when Shmuel first heard God's call, he thought it was Eli, for "your fear of your teacher should be like the fear of Heaven". Before one can be a prophet, one must first be the assiduous student of a Torah sage and a Tzaddik. Yet now Shmuel was ready to ascend to a new level beyond that of his teacher: from now on God would speak to Shmuel directly.

The fate of Eli and his sons was sealed. Shmuel's ascent to prophecy came on the eve of a terrible storm that would be so shocking that "the two ears of all who hear of it will ring and tremble" (v 11). Shmuel, while modest, eventually showed himself fearless in delivering his message to its intended recipient, Eli. God was with Shmuel and all Israel from Dan to Be'er Sheva knew that he was God's faithful prophet.

Samuel was now nationally known throughout Israel as the **Prophet**, but as yet he could not really be said to be the nation's **leader** because the people did not take counsel with him in face of the crisis caused by Philistine expansionism. It was on their own initiative that they went out to war instead of first repenting, and when they suffered their first serious defeat on the battlefield, they sent to take the Ark from Shilo without consulting either Eli or Samuel. They were still afflicted with the malady of the age of the Judges, doing what was right in their own eyes without seeking counsel from the wise.

THE ARK OF THE COVENANT

The Ark was Israel's most sacred national treasure, containing the fragments of the Tablets of Stone received by Moses on Sinai, the Second Tablets hewn by Moses, and the authoritative Torah Scroll that Moses had written. Jacob in his dream on the Temple Mount in Jerusalem had seen a **sulam** ("ladder", Gematria=130) connecting heaven and earth. 130 is also the Gematria of **Sinai** - for the Torah given on Sinai connects heaven and earth when we embrace that Torah and take it into our hearts and our very lives. Jacob dreamed that the Torah - the Ark of the Covenant with its precious contents given at Sinai - would eventually rest on the very spot where he had laid his head, the Foundation Stone around which the Temple Holy of Holies was built to house it. The purpose of the Giving of the Torah on **Sinai** was that the Torah should be at the very center and foundation of the Temple, from which it should shine to all Israel and to all the world. In the time of Eli, the Sanctuary in Shilo was the precursor of the destined Temple in Jerusalem. But before Samuel could pave the way for the building of this Temple, the Israelites first had to suffer a catastrophe in order to learn the awesome meaning of the Ark and the Covenant to which it bore testimony.

"And the people came to the camp and the elders of Israel said, 'Why has God smitten us this day before the Philistines?'" (ch 4 v 3). The elders pretended to be righteous, beating their breasts in mock self-recrimination, but they did not truly repent because they did not seek out the true reason for their defeat, which was their acceptance of the corruption of the priesthood and the resulting corruption of the spiritual life of the people, a malady delineated in the previous two chapters. Even though it was the people themselves who had complained about the irregularities practiced by Eli's two sons, Pinchas and Hofni, they did nothing about them, and indeed they suffered from a related malady, because it is clear from the ensuing narrative that they thought that carrying out the **externals** of religion is sufficient without embracing God **internally** with all their heart.

Israel had witnessed the power of the Ark of the Covenant in the time of Moses in the war against the Midianites, and again in the time of Joshua at the splitting of the Jordan and the fall of Jericho. Now in their struggle against the Philistines, they thought that it would be sufficient to take the Ark out to battle and let its "magic" "work" for them automatically without their having to break their own hearts and repent completely. However, God was to teach both the Israelites and the Philistines that the Ark is not a magic box-of-tricks that does whatever you want. The Ark is testimony to God's infinite power to make or change the laws of nature at will - according to what **He** wants.

When Pinchas and Hofni brought the Ark to the Israelite camp, the people sounded a great **teru'ah** ("blasting" ch 4 v 5), but this was not the **teru'ah** of repentance. The Philistines were disconcerted by the Israelite trumpeting, sensing that the Israelite God had come into their camp. The Philistines evidently believed in divine power, but erred in thinking that it is wielded by a plurality of forces that can be set against each other and overpowered. The Philistines thought they could beat down God by asserting their macho virility (v 9) - and God, who is very patient with sinners, allowed them to carry on thinking so by granting them victory, since the decree had already been passed against Pinchas and Hofni.

The Prophet in his unflinching reproof teaches us through our text that the responsibility for Israel's national malady lay with its corrupted leadership, and this is why Pinchas and Hofni were killed in the battle.

"AND A BENJAMINITE MAN RAN FROM THE RANKS" (v 12)

The rabbis teach that this man from the tribe of Benjamin was none other than Israel's future king Saul - who distinguished himself by his heroism this day, despite Israel's crushing defeat at the hands of the Philistines, by snatching the Tablets of Stone from the hands of the Philistine strong-man, Goliath, who had taken them when they captured the Ark. According to tradition, Saul ran anywhere from 60 to 180 miles on this one day in order to bring the Tablets back to Shilo and to tell Eli the terrible news.

Saul had a particular interest in this struggle against the Philistines as their very power over the Israelites was rooted in Abraham's oath to the Philistine king Avimelech not to betray the latter's descendants to the third generation (Genesis 21:22-31). Abraham's gift of seven lambs to Avimelech led to a decree against seven of Abraham's righteous descendants to fall at the hands of the Philistines. These were Samson, Pinchas and Hofni, and Saul himself together with his three sons, who were destined to fall on the battlefield at Mount Gilboa.

Saul now sought to break the news of the disaster to Eli as gently as possible, but Eli, although not perfect, was truly a Tzaddik and while he was unmoved by the death of his own sons, which had already been prophesied to him, the news of the capture of the Ark was such a shock that he fell backward to his death - **backward** to requite his having failed to look **forward** to the new generation of priests, his corrupt sons, whom he should have chastised.

The Philistines soon arrived in Shilo, sacking and destroying the Sanctuary, which had stood for 369 years.

Eli's daughter-in-law, Pinchas' widow, found the right term for the disaster in calling her son **Ee-Kavod**, "the opposite of Glory" (v 21) - since the Glory of Israel had gone into exile with the capture of the Ark of the Covenant.

CHAPTER 5

THE ARK TAKES CARE OF ITSELF

Eli died of shock at the capture of the Ark because he knew that he and his sons were at fault, having been charged with its safe-keeping. However, at the crossing of the Jordan, Israel had already seen that it is not man who carries the Ark, but rather the Ark that carries those who carry it.

The Philistines erred in equating the One God of the Ark of the Covenant with one of their own gods. Little is written about the nature of the Philistine god Dagon except that it was represented by the form of a **merman**, like a human from the torso upwards and like a fish from the torso downwards (**dag** in Hebrew="fish"). In this the Philistine god was apparently similar to various other mythological gods such as the Sumerian-Babylonian "Enki" and the Greek-Roman "Triton". The Philistines may have believed that their god had power over the earth and the sea. Our text suggests that they believed that there were limits to the power of the God of Israel since they evidently thought He had exhausted all His plagues on the Egyptians (ch 4 v 8).

The first time God toppled the statue of Dagon, the Philistines wanted to think it was **chance** and they put it back in its place (ch 5 v 3). When God broke off Dagon's head and hands and cast them on the threshold, they did not cease to believe in idols but instead superstitiously attributed the "accident" to some power contained in the threshold (v. 5). It was then that God showed the Philistines that His plagues were by no means exhausted on the Egyptians, and that He had the power to afflict them in their most private parts of all. Like Pharaoh in the time of Moses (who went down to the river to relieve himself at a time when nobody could see him), the Philistines liked to deny that they had human toilet needs, but now they were forced to confront their human vulnerability in the most painful way possible.

When Avimelech kidnapped Sarah, the Midrash tells that he and all his household were afflicted by having all their bodily cavities of excretion stopped up so that all the waste was held back clogged up inside them. A similar punishment now afflicted all the Philistines in the succession of towns where they tried to keep the kidnapped Ark. They kept moving the Ark from town to town, "testing" God to see if it was really the cause of their troubles.

The first blessing a Jew makes every day is **Asher Yatzar...** "Who formed man in wisdom and created in him many orifices and hollows. It is revealed and known before Your throne of Glory that if one of them is opened [when it should be closed] or one of them is stopped up [when it should be open] it is impossible to survive and stand before You for even one hour."

The **t'chorim** - hemorrhoids or "piles" - with which the Philistines were plagued were so terrible that these virile "men" suddenly found themselves staring death in the face to the point that they wanted to send the Ark straight back to the Israelites. This was in fulfillment of Moses' words: "And it was when the Ark traveled, and Moses said, 'Arise **HaShem** and your enemies will be scattered and those that hate You will flee from before You'" (Numbers 10:35).

CHAPTER 6

The stay of the Ark of the Covenant among the Philistines for **seven** months was another penalty for the **seven** lambs that Abraham had given king Avimelech (Bereishit Rabbah 54).

The story of the return of the Ark by the Philistines to Beit Shemesh subtly contrasts the attitude of the Philistines towards it with that of the Israelites who received it, serving as a reproof to the latter for failing to show the proper respect. (A similar lack of respect is often visible in present-day places of "worship".)

The Philistines consult their priests and magician-diviners as to a fitting way to return the Ark that had created such havoc in their land (a terrible infestation of mice) and in their very innards (the hemorrhoids). (According to one Midrash the mice jumped up into their anuses and pulled out their innards, making this plague no less striking than those of Egypt.) The priests and magicians answer that the Philistines must **show** that they understand that the plague was from God by offering **golden mice** and **golden hemorrhoids**. "Then you shall be healed, and **He will be known to you** - why would He then not turn his hand away from you" (ch 6 v 3).

Nevertheless, the Philistines did not quite believe in God's supreme power. They believed in a variety of divine powers and knew of the wrath of the gods, which they sought to propitiate, but they also believed in luck and chance. This was why they set up the test of the cow-drawn wagon to see if the plague might not have been chance. "And you will see, if it goes up by way of his boundary to Beth Shemesh, He did this great evil to us, but if not, we shall know that it was not His hand that plagued us, it was a **chance** that occurred to us" (v 9).

The test was set up to be as difficult as possible. Two nursing cows were brought to draw the wagon laden with the heavy wooden gold-covered ark and its contents of stone together with the golden Cherubim together with the box of golden mice and golden hemorrhoids, while their suckling calves were held back in the house behind them. The last thing a nursing cow that has never had to work wants to do is to turn her back on her new-born calf and drag an exceedingly heavy wagon in the opposite direction.

VA-YISHAR-NAH HA-PAROT, "AND THE COWS SANG" (v 12)

Rashi on this verse states that the Hebrew word **va-yishar-nah** is "**andrygonous**" i.e. a grammatical hybrid of masculine (the prefix -**yi**- indicating masculine 3rd person plural) and feminine (the suffix -**nah**, indicating feminine 3rd person plural). Without Rashi's comment, the obvious **p'shat** for anyone familiar with Hebrew grammar is that the word is not **androgynous** at all, but that the root is **yishar**, as in **yashar**, "straight", and here we simply have the feminine 3rd person plural form. I.e. the two milking cows **went straight**. However, by telling us that the word is indeed **androgynous**, Rashi is pointing to the deeper **drush**, based on the root **shar** - "sing". Not **only** did the two mother cows **sing**, but so did their **male young**, and this is why the grammatical form is both masculine and feminine!!!

The miracle of the singing cows is greatly celebrated in Torah lore (Talmud Avodah Zarah 24b), and - for Rabbi Nachman lovers - is alluded to in his story of the Exchanged Children, where the king's true son eventually gains possession of a vessel that when placed on an animal, causes it to sing.

The Rabbis indeed asked why the remarkable mouths of these cows were not included in the list of Ten Things that were created at the very end of the Sixth Day of Creation in the twilight just as the first Shabbat was beginning (Avot 5:8). They answered that it is because the mouths of the cows are **included** in the **mouth of the ass** which opened up to speak to Bilaam (Numbers 22:28). There the **aton** wife of the **chamor**, "donkey" representing **chomriut**, material physicality, spoke out the letters of Aleph Beit from Aleph to Tav - A-T-oN (the long Nun, which stretches from the top of the line down way below the bottom, signifies the 50 Gates of Understanding). When the Philistines returned the Ark, this **holy vessel** caused the very cows to **sing despite themselves** - despite their longing for their young and not to have to drag this heavy wagon.

As discussed in the commentaries on the songs of Deborah (Judges ch 5) and Hannah (I Samuel chs 1-2), the level of **song** (**Binah**) reveals that all creation is governed providentially by the One Unified God, whose commandments to the world are engraved on the Stone Tablets contained in the Ark of Testimony. Just as the Ark miraculously carried those who carried it over the waters of the Jordan, so it compelled the very cows to sing songs of praise to God.

The idolatrous Philistine captains walked after the cart watching all this in amazement, and they knew the power of God and His holy Ark, but the Israelite men of Beit Shemesh were too busy with their wheat harvest to pay more than casual attention to the passing spectacle (v 13). The Talmud (Sotah 35a) says that the men of Beit Shemesh were smitten (v 19) because (1) they kept harvesting even as they prostrated to the Ark when they should have stopped everything in face of this miracle, and (2) they made up a scurrilous rhyme asking the Ark who made it angry and what came to reconcile it.

The rabbinic discussion about whether only 70 men died but that they were equivalent to 50,000, **or** did 50,000 die who were the equivalent of the 70 members of the Sanhedrin (Sotah 35b) illustrates that such numbers given in the Biblical text need not necessarily be taken literally but are given for **drash**. In any event the men of Beit Shemesh suffered an extremely painful blow that came to teach the true, terrible **awesomeness** of the Ark of the Covenant, which signifies God's very presence among us. This is a double-edged sword, causing the righteous to rejoice while the wicked and rebellious suffer God's wrathful intolerance of evil.

So important was this **Kiddush HaShem**, Sanctification of God's name, that - surprising as it may seem - the very **box** with the **golden mice** and **golden hemorrhoids** offered by the Philistines was kept **side by side** with the Ark of the Covenant in the Sanctuary in Jerusalem throughout the period of the first Temple, until they were put away, together with the flask of Mannah made by Aaron in the Wilderness, the flask of the anointing oil, Aaron's staff and the flowering almond branch by King Josiah (Talmud Yoma 52b). As we prepare ourselves to see them again soon in our times, let us learn from this text a lesson in the proper attitude of respect and honor we must show to God's holy Ark.

CHAPTER 7

The men of **Kiryiat Ye'arim** who came to take up the ark from **Beit Shemesh** did show the proper respect for the Ark, taking it to the house of Avinadav, who dedicated his very son Elazar to guard the Ark with due honor. Present-day Beit Shemesh and Kiryat Ye'arim (Teltzstone) are considered close to the sites of the ancient settlements mentioned in our text.

The twenty-year period mentioned in our text (ch 7 v 2) as the duration of the Ark's stay in Kiryat Ye'arim extended well beyond the days of Samuel. The Talmud (Zevachim 118b) states that for ten of these years, Samuel himself reigned, then Samuel reigned jointly with Saul for one year, after which Saul reigned for two years by himself. Samuel died four months before Saul. Thereafter David reigned in Hebron for seven years before he went up to Jerusalem, and it was then that he took up the Ark from the house of Avinadav (II Samuel ch 6).

For this entire period of twenty years "the whole House of Israel **sighed** after God" (ch 7 v 2). The absence of the Sanctuary and its holy Ark caused deep yearning. The period described in the remainder of our present text, Chapter 7, covers most of Samuel's ten years of ministry, in which he physically traveled from center to center (ch 7 v 16) bringing the people to the level of Teshuvah where they would be ready for the kingship. In this ten-year ministry Samuel succeeded in reversing the blight of idolatry (vv 3-4) that had begun over three hundred years earlier after the time of Joshua.

At Samuel's national assembly of all the people at the traditional gathering place in **Mitzpah**, "they drew water and they poured before HaShem" (v 6): Yonatan in the Targum renders this as: "and they poured out their hearts in repentance like water before HaShem".

From verse 7 ("and the Philistines heard. and the officers of the Philistines went up to Israel") we learn that whenever there is an arousal to holiness and repentance in Israel, the forces of the other side (**Plishtim**=860=10 x 86, **Elokim**=severe **Dinim**, Judgments) arouse to threaten Israel not to rebel against the yoke of This-Worldly Materialism in favor of spirituality and service of God. Israel's fear of the Philistines shows how they had subjected their very selves to Philistine rule. However, now they had Samuel the Prophet, who could call upon God and receive a spectacular answer. Samuel slaughtered one female sheep (a "ruling of the hour" permitting a **female** animal as an Olah burnt-offering on a **Bamah** whereas the Olah on the Sanctuary Altar must be **male** specifically Lev. 1:3), and as Samuel offered up the sacrifice, God answered with a **thunder** that threw the attacking Philistines into consternation, turning the tables on them and enabling the Israelites to chase after and subdue them all the days of Samuel (v 13).

It had been to **Even Ha-Ezer** that the Israelites had originally taken the Ark of the Covenant from Shilo in attempting to defeat the Philistines in the time of Eli (ch 4 v 2) and it was there that the Philistines captured it. However **Even Ha-Ezer** was not yet the name of the place (see Rashi ad loc) until Samuel set up the stone (**even**) commemorating God's **help** (**ezer**) until the present (ch 7 v 12). The stone came to teach that God constantly watches His people, answering them as soon as they **pour out their hearts like water** in true repentance.

The name **Even Ha-ezer** has a special significance to those who observe the Torah in accordance with the teachings of the rabbis. This is because Rabbi Yaakov ben Asher (author of **Arba'a Turim** "The Four Rows", which provided the structure for R. Joseph Karo's definitive **Shulchan Aruch** law-code) chose **Even Ha-Ezer** as the name of its fourth section, which deals with with all the laws of marriage, divorce and family life as they apply until today. He chose **Even Ha-Ezer** as the name for this section because God created **woman** as man's "helper" (Genesis 2:20). Thus, the section of Shulchan Aruch called **Even Ha-Ezer** is the "foundation stone" of man's life with his **ezer**, "helper", i.e. his wife. The story of Samuel's memorial stone **Even Ha-Ezer** can be seen as a lesson to us that when we cast out our inner idols and base the most intimate details of our family life on God's Torah as taught in the laws of **Even Ha-Ezer** and with this **pour out our hearts like water in true repentance**, we can live at peace with those around us, and even our worst enemies will turn their backs and flee.

CHAPTER 8

VAI!!! IT WAS WHEN SAMUEL WAS OLD

The first word of Chapter 8 is **va-yehi**, "And it was." "We have a tradition handed down from the Men of the Great Assembly that wherever it says **va-yehi**, it is an expression of pain - **vai**: 'And it was when Samuel was old... and his sons did not go in his ways'" (Megillah 10b).

When Eli had told Samuel that he **must** reveal his prophecy to him on pain of being cursed, even though Samuel did in fact reveal it, nevertheless the threatened curse had its effect, and Samuel, like Eli, suffered from having children who did not live up to his own high standards (Makkot 11a).

As in the case of Eli's sons, the flaw in Samuel's sons was more subtle than might appear from a superficial reading of our text. They may not have gone in Samuel's ways, but this does not mean they were crude sinners. Their flaw was that unlike Samuel, they did not **travel around** from center to center to judge the people. Instead, they both sat at home in comfort in Be'er Sheva - in the extreme south of the Land (when one of them at least should have set up in Dan in the north), forcing all who sought justice to travel all the way there. They also allowed their staff to take fat fees for legal services (Talmud Shabbat 56a). They "inclined after gain" (ch 8 v 3) - they were criticized for **demanding** the tithes due to them as Levites instead of waiting for people to give them (ibid.; cf. Chulin 133a).

THE PEOPLE REQUEST A KING

"Set a king over us to judge us like all the nations. And the matter was evil in the eyes of Samuel" (vv 5-6).

"Israel had been given three commandments to fulfill after their entry into the Land: to appoint a king over themselves, to build the Temple and to destroy Amalek. If so, why were they punished when they asked for a king in the days of Samuel? Because they asked out of anger and not for the sake of the mitzvah" (Tosefta Sanhedrin ch 4).

The mitzvah to appoint a king is given in the Torah (Deut. 17:14-19), and Samuel's whole mission was to establish the kingship, which would inaugurate a period of divine glory and revelation through the Kingdom of God being reflected and enhanced by the kingdom on earth.

However, from our present text we see that the people had not yet reached the necessary level of understanding of the nature of the Torah kingship to be ready for kings like David and Solomon. Israel would have to endure a painful process of many years of war and civil strife in order to clarify the true meaning of the kingship.

Our rabbis taught that the elders of the people did ask Samuel for a king in the proper manner: "Give us a king **to judge us**" (v 5, i.e. to settle their disputes and make peace). However, it was the impetuous "people of the earth" (**amei ha'aretz**, ignoramuses) who were at fault, because it was they who said, "...and we also shall be **like all the nations**." (v 20; Sanhedrin 20b). Some rabbis say the people secretly hoped that with a king instead of judges they would more easily be able to revert to idolatry, which indeed came about when Jeraboam ben Nevat rebelled against King Solomon and established the kingdom of the Ten Tribes.

The people of Israel today could save themselves much war and strife by seriously seeking to clarify for themselves the true purpose of having a sovereign state to govern their affairs and the true reason for wanting Mashiach.

AND HE SAID, THIS WILL BE THE LAW OF THE KING (v 11)

God Himself commanded Samuel to accede to the people's request - for the time of the destined kingship had arrived - and ordered him to lay before them the laws of the kingship. Samuel wanted to shock this nation of independent land-owning small farmers into understanding the real implications of the Torah kingship by explaining the king's power over the people in terms that would have immediate tangible meaning for them. The king was going to be lord over the land, with the power to requisition the flower of the country's youth, males and females, for the glory of his court and to man his army, and the power to commandeer land, produce and other resources for his domestic and military needs. We will see in I Kings in the narrative about King Solomon how he did indeed use this power for the glory of God - he built His Temple - and for the glory of Israel and the House of David. But Samuel's warnings to the people that the king would be "tithing" (i.e. taxing) their seed and orchards and flocks etc. were intended to let them understand that all this would hit them hard where they would really feel it -- in their "pockets", as it were.

Samuel's address to the nation about the powers of the king is one of the primary sources in the written Torah for the laws of the kingship (as is the section in Deut. 17:14-20). These laws are discussed in the Talmud in tractate Sanhedrin (20bff) and are laid out in detail in Rambam (Maimonides), Mishneh Torah, Laws of Kings chs 1-5.

CHAPTER 9

ENTER SAUL

In I Chronicles 8:33 the name of the father of Saul's father, Kish, is given as **Ner** (=a "lamp") whereas here it is given as **Avi-el** (I Samuel 9:1). "Saul attained the kingship in the merit of his grandfather, who used to light lamps for the benefit of the public. There were dark alleyways leading from his house to the Study House, and he lit lamps in them to light the way for the public. His name was **Avi-el** but because he lit lamps for the general public, he merited to be called **Ner**" (Vayikra Rabbah 9). In other words, it was in Saul's very blood to bring Israel to study the Torah.

THE MYSTERY OF THE ASSES

The story of Saul's cross-country search for his father's asses and how it brought him to the Seer who was to anoint him as king is another example of the heavily veiled allegory of the Navi (Prophet). Again, it is the holy ARI (Rabbi Yitzchak Luria) who opens a chink in the veil with his teachings in Sefer HaLikutim on I Samuel.

"Know that the asses (**atonot**) correspond to the Ten Crowns of Impurity (the Keters of the Ten Sefirot of the unholy side of creation). And because Jacob sent asses to Esau, Esau's angel wrestled with him. The blow Jacob received on his right thigh causing him to limp brought about the cessation of prophecy. When the text says, 'And as to the asses. they have been found' (I Samuel 9:20), it means that the **Kelipot** ("husks", forces of evil) that were scattered around the world had been 'found' - i.e. the source of their accusation against the holy side has been discovered and it is possible to rectify them.

"The secret of Jacob's thigh - it was the right thigh - is that it alludes to the Sefirah of **Netzach** ("victory"), which was flawed by the Angel of Death (Samech Mem, Esau's guardian angel). Now it is from the Sefirahs of **Netzach-Hod-Yesod** that prophecy comes, but when the prophetic spirit would descend and come to **Netzach**, there was an intervening barrier closing up the channels through which the flow descends from **Netzach**. For this reason, 'The word of God was **precious** (yakar, "heavy") and no vision burst through' (I Samuel 3:1). Because Jacob prostrated 22 times to Esau, **Netzach** was very seriously flawed until **Benjamin** came - he was not yet born when Jacob prostrated to Esau. For this reason, **Mordechai** (descended from Benjamin), rectified **Netzach** and did not want to bow down to Haman.

"And he [Esau-Amalek] kept his fury for ever (**Netzach**)" (Amos 1:11). I.e. Esau's fury is against **Netzach**.

"The reason why Samuel is here called **Ha-Ro'eh**, "the **Seer**" (I Samuel 9:9 etc.) and not the **Navi**, "prophet", is because now was the time for Prophecy to be rectified through the repair of **Netzach**, but as yet the repair had not been carried out. Samuel, who was a Levite (**Gevurah**, "might") had the power to repair it with Saul, who was from the tribe of Benjamin, **ben yamin** ("son of the **right**") - for it had been Jacob's **right thigh** that was damaged.

'He will lead (**ya'atzor**) my people' (ch 9 v 17). The unusual word used here for leadership, **ya'atzor**, has the connotation, "he will stop, put on a brake". God did not say "he will **rule**, (**yimloch**)" because Saul was only able to put a temporary brake on the flaw and stop the evil Kelipah from ruling over **Netzach** anymore. But when Saul sinned with his failure to destroy the Amalekite king, the Kelipah came back and held sway again. It was only David who would be able to rectify the flaw in **Netzach**. It was because Saul failed to rectify prophecy and holy spirit that he was attacked by an impure spirit and accordingly was not answered through the Urim Ve-Tumim and the prophets. This was because his flaw lay in the sphere of prophecy and holy spirit.

"In the feast that Samuel made with the meat of the sacrifice at the Bamah (ch 9 vv. 22ff) he was sure to give Saul the portion that had been specially set aside for him - the **thigh** of the animal - for this alluded to **Netzach**, the "right thigh", i.e. the wellspring of prophecy, for this was what Saul was intended to rectify. The intention of Saul eating together with Samuel was to open the channel of prophecy, which is why immediately afterwards Saul saw a band of prophets prophesying." (ARI, Sefer HaLikutim).

CHAPTER 10

In the light of the extracts from the ARI quoted in the commentary on the previous chapter, teaching that Saul's essential mission was to rectify prophecy, the weave of incidents involving prophets and prophetic locations as narrated in our present chapter becomes a little more comprehensible.

"And Samuel took the flask of oil and poured it upon his head and kissed him" (I Samuel 10:1). The oil is, of course, emblematic of the spirit flowing down from above, yet the Rabbis pointed out that this was not Moses' **Shemen HaMishchah**, "anointing oil" but only aromatic **apharsamon** oil, and it was poured not from a **keren** ("horn") but from a **pakh** ("flask"). The **Shemen HaMishchah** was reserved for the kings of Judah, and thus David and Solomon were both anointed with it from a horn - and both saw their kingship established. However, Saul, and later Jehu, who were anointed only with **apharsamon** oil from a flask, did not see their kingship established (Horayot 11b; Megillah 14a).

Samuel's foretelling Saul of his coming journey (ch 10 vv 2-9) involves locations associated with Saul's illustrious ancestors Rachel, whose grave is mentioned though Saul was not actually to visit it (see Rashi on v 2) and Jacob, who dreamed his dream of the ladder at Luz - Beit El (v 3). The "Hill of God" mentioned in v. 5 is said in Targum to be the location of the Ark of the Covenant. It was from there that Saul would encounter a "band of prophets". RaDaK notes (ad loc.) that the illustrious prophets of those times included Elkanah, Gad, Nathan, Asaph, Heyman and Yedutun. Thus, Saul was being prepared for the kingship.

However, scarcely noticeable in verse 8 is Samuel's test to Saul. "And you shall go down before me to Gilgal. and you shall wait seven days until I come to you." In order to help us understand where Saul's going down to Gilgal as referred to here, actually comes in the sequence of events in our unfolding narrative, the commentators on this verse point out that Samuel is here referring to a visit to Gilgal by Saul and Samuel that was to come only **after** the renewal of the kingship at Gilgal as described in ch 10 vv 14-15 and ch 11 v 15. The story of the second visit to Gilgal as referred to here is only told later on, in ch 13 vv 8-14 - where we see that Saul failed Samuel's test. Here in our present text, Samuel is ordering Saul to **wait** for Samuel on that second occasion and **not** to sacrifice, because Samuel was coming to do that. However, as we shall see, Saul gave in to popular pressure, and when Samuel did not arrive, offered the sacrifice himself. For this he was deposed from the kingship. Prophecy is only possible when the student prophet is absolutely obedient to his master.

As yet, however, the text contains few direct hints of the flaw that was to undermine Saul's kingship. Here in our present chapter, we learn more of the virtues for which he was chosen as king - his exceptional modesty and humility, and his flight from honor, which actually caused honor to pursue him. Already in the previous chapter (ch 9 v 5) we heard Saul tell his attendant that he wanted to return home from searching for the donkeys lest his father "be worried about **us**" - Saul humbly put himself on the same level as the attendant. Now we hear how Saul's own uncle asked him what Samuel had told him, but Saul modestly would not tell him that he had been chosen as king (v 16). The rabbis connected Saul's modesty with his illustrious ancestress Rachel, who according to Midrash collaborated with Laban and remained silent in order to make Jacob think he was marrying Leah so that she should not be humiliated. And in the merit of Rachel and Saul, they had as their descendant Queen Esther, who modestly "did not tell her lineage".

At the assembly of the nation at Mitzpah (vv 17-25), Samuel used the method of lots to show the people that Saul had been chosen by God as their king (vv 20-21). With characteristic humility, Saul ran away and "was hiding by the vessels" (v 22). Rashi's simple **p'shat** is that the **Keilim** are the clothes and Saul was hiding where the people left their cloaks before attending the assembly. However, Rashi also brings the Midrash that the **Keilim** refer to the Urim Ve-Tumim of the High Priest: Saul would only agree to accept the kingship if they consulted the Urim Ve-Tumim!

"It is hard to rise to greatness, and as hard as it is to arise to it, so it is hard to descend from greatness. For so we find by Saul: when he was told to arise to the kingship, he 'hid by the vessels'. And when he was told to descend from the kingship, he went after David to try to kill him" (Pirkey d'Rabbi Nathan 10:3).

When the skeptics questioned how this Saul could save them, the king was silent and forbearing (ch 10 v 27 and ch 11 v 13). However, he was criticized for this. While he was permitted to be personally humble and forbearing, he was not allowed to compromise on the honor due to the king, as this would undermine the kingship.

CHAPTER 11

The first challenge of Saul's kingship was from the Ammonites. They had been routed by Yiftach (Jephthah) but since that time the Philistines had been pressing in on the Israelites from the south and west, leaving them seriously weakened and unable to defend the Israelite settlements east of the Jordan. The Ammonites thus succeeded in extending their hegemony northwards into the Gilead at least as far as Yavesh Gil'ad, which is about 60 km north west of present day Amman. The name of this ancient settlement survives in the Arab name of the local wadi - Yabbes, which flows into the River Jordan. (The names of hundreds of other settlements mentioned in TaNaKh are also evident in local Arab place-names, attesting to the great antiquity of Israel's connection with the Land.)

The town of Yavesh Gil'ad was involved in the story of the Concubine in Giv'ah (Judges ch 20) as the men of that town did not attend the National Assembly that was called to discipline the Benjaminites, and were accordingly killed. It was their 400 surviving virgin female offspring who were married to 400 of the 600 Benjaminites who survived the war of the Tribes against them, and thus although in the territories of Menasheh, the town was inhabited by Benjaminites who inherited their wives' property.

The Ammonite king Nachash (="serpent") demanded that the inhabitants of Yavesh must gouge out their own right eyes if they wanted to make peace with him. (This is very reminiscent of the demands of Israel's present-day oppressors.) His demand was intentionally humiliating (v 2). The rabbis teach that the "eyes" he wanted the Israelites to gouge out were (1) their best slingers and archers, who are the "delight of Israel's eyes", (2) the Sanhedrin, who are called the "eye" of Israel, and (3) the Sefer Torah (Yalkut Shimoni).

"And the spirit of God burst into Saul as he heard these things..." (v 6). Now Saul exhibited the **Gevurah** of kingship and swiftly mobilized the entire nation for war (vv 7-8). His tactics against the Ammonites, dividing his forces into three, are reminiscent of Gideon's tactics against the Midianites (Judges 7:16). His surprise attack brought about a God-given victory which showed all the people that he was truly God's chosen king. Samuel therefore called all the people to Gilgal (for the **first** visit, not the **second**, see above ch 10 v 8, which was to be Saul's test) in order to "renew the kingship" (ch 11 vv 14-15). Although Saul had already been chosen by the lottery and Urim Ve-Tumim and acclaimed by the people, his kingship was not established until after his victory over the Ammonites and this is why the kingship was now "renewed" at Gilgal.

CHAPTER 12

*I Samuel 11:14-15 and 12:1-22 is read as the Haftarah of **Parshat Korach**, Numbers 16:1-18:32*

Samuel's address to all Israel assembled in Gilgal to "renew the kingship"(ch 12 vv 1-25) displays an apparent ambivalence about the kingship. It is a Torah mitzvah to appoint a king, yet Samuel castigated the people for asking for one even though he himself appointed him. This is because Samuel saw that the people's conception of the nature and purpose of the kingship as being primarily for the sake of what today is called "national security" was inherently flawed. His intent in his address was to correct their misconceptions.

A LESSON IN GOOD GOVERNMENT

"I have become old" (v 2). Samuel was only 52 when he died, but the rabbis said that "old age jumped upon him" so that he should not see Saul's destined death in his lifetime (Ta'anit 5b).

In his "retirement farewell" address to the whole people, Samuel asked them to testify to his impeccable integrity throughout the years he ruled, neither oppressing nor exploiting the people and never taking bribes or twisting justice. The rabbis said that Samuel was independently wealthy (Nedarim 38a) which should perhaps have made him less susceptible to the temptations of corrupt government, yet even the ownership of substantial wealth has not stopped numerous past and contemporary government figures from flagrantly pursuing their private interests through their endeavors in the "service" of the public. None of the assembled Israelites could deny Samuel's integrity, "…and **he said** [I am] a witness" (v 5) Based on the use of the singular verb at the end of verse 5 where we would have expected the plural - "and **they** (the people) said" - the rabbis taught that a **Bat Kol** (lit. "daughter of a voice" - a heavenly "echo") proclaimed, "**I am the witness**". Even Heaven could testify to Samuel's absolute integrity. Perhaps the reason Samuel felt no need to take from others was that he was truly wealthy - i.e. satisfied with his portion (Avot 4:1) - which cannot be said for the power-hungry, wealth-seeking "leaders" of today.

THE LESSONS OF HISTORY

The key point in Samuel's sweeping survey of the history of Israel is that in Egypt, "your fathers **cried out** to God…" (v 8) and in the Land, after being "sold" to their enemies, "they **cried out** to God and said, 'We have sinned...'" (v 10). The lesson is that when Israel turns to God, they are saved, but if they put their trust in some powerful king or government or military strength alone, they are abandoned.

Samuel compares Moses, Aharon and himself in their generations to "Jerubaal, Bedan and Yiftach" in theirs. Jerubaal is Gideon, while Bedan is Shimshon (Samson), who was from the tribe of **Dan** (= BeDaN, "in Dan"). Compared to Moses, Aharon and Samuel the prophets, Gideon, Jephtah and Samson were **kaley olam**, "lightweights", yet Samuel mentions them together - teaching that even though Israel's Torah leaders in the later generations may seem much less authoritative than the outstanding giants of the past, we must still rely on our leaders if they truly speak in the name of the Torah (see Rashi on v 11).

A RAINSTORM AT HARVEST TIME

"And Samuel **called** to God, and God gave thunderclaps and rain on that day" (v 18). Samuel gave the people a most frightening, practical demonstration of the great power of prayer in order to prove his point that the strength of the people of Israel in the face of all their enemies lies only in **crying out to God**.

In Israel, the rainy season comes to an end in Adar (March) with only a few late showers in Nissan (April), and by the time of the wheat harvest, which is after Pesach during the months of Iyar-Sivan (May-June) any rain is a freak occurrence. Indeed, rain after Nissan is a curse (Ta'anit 12b) because it spoils the wheat. Nevertheless, when Samuel called upon God, He answered him at once. Samuel's purpose was to shock the people into understanding that their entire salvation depended only on prayer. He also was hinting to them that just as his few words of prayer had the power to unleash a terrible storm, so too their few wrongly-motivated words in requesting for a king could let loose a torrent of destructive consequences (Me'am Lo'ez). We need to know what we should be praying for (which we learn from the Torah), and then we need to pray for it.

CHAPTER 13

Ben-shanah Sha'ul be-molcho (ch 13 v 1). The literal meaning of the Hebrew words is: "Saul was **one year old** when he reigned", although the commentators explain that the intent is that the "renewal of the kingship" described in the previous chapter took place a year after Saul's induction as king. However, the rabbis darshened from the literal meaning of these words that Saul was **like a one-year-old** babe when he became king, because just as a baby is clean of all sin, so a leader is forgiven all his sins on his induction (and from other verses they learned that so too a sage on his induction and a bridegroom - and his bride - on their wedding day are forgiven all their sins).

The same verse also states that Saul's reign over Israel lasted only two years (v 1), at the end of which he died in battle against the Philistines. This may seem surprising when we consider that the nineteen chapters from here to the end of I Samuel seem to cover a very great variety of incidents which one might have expected to have taken place over a longer period of time. We should bear in mind the timeframe as we proceed with our study of the later sections of this book.

ENTER JONATHAN

In verses 2-3 we are first introduced to one of the most noble characters in the Bible, Saul's son Jonathan, who should have inherited the kingship, and who displayed spectacular boldness and courage from the very start of his career by assassinating the Philistine governor of the Benjaminite territories - emblem of the foreign oppressor -- thereby triggering the Philistine war to quash the Israelite "rebellion". Despite the fact that Jonathan "lost" the kingship to David, he showed not the faintest trace of jealousy of his beloved friend, for whom he was ready to endanger his very life.

RaDaK (on verse 2) notes that from the beginning of the book of I Samuel until ch 18 v 1 his name is written as **Yonatan** except for two occasions (ch 14 vv 6 & 8), where it is written as **Ye-ho-natan**, as it is from ch 18 v 1 onwards. In Hebrew, the difference is the result of the addition of only one letter - a **Heh**. The addition of this letter, as in the change of Abram to Abraham and the addition of a **Yud** in the name of Pinchas, indicates the attainment of a higher spiritual level.

THE PHILISTINE OPPRESSION

Chapter 13 illustrates the dire plight of the Israelites under Philistine "occupation" in the times of Saul and Samuel. While the Philistines could field an army of 30,000 chariots and 6,000 horsemen and "people like the sand of the shore of the sea in multitude" (v 5), the disorganized Israelite small farmers had been intentionally disarmed by their foreign masters, who banned the Hebrews from engaging in any kind of metalwork so as to be unable to make swords and spears (v 19). The Israelites were forced to go down to the Philistines to repair their plows and other agricultural implements (v 20) or else they had to make do with the most primitive self-help methods to sharpen their instruments (v 21, see commentators). [Ironically, contemporary Israel is one of the world's leading weapons manufacturers, yet the nations of the world led by the country's closest ally generally prevent Israel from actually using any of her sophisticated armory with real effect, thus leaving the people of the country at the mercy of enemy rockets and missiles etc.]

SAUL: FLAWED OR TOO PERFECT?

It is hardly surprising that most of the people felt completely helpless and went into caves and holes, etc. (v 6) or emigrated to safer areas (v 7). Even when Saul gathered his bands at Gilgal to wait for his **second** meeting there with Samuel as instructed by the prophet (see ch 10 v 8 and the commentary thereon), people started deserting and scattering (ch 13 v 8). Saul had been commanded not to sacrifice at Gilgal but to wait for Samuel to do so on the seventh day. However, when Samuel did not arrive on the morning of the seventh day, Saul felt compelled to stall the people's increasing restiveness by officiating at the sacrifice himself. He was not at fault for serving at the Altar even though he was not a priest, because a **Zar** (non-priest) is permitted to serve at a **Bamah**. (Indeed, Samuel himself was not a priest but a Levite.) Saul's error was to succumb to popular pressure and stop waiting for Samuel, even though the latter had prophesied that he would arrive, which he did, albeit late in the day. Samuel's delay was a very hard test for Saul, but the Torah writes that the king "must not turn aside from the **Mitzvah** to the right or the left in order that he may extend his days..." (Deut. 17:20), and since the same passage previously states that he must "keep all the words of this **Torah**", we infer that the **Mitzvah** can only refer to the order of a prophet, which is also from God (see Rashi on v 14). Unlike democratic politicians, the leader of Israel must not pay attention to **vox populi** but only to the word of God and His prophets.

Paradoxically, the rabbis stated that Saul was deposed from the kingship not because he sinned but because he was **too perfect**. "Rav Yehudah said in the name of Shmuel, 'Why did the kingship of the house of Saul not endure? Because it contained no reproach' (i.e. Saul's pedigree was impeccable), for R. Yochanan said in the name of R. Shimon son of Yehotzedek, 'A leader is only appointed over the community if he has a box of unclean creatures hanging from his back so that if he becomes too arrogant they can say to him, Take a look behind you. '" [Thus, David's great-grandmother wasn't even born Jewish as she was a Moabitess, and this was the "box of unclean creatures" hanging over his back!!!] (Yoma 22b).

Despite having been told by Samuel that his kingship would not endure, Saul did not flinch from carrying out his duty and going to war against the Philistines despite the fact that **none of his people had any weapons** (v 22). Only Saul and Jonathan miraculously found weapons (Rashi on v 22), and with these they prepared to face the Philistine hosts at Michmas.

CHAPTER 14

There are many mysterious twists and turns in this chapter's narrative about Israel's war of rebellion against Philistine domination in the reign of Saul, which was largely initiated by his bold and courageous son Jonathan. Despite the presence of Achiyah the High Priest and the **Urim Ve-Tumim** with Saul, Jonathan did not wait for an answer through this channel (which in any case was not forthcoming) before setting off on what would have been a suicide mission were it not for his total trust in God.

Jonathan was going to expose himself and his sole attendant to the entire Philistine garrison and decide if he would remain stationary or advance based on their reaction on seeing him. Jonathan's making a sign for himself in this way was compared by the rabbis to Abraham's servant Eliezer's making a sign at the well as to which maiden would be suitable as Isaac's wife (24:13-14). The question of whether such signs are legitimate or proscribed as divination is discussed at great length by RaDaK (on v 9). If the Philistines advanced towards Jonathan, he would know that they were not afraid, but if they told him to come up to them he would know that "the fear of God was in their hearts and they were afraid to move from their place" (Rashi on v 10).

Jonathan was not afraid to go into the very midst of the Philistines for hand-to-hand combat despite the odds being so heavily weighed against him, for "there is nothing to prevent HaShem from saving whether through a multitude or through a little" (v 6). Jonathan's foray and his rapid massacre of the enemy garrison led to the mass flight of the Philistine army in total disarray.

When Saul's watchers reported this, he sought divine guidance through the **Urim Ve-Tumim** as to whether to chase after them (v 18), but there was no time even to wait for an answer (having disobeyed Samuel at Gilgal, Saul was unable to elicit answers through holy spirit any more) and the war against the Philistines started in earnest. From v 21 we learn that Philistine domination had been so powerful that many Hebrews were actually present helping their forces, but when the Hebrews saw the success of the Israelite rebellion they went over to Saul. [Similarly, in the war of Gog and Magog it is prophesied that even Jews will come with the hordes of Gog against Jerusalem, but their hearts will go out to their Jewish brothers under the siege, Zechariah 12:2, see Targum and Rashi ad loc.]

"AND SAUL PUT THE PEOPLE UNDER OATH (v 24)

The key to understanding some of the mysterious twists of this chapter is to recognize that Saul wanted to bring the people to exceptional levels of spiritual discipline, even under the exigencies of a war against an enemy they perceived as being overwhelmingly powerful.

Thus, Saul put the people under an oath not to eat until the evening - despite the fact that they were engaged in a life and death battle! Jonathan, who was absent when Saul declared the ban, tasted some "honey"(=cane sugar), and, when told of the oath his father had imposed, was not afraid to express his true opinion that Saul had gone too far (vv 29-30): "he has upset their minds and their salvation like turbid waters" (Rashi on v 29).

At the end of the day the ravenous people flew upon the booty and took sheep and cattle "and slaughtered them on the ground and the people ate upon the blood" (v 32). The rabbis offer various opinions about the nature of the "sin", with some saying they did not allow the blood to drain properly from the meat before eating it as required by the laws of Kashrut, and others saying that they offered **Shelamim** (peace) offerings but ate the meat before the blood was sprinkled on the Altar. Rashi's opinion is that they slaughtered mother animals and their young on the same day, which the Torah forbids.

Saul's emergency measure of setting up a **Bamah** Altar and sacrificing even at night (which is not permitted in the Temple but was permissible on such a **Bamah**) was intended to rein the people's animalistic lusts as part of his campaign for heightened self-discipline.

Failing (again) to get an answer from the **Urim Ve-Tumim** about taking the war into the Philistine areas (v 37) Saul realized there was a flaw that had to be exposed, and he resorted to casting lots in order to discover where it lay. The perfection of Saul's governmental ideals is expressed in his declaration that even if the fault lay with his very son he would kill him (v 39). Why Saul received no answer from the **Urim Ve-Tumim** despite the fact that Jonathan at worst violated the oath **unwittingly** since he had not heard it (as v 27 testifies) is explained by Rav Saadia Gaon (brought in RaDaK on v 45). He suggests that if Saul had received an answer despite the fact that his son was somehow at fault, this would have made people feel Jonathan was getting preferential treatment as son of the king whereas someone else would have been punished for violating the king's ban. The public would then not have become aware that Jonathan had not even been present when the ban was declared. Since Saul was not answered by the **Urim Ve-Tumim**, he was forced to cast lots to establish where the problem lay, and when Jonathan was "caught" the people were forced to investigate what really happened and thus they all found out that Jonathan had indeed not been present and was quite innocent.

"AND WHEREVER HE TURNED HE CAUSED TERROR" (v 47)

The closing section of Ch. 14 summarizes the many-fronted wars waged by Saul in his brief two-year reign, and introduces the names of his family members and Chief of Staff, several of whom play leading roles in the narrative in the chapters to come.

Saul is a very paradoxical figure, but without doubt he was a man of outstanding **Gevurah**. He fought on so many fronts, and "wherever he turned he caused terror" (v 47). An illuminating comment based on this verse is found in Talmud Eiruvin 53, where Ravina states that "David revealed his **Masechta** (the tractate of Torah that he learned), and his kingship endured, for 'those who fear You see me and rejoice' Ps 119:74, while Saul did not reveal his **Masechta** and his kingship did not endure, 'and wherever he turned he caused terror'." This seems to suggest that David (like his descendant, Hillel) reached out to the people and spoke on their level, while Saul, who was "head and shoulders above everyone else" (see ch 10 v 23), wanted to bring the people up to his own high levels of stringency (like Beit Shammai) - and this was why his kingship did not survive.

CHAPTER 15

The account of Saul's war against Amalek and its tragic consequences is familiar as the Haftarah of Shabbat Zachor immediately before Purim, when we remember Amalek's evil, murderous and entirely unprovoked attack on the Israelites as they came out from slavery in Egypt.

The mitzvah to extirpate Amalek is one of the three that Israel were commanded to carry out on entry into the Land, together with the appointment of a king and the building of the Temple. Amalek's continuing war against Israel was a war against the very name of God Himself, which this **Kelipah** (husk) seeks to hide from the consciousness of the world, and thus it must be removed in order for the glory of God to shine to perfection from His Temple in Jerusalem.

"AND NOW LISTEN TO THE VOICE...." (v 1)

Saul had already deviated once from Samuel's instructions when the prophet told him not to sacrifice at Gilgal but to await his arrival (ch 10 v 8). Now Saul was given one last opportunity to redeem himself and his kingship - but he failed, and the decree against him was sealed. God finally rejected him completely and gave the kingship "to your companion who is better than you" (=David; ch. 15 v 28). It was only many generations later that Saul's descendant Esther came to the throne in Shushan when Vashti was displaced, and the king gave her royal position "to her companion who is better than her" (Esther 1:19), and Esther rectified Saul's fault by working with Mordechai to destroy Haman the Aggagite-Amalekite.

Samuel gave Saul exact instructions to destroy not only the Amalekite men, women and children but even their animals. (Rashi on v 3 states that the Amalekites were masters of witchcraft and changed themselves in such a way that they resembled animals - which is somewhat reminiscent of the kind of media wizardry of our day that causes humans to seem and behave like animals.) However, after Saul's victory over the Amalekites, "and Saul and the people had pity on Agag and on the choice of the flocks and cattle etc." (v 9). Rashi (on vv 5 and 24) explains that it wasn't just that they said what a pity it would be to kill all these fat cattle. "And he struggled in the **valley** (nachal)" (v 5) Rashi explains to mean that Saul went through a deep inner debate about the justice of killing innocent men when the Torah itself commands us to atone for spilt blood and avoid further bloodshed through the mitzvah of the **Egla Arufah**, breaking the neck of a heifer, which is performed in a **valley** (Deut. 21:4). It was not just the mass of the people who questioned the justice of the Prophet's command - it was no less than **Do'eg Ha-Edomi**, the outstanding Torah scholar of the time, who was so great that he was equivalent to the whole people (see Rashi on v 24). Do'eg is portrayed by Rabbi Nachman of Breslov as the archetype of the brilliant, constipated Torah scholar who is all intellect without heart (Likutey Moharan I, 61) - Do'eg was later responsible for Saul's persecution of David, and here we find that Do'eg's advice brought about the collapse of Saul's kingship.

When Samuel questioned why Saul spared the flocks, the latter was quick to provide extensive rationalizations - he talked too much - and Samuel put a stop to this, telling him that his rebellion against the words of God's prophet was quite as bad as the very sorcery that Saul tried to stamp out in Israel, and that his excessive talk was as bad as the divination he prohibited (v 23). "Does God receive pleasure from burnt offerings and sacrifices as from listening to the voice of God?" (v 22).

"The Eternal of Israel (**Netzach Yisrael**) will not lie and will not repent" (v 29). As explained by ARI (see commentary on I Samuel ch 9) this verse was said precisely because Saul's flaw was in the Sefirah of **Netzach**, from which the prophets "suckle", and since **Netzach will not lie or repent**, the decree against Saul was now sealed and unchangeable. As soon as he heard the decree, Saul acknowledged his sin - but it was too late. From this time on, despite his great **Gevurah** Saul was almost like a ghost of a king, and we are left with feelings of deep mourning - like those of Samuel - about how a character so noble and exalted could fall. Saul had erred with an excess of kindness - but when kindness is bestowed upon those who are evil, such as Amalek, it turns into the worst cruelty.

CHAPTER 16

THE ANOINTING OF DAVID

We find little in our text about Saul's greatness and good qualities despite his perfection and outstanding saintliness (**Chassidut**), while we find a great deal both in the Bible and in the words of the sages (Berachot 4a) about David. This is because Saul's soul is rooted in the World of Concealment (Nekudat Tzion, Yesod of Imma, the "World of the Male"), while that of David is from the Revealed World (Yesod of Nukva=Nekudat Tzion ViYerushalayim). For this reason, Saul was modest (hidden) and he calls David "my son" and became his father-in-law.

Saul's root lay in the Yesod of the Kings of Edom who died (see Genesis 36:37: the **sixth** king of Edom was called **Sha'ul**). Thus Saul "reigned… and died." His kingship, being from the world of **Tohu** ("devastation"), could not endure. David, on the other hand, is rooted in the world of **Tikkun** ("repair"), and for this reason his kingship endured. (ARI, Likutey Torah I Samuel 17).

God commanded Samuel to go to the house of Yishai to anoint his son as king, but although Samuel had said "I am the seer" (ch 9 v 19), even he was unable to **see** who was really **Mashiach**, "for it is not as man sees, for man sees according to the eyes but God sees into the heart" (v 7). From the outside, Yishai's first-born Eliav seemed outstanding, but God knew that he was given to lose his temper (ch 7 v 28) and was not fit to be king.

Nobody could have imagined that Yishai's "small" shepherd son was the one, because Mashiach is necessarily clothed in darkness and mystery and surrounded by the most powerful opposing forces, including even those who are apparently very wise, and even those who are closest to him.

David is nothing less than the reincarnated soul of **Adam** (ADaM=Adam-David-Moshe). As we read the beautiful narrative about this most breathtakingly enchanting of all the Biblical heroes, we must constantly bear in mind that while the stories show us the **Chitzoniut** ("externality"), the true **Pnimiut** ("inner face") of David is to be found in his immortal **Tehilim** (Psalms), which are the very foundation of the spiritual life of Israel until today. A substantial part of the prayer services in the Siddur (Jewish prayer book) is made up of Psalms, and it was these songs that were and will be sung in the Temple in Jerusalem. David taught mankind the true path of **return** and **repentance** (Psalm 51:15).

It is said that Samuel was terrified when he saw that God's chosen was **admoni** ("ruddy", from the root Edom, v 12) - saying that this one too was a shedder of blood like Esau (=Edom) - until Samuel saw that this came "with beauty of the eyes". The "eyes" of Israel are the Sanhedrin: everything David did, including all the wars and bloodshed, were carried out in accordance with Torah law and the guidance of the Sages (Bamidbar Rabbah 63:8).

When David stepped forth, the very oil jumped out of Samuel's horn to anoint him. This was Moses' anointing oil, which was kept by the Ark in the Sanctuary, from where Samuel took it to anoint Israel's true king.

As soon as David was anointed, Saul became afflicted by an "evil spirit" - the penalty for his having failed to obey the voice of holy spirit that spoke through Samuel ordering him to wipe out all Amalek. The intention of that "one of the lads" who advised Saul to take a musician to play to him was far from pure. This was Do'eg Ha-Edomi, the "unique **one**" among Saul's "lads", Do'eg the brilliant trouble-maker. The Talmud (Sanhedrin 93b) shows how every one of his words to Saul (v 18) was designed to bring him to jealousy of David. "He knows music" - "he knows how to ask". "Mighty" - "he knows how to answer". "a man of war" - "that knows how to give and take in the war of the Torah"- "and HaShem is with him" - **"The Halachah is like him**!!!" "And when Do'eg told Saul that 'HaShem is with him - which was not so in Saul's case - he became disheartened and became jealous of him" (Sanhedrin ibid.)

Yet the pure, innocent David came from the world of **Tikkun** and was therefore able to heal Saul. "And he would play **with his hand**" (v. 23). His **hand**=YaD, made up of the letters **Yod** (10) and **Dalet** (4) = 14. For Kohelet (Ecclesiastes) speaks of the 14 good times and 14 bad times. David would play only in the 14 good times. This is because David is the mystery of the waxing moon, which grows from the slenderest crescent to fullness in the first 14 of the 28 days in which the moon can be seen each month. The **yad** (14) with which David played derived from the 4 letters of **HaVaYaH** plus the 10 letters of the Milui of **HaVaYaH**=14=YaD. David's power to heal and repair comes from his pure radiation of the light of HaShem.

CHAPTER 17

The story of David and Goliath must be one of the most famous and inspiring of all biblical tales and has been illustrated countless times (see Shulchan Aruch, Orach Chayim 307:20).

Targum on ch 17 v 8 brings out the force of Goliath's taunts against Israel. "I am Goliath the Philistine from Gat that killed the two sons of Eli the Priest, Pinchas and Hofni, and I captured the Ark of the Covenant of HaShem and brought it to the house of Dagon my idol. and in every battle that the Philistines waged I went out at the head of the army and was victorious in battle and I cast down dead corpses like the dust of the earth... and as for you, Children of Israel, what might has Saul son of Kish from Giv'ah that you appointed king over you done for you? If he is a mighty hero, let him engage in battle, and if he is a weak man, choose someone else to come down against me".

If the Philistines represented the ultimate of unholy **Gevurah** (**Plishtim**=860=10 x 86, **Elokim** =severe **Dinim**, Judgments), Goliath was the very epitome of this utter concealment. According to rabbinic tradition, **Horpah** who is mentioned as Goliath's mother (II Samuel 21:16ff and commentators ad loc.) was none other than **Orpah**, daughter-in-law of Naomi, who when her sister-in-law Ruth, David's great-grandmother, converted, refused to do so.

The ARI explains that Ruth and Orpah parallel Rachel and Leah. Leah was marked out for the unholy Esau (**Sitra Achra**) but had the ability to attach herself to the side of the holy (Jacob, **Sitra Di-Kedushah**), which she took, thereby becoming the "chariot" of the World of Concealment while Rachel was the "chariot" of the World of Revelation. Like Leah, Orpah could have attached herself to the Side of Holiness had she converted, but she refused, turned her back (**oreph**) and instead became consort of the Angel of Death. All of the holiness contained in Orpah went to Ruth, while all the unholiness contained in Ruth went to Orpah. Thus, Ruth was blessed to be **like Rachel and Leah** (Ruth 4:11). Orpah on the other hand opened herself indiscriminately to all the Philistines (see Rashi on ch 17 v 23) and from in between them all came forth Goliath, who is therefore called "the man in between" (ch17 v 4). The unholy side is the evil mirror-image of the side of the holy, and thus Goliath is on the side of the unholy, while David is on the side of the holy. (ARI, Likutey Torah on I Samuel ch 17).

Rabbi Nachman of Breslov explains that the "greaves of brass (**nechoshet**) on his legs" (ch 17 v. 6) allude to the God-concealing ideology which attributes everything to natural causes (the "legs") that Goliath represents. This is the ideology of the serpent (**Nachash**). (Likutey Moharan Vol II, Torah 4:7-8).

According to natural law and science it was completely ridiculous that a tender, inexperienced youth like David could conquer a mighty giant like Goliath who was armed to the teeth. This was why David's brother Eliav was so angry with him for coming to join the "action" on the battlefield (v 28), and Saul too could not believe that David could be victorious. However, David had already conquered "the lion and the bear" (actually there were 3 lions and 3 bears according to the Midrash brought by Rashi on v 34). These wild animals allude to the evil philosophers of materialism and natural cause who have preyed upon Israelite souls, turning them into atheists (see Likutey Moharan loc. cit.).

"And David said to the Philistine, 'You come to me with a sword and a spear and a javelin, but I come against you in the name of the Lord of Hosts.'" David's purpose was that "all this Assembly shall know that it is not with the sword and the spear that God saves." (v 47).

The shepherd's satchel in which David took his stones alludes to **Malchut**. The "five stones" are **Chesssed-Gevurah-Tiferet-Netzach-Hod**. He took them from the **nachal**=**Yesod**. David made these attributes into a unity - one stone. This is the **even shelema Retzono** - "a perfect stone [is] His will" (Proverbs 11:1), alluding to God's **Will**, which has power over **everything**, including all the powerful natural causes that Goliath flaunted.

The stone with which David killed Goliath is bound up with the mystery of the stone that Nebuchadnezzar saw in his dream, which was hewn out without hands and which struck the great statue he had seen, causing it to collapse and be ground up, signifying the destruction of the empires that subject Israel heralding the everlasting kingship of Heaven (Daniel 2:34 & 44-5).

David showed that despite seemingly overwhelming odds, God's **Will** rules over everything. David is the secret of prayer, in which we pray that "He should carry out our will as His will". David's conquest over Goliath was his first lesson to Israel in the power of prayer.

But Mashiach cannot be revealed more than momentarily each time. No sooner had David conquered Goliath than the **machloket** - the controversy and opposition that attended him throughout his life - began to develop in earnest. The verses in Chapter 17 vv 55-8 in which Saul starts enquiring who David really is are interpreted in the Talmud (Yevamot 76b) as alluding to the dispute about whether David's Moabite pedigree on Ruth's side even allowed him to enter the Assembly of Israel since "a Moabite shall not come to you in the Assembly of the Lord" (Deut. 23:4). Once again it was the sinister Do'eg who stirred up the trouble. While Saul and Avner opined that only a Moabite was forbidden to enter but not a Moabitess, Do'eg argued that the same reasoning could be used to permit a **Mamzerah** (illegitimate female) into the Assembly since the verse apparently only forbids a male **Mamzer**. (Deut. ibid. v 3). With Saul and Avner silenced, a cloud of doubts and questions settled over the little shepherd David.

CHAPTER 18

DAVID AND JONATHAN

"And the soul of Jonathan was bound with the soul of David" (ch 18 v 1).

The ARI (Likutey Torah I Samuel 18) explains: Jonathan's love for David was "more wondrous than the love of women" (II Samuel 1:26). For it was from Jonathan that the flow of blessing (**shefa**) came to David, because the first three letters of Jonathan's name are Yud-Heh-Vav, the first three letters of the Tetragramaton, the "essential" name of God, while the last three letters are NaTaN, "he gave", indicating the **Mashpia**, who influences another. The gematria of NaTaN is 500, because Jonathan's soul was rooted in Tiferet of the Kings that Died (Genesis 36:31-39), and Tiferet receives the influence of Binah, "understanding", whose Fifty Gates each contain 10 Sefirot: 50 x 10=500. Being rooted in the Seven Kings that Died, Jonathan's kingship could not endure. Understanding that his role was to give over his influence to David, he embraced his destiny with love and "made a covenant" with him, giving him his coat and all his symbols of royalty - his sword, bow and belt (ch 18 v 4).

THE CYCLE OF JEALOUSY AND HATRED

The song of the women who came out dancing with instruments to hail Saul could have been construed as an honor to Saul - that while Saul only needed to go out with thousands to conquer the Philistines, David had to go out with tens of thousands. However, when a person has already been "bitten" by an evil spirit, he tends to construe everything negatively, and thus Saul took the women's song as an insult to his honor, and from that time on the poison of his jealousy of David festered and grew.

"And it was on the next day that an evil spirit from God swelled in Saul, and **he prophesied** in the house" (v 10). The Hebrew word **vayit-nabei** is from the same root as **Navi**, a "prophet", but here Targum Yonatan renders it not as "he prophesied" but "he went mad" (**ve-ishtati**). For without the perfect discipline required of the prophet, his prophetic spirit easily turns into madness. "A prophet and a madman both speak in hints that are not understood" (Rashi ad loc.).

Saul's jealousy was only increased when he saw that David was divinely protected from all his efforts to spear him, making Saul afraid and even more full of hatred. Saul's mix of jealousy, fear and hatred is very reminiscent of similar syndromes found in many Jews who have gone more or less off track in relation to those who remain genuinely faithful to the Torah pathway, whose joyous determination and success cause them profound vexation and irritation. Just as Saul tried every method, direct and indirect, of killing David, so too some lapsed Jews are tireless in their efforts to thwart the Torah community - and they will fail just as Saul failed to harm David.

Saul's stratagems to try to get David killed are reminiscent of the kinds of stratagems often used today by those in positions of great power in order to get their enemies knocked off indirectly or seemingly by accident.

Saul hoped that by dispatching David to bring the foreskins of 100 Philistines as the "dowry" for his daughter, he was sending him to a quick death - yet with typical loyal obedience, dauntless courage and great alacrity, David brought back **double** the number of foreskins. Cutting off the enemies' foreskins may seem to be a particularly gruesome way of humiliating them and taking vengeance - though the same was practiced on Israel by their enemies (see Rashi on Deut. 25:17). Perhaps a less gruesome modern equivalent would be the endeavors of contemporary outreach workers to outdo each other in removing the mental and emotional "foreskins" from as many irreligious Jewish hearts as possible and turning them into **Baal Teshuvahs!**

CHAPTER 19

The vicious cycle of Saul's jealousy and hatred for David deteriorated into a mad paranoia that had him telling all his ministers and servants and even Jonathan to kill him. Jonathan succeeded in temporarily mollifying Saul, who exhibited all the symptoms of severe mood-swing. The fact that Saul's son Jonathan and his daughter Michal continued to show the utmost loyalty to David proves that they saw clearly that he was completely guiltless. David did nothing to provoke Saul: all the suffering that came upon him was sent to him from God to prepare him for leadership, for the broken heart of one who has suffered is filled with compassion for others who are suffering. David gave expression to his pain and search for fortitude in God in his Tehilim (Psalms), which speak for all Israel and are our greatest source of solace in face of the jealousy of the nations.

When indirect methods of assassination did not work, Saul sent a squadron of messengers directly to David's house to capture him in order to kill him. In this Saul was criticized for being even worse than Jezebel, who was not Jewish (she was the daughter of idolatrous priests) yet when she sent to Elijah saying, "At this time tomorrow I will make your soul like the soul of one of them [i.e. the prophets she had already killed]" (I Kings 19:2) she at least gave him a day's notice so that he had the opportunity to flee.(Yalkut).

The present-day Israeli government does indeed normally give advance notice to Arab terrorists of their intent to conduct bombing operations against specific hide-outs etc. thereby enabling the occupants to flee or take other precautions. However, this same government tends not to display a similar indulgence when sending police in to deal with protesting Jewish settlers, chareidim, disenchanted Ethiopian immigrants, etc. Thus, it is that those who show kindness where it is unwarranted end up showing cruelty where it is unwarranted.

THE TERAPHIM

After Michal let David down through the window to escape, she put the **teraphim** in his bed to seem like a body together with a goatskin to seem like hair, so that Saul's guards would think it was David. When Jacob fled from Laban, Rachel took her father's **teraphim** (Genesis 31:19), which were clearly idolatrous statues. In the case of the **teraphim** taken by Michal, most of the commentators agree that they were some kind of statue or mannequin in human form but bring a variety of interpretations as to what such a statue was doing in the house of David. RaDaK (on v 13) states that it is quite unthinkable that David would have had any kind of idolatrous statue in his house and inclines to Ibn Ezra's opinion that these **teraphim** were a diagrammatic emblem of the human form that could be used for channeling angelic power. According to this interpretation, Michal would have used them to bring some kind of protection against Saul's messengers. Metzudat Tzion's explanation is that while some **teraphim** were indeed idolatrous statues, others were made by devoted wives in the form of their husbands so that they could look upon them lovingly.

PLANNING THE TEMPLE

David fled to Samuel, who had anointed him king. And at this moment of supreme crisis, when his very life was hanging in the balance, how did David occupy himself with Samuel? The rabbis said that in this one night when he fled from Saul, David learned more from Samuel than a seasoned student could learn from his teacher in a hundred years. They could find nothing better to do than determine the site of the Temple and lay plans for its building. [Similarly, in the 1720's, at the very height of the persecution of the 22-year old R. Moshe Chayim Luzzatto, Ramchal, by the rabbis of Italy and Germany, he could find nothing better to do than write **Mishkeney Elyon**, "Secrets of the Future Temple", explaining the meaning of the form of the Third Temple as prophesied by Ezekiel chs 40ff.]

"And he and Samuel went and they sat in **Noyot**" (v 18). The rabbis taught: "What connection does **Noyot** have with Ramah? What the text means is that they sat in Ramah and engaged in the **beauty** (**noy**) of the world. [The Hebrew word **be-nayot** in vv 18 and 19 is written in the parchment - **ktiv** -- differently from the way it is pronounced - **kri**. The **ktiv** has the connotations of both **beauty** and **building**.] They said that since the Torah writes that 'you shall go up to the place' (Deut. 17:8), it must be that the Temple is higher than all the land of Israel and the Land of Israel is higher than all the lands, but they did not know the exact site of the Temple, so they brought the book of Joshua. In all the descriptions of the territories of the tribes it says the border 'goes down… and goes up.' but in the case of the territory of Benjamin it is written that 'it goes up' but not that 'it goes down' (Joshua 15:8). They said that from this we can infer that this is the proper place of the Temple. They discussed whether to build it in Eyn Eytam, which is high, but they said they should go down just a little, as it is written, 'He dwells **between his shoulders**' (Deut. 33:12)" (Talmud Zevachim 54b).

The presence of Samuel and his students, the "sons of the prophets" engaged in such exalted prophecy brought even Saul to the level of true prophecy. In verse 23 the word **vayitnabei** is rendered by Targum Yonatan as referring to true prophecy: "also on him there dwelled the spirit of prophecy from HaShem". Saul's stripping off his clothes and falling "naked" (v 24) does not mean that he was literally without any clothes, but that in his prophetic ecstasy he removed his royal robes - for at this moment of truth and prophetic lucidity, he knew then that David was the true king of Israel.

CHAPTER 20

"BUT A STEP BETWEEN ME AND DEATH"

David had barely escaped being killed with Saul's spear by stepping aside at the crucial moment. He felt himself to be in extreme danger from Saul, and the present chapter narrates the final test which Jonathan set up to see if Saul intended the worst or not.

The constant danger attending the Messianic king is reflected in the epithet given to Mashiach in the Talmud, "**Bar Nofli**" (Sanhedrin 96b). While on one level this alludes to how the future Mashiach will raise the **fallen** (**nafal**) Tabernacle of David, it also indicates that Mashiach is all but a **nefel** - an "abortive foetus" that has only a slender hairsbreadth chance of surviving. David almost had no life at all, except that Adam gave him 70 his own allotted 1000, and thus Adam lived only 930 years. Mashiach is in constant danger because of the fierce opposing forces that ever seek to swallow him up. Only by hiding himself in the baffling depths of concealment and secrecy can Mashiach survive.

Jonathan too was in great danger from his demented father, who indeed tried to kill him (ch 20 v 33). However, Jonathan knew that David was truly destined to be king and therefore swore an eternal covenant to help and protect him, in exchange for which David was duty bound to protect Jonathan and his family. [David paid a heavy price for violating this covenant when he took half of Saul's son Mephiboshet's estate and gave it to the latter's servant Tziva, see II Samuel 19:30: as a result, a heavenly voice declared that David's kingdom would be divided between his grandson Rehaboam and the rebel Jeraboam.]

THE NEW MOON

Verses 18-42 of our present text are familiar as the special Haftarah read in place of the regular Shabbat Haftarah whenever Rosh Chodesh (the New Moon) falls on the following day, i.e. the Sunday, for "tomorrow is the New Moon" (v 18).

David (=**Malchut**, Kingship) is bound up with the mystery of the Moon, which wanes steadily after the 15th of the month until it disappears completely at the very end of the month, and cannot be seen again until a very slender crescent appears on the western horizon for a few minutes after the sunset of the last day of the month. The appearance of the "new" moon heralds the arrival that night of Rosh Chodesh, the first day of the new month, and from then on, the moon steadily waxes day by day - corresponding to the steadily growing light of Mashiach after its initial total concealment. The constant renewal of the moon is a sign of the ever-renewed vitality of Mashiach (and thus when we bless the new moon after Rosh Chodesh in the ceremony of **Kiddush Levanah**, "Sanctification of the Moon", it is customary to recite three times "David, king of Israel is alive and enduring").

Jonathan used the sign of the three arrows at his secret tryst with David (vv 20-22 and 36-39) because in relation to David's **Malchut**, the "receiving" attribute, Jonathan is rooted in the mystery of **Yesod**, the **Mashpia**, the giver of influence, which is allusively called the **Keshet**, the "bow", connoting both the 3-colored rainbow and the archer's bow. **Yesod**, the power of procreation, "shoots like an arrow".

The news was not good and David had to flee. Saul was so paranoid that he besmirched his own wife in accusing Jonathan of being illegitimate and therefore favoring Saul's enemy. But Jonathan knew the truth and took God as his witness that his covenant with David would be eternal.

After the destruction of the Sanctuary in Shilo in the days of Eli the Priest, the Sanctuary was re-established in the city of Nov, which was entirely given over to Kohanim (priests). Achimelech, who ministered as the High Priest in the Sanctuary, is identical with Achiyah mentioned in I Samuel 14:3 (see also 22:9).

David was in flight from Saul when he came to Nov - alone and unarmed, and apparently starving to the point of being in mortal danger. Numerous halachic questions surround David's eating of the "holy" bread in the Sanctuary since Achimelech stated that there was no "profane" bread (=**Chulin**) available. RaDaK (on v 6) offers his father's opinion that the bread that Achimelech gave David was from the loaves of a **Todah** (thanksgiving) offering, which are permitted to a **Zar** ("stranger", non-Kohen) as long as he is ritually pure (and this is why Achimelech tactfully checked that David had not been with his wife recently, which would have made him defiled with **Tum'at Keri**, vv. 5-6). However, RaDaK evidently prefers the more obvious though halachically difficult **p'shat** of this passage, adopted by the Talmudic sages (Menachot 95b), which is that the "holy bread" that Achimelech gave David was actually the **Lechem HaPanim** ("showbread") from the Golden Table in the Sanctuary. Twelve new loaves were placed on the Table each Shabbat, while the loaves that had sat there for the previous week were removed and divided up between the High Priest (who took six loaves) and all the other priests (who shared the rest; see Leviticus 24:5-9.)

The priests were only allowed to eat the showbread **after** the incense in the golden spoons that sat on the table side by side with the bread all week had been burned on the Altar (as the **Azkarah**, "memorial" Lev. 24:7 - for the Altar had no share in the showbread itself). This is the meaning of David's words to Achimelech (v 6) "and it is by way of profane" - i.e. the incense had **already been burnt**, thereby releasing the bread for consumption. David went on to say, "…even if today it had been sanctified in the ministering vessel" (ibid.) meaning that in any case, even if this was the new bread that had only just been sanctified for putting on the golden table, he would still have been permitted to eat it because of **Sakanat Nefashot** - a danger to life. All the commandments of the Torah (except for the prohibitions against idolatry, murder and fornication) are suspended if there is a danger to life.

RaDaK also explains why Achimelech could not provide David with any other bread despite the fact that there must have been bread somewhere in the city of Nov. Nov was a city of priests, whose main food is Terumah. The penalty for a **Zar** who eats Terumah is death at the hands of heaven, and although David would have been permitted to eat Terumah because of **Sakanat Nefashot**, it is preferable, where there is a choice, to feed the person in danger with the less serious of two prohibited items. While a **Zar** is also forbidden to eat the Showbread, doing so does not carry the penalty of death at the hands of heaven like Terumah.

Thus, it was that David, although not a Kohen, tasted from the **Lechem HaPanim**, the "bread of the inner face", which remained hot on the Sanctuary Table for over a week from the day it was baked before Shabbat until the time the priests ate it on the following Shabbat (v 7 as explained in Menachot 96b). The heat of the bread is the same as the heat of the sun which God took out of its "scabbard" after Abraham circumcised himself and sat at the door of his tent "in the heat of the day" (Gen. 18:1). Circumcision strips off the thick concealing outer **Orlah** foreskin from the world, exposing and revealing the inner **Pnimiut** ("interiority") that governs everything. The "heat" of the sun of revelation burns up all God's enemies (see Likutey Moharan I, 30:9).

The Talmud (Menachot 95b) comments on the enormous good that comes from feeding a needy person even a mouthful. If Jonathan had had the good sense to provide David with a couple of loaves of bread when he fled, the priests of Nov would not have been slaughtered, Do'eg the Edomite would not have been driven out from the life eternal, and Saul and his three sons would not have been killed.

As it was, David, who was starving and in mortal danger, had no choice but to stop at the Sanctuary to eat the **Lechem HaPanim**, and while there he was seen by the sinister **Do'eg**, who as discussed previously is emblematic of Torah brilliance turned perverse. Thus, he was called an Edomite, not only because Edom was the name of his town, but also because he was jealous of David, who was called **admoni** ("ruddy"), and because he ruled that the priests of Nov should be massacred, that David's wife could be given to another man and that Agag should not be killed - he turned everyone's face red with shame in face of his "brilliant" rulings and tried to consume David's merits like the red thread that swallows up the merits of Israel (Yalkut). The text states that Do'eg was "**ne-etzar** before Hashem" (v 8) - i.e. he was "detained" at the Sanctuary in Nov. **Ne-etzar** also carries the connotation of "was closed up, constipated" - the Sages taught that Do'eg did not purify his body of waste when he studied, and this was the reason for his perversity (See Likutey Moharan I, 61.)

THE BENEFITS OF MADNESS

In a further intensification of mystery and darkness, David was forced to flee to the territory of Israel's very enemies, the Philistines (v 11). The Midrash states that the attendants of Achish king of Gat were Goliath's brothers and wanted to avenge his blood by killing David. However, Achish answered that Goliath himself had challenged David to kill him. If so, they replied, Goliath's stated condition was that whoever overcame him would rule the Philistines, in which case Achish should step down in favor of David. This is why they called David "king of the land" (v 12).

David - who was **maskil** ("intelligent") in all his ways (ch 18 v 14) - could not understand why God created madmen, until he found himself in mortal danger in Gat and discovered that the best cover was to make it appear as if he was crazy. The Midrash states that Achish's wife and daughter were both mad and would rant inside his house while David would rant outside. This is why Achish asked, "Am I lacking in madmen?" (v 16). David's true inner face in this moment of crisis is expressed in the Psalm he wrote at the time: Psalm 34, "David's prayer when he changed his personality before Avimelech and he sent him away and he went". Avimelech was a generic name for the Philistine king just as Pharaoh was the generic name of Egyptian kings (RaDaK on ch 21 v 11).

CHAPTER 22

Realizing he was unsafe with the Philistines in Gat, David went east to Adulam, where his ancestor Judah had also gone when he "went down" from his brothers (Gen. 38:1). Adulam and nearby Ke'eela, which are among the places David went to escape as narrated in the present chapter and the earlier part of the next, are located in the hilly region a little south of present-day Beit Shemesh. Meanwhile, Saul was in Giv'ah, a little to the north of the present-day Jerusalem suburb of Ramot, which is immediately south east of Ramah ("Nebie Samwil"), where Samuel lived. The town of Nob was further east, near the road to Ramallah.

There in Adulam, the charismatic David attracted a bedraggled band of what may have somewhat resembled today's Baal Teshuvahs, each in their tight corner with their debts, physical and spiritual, and each bearing their own pack of sorrows!!!

From Adulam, David went east of the Dead Sea into Moab, where he had a family connection with the king through his convert great-grandmother, Ruth, who was daughter of Eglon king of Moab. Realizing that Saul was out to destroy him and his whole family, David sought to find a safe place in Moab for his parents, but as Rashi brings on v 4, the hoped-for haven was safe only while David was in Metzudah, but afterwards the king of Moab killed his mother, father and all his brothers except for one.

It was the prophet Gad who told David not to dwell in Metzudah but to return to the Land of Israel to his native tribal territory of Judah (v 5). Unlike Saul, we see that David had scrupulous respect for the prophets and carried out their words to the letter. Likewise, he consulted with the **Urim Ve-Tumim** on all critical questions and - unlike Saul - received answers from God, as we see in the ensuing narrative.

The Midrash states that Giv'ah and Ramah mentioned in v 6 as where Saul was located at this time are actually two separate places, and that Saul was physically in Giv'ah, but he lived there in the merit of the "Tamarisk (**Eshel**) in Ramah", namely the prophet Samuel, who did not cease to pray for him (Rashi on 6).

Nevertheless, the divine decree against Saul was sealed and he descended ever-deeper into his paranoid delusions, seeing conspiracies against him from all around. In Saul's eyes David was a **Moreid Be-Malchut**, a "rebel against the throne", a national traitor, particularly now that he was evidently attracting a growing following from among the disaffected.

"AND DO'EG ANSWERED..." (v 9)

Once again, the sinister brilliant Torah sage Do'eg steps in to further stir the pot of evil by disclosing that he had seen David at the Sanctuary and that Achimelech the High Priest had fed and armed him. Do'eg's telling on Achimelech - which led to Achimelech's death and that of all the priests of Nov - is seen as the archetype of **Rechilut** - "tale-bearing", one of the main categories of **Lashon Hara**, "evil speech". Even if the story is true, it is forbidden to tell it to anyone when this is likely to lead to any kind of harm to the person involved.

From the interchange between Saul and Achimelech (vv 12-15) we learn that the main issue was why Achimelech had consulted the **Urim Ve-Tumim** for David. Do'eg maintained that only the king was allowed to consult the **Urim Ve-Tumim**, making Achimelech guilty of high treason, but the majority of the Sanhedrin followed the tradition that "they may be consulted for the king, the Sanhedrin, and for an individual who is needed by the community", and David came into the last category since his victory over Goliath. The other members of the Sanhedrin at this time were Avner and Amasa: they are the "runners" standing by the king in v 17: these are "the king's servants", who "**did not want to put forth their hands to strike the priests of HaShem**". They were not willing to strike because they did not believe it was justified.

Since Do'eg was in the minority, when Saul challenged him to strike the priests and he did so, he became a **Zaken Mamre**, an elder who maintains his ruling in face of the majority of the Sanhedrin, who incurs the death penalty (Deut. 17:12). The Midrash tells that Do'eg ended up forgetting everything he had ever taught his students, who realized he was "ruling the pure to be impure and the impure to be pure" and put chains on his legs and dragged him away (Midrash Yelamdenu).

The consequence of Do'eg's evil words was that he ended up personally killing 85 Kohanim "bearing the linen **Ephod**" (v 18, i.e. each was **worthy** to be High Priest) - from this we see Do'eg's strength - as well as the entire population of Nov, men, women, children and suckling babes, oxen, donkeys and sheep. In other words, Saul's regime, having **failed** to carry out God's command to completely destroy Amalek, now vented its frustration on the Israelites - the very holiest of them! In the words of Kohelet (Ecclesiastes 7:16-17) "Don't be too righteous..." (in sparing Amalek) "...and don't be too wicked" (in destroying Nov; Talmud Yoma 22b). [The present-day Israeli high court and successive governments since Oslo have mirrored this behavior - also on the basis of a chronic campaign of malicious slander - in favoring the enemies of the Jews while victimizing the settlers, the chareidim and anyone who stands up for Torat Moshe and the Halachah, which is according to David.]

Psalm 52 gives expression to David's response to Do'eg and his slander.

EVIATAR BEN AVIMELECH

Only one son of Avimelech escaped the massacre of the priests of Nov and fled to David, who received him with his characteristic noble eloquence: "he that seeks my soul seeks your soul" (v. 23), which can be understood to mean either "he who seeks to kill," or "he who seeks the good of" both of us (Targum, Rashi). Thus, the bond between the kings of Judah and the priesthood - which began when Aaron married Elisheva sister of Nachshon prince of Judah (Exodus 6:23) - was further strengthened in preparation for the building of the Temple.

CHAPTER 23

David was fleeing for his life against a murderous enemy, but as soon as he heard that Philistine marauders were fighting his brothers in Ke'eela and stealing all their hard-earned harvested produce (ch 23 v 1), he lost no time before consulting the new High Priest's **Urim Ve-Tumim**, not to ask if it was right to strike the Philistines - this he knew - but whether he would succeed. He repeated his question twice, not because he doubted the answer the first time, but in order to reassure his disheartened men (vv 3-4).

David went to Ke'eela and delivered the city but in spite of his courageous campaign on their behalf, the "bosses" of Ke'eela showed treacherous ingratitude in their willingness to hand him over to Saul, who was mobilizing the entire nation for war against David. Again, consulting the **Urim Ve-Tumim**, David vacated Ke'eela, and went with his expanded following of 600 men to the Wilderness of Zif. Thus, the action now moves eastwards from Ke'eela, an inhabited agricultural area which, as stated in the commentary on the previous chapter, is a little south of present-day Beit Shemesh, into the mountainous wilderness region south east of Hebron in the direction of Arad. Saul "sought him all the days, but God did not give him into his hand" (v 14), and the one who was closest to Saul - Jonathan - never let his filial duty to his father make him lose sight of the truth. Jonathan, and even Saul himself (perhaps unconsciously) knew that David would rule (v 17).

The people of Zif's betrayal of David by reporting his whereabouts to Saul is the subject of Psalm 54, which shows David's dauntless faith in God. Saul welcomed the men of Zif as being "blessed to HaShem", but although Saul spoke the **language** of faith and prayer, in **actuality** he used only **tachbulot**, man-devised strategies, while God was not with him but with David. Saul was rapidly closing in on David (v 26), but at the critical moment a **Mal'ach** ("mamash" says Rashi on v 27, an "actual" angel) came to tell Saul that the Philistines were invading the entire country. Saul was divided in his own mind as to whether to go off to fight the national enemy or continue pursuing his own perceived demon-enemy (Targum and Rashi onv 28), which is why the place was called **Sela Machloket** ("the rock of conflict"). Similarly, the present-day Israeli government is unable to make up its mind whether to fight the country's real enemies or continue persecuting Jews who are loyal to Israel and its Torah.

CHAPTER 24

Saul's massive military pursuit of David now moves to the wilderness of Ein Gedi, an area of enchanting natural beauty familiar to many visitors to the "Dead" Sea area, some of whom may in a quiet, still moment have caught sight of the nimble, exquisitely graceful but very shy mountain goats (ibex) that are to be found in the hills and rocky crags (v 2).

When Saul modestly entered the recesses of a cave to attend to his bodily needs, it would have been permissible for David to kill him since "if someone is coming to kill you, you should kill him first" (Sanhedrin 72a based on Exodus 22:1). David must have been very tempted, and his men were encouraging him, yet even after merely cutting the corner of Saul's garment, David was smitten by his own heart (v 5) - the sign of a truly humble Tzaddik who after doing something even only mildly improper feels deep contrition. David then "tore his men apart with words" (v 7), showing that he would not allow himself to be swayed by "public opinion", unlike Saul, who listened to the people when they told him to spare the Amalekite king and flocks.

When Saul, having sinned by doing so, had gone after Samuel, "he took hold of the corner of his coat and it was torn" (ch 15 v 27). The text there is ambiguous, and it is not clear whose coat was torn, Saul's or Samuel's (see Rashi ad loc.), but either way Samuel took it as a sign that "God has torn the kingship of Israel from you today": he gave Saul a sign that whoever would tear the corner of his garment would rule in his place.

David's speech of self-defense before his persecutor, Saul (vv 9-15) is another example of David's outstanding nobility and eloquence. He would not set his hand against Saul even when he had the opportunity: he knew and trusted that God would vindicate him and that "as the proverb of the ancients says, Wickedness proceeds from the wicked and my hand shall not be against you". The "proverb of the ancients" (v. 13) refers to the Holy Torah, which states that God Himself brings death upon the wicked (Exodus 21:13, see Rashi there and on our verse, I Samuel 24:13; see Talmud Makkot 10b).

When Saul heard the actual **voice** of David (v 16), it was a "reality check" that temporarily put to flight the paranoid madness that constantly fed him with demonic fantasies about his imagined persecutor and his evil designs. The actual presence of David had from the beginning had the power to cure Saul of his evil spirit and bring him back to sanity and lucidity (see ch 16 v 23). For while Saul's soul was rooted in **Olam HaTohu**, the "world of devastation", David was rooted in **Olam HaTikkun**, the "world of repair", and he therefore brought healing wherever his true influence was felt. However, as soon as Saul left David's healing presence and went back to his home, his madness came to the fore again.

CHAPTER 25

Samuel had become old prematurely (ch 8 v 1) and he died at the age of only 52, in order that he should not see the first king that he had anointed die in his own lifetime. The death of Samuel thus opened the way for the death of Saul, which came only seven months later. David therefore now stood on the very threshold of kingship. Samuel was buried at his home in Ramah, and the hilltop mosque that marks his tomb is a prominent landmark until today and is clearly visible to travelers on the Jerusalem-Tel Aviv highway near the entrance to Jerusalem.

NAVAL

It is necessary to bear in mind throughout the narrative of Saul's reign that it lasted a total of only two years (see ch 13 v 1) and that the events described followed very closely on the heels of one another.

Since Samuel had been born on Rosh HaShanah (the New Year) in answer to Hannah's prayer, he died on the same day, because God "completes the years of the Tzaddikim" to the very day. The rabbis dated David's request to Naval for sustenance to the eve of the same Rosh HaShanah (see Rashi on v 8), and thus Naval's "heart failure" (v 27) occurred on the morning of Rosh HaShanah, the Day of Judgment, and his death ten days later came on Yom Kippur, when God's decree is sealed if the sinner does not repent.

Naval's town of Ma'on and the "Carmel" where his affairs were concentrated (v 2) were both in the mountainous area west of Ein Gedi, some way to the southeast of Hebron. Thus, the Carmel in our present text cannot be identified with Mount Carmel in the north of Israel by Haifa, the site of Elijah's challenge to the priests of Baal generations later.

The Judean Carmel was a grazing region where Naval evidently became extremely prosperous: he is depicted as the archetype of the wealthy, selfish, arrogant, mean-eyed villain. The ARI states that the soul of Laban was incarnated in Naval: the Hebrew letters of the two names are identical. There are many parallels between Laban's attitude to Jacob and Naval's to David. Our text counterpoints the paradigm case of the **Evil Eye** against the messianic David, who had "beautiful eyes and good vision" (ch 16 v 12). David's intrinsic nature was to see and reveal goodness everywhere, while his worst enemies (Saul, Do'eg and now Naval) had the opposite nature and saw only negativity and evil all around them. [The conceptual interrelationship between the evil eye and the death of the heart on the one hand and messianic goodness on the other is analyzed by Rabbi Nachman in Likutey Moharan I, discourses 54 and 55.]

When David sent his emissaries to Naval he told them to open with a beautiful blessing for Naval's future prosperity and peace (v 6): this is included in the passages of blessing customarily recited on Saturday night after the departure of the Shabbat. Despite his gracious overture to Naval and despite the fact that David was indeed his relative since Naval was from the Judean house of Caleb (v 3), Naval contemptuously brought up the issue of David's "tainted" Moabite lineage and snidely dismissed him as yet another of the rash of upstart servants who in recent times had taken to rebelling against their masters (v 10, see Rashi).

David and his men had heroically helped and supported Naval's shepherds, as testified by one of Naval's own "lads" (vv 15-16), yet Naval found it offensive that he should be asked to give any of **his own** bread, **his** water and **his** succulent fresh meat "to men that I have no idea where they come from" (v 11). Many of the Jews forced to demean themselves by going from door to door to beg funding for needy Torah institutions from some of the rich "fat cats" of today can testify from personal experience that Naval's attitudes still persist.

"And David said to his men, 'Let each one gird his sword, and each one girded his sword and David too girded his sword'" (v 13). Naval's contemptuous refusal to help David and his "servant" smear made Naval a **Moreid Be-Malchut** (rebel against the kingship) because all Israel now knew that Samuel had anointed David to be king (RaDaK on v 13). Yet although this was a capital case, David girded his sword only **after** asking his men to do so. From this we learn that in capital cases before a Beit Din (rabbinical court) the head of the court states his opinion only **after** all the other judges have stated theirs, starting with the most junior. For if the head of the court were to state his opinion first, none of the other judges would have the audacity to openly disagree with him (Sanhedrin 36a).

AVIGAIL

A bloody massacre was averted only through the shrewdness and presence of mind of Naval's wife Avigail, who is counted as one of the seven outstanding prophetesses of Israel together with Sarah, Miriam, Deborah, Hannah, Huldah and Esther (Megillah 14b). In our present text we see that Avigail prophesied the imminent death of Naval when she said that all David's enemies should end up like him (v 26).

Just as Laban's daughters Rachel and Leah had no illusions about the character of their father (Genesis 31:14-15), so Avigail, despite being married to Naval, preserved her integrity and knew exactly how despicable he was. Matching David himself in the eloquence and subtle, tactful delicacy with which she deflected the threatening storm, Avigail saved him from unnecessary bloodshed that would have put a dark stain on his kingship.

Avigail's blessing to David, "Let the soul of my master be bound up with the bond of life" (v 29) alludes to the life eternal, and a slightly modified version is customarily included in the form of the initial letters of each of the Hebrew words in the phrase "Let the soul be bound up with the bond of life" (**Tav Nun Tzadei Beit Hei**) as the last line of inscriptions on Jewish gravestones or dedications in memoriam. Likewise, Avigail's curse that the soul of David's enemies should be "shot from the sling" (ibid.) is the foundation for the concept of the **Kaf HaKelah** (the "pouch of the sling") from which the souls of the wicked are slung by vengeful angels from one end of the universe to the other and back again (Talmud Shabbat 152b).

Naval had what today would be called a massive heart attack on hearing the news of the gift given to David (one wonders if the epidemic of heart disease among today's fat and wealthy is related). Naval lingered for 10 days but still did not repent, and he died on the day of God's sealing of His judgments, Yom Kippur. David subsequently took the outstanding **Tzaddeket** - prophetess Avigail as his wife, as well as Achino'am from Jezre'el (who interestingly has the same name as Saul's wife, see ch. 14 v 50). How Saul could have given his daughter Michal, who was already married to David, to Palti ben Layish, and how David could have taken her back afterwards is the subject of extensive discussion in the Talmud and commentaries (Sanhedrin 19a; see RaDaK on v 43) but we will have to leave the intricacies of this discussion for some other time!

CHAPTER 26

The men of Zif now betrayed David to Saul for a second time, and the king - instantly forgetting his earlier repentance and contrition - hurried off with 3000 choice soldiers in pursuit of his bugbear. The ensuing action once again took place in the barren mountain wilderness area southeast of Hebron towards the "Dead" Sea area.

If David had spared Saul's life only the one time when he went to relieve himself in a cave, as narrated in Chapter 25, it could have been seen as some kind of fluke. However, his doing so a second time - even though he knew beyond any shadow of a doubt that Saul was out to kill him - makes it clear that David's forbearance stemmed from true nobility and perfect integrity. David "**saw** that Saul was coming after him to the wilderness" (v 3) - his very **soul** saw it - yet he had the utmost respect for the sanctity of the kingship and for the authority of his own teacher, Samuel, who had anointed Saul. Even when the latter was literally delivered into his hands, David would not strike God's anointed.

Saul and all his men were all **fast asleep**. While it is said of David that, like a horse, he never slept for longer than it takes to breathe sixty breaths (Berachot 3b) - which is typical of the true Tzaddik, who is constantly awake, alert and advancing in his service - Saul and his top ministers had ceased moving forward and had fallen into a deep spiritual slumber and complacency.

On entering Saul's camp together with Avishai, David initially invited his companion to take the king's spear and water flask (v 11). However, David evidently did not trust Avishai not to give way to his desire to kill Saul and therefore David took them himself (v 12) in order to be able to prove his loyalty to Saul by showing him that he had stood right by the sleeping king yet still did not kill him.

It was a veritable "slumber of God" that had fallen upon Saul and his men. One Midrash tells that David was actually saved by a stinging wasp. It is said that the stinging wasp was one of three creatures the purpose of whose creation had always puzzled David, the other two being the madman and the web-spinning spider. David had already discovered the benefits of madness when he used feigned madness for self-protection during his first stay with Achish king of Gat (ch 21 v 13). He discovered the benefits of spiders' webs when once forced to hide in a cave, over the entrance to which a spider spun a web, making those searching for David assume he could not have entered the cave. Now, as he entered the circle of Saul's sleeping henchmen, Avner moved his leg in his sleep, barring David's exit. Had anyone woken up while David was thus trapped, he would have surely been killed. There was no way for him to escape - until God sent a wasp that stung Avner in the leg, causing him to move his leg again while remaining fast asleep, thereby making a gap in the circle that enabled David to escape (Midrash). God was protecting David at every step of the way, but it was through the minute details of His all-encompassing providence that David had to learn to believe it.

After snatching the spear and water flask and making his getaway, David called to Avner, chiding him for sleeping while supposedly being on duty "guarding" God's anointed. When Saul woke up and again heard the **voice** of the noble, saintly David, his sanity and lucidity returned once again, and he knew that he had sinned (v 21). So great was David's power of **tikkun** that whenever Saul actually came into direct contact with him, his madness was immediately dispelled.

Among David's complaints to Saul were that accursed men were seeking to "drive me out today so as not to be attached to God's inheritance, saying, 'Go, serve other gods'" (v 19). The rabbis asked, "Who ever told David to go and serve other gods? Rather, this comes to teach you [since they were trying to force David to live outside the Land of Israel, which he considered tantamount to "serving other gods"] that everyone who dwells outside the Land is as if he had worshiped idols" (Talmud Ketubot 110b). I quote this not to upset readers who live outside of Israel, but only to encourage you to think carefully what your purpose is in being there.

Saul relented and said he would do David no further harm (v 21) - and indeed the dire situation caused by the imminent massive Philistine war gave Saul no further opportunity to go after David even if he had wanted to. Nevertheless, while "David went on his way" (v 25) - continuing to ascend constantly, rising from level to level - "Saul went back to his place" (ibid.): not only was he not moving forwards, he was going backwards!

CHAPTER 27

Saul's end was rapidly approaching, and with it the dawn of David's kingship. In the period of barely more than four months before Saul was killed and David became king, the latter took one of those mysterious twists that characterize the dark cloak of concealment which accompanies the revelation of Mashiach by going across to the Philistines and appearing to collaborate with them.

[Could this mean that the puzzling behavior exhibited by certain "Neturey Karta" adherents in turning out for marches in London and Washington to demonstrate **against** Israel and **for** the "Palestinians" - which thoroughly disgusts many of their fellow Jews - is actually in some sense a sign of the imminence of Mashiach??? Likewise, many Jews to the left and far left of the political spectrum can also be found supporting Israel's sworn enemies, but perhaps it is because they are so assimilated and hardly identify as Jews that they do not arouse the same disgust.]

Thus, David now returned to the territory of the Philistines to stay with Achish king of Gat. On his earlier visit he had felt so insecure that he resorted to feigning madness and fled soon afterwards (ch 21 vv 13ff and ch 22 v 1), but now he was no longer alone as he had been before. This time he arrived with an army of 600 men as well as his entourage of wives, and moreover, it was common knowledge that Saul and the whole army of Israel "abhorred" him (v 12) and had been chasing after him, and this was enough to persuade Achish that David was not a danger to the Philistines.

Achish gave him the city of Tziklag where he could reside with dignity, but David preferred to spend his time operating as a kind of Israeli undercover agent, ostensibly protecting the Philistines from their enemies in the desert regions of the Negev but actually campaigning against Israel's own endemic enemies, including Amalek. David was wise enough to kill off all he fought against so that there would be no survivors to come and tell Achish what was really going on. Thus, Achish thought he had David "in his pocket" (v 12), but the Philistine king was merely deceiving himself.

CHAPTER 28

"And it was in those days that the Philistines gathered their camps to go to war against Israel." (I Samuel 28:1).

The Philistines were mobilizing for what they intended as a full-scale invasion of the very heartland of Israel. It is noteworthy that David's imminent ascent to the kingship of Israel came at a moment of direst peril for his own nation in their very homeland - the Philistines certainly intended to enslave them -- and that precisely at this time of supreme crisis God's anointed king was actually present with one of the enemy Philistine rulers, ostensibly "helping" him! This mysterious twist may indicate that in our times too, the arrival of Mashiach will be signaled by a situation of dire threat to the connection of the people of Israel with their land, and that Mashiach himself may turn out to be somewhere that no-one would ever have expected him to be.

The Philistine assault was focused in the area between the Jezreel valley (between Haifa and the central mountain chain) and the valley of Beit She'an (south of Lake Tiberias west of the R. Jordan). Canaanite settlements still survived in these valleys, and the Philistines, entering from the Mediterranean coastal regions of the Land, evidently intended to foment a Canaanite revolt against the Israelites and then march southwards into the central mountain chain in order to overwhelm and subjugate the Israelite settlements of Mount Ephraim (present day Shomron) and the mountains of Judah, which were the heartland of the country.

While Saul's pursuit of David had been concentrated in the territories of Benjamin and Judah, he now marshaled his army, which comprised forces from all the Tribes of Israel as well as the king's standing army. This was a national war. Saul camped on the slopes of Mount Gilboa near the town of Jezreel, which was the key to the control of the Jezreel valley and the road to the valley of Beit She'an and Israelite settlements on the east bank of the Jordan.

Prior to this critical battle, Saul fully understood the seriousness of the situation. After only two years as king he could see that the entire future of Israel as a free nation in their land was threatened. After having killed the High Priest and a whole city of Kohanim, Saul could not expect any answers about his fate through the **Urim Ve-Tumim**, or from prophets or experts in asking "dream questions" (a skill that is known to certain kabbalists until today).

There is deep pathos in the picture of Saul on the night before his death in battle turning to the very kind of forbidden sorcery that he had spent the two years of his reign trying to eradicate from Israel. (Although the narrative about Saul's reign concentrates primarily on his persecution of David, we can infer from various hints in our text that he succeeded in organizing Israel's first standing army and also sought to continue Samuel's work of weaning the people from idolatry and occult practices. Although Saul was afflicted by an evil spirit in relation to David, this should not be taken to imply that he was not sane or fit to govern in other respects.)

The Torah states clearly that "any man or woman that has in them an **Ov**... shall surely die." (Deut. 18:11). The **Ba'al Ov** - "master of the Ov" - is a sorcerer who uses special rituals and incantations accompanied by certain bodily movements to divine the future by eliciting a low, almost inaudible voice allegedly coming from some dead soul to whom questions may be addressed (see RaDaK on v 24 for a detailed analysis of the different opinions among the sages about the Ba'al Ov).

Members of the Sanhedrin were expected to be familiar with the various different forms of witchcraft, sorcery and divination and to understand exactly what is prohibited by the Torah. It is not that the Torah views such practices as inefficacious: the Torah recognizes that God has placed the power of witchcraft in the world, just has He has placed many other kinds of impurity in creation for His own inscrutable purposes. It is just that despite their possible efficacy, the Torah has forbidden Israel to resort to such methods.

Somewhat paradoxically, RaDaK (on v 7) states that the surviving female **Ba'alat Ov** that Saul's men found for him in **Eyn Dor** (="the eye of the generation") was none other than the wife of Tzephaniah, mother of **Avner** - who was Saul's own chief of staff, and who was according to rabbinic tradition one of the two men who accompanied Saul on this eerie mission. After all Saul's cleansing efforts, impurity remained so close to the throne!

She did what she did, "And the woman saw Samuel and she screamed with a great cry and the woman said to Saul why did you deceive me?" (v 12). How did she know that the man who had come to consult her was Saul? The rabbis explain that the woman knew her disguised questioner must be the king because normally dead souls would rise up from beneath the earth feet first, while Samuel arose head first in honor of the king (Tanchuma). "And the woman said, "I saw **Elohim** ascending from the earth". While **Elokim** is one of the names of God, **Elohim** can also mean mighty angels or human judges (cf. Genesis 6:4 and Exodus 22:8). Here, since the verb **olim** (ascending) is plural, it cannot refer to God. The rabbis stated that it refers to Samuel and a companion - no less than Moses - whom Samuel brought with him because when he was suddenly disturbed from his eternal rest he thought he was being raised for the final judgment and wanted Moses to testify that there was not a commandment in the Torah that he had not fulfilled (Chagigah 4b).

The news was very grim for Saul, yet Samuel still told him that "tomorrow you and your sons will be **with me**" (v 19) - i.e. within Samuel's own **Mechitzah** (boundary of holiness) in Heaven (Rashi ad loc.), which at least meant that although Saul and his sons were being taken from **Olam Ha-Zeh** ("this world") they would have a glorious **Olam Ha-Ba** ("world to come") in virtue of their great saintliness. 'Saul had sinned but he was still an outstanding tzaddik whose tragic end should make us weep.

Despite having been told that he was to die the next day, Saul - to his credit - did not flinch from the call of duty. "When Avner and Amasa, his two companions, asked him what Samuel had said to him, Saul replied that he had told him he would be victorious and that his three sons would ascend to greatness. Said Reish Lakish: At that moment, the Holy One blessed be He called to the ministering angels and said, 'See what a creature I have in my world. Normally a man won't even take all his sons to a party for fear of the evil eye, but this one knows he is going to be killed in battle, yet he still takes his sons out to war and rejoices in the Attribute of Justice!'"(Midrash Rabbah Vayikra 26).

CHAPTER 29

Meanwhile David was ready to go out with king Achish and the Philistines to war. We are not told how David intended to act as a "fifth column" in the war in order to subvert the Philistine plans. However, in the event he did not have to do so because Achish's Philistine co-patriots were much more suspicious than he was of David and told him to send David away. Thus, the latter was saved from having to take part in a battle against his Israelite brothers and he returned to the land of the Philistines while the Philistines went up to Jezreel to fight Saul.

CHAPTER 30

Due to the suspicions of the Philistines that David was a fifth-columnist, Achish king of Gat had sent him away while Achish himself marched northwards together with the rest of the Philistine armies to Jezreel for the coming onslaught against Saul and his forces (chapter 29 v 11).

Our present chapter thus narrates how David returned to the Negev to Tziklag, the city Achish had given him (which was between Gaza and Be'er Sheva in the region of present day Netivot, north of Ofakim) only to find that the city had been sacked by the ever-opportunistic national enemy of the Israelites, the Amalekites, who took advantage of Israel's disarray at that time to kidnap all the women and children that David and his men had left behind. It was only through God's mercy on David that the women and children were not killed despite the fact that David himself had left no survivors on his undercover missions against the Amalekites and the other tribes of the southern wilderness regions (ch 27 v 9, see RaDaK on ch 30 v 1).

As yet, however, David and his men had no information about the fate of their kidnapped women and children and could only fear the worst. This was a critical moment for David because the people wanted to lynch him out of grief and anger at David's "antics" in going off with Achish in the first place, which had left the unguarded women and children exposed to the kidnapping. The people's readiness to stone David is reminiscent of the people's readiness to stone Moses when they found no water in the wilderness at Rephidim, which was also one of the locations where Amalek attacked (Exodus 17:4).

"And David was in very sore straits. but David strengthened himself in HaShem his God" (v 6). This was typical of the noble David, who immediately called for the High Priest to bring the Urim Ve-Tumim to ask if he should pursue the Amalekites (v 7-8).

It was through divine providence that David and his men found the starving Egyptian slave of an Amalekite who because of weakness had been left by his master to die in the wilderness - typical of hard-hearted Amalekite mercilessness. David found the Amalekites feasting and drinking in celebration of their predations (cf. the celebrating bands trying to get up the mountain in Rabbi Nachman's story of the Spider and the Fly). David was able to restore all those who had been kidnapped and take all the Amalekite booty and kill all the Amalekites except for 400 young men who rode off on camels and escaped (v 17).

The Midrash comments that these four hundred survived in reward for the fact that the four hundred men that Esau brought with him against Jacob (Genesis 32:6) all slipped away and are not mentioned again in that narrative. They went off because they had the good sense not to want to get scorched by the burning coal of Jacob (Bereishit Rabbah 75). This Midrash seems to imply that the four hundred who escaped in David's time were incarnations of the four hundred who slipped away in the time of Jacob - indicating that history constantly revolves in interrelated cycles.

Thus, Saul's career as king had begun with his unsuccessful search for his father's **atonot** ("donkeys") which according to the ARI allude to the husks of Amalek (see commentary on I Samuel ch 9), while David initiated his career as king with the restoration of all that was lost to the Amalekites - because David's constant trust in God earned him His aid.

DIVIDING THE SPOILS

The Amalekites had been looting the Philistines as well as the Israelites (v 16), leaving an enormous booty to be divided up among David's victorious forces.

"And every evil and worthless (**beliya'al**) man spoke up from among the men who had gone with David and said, 'We shall not give any of the spoil to those who did not go with us'" (v 22). These "evil and worthless" men exhibited exactly the same kind of mean-eyed selfishness as Naval, who is described with exactly the same epithet of **beliya'al** (ch 25 v 25): in not wanting to share any of the booty with those who were too weak to go out to war, they violated the fundamental Torah value of collective social welfare, which saves us from the cruel inequality that comes when the strongest take all.

"And it was from that day **and above** that he made it as a statute and a judgment for Israel..." (ch 30 v 25). The unusual phrase "from that day **and above** (**va-ma'alah**)" where we would have expected "from that day **onwards**" alludes to the fact that sharing the spoil equally between those who fought and those who stayed at home was not instituted by David himself but revived from the ancient practice of Abraham, who after his victory in the war of the four kings against the five (Genesis ch 14) insisted that those who had stayed guarding the equipment should take a share in the booty just like those who had gone out to fight the enemy (ibid. v 24; see Rashi on I Samuel 30:25). In everything David did, he followed the Torah.

"And David came to Tziklag and he sent from the booty to the elders of Judah..." (v 26). Thus, David consolidated his leadership over his own tribe of Judah as he prepared to become the new king of Israel.

CHAPTER 31

The ascent of the Messianic David to the kingship came at a moment of cataclysmic national crisis. First the Philistine forces killed Saul's three sons, and their archers then cornered Saul. Seeing that the end was at hand Saul was deeply fearful of the Philistines, and knowing the vengeful cruelty they were sure to display against him, he preferred to end his own life first.

RaDaK (on verse 5) points out that Saul did not sin in killing himself despite the fact that the Torah writes, "But I will require your blood for your souls" (Genesis 9:5), which means "I will require your blood if you kill yourselves". Nevertheless, Saul did not sin because he had already been told by Samuel that he was going to die in the battle and moreover, once he saw that he was surrounded by the Philistine archers and would be unable to escape, it was better that he should kill himself than allow himself to be abused by the uncircumcised Philistines (cf. Yalkut Shimoni on Genesis ch 8 Remez 61).

DISASTER

The death of Saul and his three sons on Mount Gilboa and the routing of the Israelite forces left the nation in total disarray. The Israelites in the Jezreel valley region and on the east bank of the Jordan felt so threatened by the Philistines that they simply abandoned their cities and fled, leaving the enemy to occupy strategic areas of the Land.

Manifesting a blood-thirsty vengefulness that also typifies the "Palestinians" who have adopted their name in modern times, the Philistines gleefully mutilated the bodies of Saul and his sons, taking his skull to the temple of their god Dagon (I Chronicles 10:10) and hanging his body on the fortified wall of Beit She'an.

The Israelite inhabitants of Yavesh Gil'ad (who were from the half tribe of Menasheh that took their portion east of the river Jordan) had a special motive for their daring exploit in rescuing Saul's body and those of his sons from where the Philistines were exhibiting them on the wall of Beit She'an. This was because Saul's very first act as king had been to come to the rescue of the inhabitants of Yavesh Gil'ad when they had been presented with an impossibly cruel ultimatum by Nachash, king of Ammon (I Samuel ch 11 vv 1-11).

Because of the kindness of the men of Yavesh Gil'ad (**chessed shel emet** - **true** kindness), God said, "You have dealt kindly with Saul and his children, so shall I give your reward to your children. In time to come, when the Holy One blessed be He is destined to gather in Israel, the very first He will gather in will be the half tribe of Menasheh, as it is written, 'Mine is Gil'ad and Mine is Menasheh'" (Pirkey d'Rabbi Eliezer 17). [A little over a week before the writing of this commentary, it was reported in the Israeli media that about 250 members of Bney Menasheh flew from the remote areas of eastern India near the border with Bangladesh where they have been living for thousands of years and made Aliyah to Israel! This is surely a sign that the ingathering of the Ten Tribes is happening before our very eyes!]

With the respectful burial of Saul's bones, the First Book of Samuel ends on the theme of the honor that must be shown to the king even after his death - for this book has traced the steady transition from a state in which "each man did what was right in his own eyes" to one in which Israel had a kingship.

"And Samuel was dead…" (ch 28 v 3). The rabbis asked how this squares with the tradition that Samuel wrote the book called by his name. They answer that the Book of Samuel (including what we call II Samuel, which tells the story of the kingship of David, whom Samuel had anointed) was completed by Gad the Seer and Nathan the Prophet (Bava Batra 15a).

II SAMUEL CHAPTER 1

The norm today in the political life of most nations is that after a regime-change, the new ruler does everything possible to smear and destroy the reputation of his predecessor.

Thus, the Amalekite lad who came to announce to David that he had killed his greatest persecutor assumed that David would rejoice in the news. Not so: despite David's being surrounded by bloody conflicts on every side, he never lost sight of his noble aspiration for true peace and reconciliation.

The Amalekite says, "I **chanced** to be on Mount Gilboa..." (v 6). This is because Amalek denies the unity of God and His ubiquitous providence. Accordingly, for him, everything is pure chance (cf. Deut. 25:18: Amalek "**chanced** upon you" - same Hebrew root as here). However, Saul, who had already fallen on his sword and was in his death throes, realized that the presence of the Amalekite at this critical moment was no chance. The king asked the Amalekite to finish him off before the Philistines could get to him and abuse him (v 9 see Rashi) - as if Saul knew that he had to execute the divine judgment upon himself for his failure to wipe out Amalek when charged to do so by the prophet. The Amalekite stripped Saul of "the crown on his head and the ornament on his arm" (v 10) - i.e. his head and arm **Tefilin** - and brought them to David expecting a rich reward.

But far from rejoicing over Saul's death, David immediately rent his garments mourning over the slain head of the nation's Sanhedrin and his son Jonathan, David's dearest friend. He publicly eulogized them, and wept and fasted until the evening, after which he swiftly meted out fitting justice upon the head of this Amalekite, who had shown no respect for God's anointed king.

DAVID'S LAMENT

It was Saul who had "lost it" in persecuting David, but despite the pain and suffering David had endured at his hands, he never wavered in the slightest from his loyalty, love and devotion for his master, God's anointed king, who had been head and shoulders above the rest of the nation in sanctity and righteousness.

David's immortal lament for Saul and Jonathan is the very height of sublime eloquence, expressing his pain at the death of two outstanding heroes who had been unflinching in their war against the uncircumcised Philistines and their idols. It was as if the "high places" of Israel had become an Altar of atonement through the slaying of these warriors: "How are the mighty fallen!" (v 19).

The phrases of verse 23 of David's lament are included in the **Av HaRachamim** prayer in memory of the Jewish martyrs in all ages recited in the Synagogue on Shabbat after the conclusion of the reading of the Torah and Haftarah just before **Ashrei**.

"Daughters of Israel, weep for Saul, who clothed you in scarlet..." (v 24). "Rabbi Yehudah says these are the actual daughters of Israel, for all of whose needs Saul provided when their husbands went out to war. Rabbi Nehemiah says, The Daughters of Israel are the sages of the Sanhedrin, and they should cry because when Saul would hear the explanation of the reason for a law from the mouth of a Torah scholar, he would rise and kiss him on his mouth!" (Talmud Nedarim 31b). Thus, we see the greatness of Saul, the warrior king who organized Israel's first army so humanely and who showed constant honor, love and devotion to the Torah.

Through the Urim Ve-Tumim of the High Priest, God told David to go up to Hebron to rule over Judah. It was necessary for David to reign for seven years in Hebron (v. 11): this was because David is the "fourth leg" of the Throne of Glory, the three other legs being the patriarchs Abraham, Isaac and Jacob. Before David - the **receiving** vessel of Malchut - could reign over all Israel, he first had to attach himself to the Patriarchs (buried in the Cave of Machpelah in Hebron) and receive from them the spiritual influence that he would bestow upon the people. David had to be in Hebron for **seven** years, because the attribute of **Malchut** consists of **seven** Sefirot of Building (Chessed, Gevurah, Tiferet, Netzach, Yesod, Hod and Malchut) and each had to receive the influence of the three Patriarchs.

Although as yet David reigned only over his native tribe of Judah, he still acted as king over all Israel, as illustrated in his magnanimous message to the men of Yaveish Gil'ad who had buried the bodies of Saul and his son. "And now strengthen your hands and be men of valor, for your lord Saul is dead, and the house of Judah have anointed even me as king over them" (v 7). Metzudat David (ad loc.) explains that David was guaranteeing the men of Yaveish Gil'ad that he would help them no less than Saul if they came under attack from Israel's enemies.

CIVIL WAR & NATIONAL RECONCILIATION

The people of Israel were teetering on the very brink of civil war. Avner ben Ner had been Saul's commander-in-chief as well as his first cousin, and Avner now saw it as obvious that Saul's successor should be his surviving son Ish-Boshet (the Hebrew name means Man of Shame - shame in the sense of deep modesty, a virtue greatly treasured by Saul). It is a Torah law that when a king is anointed, he gains the kingship for himself and his children for ever, because the kingship is hereditary" (Deuteronomy 17:20, Rambam, Laws of Kings 1:7). Although Avner surely knew that David had been anointed as king by Samuel, the rabbis teach that Avner darshened from God's promise to Jacob that "**kings** will go out from your loins" (Genesis 35:11) (a promise that was given when only Benjamin still remained to be born) that at least **two** kings were destined to come from the tribe of Benjamin, i.e. Saul and Ish-Boshet (see RaDaK on v 8).

Ish-Boshet emerges as a weak and rash-minded figurehead. Avner first took him to Machanayim, a strategic town east of the River Jordan (safe from the Philistines) on the very boundary between the territories of the tribes of Gad and Menasheh. Although the places to which subsequently Avner took his candidate for the kingship are enumerated in only a single verse – v 9 - in fact the spread of Ish-Boshet's regime took place in successive stages over a period of several years. Gil'ad is the collective name for all of the Israelite territories east of the Jordan. The **Ashuri** most probably refers to the territory of the tribe of Asher in the western Galilee, while the successive spread of Ish-Boshet's regime southwards to Jezreel, Mount Ephraim and the territories of Benjamin brought his kingship to the very heartland of Israel.

Just as Saul's commander-in-chief Avner was also his close relative, so too David's commander-in-chief, Joab son of Tzeruyah, was his own nephew: Tzeruyah was David's sister (I Chronicles 2:16). A superficial reading of our narrative may leave the impression that Avner on the one side and Joab and his brothers on the other were some kind of swash-buckling warriors, but in fact their internecine battles were not necessarily purely physical but also spiritual: embedded in our present narrative is the prehistory of the later **machloket** (conflict) over the general contours and details of the Halachah as conducted among the Tannaim (sages of the Mishnah) and Amoraim (sages of the Talmud).

Thus, when Avner invited Joab to allow twelve representatives of each side to engage in a gladiatorial struggle to the death, "each one took hold of his fellow's **head**" (v 16). This seems to indicate that this was on one level an intellectual battle between potential representatives of the Twelve Tribes for spiritual dominion over the nation.

"For the race is not won by the swift" (Ecclesiastes 9:11). Asa'el was reputed to be so fleet of foot that he could run over the very tips of the ears of corn in a field without breaking them. Even so, his swiftness did not help him on the day he chased after Avner (Kohelet Rabbah 9). The latter offered him to make an honorable getaway, but when Asa'el refused, Avner speared him through the rib into his liver and gall bladder and killed him.

This put Asa'el's brothers Joab and Avishai into the role of **Go'el Ha-Dam**, "avenger of the blood" (Deut. 19:12 etc.) of their slain brother. This in itself threatened the nation with a vicious spiral of bloodshed (vv 24-25) but Avner had the good sense to make an overture for peace - "Shall the sword devour forever?" (v 26) - and although he himself had initiated the bloody violence (v 14), Joab still agreed to call a halt for now, and the two parties returned to their respective bases.

"And the light shone to them in Hebron" (v 32): with the Messianic king now installed in Hebron, there was hope that despite the potential for a protracted bloody civil war, it would indeed be possible to forge true peace and national reconciliation.

CHAPTER 3

Before continuing with the account of the decline of the house of Saul, our text (vv 2-5) lists the sons who were born to David during the seven years that he reigned in Hebron. Of these sons, Amnon, Avshalom (Absalom) and Adoniyah all play leading roles in the ensuing narrative of the life of David.

In verse 3 we learn that Avshalom - who was later to rebel against and almost snatch the very kingship from his father - was David's son from Ma'achah, daughter of Talmi ("Ptolemy"?), king of Geshur. The rabbis teach that Ma'achah was captured in war (I Samuel 27:8 refers to David's campaign against the Geshurites) and was thus in the category of **Eishet Yefat To'ar**, the "beautiful captive woman" that her Israelite captor is permitted to marry under certain conditions (Deuteronomy 21:11). However, written directly after this mitzvah in the Torah is the law of **Ben–Sorer U-Morer**, the "rebellious gluttonous son" (ibid. vv 18-21), who must be stoned to death. Avshalom is the prime exemplar of the case of the rebellious son born to the **Yefat To'ar**.

The rabbis taught that **Egla** the wife of David mentioned in v 5 is none other than Michal daughter of Saul, whom he betrothed with 100 Philistine foreskins and who was beloved to David like a favorite calf (cf. Judges 14:18 where Samson alludes to his wife as a calf).

DECLINE OF THE HOUSE OF SAUL

The civil war between the House of Saul (Benjamin) and the House of David (Judah) was part of a protracted historical process which began in the time of Joseph in Egypt when Judah stepped forward to become protector and guarantor of Jacob's youngest son, Benjamin (Genesis 43:9; 44:18ff). Benjamin was unique among the twelve tribal founders inasmuch as he was the only "Sabra" - he was the only one of Jacob's children who was actually born in the Land of Israel (Genesis 35:16). Home-born Israelis are called Sabras after the prickly, thick-skinned desert cactus fruit that is so sweet and refreshing inside! The tribe of Benjamin showed their prickly nature in their war against the other tribes in the aftermath of the gang-rape of the Pilegesh in Giv'ah (Judges chs 19-21), while Saul showed similar tough-skinned Gevurah ("might") throughout his reign.

Nevertheless, as explained by the ARI, the House of Saul was rooted in Olam HaTohu, the "World of Devastation", and their kingship could not endure, for the **tikkun** ("repair") was to come about only through the House of David. Indeed, later on, it was only through identifying himself with Judah that Saul's Benjaminite descendant Mordechai - known as HeYehudi, "the Judah-ite" (Esther 2:5) - was able to rectify Saul's flaw by destroying Haman the Amalekite. (**Yehudah** has the connotation of denying idolatry, see Likutey Moharan I, 10.) The conflict between the House of Saul and the House of David was later expressed in the conflict between Beit Shamai and Beit Hillel.

The fall of the House of Saul in David's time came about through the rashness of his son Ish-Boshet, who vented his suspicions that Avner was involved with Saul's concubine. If this was true, it was forbidden by Torah law (Rambam, Laws of Kings 2:1-2), which prohibits anyone else marrying a dead king's widow (see RaDaK on II Samuel 3:7). Avner greatly resented these suspicions after he had resolutely stood up for the House of Saul, and this gave him a strong motive to go to make peace with David and bring over the rest of Israel to support his kingship.

David made his acceptance of Avner's overtures conditional on the return of his wife Michal, whom Saul had given to Palti son of Layish (I Samuel 25:44). As indicated briefly at the end of the commentary on the above-referenced chapter, the halachic ramifications of Michal's "marriage" with Palti are very complex as normally a woman who marries a second husband is thereafter forbidden to return to her previous husband (Deut. 24:4), although Saul had no right to take Michal from David and give her to another man. In any event, the rabbis taught that Paltiel understood that he was not free to be with Michal as a husband, and that he drove a sword between himself and her in bed in order to remind himself that if he so much as touched her the sword of divine punishment would be unleashed against him. Paltiel's going out after Michal weeping (I Samuel ch 3 v 16) is darshened as referring to his weeping over having lost the great mitzvah of abstention from a tempting but forbidden relationship that was now being taken from him (see Rashi ad loc.).

Although Avner had a personal motive for ceasing to support the House of Saul, he showed great courage and true statesmanship in setting national unity above any partisan interests he may have had as Saul's commander-in-chief.

When Avner visited David in Hebron to talk about national reconciliation, Joab was absent fighting and pillaging the Philistines. On hearing of these negotiations on his return, Joab suspected that Avner had ulterior motives and had come to Hebron to spy on David and check out the weak points in his regime (v 25). Joab had good reason to mistrust Avner, who had killed Joab's brother Asa'el as told in ch 2 v 23.

Thus, Joab and his brother Avishai were under Torah law in the role of **Go'el Ha-Dam**, "avenger of the blood". Joab succeeded in assassinating Avner by waylaying him inside the gate of Hebron. The "gate" alludes to the Sanhedrin, where Joab challenged Avner as to the legality of his killing of Asa'el. Avner is said to have replied that he was justified in doing so since Asa'el had been pursuing him and thus came into the category of a **Rodeif** ("pursuer"). Joab replied that where possible a person being pursued should strike the **Rodeif** only hard enough to deflect him but not to needlessly kill him. Avner replied that he had not been able to aim sufficiently accurately, at which point Joab asked him how come he was able to aim for Asa'el's fifth rib. Avner had no reply to this.

The text states that Joab took Avner aside "to speak to him **basheli**". This unusual Hebrew word has the connotation of "innocently" - indicating that Joab did not let Avner understand what he was intending to do. The rabbis state that Joab asked Avner a complex halachic question (which as deputy leader of the Sanhedrin in the time of Saul, Avner had the authority to answer). The question was how a girl with a stump-arm can carry out the mitzvah of **Chalitzah** (removing the sandal of her dead husband's brother if the latter does not want to perform the levirate marriage with her, see Deut. 25:9). Avner crouched down to demonstrate how such a girl could release the straps of her brother-in-law's sandal using her teeth, at which point Joab took his opportunity to drive his sword into Avner's fifth rib to avenge his brother's blood. [In Exodus 3:5, God's command to Moses to **remove** his shoes uses the word **shal**, "take off", which according to the drush is alluded to in the word **ba-shel-i** in our present verse. See RaDaK on II Samuel 3:27.]

David immediately dissociated himself from the assassination of Saul's commander-in-chief, and went on to curse Joab very severely, although the latter remained his commander-in-chief almost to the end of David's life. It is ironic that the curses called down upon Joab and his descendants by David - who as king embodies the attribute of **Malchut**, associated with severe Judgment - were all visited on David's own descendants. Rehaboam was a **Zav** (a man suffering a morbid flow from his member); Uzziah was a leper; Asa went with a stick because of illness in his legs; Josiah died at the sword, while Jehoachin was lacking bread. These curses fell on David's descendants because David intended to kill Joab and should not have cursed him as well (RaDaK on v 29).

A king does not normally attend funerals (Rambam, Laws of Mourning 7:7; Laws of Kings 2:4) but David made an exception in the case of Avner to demonstrate publicly that he had had no hand whatever in his assassination and wanted to avoid any further escalation of the civil war and on the contrary, was anxious to bring it to a close. David's statesmanlike behavior indeed found favor in the eyes of all the people (v 36) and contributed greatly to the resolution of the conflict.

CHAPTER 4

With the death of Avner, the House of Saul was further weakened, and besides Saul's son Ish-Boshet, the only surviving member of any significance was the young son of Jonathan (who had been Saul's "crown prince") – **Mephi-boshet**, who as a child escaping from the Philistines after Saul's defeat had fallen and become lame. Mephi-boshet appears again in the narrative later on (ch 9 etc.).

The perpetrators of the bloody daytime assassination of Saul's son Ish-Boshet during his afternoon rest thought that their act would win them favor in the eyes of David, whom they perceived as being no different from the normal run of new rulers, who are anxious to "neutralize" all possible rivals.

However, David's eyes were always to God (v 9), and he had no more patience for this kind of murderous criminality than he had shown to the Amalekite who prided himself on having dispatched Saul (ch1 v 15-16). David had no intention of founding the kingship that was to lead to the building of the Temple and the establishment of the Sanhedrin by its side upon the bloody assassinations of all perceived opponents. (It would greatly benefit the world if today's political assassins would learn the lesson.) David made a gory public example of the killers of Ish-Boshet in order to deter others, and had the severed head of Ish-Boshet buried in the grave of Avner in Hebron. The site of the grave of Avner is just a few minutes' walk from the graves of the Patriarchs in Hebron and can be visited until today.

CHAPTER 5

With the death of Ish-Boshet there was no other serious contender for the kingship besides David, who had already won the love of the nation when he killed Goliath. There was no prophet of the stature of Samuel to publicly "crown" David similarly to the way in which he had publicly appointed Saul, but everyone knew that in his lifetime Samuel had already anointed David, and the latter's public acceptance by all the Twelve Tribes (ch 5 vv 1-3) was the final seal on his kingship.

"AND THE KING AND HIS MEN WENT TO YERUSHALAYIM" (v 6)

David was in Hebron when he was accepted as king by all the tribes. His very first move without delay was to go to Jerusalem. In our present text, it says that David "**and his men**" went up to Jerusalem, making it appear that David's main support was coming from his existing following. However, this was not at all the case: in I Chronicles 11:4 speaking of the move to Jerusalem, it says, "And David **and all Israel** went...". In other words, **all Israel** were now David's men: he was king without any opposition. (The overall purpose of the Book of Chronicles is not merely to repeat historical narratives but primarily to establish the primacy of the House of David, yet it does contain numerous parallel accounts of the events described in I & II Samuel and I & II Kings, often with important supplementary details.)

It was now necessary to conquer the citadel of Jerusalem from the Jebusites, because the Israelites had a tradition that Zion would be the capital city of the kingdom of Israel and that it would only be captured by one who was king over all Israel. Until that time, no-one had been truly king over all Israel, because Saul's kingship did not endure (RaDaK on verse 6).

As discussed in the commentaries on Joshua and Judges, "the children of Judah were **not able** to drive out the Jebusite inhabitants of Jerusalem" (Joshua 15:63), **not** because they did not have the power to do so, but because they were still constrained by the oath of Abraham to Avimelech (from whom the Jerusalem Jebusites were descended) not to harm his grandchildren or great-grandchildren. This oath had been extracted by the Canaanites in exchange for agreeing to sell the Cave of Machpelah to Abraham - his first acquisition of property in the Holy Land.

When David tried to enter Jerusalem, the Jebusites taunted him that he would have to remove "the blind and the lame" (v 6). One explanation of this is that the Jebusites had placed their idols on the walls of their city for protection - idols are called "blind" because "they have eyes, but they do not see" and "lame" because "they have legs, but they do not walk" (Psalms 115:5 & 7). The Midrashic explanation is that the Jebusites had placed great copper statues on the wall - one of them blind to represent Isaac (Genesis 27:1) and another lame to represent Jacob (Genesis 32:31) - with scrolls coming out of their mouths inscribed with Abraham's oath to Avimelech. However, since the oath was limited to his grandchildren and great-grandchildren, it had already expired, and David was free to capture the city. I Chronicles 11:6 relates that it was Joab who actually succeeded in getting up onto the fortified wall and destroying the idols ("detested by the soul of David" v 8). The Midrash relates that he got up onto the wall by driving a tall poplar tree into the ground outside the city, pulling its top branch down onto the ground, climbing up on David's head and using the tree as a kind of catapult to shoot himself up onto the wall (see RaDaK on vv 6-8).

Something as important as the capture of Jerusalem - eternal City of David from which the word of God will ever go out to the whole world - could not but come about with a great leap!

"AND DAVID KNEW..." (v 12)

David knew that God had given his kingship a firm foundation when he saw his miraculous success over Israel's endemic enemies. The gift by Hiram king of Tyre of timber together with craftsmen in wood and stone to build David a house was a sign of the growing international recognition of the House of David that would culminate in the time of Solomon, whose Temple Hiram also helped to build and to whom all the kings of the earth came to pay their respects.

Although Solomon is mentioned in our present chapter in the list of David's sons born in Jerusalem (v 14) the circumstances of his birth are narrated in detail later on.

"AND THE PHILISTINES HEARD..." (v 17)

Although the Philistines had defeated the Israelites at Gilboa and subsequently occupied many of their abandoned cities, they do not appear to have made serious efforts to press their military advantage thereafter: perhaps they saw the conflict between the House of Saul (Avner and Ish-Boshet) and the House of David as one that would automatically weaken the Israelites, and in any case, when in flight from Saul, David had **acted** as some kind of "ally" of the Philistines, or at least of Achish king of Gat.

But now that David had taken Jerusalem from the Canaanites, causing a great arousal of holiness, it was inevitable that there should be a corresponding arousal of the forces of unholiness (for "God has made the one against the other" Eccles. 7:14). Similarly, the ingathering of Israel to their land in the last few hundred years has been accompanied by a steadily growing arousal of enmity on the part of those who see themselves as the successors of the Canaanites and Philistines.

From the accounts in our present text and other texts in II Samuel and I Chronicles, it can be inferred that in David's reign there were three major battles between the Israelites and the Philistines with a number of secondary skirmishes. The first two battles took place in **Emek Refa'im** ("valley of the giants") which is south west of the Citadel of Jerusalem and which is familiar to those who know the present-day Jerusalem, being the name of one of the city's most important arteries leading from the Baka district, where the old Jerusalem Railway Station is located, to the southern suburbs. This road actually runs through the valley after which it is named. The south west end of **Emek Refa'im** joins Nachal Shorek, through which the railway passes on the way to Beit Shemesh.

It would appear that the Philistines came up from their habitations in the coastal and lowland regions through Nachal Shorek in order to advance on Jerusalem and were massed in Emek Refa'im when David -- on the instructions of the Urim Ve-Tumim - successfully struck them and destroyed their idols (vv 17-21). This defeat did not deter the Philistines, who advanced a second time (vv 22-25). This time the Urim Ve-Tumim answered David that he was **not** to attack them "until you hear the voice of treading on the heads of the mulberry trees" (v 24). According to the Midrash, the Philistines were within four cubits of the Israelites but still David would not allow them to advance even if it meant they would die ("better to die righteous and not die wicked"). This showed enormous faith in God (unlike Saul, who did not carry out God's words to the last detail), and at last the Israelites saw the mulberry trees waving - protective angels were walking on the foliage - and successfully attacked the Philistines (Yalkut Shimoni).

CHAPTER 6

David's foremost goal was to build the Temple in Jerusalem in fulfillment of Jacob's prophetic dream of the Ladder on that very site. The Hebrew word for "ladder" is **sulam**, the letters of which have the same numerical value as those of **Sinai** - for the very center point of the Temple was the **Even Shetiyah** ("Foundation Stone") upon which Jacob had rested his head, and this was the destined resting place of the **Aron** - Ark of the Covenant - which contained the Tablets of Stone Moses received at Sinai. The Temple is not only a place of worship but one from which Torah is to shine forth to all the world.

Thus, after the conquest of Jerusalem, it was now necessary to bring the Ark of the Covenant up from Kiryat Ye'arim (=Baaley Yehudah in v 2) where it had remained ever since it had been brought up there from Beit Shemesh after its return from captivity among the Philistines (I Samuel chs 6-7).

DAVID'S ERROR

"David erred in something that even little school-children know, that the Ark must be carried **on the shoulders of the Levites** (Numbers 7:9) and not on a wagon. However, David said "Your statutes have been **songs** to me in the house of my sojourns" (Psalms 119:54) - this was considered somewhat too light-hearted an attitude to God's laws, and David was penalized by making the mistake of transporting the Ark on a wagon, thereby indirectly causing the death of Uzza when he thought it was about to fall and put out his hand to steady it" (see Rashi onv 3).

This harsh blow on what was supposed to be an occasion of consummate national joy (parallel to the deaths of Aaron's sons Nadav and Avihu on the day of the consecration of the Sanctuary in the wilderness, Leviticus 10:1-2) made David's face "change into a charred oven-cake" (Sotah 35a) - he was ashen with fear of God. By putting out his arm to "steady" the Ark, Uzza betrayed a fundamental misconception - that man needs to protect the Ark, whereas the truth is that the Ark protects itself. It appears that man carries the Ark, but in fact the Ark carries those who carry it - and the same applies to the entire Torah. While it appears that we have to "carry" the Torah through our observance of its commandments, in fact the Torah carries us every day of our lives.

On the great blessing that came to Oveid-Edom when the Ark was in his house for three months (his wife and eight daughters-in-law each had sextuplets, which is why he had a household of 62=8 sons + 9 x 6 babies, I Chronicles 26:8) the Talmud comments: If this is the reward of one who takes in the Ark, which neither eats nor drinks, how much more is the reward of one who gives hospitality to a Torah sage in his home and gives him to eat and drink" (Berachot 63b).

MUSIC AND DANCE

Many secrets of the Temple music are embedded in this chapter, which enumerates some of the Temple instruments. When the Philistines returned the Ark in a wagon drawn by nursing cows, contrary to nature the cows and even their calves began to sing - because the Ark creates music everywhere: the music of God's providence, where everything is interconnected. Likewise, David accompanied the taking up of the Ark to its resting place in the eternal city of Jerusalem with ecstatic music and dance.

David's own dancing was far superior to that of any dervish, yet it elicited the sarcastic derision of his wife Michal, Saul's daughter, who saw it as undignified. Similarly, since the beginnings of the Chassidic movement, which gave birth to an explosion of fervent devotion accompanied by much dancing, some have tended to look scornfully upon the "antics" of the Chassidim as lacking in dignity. (Thus, when Rabbi Avraham Kalisker, who had been an outstanding student of the Gaon of Vilna, became attached to the Baal Shem Tov and began dancing for joy in the streets of Vilna, the Gaon never spoke to him again - yet Rabbi Nachman, who saw R. Kalisker in the latter's old age, described him as the only truly perfect Tzaddik he had ever seen.)

The House of Saul were indeed modest in the extreme, and the rabbis in the Midrash said that Michal told David that no one in her father's house would let so much as a tiny portion of a hand or foot be exposed. However, David replied that her father's house ignored the glory of Heaven and were mainly concerned with their own glory, while his dancing was purely to glorify God (see RaDaK on v. 20). Let us abandon our concerns about our own dignity and take a lesson from David about how to throw ourselves into the service of God with true fervor.

* * * The sections in II Samuel 6:1-23 and 7:1-17 are read as
the Haftarah of Parshat **Shemini** Exodus 9:1-11:16 * * *

CHAPTER 7

"AND IT WAS WHEN THE KING SAT IN HIS HOUSE..." (v 1)

"...And God gave him rest from all his enemies round about" (v 1). David's victory over the Philistine invaders at the battle of Emek Refa'im (ch 5) brought to an end the wars that had afflicted the Israelites in their own home territories since the beginning of the period of the judges. Although David still fought many wars (as we see in Chapter 8), from now on all the battles were in enemy territory, and this was the "rest" that God gave David "from all his enemies roundabout".

The Torah commands that "when He will give you rest from all your enemies roundabout and you dwell securely. And it shall be that the place that the Lord your God shall choose to cause His Name to dwell therein ..." (Deut. 12:10) - that place "...shall you search out" (ibid. v 4).

From these verses David learned out that as soon as peace came to the Land, it was a sign that it was time to fulfill the mitzvah to build the Temple. David felt uncomfortable living in his own magnificent house built with timber sent by Hiram of Tyre while the Holy Sanctuary in Giv'on was merely a temporary structure and the Ark newly brought up to Jerusalem had no proper home. (Those who live in extravagant homes while the Temple remains in ruins should take note.) David therefore consulted Nathan the prophet - for all David's actions were based on the guidance of the prophets or the Urim Ve-Tumim - and Nathan felt that the logic of David's understanding of the passage in Deuteronomy was compelling and told David to go ahead.

Notwithstanding this logic, Nathan's **intuition** proved incorrect, and God sent him **prophecy** that very night telling him to put the brakes on David. The rabbis taught that David was so eager that without this immediate prophecy he would have started building the Temple at once and David was the type who could well vow not to eat or drink until it was completed (cf. Psalms 132:2). Since David was not destined to build the Temple, he would have lost out badly had not God immediately sent Nathan to stop him (see RaDaK on v 2 & Rashi on v 4).

Nathan's prophecy centers on the appointment of David and his offspring for ever as the true royal house of Israel (vv 8-11), and prophesies the birth of Solomon, to whom God would be a "father" while he would be God's "son" and would actually build the House to His Name (vv 12-15). In verse 12 God announces to David that "I will establish your seed after you **that will come from your loins**...." This is the sign that the son who would build the Temple was not Absalom or Adoniyah since they had already been born in Hebron, while the builder of the Temple had yet to come forth from David's loins. The story of the mysterious chain of events whereby the soul of the wisest man that ever lived came into the world will begin in chapter 11.

"AND KING DAVID CAME AND SAT BEFORE HASHEM..." (v 18)

In response to Nathan's eloquent prophecy about the glorious destiny of the House of David, the king "sat before HaShem" - i.e. he sat in meditation and prayer before the Ark of the Covenant (only kings of the House of David are permitted to sit in the **Azarah**, which is the main Temple courtyard, while all others, including even the High Priest, must stand) - and there he poured forth his equally eloquent, humble prayer of praise and thanks and his supplication for future divine protection.

"AND THIS IS THE TORAH OF ADAM..." (v 19)

While David's literal meaning in these words may be understood to be that he humbly recognized that his destiny as spelled out in Nathan's prophecy was fit for a great man and not a lowly one such as himself (Metzudat David, RaDaK), his words also imply that he was granted a vision of all the future generations just like Adam (Rashi on v 19), and also that David was comparable to Moses (RaDaK on v 19). Just as Moses was the greatest of the prophets, so David was the greatest of the kings. Moses took Israel out of Egypt while David released them from servitude to the nations. Moses split the Red Sea, while David split the waters of Aram Naharayim (Psalms 60:2). Moses gave Israel the Five Books of the Torah, while David gave us the Five Books of Psalms. (RaDaK ibid.)

David's prayer, with its many memorable phrases (v 23 is included in the Shabbat afternoon Amidah prayer) concludes with his supplication for God's future blessing and help - all to enhance the glory of His Name.

David had been planning the Temple since his initial flight from Saul (I Samuel 19:18 as darshened in Zevachim 54b). From this time on, he studiously gathered in all the booty from his wars to Jerusalem, as described in the next chapter, in order to amass all the necessary materials to enable Solomon to build the Temple without delay on ascending to the throne.

CHAPTER 8

In the last decades, the Jewish people have witnessed the alarming tendency for historians to rewrite and revise established history in order to suit later opinions and points of view. Thus, holocaust denial has been a favorite theme of anti-Semitic writers and publicists until this very day, while the actual history of the birth and growth of the Jewish **Yishuv** ("habitation") in the land of Israel hundreds of years before the Zionist Congress of Basle and the 1917 Balfour Declaration until today has been totally distorted by the Arabs and their supporters in the mass media and academia worldwide.

Likewise, it appears that the true greatness of the Israelite empire and sphere of influence as established by David and Solomon, which stretched "from the river [Nile] to the river [Euphrates]" and endured for much of the period of the later kings, was long ago willfully erased from the annals of history as presented by the chroniclers of the nations. Yet despite what seems to have been deliberate revisionism on the part of Israel's enemies, it is possible to reconstruct a picture of the true extent and nature of this glorious empire with its sphere of spiritual and cultural influence from various passages in II Samuel, I & II Kings and Chronicles, including our present chapter.

All of the wars described in this and the ensuing chapters took place outside the boundaries of the Israelite's existing habitations. **Meteg Ha-Amah** in verse 1 is identified by the commentators with Gat (see RaDaK on v 1), which was the leading Philistine city since it was the only one whose ruler was called "king" (such as **Melech** Achish) as opposed to "captain" (**seren**). Gat was indeed part of the tribal territory of Judah but had for centuries fallen under Philistine occupation until the time of David.

His campaign in Moab and the harsh punishment he meted out there (v 2) were in revenge for the killing of his parents by the king of Moab (see Rashi here and on I Samuel 22:4).

The people over whom King Hadad-ezer (vv 3ff) ruled were Arameans - descendants of Noah's son Shem - who originally dwelled in eastern Turkey and Armenia and subsequently migrated in waves southwards into Mesopotamia and westwards from the Euphrates in the direction of the Mediterranean. The Arameans comprised a number of different streams (including the family of Abraham's brother Nahor and of Laban and Bilaam), and their language, Aramaic, was the lingua franca of the entire region. Laban's agreement with Jacob as described in Genesis 31:44-53 was a covenant demarcating their respective spheres of influence.

It was only during the period of the Judges that the Arameans migrated into what is now Syria and Lebanon, where they rapidly built up their city-based principalities into strong metropolises that wielded power over extensive belts of territory. Throughout the period of the kings of Israel, the Arameans were one of the main scourges from which the nation suffered.

From various verses in our present text and in the parallel account in Chronicles we can piece together a picture of David's wars against Hadad-ezer, whose home-base of Tzova was in the **Bik'ah** ("valley") of Lebanon, while his sphere of influence extended to Damascus. David's breaking the legs of the Aramean horses (v 4) was designed to make it impossible for them to use their main military resource in future as well as to avoid taking the horses for himself, which would have violated the Torah prohibition against the king's "multiplying horses" (Deut. 17:16). David placed Israelite garrisons in the Aramean territories in Lebanon and Syria, thereby turning them into Israelite colonies (v 6). These territories (including the Golan Heights) had large Israelite populations throughout the periods of the First and Second Temples and well after the Jewish exile from Israel. In the language of the Mishnah and Talmud, these territories are collectively called "Suria" (=Syria). Had David conquered them **after** completing the conquest of all the territories comprising the actual Promised Land, Syria would also have been incorporated into the Land and all of the **Mitzvot Taluyot Ba-Aretz** (agricultural and other commandments that apply in the Land) would also have been applicable in Suria. However, since David's conquest of Suria came **before** the conquest of all of the Promised Land, these laws do not apply there in full but only partially. The roots of the present conflict between Israel and Syria over the Golan Heights and Lebanon lie in David's conflicts with the Arameans millennia ago.

As indicated earlier, David transported all the gold, silver and copper and other booty captured in his wars to Jerusalem in readiness for the building of the Temple.

"And David made a **name** when he returned from striking Aram...." (v 13). The rabbis taught that the **name** that made David famous among all the surrounding nations came in virtue of his unique behavior in his foreign wars (long before the "Geneva Convention"). Whereas other nations would leave their slain enemies lying on the battlefield for the vultures to eat, David had his generals **bury** them with dignity (see I Kings 11:15), just as the Israelites are destined to bury the fallen hordes of Gog and Magog in time to come (Ezekiel 39:13).

David's placing of garrisons in the territory of the Edomites and his turning them into a subject nation (verse 14) signifies the end of the World of Devastation in which the kings of Edom (=the "broken vessels" of Shevirat HaKelim) ruled before there was a king over the Children of Israel (Genesis 36:31), thereby initiating the order of **tikkun** (repair). "And David ruled over all Israel...." (v 15).

"...And David practiced justice and charity to all his people" (ibid.) It was precisely this "justice and charity" that constituted the repair. The Talmud asks what kind of justice it is that involves charity -

surely strict justice and kind charity are opposite attributes? The answer is that a legal **peshara** ("compromise"=**win/win**) is a judgment that is sweetened with kindness and charity (Sanhedrin 49a). Instead of fighting one another, people were willing to make concessions, and this is what leads to true peace within the nation.

CHAPTER 9

The rabbis advised to "be careful of the government, because they only reach out to a person to serve their own need and appear to show him love only so long as they have benefit from him but do not stand up for him in his hour of hardship" (Avot 2:3). King David showed himself a notable exception to this mode of government, displaying his truly royal nature in searching for any surviving members of the House of Saul that he might be able to help despite the fact that he had nothing whatever to gain from showing them favor.

David remained loyal to the covenant he had struck with Jonathan at the very beginning of their acquaintance (I Samuel 18:1-3) and which had been renewed several times with both Jonathan (I Samuel 23:18) and Saul himself, to whom David had promised that he would never cut off his seed (I Samuel 24:21-2).

Tzeeva, the "servant of the House of Saul" whom David called for information about surviving members of Saul's family, evidently had the status of **Eved Kena'ani**, a "Canaanite slave", who according to the law of the Torah remains a slave unless his master frees him and who is part of his master's estate, passing on his death into the possession of his inheritors (see Leviticus 25:44-6 and RaDaK on II Samuel 9:2). Unless he or she is freed, the Canaanite slave is not permitted to marry a free Israelite and enter the Kahal ("Assembly") but is nevertheless a member of the Covenant and is bound by all of the commandments that Israelite women are obliged to fulfill. (Thus, the Canaanite slave must observe Shabbat, eat kosher, share in the Paschal lamb, etc. but does not wear Tefilin or pray the set daily prayer services etc.)

With the death of Saul and his three sons in the war against the Philistines and the subsequent assassination of his fourth son, Ish-Boshet, the only male survivor of Saul's house was the son of his first-born Jonathan - Mephiboshet -- who had been a small child at the time of the Philistine war and who while being evacuated by his nursemaid had fallen and injured both legs, leaving him permanently lame (II Samuel 4:4, see RaDaK there). His lameness is symbolic of the collapse of Saul's house.

It appears that Saul's family estate now legally belonged to King David because Saul's son Ish-Boshet was **Moreid Be-Malchut**, a "traitor against the kingship", since with Avner's encouragement he had acted as king despite the fact that all Israel knew that Samuel had anointed David to be king after Saul. Under Torah law, the estate of a traitor falls to the crown, and thus David's kindness to Mephiboshet lay in returning the estate to the family, which he was not legally obliged to do (see RaDaK on v 7). David thus appointed Tzeeva as **atropus** ("adult executor" or "guardian") over Saul's estate for the benefit of the young Mephiboshet. Tzeeva and Mephiboshet will enter the narrative again in II Samuel ch 16.

CHAPTER 10

After the death of Nachash king of Ammon, David wanted to "practice kindness" with his son Chanoon - i.e. to send a delegation to comfort him in his mourning - because "his father practiced kindness with me" (v 2). Nachash's "kindness" to David lay in taking in the one member of his family who survived when the king of Moab killed all the others after David had taken them there when he fled from Saul (I Samuel 22:1-6; see Rashi on II Samuel 10:2).

The Torah commands Israel not to seek out the peace and goodness of the Ammonites or Moabites "all your days forever" (Deut. 23:7) because far from hospitably coming out with bread and water to help their Israelite cousins in their journey from Egypt through the wilderness to their land, they even hired the Aramean Bilaam to come and curse them.

The rabbis criticized David for showing kindness to those who were intrinsically unkind, pointing out that it led only to a humiliation for David and his delegation that escalated into a full-scale war (see RaDaK on ch 10 v 2). [Similarly, contemporary attempts to appease angry terrorists and their supporters have only led to escalating terror and violence.]

The new Ammonite king's advisors convinced him that David - whom they presumably perceived as a menacing expansionist - was seeking to spy on them in order to prepare to incorporate them into his growing empire.

In view of the history of Jewish costume in the last few hundred years, it is interesting to note that the humiliation which the Ammonites chose to inflict on the Israelite delegation was to shave off their beards and cut their garments in half over the buttocks. Similarly, in 19th century Germany, the first acts carried out by Jews wanting to dissociate themselves from traditional European Jewish culture were the removal of their beards and the drastic shortening of their coats, turning them into jackets that barely covered their buttocks, earning for Jews of German origin until today the nickname of **Yekkes** ("short jackets").

Realizing that their blatant provocation of David was likely to elicit a very firm-handed military response, the Ammonites repeated their ancestral ploy of calling in help from Aram. Since the times of Bilaam, the Aramean clans had spread westwards from Mesopotamia into the territories of modern-day Syria and Lebanon, and the Ammonites summoned Aramean mercenaries from there to attack David's forces from the rear when they advanced against the capital city of Ammon.

HOW DAVID'S MEN MADE WAR

The serious military crisis in which David's commander-in-chief Joab found himself in the war with the Arameans and Israel's other enemies is reflected in Psalm 60. The Ammonites intended to coordinate with the Arameans in order to stage a pincer attack on the Israelite forces, who saw the war closing in on them "from in front and from behind" (v 9). It is noteworthy that Joab did not merely raise his hands to God and hope for the best: first he carried out his **hishtadlut** ("effort in the world of practical action"), dividing the Israelite forces into two, sending his brother Avishai against Ammon while he himself marched against the Arameans, who because of their numbers and training were the more serious threat. Only after making a pact of mutual support with Avishai (v 11) and giving him a powerful "pep talk" on being courageous "for the sake of our people" (that they should not be captured) and "for the sake of the cities of our God" (that they should not be sacked) did Joab then entrust the outcome of their efforts into the hands of God (v 12).

This trusting believer's way of making war met with a positive outcome, and the Arameans fled from Joab while the Ammonites fled from Avishai (vv. 13-14). Hadad-ezer, the king of Aram Tzova (in the **Bik'ah** of Lebanon) now sent for Aramean reinforcements from east of the Euphrates, but David went out against them with the entire Israelite army and forced the Arameans into submission (v 19). This gave David's kingdom supremacy in the entire region, opening the way for the conditions of peace in which the future builder of God's Temple in Jerusalem could be born through the mysterious chain of events that is the subject of the ensuing chapters.

CHAPTER 11

"AND IT WAS AT THE RETURN OF THE YEAR..." (v 1)

Unlike traditions whose saints are presented as totally flawless halo-wearing supermen, the Torah does not seek to hide the sins of even a Moses or a David. The Torah testifies that Moses sinned once - and once only - by striking the rock for water instead of speaking to it, for which he was strictly penalized by not being allowed to lead the Children of Israel into their land (Numbers 20:12; Deut. 32:51). Likewise, the prophet does not spare even David, the Messianic king, who is not some kind of perfect angel having no connection with the material world but a real man of flesh and blood with very human desires and impulses. David is Messiah not because he never sinned but because having sinned, he acknowledged his wrong-doing and repented completely, and then went on to teach all mankind the path of true repentance.

If David sinned, it was not the kind of gross carnal sin that average people stumble into time and again. In the words of the rabbis, "Anyone who says that David sinned is simply mistaken" (Shabbat 56a). We cannot expect to understand the true nature of what for David on his level was a "sin", any more than we can clearly understand anything else about the fathomless depths of the soul of Messiah. It was in order for David to teach the world the path of repentance that there was some kind of heavenly necessity for David to sin. Before trying to get a glimpse of where his sin may have lain, let us first understand what it was **not**.

Rabbi Nachman of Breslov remarked that someone who does not understand why the Land of Israel had to be in the hands of the Canaanite nations before it came into the hands of the Children of Israel will also not be able to understand why Batsheva had to be married to Uriah the Hittite before she was married to David (Sichot HaRaN). From these words, we may infer that Batsheva was intended for David - for it had been prophesied to him already that he was destined to have a son who would build the Temple (II Samuel 7:12-13), and only a unique woman could mother the wisest man that ever lived. (Batsheva proved her strength of character in various ways, see I Kings 1:15ff; moreover, the Midrash says she had no compunction about chastising Solomon even after he became king.)

The greatness of the **tikkunim** ("repairs") that were destined to result from the union of Batsheva with David was such that the two could only come together in a manner overshadowed with darkness and mystery. David's sin was not the common man's sin of going into a woman who is **Niddah** ("menstruant"), because Batsheva was purifying herself in the Mikveh ("ritual pool") at the very moment when David saw her (v 2). Nor does the fact that the text makes it appear she was married to Uriah the Hittite mean that she was simply in the category of **Eishet Ish** ("a man's wife"). Although on the surface it looks as if David was guilty of adultery, this is not so. In David's time, it was the practice of all men prior to going out to war to give their wives a **Get** ("bill of divorce"). The purpose was to ensure that if the husband went missing in the war, his wife would not become an **Agunah** ("anchored women", unable to marry anyone else) and that if he was killed and left no children, she would not be subjected to the humiliation of **Yibum** or **Chalitzah** (levirate marriage). Soldiers could thus wholly throw themselves into fighting the war without having to worry what might happen to their wives if they lost their lives. The formula of the **Get** followed the standard formula of a **Get Al Tenai** ("conditional divorce") that made the divorce retroactive to the time of the giving of the **Get** in the event that the husband died in the war (Rashi on v 4; Talmud Ketubot 9b; Rambam, Laws of Divorce ch. 8).

When Batsheva informed David that she had conceived, he sent for Uriah and ordered him to go into Batsheva (v 8) so that when the child was born Uriah would think it was his own, which would help cover up the scandal. It was only when Uriah refused to go into Batsheva while his brother Israelites were fighting a war that David contrived to have him killed. The death of Uriah in the war would cause his **Get** to Batsheva to come into effect retroactively, as explained above, meaning that at the time of David's relations with her she was technically **not** a married woman.

If the sin was **not** that Batsheva was a Niddah or a married woman at the time of the relations, what was it??? Did David sin in ordering Joab to send Uriah to a battle-position in the continuing Ammonite war in which he would certainly be killed? Our rabbis teach that Uriah was indeed guilty of a capital offense in refusing to carry out David's order to go into Batsheva. This made him **Moreid Be-Malchut** ("a traitor to the kingship") the penalty for which is death.

Where David sinned was in contriving for Uriah to be killed in such a way as to make it seem that he was merely a war casualty, whereas in fact David should have taken Uriah before the Sanhedrin and had him publicly condemned to death (Shabbat 56a). However, David did not want to do this as it would have drawn public attention to the questionable circumstances of his relations with Batsheva.

It was not that Batsheva was not meant for David and that he took what was not his. The sin was that having caught a glimpse from his roof-top of the mother of Solomon, he took her by force and tried to hide what he was doing instead of waiting for God to bring her to him in the course of time. In this respect, there is a certain parallel between David's sin and that of Moses' impatiently striking the rock for water instead of speaking to it.

CHAPTER 12

The real meaning of Nathan's reproof for David personally is not even our business. The average individual cannot expect to grasp the exact nature of David's sin. The prophet's reproof to the saintly David is directed at **us**, the average readers, who are to learn from it how to recognize our own sins and how to repent in order to rectify them. From verse 4, which successively refers to the rich man's visitor as a **heilech** ("passer-by"), then an **ore'ach** ("visitor") and finally an **ish** ("man of stature"), the rabbis learned out that the nature of the evil inclination is first to drop in casually as a passer-by, then to install himself within us as a long-term guest, until he finally takes over the entire house and acts as the **Baal HaBayit** ("owner of the house"; Succah 52b).

Nathan the prophet used the parable of the rich man's taking the poor man's lamb in order to prompt David to see for himself where his sin lay and how he should be punished. Had Nathan simply asked David to consider his behavior and ask himself if he had done anything wrong, the king may have tried to rationalize away his actions. Instead, Nathan told David a graphic story about somebody else's gross behavior and asked him to give a quite impartial evaluation of this kind of behavior that would not be colored by the need to justify himself. Rabbi Nachman (Likutey Moharan I, 113) teaches that this is the method whereby God consults sinners about how they should be punished. If He were to ask them directly about their own behavior, they would never give an impartial reply and would always judge themselves too leniently. He therefore shows them someone else's behavior which is parallel to their own and then asks them how they judge it. According to their evaluation of the other person's deeds and how they should be penalized, so God judges and penalizes their own, and this is the meaning of the rabbinic statement that "a person is punished with his knowledge (**mi-da'ato**) yet without his knowledge" (**Shelo mi-da'ato**)" (Avot 3:16). We should be very careful when looking at and judging the behavior of others in case we are unknowingly being invited to decide our own fate.

In angrily demanding that the rich man pay fourfold, David sealed his own fate: he suffered by losing four children - Batsheva's first baby, Amnon, Tamar and Absalom (Rashi on v 6).

"Why have you despised the word of God to do evil in His eye?" (v 9). As explained above, the evil was not that Batsheva was already married or that she was not intended for David. The evil was that while knowing Batsheva was intended for him, David still contrived to take her using subterfuge. If Batsheva had not been intended for David, why after punishing him with the death of the baby did God allow Batsheva to conceive and bear a child of whom our text states that "HaShem **loved** him" (v 24)? According to the Midrash based on the **ktiv** "**he** called" and the **kri** of "**she** called" in v. 24, it was not Batsheva but God Himself who called the child's name **Shlomo**, which is also the Name of God throughout Song of Songs. If David's relationship with Batsheva was inherently evil, how could it be that the one who built God's very Temple was born as a result?

David acknowledged that he sinned (v 13), and he fully repented: Psalm 51 is eloquent testimony to the depth and sincerity of David's repentance and his ability to turn the very sin into merit by using it to teach others the path of repentance. Whereas King Saul's sins led to his deposition from the kingship, David's kingship was not undermined by his sin, which indeed added a new dimension to David's Torah, showing that even a Tzaddik can sin and that even a Rasha (wicked person) can repent.

With the birth of Solomon (who does not enter the narrative again until the very end of David's life), the protracted war against the Ammonites came to an end with David's capture and destruction of the capital city and his cruel punishment of the Ammonites (v31). This was particularly severe because the Ammonite god alluded to in verse 30 ("the crown of **Malkam**") and in the **ktiv** of verse 31 (**Malkam** as opposed to the **kri** of **Malbein**) is none other than **Molekh**, whose worship through passing children through the fire is strictly proscribed by the Torah (Leviticus 18:21, see RaDaK on II Samuel 12:1).

How David could have placed the crown of an idol on his own head when the appurtenances of idolatry are normally strictly forbidden is explained by the rabbis as having been made possible through the prior nullification of the Ammonite idol by a non-Israelite (Talmud Avodah Zarah 44a). How David could have balanced such a heavy crown on his head (it weighed a talent of gold) is also discussed by the rabbis, some of whom say that it had a magnet in it that caused the crown to be self-suspended in the air! This is by no means the least of the weighty mysteries embedded within the fathomless allegory of these chapters.

CHAPTER 13

After David's sin in taking Batsheva, Nathan the prophet had told him: "For so says God: 'behold I will raise up evil against you from your **house**'" (I Samuel 12:11). Immediately afterwards and for the rest of his reign, David was afflicted with a succession of intrigues, scandals and rebellions from within the royal household itself. The rabbis said: "Harsher is the effect of bad upbringing of children in a man's house than even the war of Gog and Magog" (Talmud Berachot 7b). The rabbis learned this from King David's expression of pain in Psalm 3, "A song of David when he fled from Absalom his son", while there is no similar expression of pain in Psalm 2, which speaks of the war of Gog and Magog.

The rape of Absalom's sister Tamar, narrated in our present chapter, set off the chain of events that eventually led to Absalom's later rebellion against David, in which the latter came very near to losing the throne. After we heard in the previous chapter about the birth of Solomon, what we see in the ensuing episodes in David's life is how three of Solomon's older brothers excluded themselves one after the other from the succession. In raping and then rejecting Tamar, Amnon, who was David's first-born son from Achino'am the Jezreelitess (II Samuel 3:2), earned him Tamar's brother Absalom's implacable hatred, resulting in Amnon's death. It was David's rejection of Absalom in the aftermath of his killing of Amnon that led him to rebel and try to seize the throne. Later on, at the very end of David's life, his fourth son Adoniyahu tried to take the throne but was thwarted. Thus, all other serious contenders to the throne were rejected from the succession in favor of Solomon, who was born out of the highly questionable union of David with Batsheva. Having tried to cover over his own private scandal, David now had to face a succession of public scandals.

According to Torah law, Amnon would have been permitted to marry Tamar, because according to rabbinic tradition, Tamar was born from David's first union with Ma'achah, daughter of Talmai king of Geshur (II Samuel 3:4). Ma'achah was a **Yefat To'ar** (the "beautiful captive woman", Deut. 21:11), with whom an Israelite warrior is allowed to have relations one time when he first captures her, but thereafter he must abstain from all further physical relations with her until he converts her and marries her as his full wife. Ma'achah had conceived Tamar from her first union with David (and thus Tamar was not "born in holiness" and was not an Israelite woman but had to convert), while Tamar's brother Absalom was Ma'achah's son from David **after** Ma'achah's conversion and formal marriage, making Absalom a home-born Israelite.

Amnon, who was David's son from his first wife, Achino'am, was still permitted to marry Tamar despite the fact that they both had the same father, because Tamar's mother was in the category of a captive slave woman when she conceived Tamar, and "slaves have no **yichus**" (pedigree), i.e. even the closest incest prohibitions do not apply to freed slaves who convert even when biologically related with the exception of the prohibition of a son marrying his mother or her immediate blood relatives. The same technically applies to all gentile converts (Rambam, Laws of Forbidden Relationships 14:13). Thus, even though it was known that David was Tamar's biological father, it still was halachically permitted for Amnon to marry her.

The rabbis taught: "In any case where love depends on something in particular, when that something is no longer present, the love also goes away, whereas when love is not conditional upon anything, it never goes away. What is an example of love that depended on something? The love of Amnon for Tamar, while the example of unconditional love is that of David and Jonathan" (Avot 5:16).

Despite the permissibility of Amnon's marrying Tamar, this was not what interested him. He was infatuated with her beauty - she was, after all, the daughter of a **Yefat To'ar** - and just as David had taken Batsheva by force, so Amnon contrived to take Tamar by force.

Rambam writes (Hilchot Yesodey HaTorah, "Foundations of the Torah" 5:9): "If someone has set his eyes on a woman and becomes so sick as a result that he is in mortal danger, even if the doctors say he will not be able to be cured until he has relations with her, he should die and she must not be allowed to have relations with him even if she is unmarried. One may not even permit him to speak with her from behind a barrier, and he should die rather than be permitted to speak to her in order that the Daughters of Israel should not be **hefker** ('free for anyone to grab') resulting in the breakdown of the incest prohibitions."

Thus, it was very evil for David's nephew Yonadav to advise Amnon to contrive to get Tamar to prepare him **bagels** (boiled-fried doughnuts) as a cure for his sickness in order to be alone with her and rape her. Yonadav was "very wise" (v 3) - "to do evil" (Avot d'Rabbi Nathan 9:4).

Unfortunately, cases of cruel rape have today become so common that they have ceased to cause shock and horror. However, in earlier, more innocent times, the Biblical account of Amnon's rape and subsequent betrayal of Tamar was considered so shocking that in the days when the Bible was publicly studied in the Synagogues and a **Meturgeman** ("translator") would explain the text to the assembled people in the Aramaic vernacular, he would refrain from publicly translating the story of Amnon and Tamar (Rambam, Laws of Prayer 12:12). The only time the story would be read publicly was in the

Temple, when it was read to the **Sotah** (a wife whose loyalty had been called into question) to show her that sexual impropriety can take place even among royalty in order to encourage her to confess (Rambam, Laws of Sotah 3:2).

The only one who comes out clean from this story is Tamar herself, who was a model of modesty. As an unmarried girl, she would normally stay cloistered in the home and it was precisely because Amnon knew he would never catch her alone that he manipulated his father into ordering her to come to him to tend him in his illness.

The rabbis say that after having raped her, the reason why Amnon suddenly hated her more intensely than he had ever loved her was because during the act he caught his member on one of her hairs and it was partially severed, disqualifying him from entry to the Assembly (Deut. 23:2; Sanhedrin 21a).

Thus, Tamar was ruined and Amnon was ruined, and "when King David heard all these things it made him very angry" (v 21). Our rabbis taught that at that very hour, King David and his **Beit Din** ("court") decreed the laws prohibiting **Yichud** ("being alone together in private") between men and women even where both are unattached and not forbidden to one another through incest prohibitions (Sanhedrin 21a; Rambam, Issurey Bi'ah 22:3).

Thus, we see how a Biblical passage - the story of Amnon and Tamar - throws light upon the reason for an institution that is one of the pillars of Torah sanctity and modesty. Although the prohibition against **Yichud** is **Mi-DeRabbanan** ("instituted by the rabbis"), it is necessary to understand that the "rabbis" who instituted it were not some kind of dark-coated medieval clerics: they were none other than King David and his **Beit Din**!

Tamar's brother Absalom had good reason to feel aggrieved over the despicable treatment of his sister by Amnon, but instead of making a public complaint to the king over the matter, he hid his feelings and now contrived to take vengeance on his older half-brother. We learn in the next chapter (ch 14 v 25) of Absalom's perfect physical beauty - he too was the son of the same **Yefat To'ar** as Tamar - and through his endearing presence combined with his skill in manipulation, he succeeded in persuading David to send Amnon to take part in Absalom's forthcoming sheep-shearing celebrations (ch 13 v 27). It is interesting that Absalom ordered his servants to kill Amnon while the latter was drunk with wine, because Absalom himself was a Nazirite (ch 14 v 26) and was not allowed to drink wine himself.

The public assassination of the king's oldest son during a sheep-shearing celebration caused consternation among the other members of the royal household, who fled on their mules (see Bartenura on Mishnah Kil'ayim 8:1), while Absalom fled to his mother's native country of Geshur, where his grandfather was the king.

CHAPTER 14

David longed for Absalom even more than a normal father longs for a son, because David was king of Israel, and while Solomon's wives later "led him astray", David surely hoped that his own fulfillment of the Biblical commandments, including that of marrying the **Yefat To'ar**, would lead to the glorification of God and bring righteous gentiles into the community. All the time that Absalom was back in his mother's native, idolatrous Geshur, it was an affront to the very kingship of heaven that David hoped to establish on earth.

THE WISE WOMAN OF TEKO'A

Joab had already been in trouble with David over the very same kind of cycle of bloodshed and revenge that now afflicted the king, since Joab had killed Avner in revenge for his having killed Joab's brother Asa'el, thereby invoking David's curse for continuing the bloody war against the House of Saul.

Seeing that David was torn with longing for Absalom, Joab wanted to persuade the king to re-instate him but felt unable to approach him directly (it cannot have been easy to try to counsel a King David). Joab therefore turned to the mysterious Woman from Teko'a in order to take Nathan the Prophet's method of clothing reproof in allegory one step further. In Chapter 12 we saw how Nathan told David the story of the Rich Man who stole the Poor Man's only lamb in order to reprove him over his having taken Batsheva. Now Joab calls on a wise woman (rather differently from the way Avner had taken Saul to the woman who raised the ghost of Samuel) and Joab coaches her in pretending to be involved in a saga carefully calculated to touch David's compassionate heart. The appearance of this Wise Woman is reminiscent of certain other mysterious women who appear in the Bible having the good sense to take dramatic action in order to reverse serious cycles of violence in Israel. Another case is that of the woman who stopped the rampages of Avimelech son of Gideon by smashing his head with a millstone (Judges 9:53): that woman was specifically mentioned by Joab himself in II Samuel 11:21.

The town of Teko'a is in the territory of Judah south of Jerusalem a short distance east of Efrat/Bethlehem. Teko'a was noted for its wonderful olive trees, and because the locals habitually consumed the excellent olive oil, wisdom was found among them (Menachot 85b).

The main point of the claim of the woman of Teko'a to David was that even though one of her fictitious sons had killed the other, it was not legal for other members of the family - as **Go'el Ha-dam** ("avenger of the blood") - to continue the bloody cycle by killing the killer, because as she pointed out, "there was no one to save between them" (v 7) i.e. there had been **no witnesses** to the original killing (see RaDaK on v 6). She implied that the only reason why the other family members wanted to kill the killer was to eliminate all her late husband's direct heirs and thereby get their hands on his estate!

Having presented her parable in the form of the case of her two purported sons and manipulated David into swearing he would save the "killer" (v 11), the Wise Woman of Teko'a went on to use her artful eloquence to show David that Absalom should likewise be reinstated without being punished for the killing of Amnon, because there had been no witnesses to prove that he was responsible. "For we shall surely die, and like the waters that are drawn down towards the ground and cannot be gathered again, so God will not take bribes, but He thinks up thoughts so that even one rejected will not be rejected by Him" (v 14). The Wise Woman of Teko'a was appealing to David to leave Absalom alone and let God decide whether he deserved punishment or not. Having sworn to her, David could not backtrack from his oath and agreed to allow Joab - whose hand he quickly recognized in all this - to recall Absalom to Jerusalem, although he would not admit him into his presence.

The return of the aggrieved Absalom laid the ground for his subsequent rebellion against David, for which he patiently and skillfully prepared by nagging Joab repeatedly for several years to give him admission to David. When Joab did not respond, Absalom showed his manipulative skills by telling his servants to burn Joab's barley crop (v 30), forcing him to go to David to plead for Absalom's reinstatement, to which David agreed.

In verse 27 of our present chapter we learn that Absalom had three sons, while in II Samuel 18:18 we are told that he had none. The rabbis reconciled this apparent contradiction through the tradition that

Absalom's sons died as a punishment for his burning Joab's crops, because "anyone who burns his neighbor's crops does not leave a son to inherit him" (Sotah 11a).

CHAPTER 15

Verse 7 of our present chapter dates Absalom's rebellion "**at the end of forty years**". This cannot mean at the end of forty years of David's reign, since he reigned for only forty years altogether while the ensuing narrative deals with numerous events that took place after the quelling of the rebellion. Thus, our rabbis stated that this verse means "forty years from the time the Children of Israel first asked Samuel for a king" (Talmud Temurah 15a). For one year, thereafter Samuel reigned jointly with Saul, after which Saul reigned alone for 2 years. "At the end of forty years" thus brings us to the thirty-seventh year of David's reign, three years before he died.

The closing years of David's reign were thus wracked with troubles, of which Absalom's rebellion was one of the most serious, coming very close to succeeding.

Absalom was the archetype of the self-seeking, power hungry narcissist whose evil eye was turned against his father's kingship (see Likutey Moharan I, 55). Absalom built his power-base in precisely the same way as a populist politician, telling everyone exactly what they wanted to hear. He would give everyone who was aggrieved and disenchanted the feeling that he was totally on his side and would give him his full support, subtly smearing the established regime as being indifferent to people's suffering (vv 3-4). Like present day political campaigners, Absalom literally went around hugging and kissing the crowds (v 5).

This was how "Absalom stole the heart of the men of Israel". "Stealing the heart" is the same as what in rabbinic literature is called **G'nivat Da'at**, "stealing the mind" by craftily deceiving other people into thinking exactly what one wants them to think. The Talmud comments that Absalom "stole" **three** hearts: that of his father David, that of the Beit Din (the court of law) and that of all Israel, and he therefore died having **three** stakes driven into his heart (Sotah 9b).

Absalom deceived his unsuspecting father into allowing him to go to Hebron, the very heartland of Judah, where he staged a carefully contrived plot to spring a sudden coup d'etat on everyone. Rashi (on v 11) brings a midrash from the Jerusalem Talmud Sotah stating that Absalom asked David to give him a written slip ordering any two men that he invited to go with him to do so. Absalom kept showing the same slip to more and more pairs of men, until he ended up with a most impressive band of men following behind him.

Absalom's greatest "catch" was Achitophel, who emerges as another mysterious, sinister, outstanding Torah genius somewhat reminiscent of Do'eg Ha-Edomi in his power to cause harm. Not only was Achitophel the leading sage and counselor of the time, whose advice to Absalom - had it been followed - would certainly have led to the defeat of David. Even more surprising is that Achitophel was actually the grandfather of David's own wife, Batsheva! Batsheva's father, Eli-am (II Samuel 11:3), was the son of Achitophel (II Samuel 23:34). The rabbis taught that it was Achitophel's own **Mazal** ("destiny") that deceived him into siding with Absalom. Achitophel thought that he himself was going to be king, and intended to trick Absalom into killing David in order that Achitophel would be able to condemn him in the Sanhedrin and thereby depose him. What Achitophel did not understand was that the kingship was not destined to come to himself but to his granddaughter Batsheva's son Solomon.

DAVID'S FLIGHT

Absalom's "coup d'etat" put David in extreme danger. Realizing that Absalom's flaw was that of turning **Malchut**, "kingship" into **arrogant self-seeking**, David took refuge in the opposite quality of supreme humility, taking his entire household on foot from Jerusalem into self-imposed exile.

David evidently did not believe that he had the power to overcome Absalom's nation-wide rebellion even in his own capital city. Instead, he made for the east bank of the Jordan (Gil'ad) where the Israelite population owed a debt of gratitude to David for providing them with security through his successful campaigns against the neighboring peoples of Mo'ab and Ammon.

David went into exile accompanied by a sizeable contingent including his "mighty warriors (ch 15 v 16-18), "all the **kereiti** ('archers') and all the **peleiti** ('slingers')" and "six hundred men that came on foot from Gat", who may have been Philistine mercenaries. The rabbis state that the **kereiti** and **peleiti** actually allude to the Urim Ve-Tumim (Talmud Berachot 4a): even in his hour of dire crisis, David sought guidance only from God. The rabbis teach that David first turned to Eviatar the High Priest to ask guidance from the Urim Ve-Tumim, but Eviatar received no answer and was thus deposed from being High Priest. This was in accordance with God's decree, as Eviatar came from the rejected line of Eli the Priest, who was descended from Aharon's fourth son, Itamar. It was then that Tzadok, who was from the line of Aharon's third son, Elazar, became High Priest (RaDaK on v 23).

David ordered Tzadok to take the Ark of the Covenant back to Jerusalem, where in fact the priests would be able to spy on Absalom for David's benefit. And "if I find favor in the eyes of God, he will bring me back and show me the Ark and its resting place. And if He says thus, 'I do not desire you', here I am, let Him do to me as is good in His eyes" (vv 25-26). Thus, David surrendered himself to God completely, praying that He should thwart Achitophel's counsel (v 31).

CHAPTER 16

Even in his hour of supreme crisis, David had certain allies and helpers who proved themselves true friends in his time of need.

One who was less than truthful, however, was Tzeeva (ch 16 v 1), who certainly owed a debt of gratitude to David for having appointed him manager/director over all the estates of Saul for the benefit of the late king's only surviving grandson, Mephiboshet, as told in I Samuel ch 9. When Tzeeva now arrived in the wilderness with badly needed supplies of food for David and his men, he answered David's question about the whereabouts of Mephiboshet by accusing him of having stayed in Jerusalem with the intention of using the upheaval caused by Absalom's rebellion to take back the throne for the House of Saul. According to the rabbis, this was **Lashon Hara** (unwarranted slander) on the part of Tzeeva, yet David accepted it (Talmud Shabbat 56a). Under the influence of this slander, David awarded Mephiboshet's estate to Tzeeva (which is presumably exactly what the latter intended), but later Mephiboshet was to come to David to argue that he was innocent (II Samuel 19:25).

THE CURSES OF SHIMI BEN GERA

Shimi ben Gera, who came out cursing David in his flight and throwing stones and mud on the king and his men, was far from being some lowly foul-mouthed ruffian. He was a prominent member of the family of Saul as well as head of the Sanhedrin (Rashi on ch 16 v 10). He execrated David as "a man of blood" (v 7), accusing him of having engineered the deaths of Saul's son Ish-Boshet and his commander-in-chief, Avner as well having killed in order to take Batsheva (see RaDaK on v 7).

Shimi ben Gera's insults were intended to further increase David's pain and humiliation, yet when Avishai asked David for permission to strike him down, David refused, teaching that even though this humiliation was coming to him through the instrumentality of a human being, in fact it was God who had put Shimi ben Gera up to it and that it would be better for David to bear the humiliation with patience than to rebel against God's chastisement. It is indeed a great level to be able to discern the hand of God in the suffering that comes to us through other people. David prayed that God would see his humble resignation and pay him back with goodness in exchange for bearing these curses (v 12).

HUSHAI THE ARCHI

Various characters enter our narrative about whom we have little or no supplementary information from other sources. Among these is Hushai Ha-Archi (ch 15 v 32), who was apparently one of David's leading advisors yet succeeded in entering into Absalom's innermost circle of advisors as David's "plant", and in that position, he was indeed able to thwart Achitophel's counsel, thus saving David's kingship from collapse (Yalkut Shimoni).

ACHITOPHEL'S ADVICE

When Achitophel advised Absalom to go into his father's concubines, he was not telling him to commit an actual sin. Under the Torah laws of forbidden incest relationships, for Absalom to have relations with his father's concubines was not technically a sin, because it is only a woman who is formally married to a father that is forbidden to his son: the prohibition of marrying a father's wife does not apply to a woman **raped** or **seduced** by the father (**Anusat** or **Mefutat Aviv**) and the **Pilegesh** ("concubine") comes into this category (Yevamot 11:1, see RaDaK on II Samuel 12:11).

The reason why Achitophel advised Absalom to go into his father's concubines was because only a public demonstration of this order would convince the people that Absalom was fully determined to carry his rebellion through relentlessly to the very end. Had people thought that he was not serious, they would have abandoned him. The Torah law of kings forbids anyone except the new king from taking the wives of a former king for himself. Going into David's concubines was thus Absalom's way of publicly asserting his ascent to the throne, which was an act so treasonable that David would never be able to make peace with him.

CHAPTER 17

Having advised Absalom to go in to his father's concubines in order to force an all-out conflict, Achitophel now offered his second piece of advice - that Absalom should send him with a strong army to hunt down David **immediately** before he had a chance to get far away and muster more forces. Achitophel promised a swift, decisive operation that would avoid unnecessary bloodshed - and his advice would have been accepted and would undoubtedly have proved effective except that "God commanded to thwart the counsel of Achitophel" (v 14), for God was with David, despite chastising him so sorely.

As we read in ch 15 vv 32ff, David had planted his other outstanding advisor, Hushai Ha-Archi, in Absalom's court, and Hushai skillfully undermined Achitophel's plan for **immediate** action by proposing a far larger operation **later on**, thus gaining time for David to make his escape from the Jerusalem region. Carefully reminding Absalom of David's great strength and courage and raising specters of a set-back for the pursuers that could radically demoralize Absalom's army, Hushai appealed to his vanity in proposing that the entire nation should gather so that he would be able to march proudly at the head of a great Israelite army (see Rashi on v 11).

This idea was highly attractive to Absalom, who went cold on Achitophel's idea of going off himself immediately to finish the job in a low-profile way. Thus, while Absalom began to dream of his coming glory, Hushai sent inside information from Absalom's court using the sons of the two high priests as runners. Having heard Achitophel's advice to go in hot pursuit, Hushai urged David to make as quick a getaway from the region as possible in case Absalom changed his mind again.

Having much earlier in his life had to flee from the persecutions of King Saul, David once again found himself in flight - this time to escape his own son! Chapter 15 vv 23-30 traced David's escape from the city of Jerusalem prior to Absalom's arrival there. David had then crossed over the Kidron Valley (directly to the east of the Temple Mount) and climbed up the Mount of Olives (from where he could still gaze back upon the Tent of the Ark of the Covenant). Chapter 16 then narrated his journey to Bachurim, a Benjaminite town a little south of Jerusalem, from which Shim'i ben Gera went out to curse and stone him. During this time, Absalom had arrived in Jerusalem and went into David's concubines, after which Achitophel wanted to go straight after David. This was when Hushai advised David to flee the Jerusalem area altogether, and David now went eastwards past Jericho to the Jordan, which he crossed as told in our present chapter v 22. He then advanced northwards into Gil'ad (the generic term for the territories of the tribes of Reuven, Gad and half Menasheh east of the Jordan) to the city of Machanayim.

The mark of a wise man is that he sees what is developing (Avot 2:9), and Achitophel saw that with his own advice unheeded, Absalom would be unable to overcome the mighty warrior David. Achitophel realized that as soon as David was restored to the kingship, he himself would be first in the firing line for treason. He therefore went to his home in Gilo (after which the present-day south-Jerusalem suburb of Gilo is named owing to its proximity to the original town), delivered his last will and testament to his children (telling them to keep out of **machloket**, "conflict", not to rebel against the kingship of the House of David, and to use the sign of a clear summer's day on the festival of Shavuot to know that the wheat crop will be successful, Bava Batra 147a) and then hanged himself.

David's escape to Gil'ad forced Absalom to take his forces out of the Land of Israel proper to the less favorable territories east of the Jordan, where David was receiving reinforcements and abundant supplies of food (vv 27-29).

CHAPTER 18

In Machanayim, David marshaled his forces and followed the classic strategy known from the times of the judges of dividing them into three. David was ready to go out to battle (v 2) but the people would not hear of this, advising him to stay in the city to pray for their success.

We suddenly see a picture of David at the age of 67 - the old king - no longer going out to battle but yielding to the will of the people and watching over their fortunes from the city.

David's love and compassion for Absalom despite his having rebelled and now being in hot pursuit of him - defy reason, just as does the love of any father for a miscreant son. David no doubt saw to the very roots of Absalom's soul and still hoped a way could be found to rescue him from the hell awaiting him because of his rebellion, so that, in the words of the Wise Woman of Teko'a, "even the rejected shall not be rejected from Him" (II Sam. 14:14). Thus, David begged his generals to go easy with Absalom if they found him (v 5).

"…And the war was in the Forest of Ephraim" (v 6). Rashi (ad loc.) asks, "How come Ephraim had a forest on the east bank of the Jordan when the only tribes who received a share there were Gad, Reuven and Menasheh? The answer is that one of the conditions on which Joshua gave the tribes their portions in the Land was that anyone from any tribe could graze their flocks in any forest. The forest in question was near to the territories of Ephraim except that it was on the other side of the river Jordan, and they used to graze their animals there, which is why it was called the Forest of Ephraim."

From the description of the forces gathered on both sides, we can build a picture of the magnitude of this civil war between David and his supporters on the one hand and Absalom and all Israel, including Judah, on the other. As Absalom's commander-in-chief to replace Joab (who was with David), he had appointed Amasa, who was married to David's **own sister** (ch 17 v 25, where Nachash=Yishai/Jesse, who was so called because he was one of the four who died not because of sin but purely because of the "bite of the serpent": Nachash="serpent", Talmud Bava Batra 17a).

Despite Absalom's impressive line-up of all Israel and the leaders of Judah, God was against him and his forces were ravaged by the wild animals of the forest (Targum on v 8).

One of the most famous scenes in the Bible is the specter of the mule-riding Absalom getting his Nazarite's long hair hopelessly entangled in the branches of a great tree, leaving him "suspended between heaven and earth as the mule passed on from under him" (v 9). Had Absalom taken his sword to cut his hair, he might have escaped, but only at the cost of violating his Nazirite vow. The rabbis stated that he drew his sword and saw Gehennom open underneath him! (Sotah 10b brought by Rashi on v 9). The very hair about which Absalom had been so vain now proved to be his undoing! (RaDaK on v 9)

David - the distraught, loving father - had pleaded with his generals to go easy on his rebel son, but Joab had no patience for the aged king and his illusions that Absalom might somehow be rehabilitated. Joab knew that Absalom would be a terrible danger to David as long as he was alive. When the soldier who found Absalom refused to kill him, Joab himself went and drove three stakes into his heart (in revenge for Absalom's having stolen the hearts of David, the Law Court and all Israel) while Joab's ten attendants (corresponding to the ten concubines of David whom Absalom went into) finally put him to death.

Yad Avshalom - the Monument of Absalom mentioned in v 18 -- is identified with the famous, impressive and much-photographed carved stone monument that can be seen in the Kidron valley until today.

The news of Absalom's death, which spelled the end of the rebellion, had to be taken to David, but Joab knew that he would take it very hard, and in trying to dissuade the swift-footed priest Achima'atz from going to tell the king (vv 19-23), Joab teaches that one should avoid telling bad news and always strive to relay good news.

CHAPTER 19

"And the king raged..." (v 1). David was beside himself with grief over the loss of Absalom, whom he still loved in spite of everything. The rabbis state that with the first seven of his eight repetitions of "My son, my son" (verses 1 & 5), David elevated Absalom's soul from all seven levels of hell, and with the eighth, he brought him to the life of the world to come (Sotah 10b brought by Rashi on v 1).

David's grief put a complete damper on the joy that should have accompanied his restoration to the kingship, and when the people returned to Machanayim from the battlefield, they slunk back into the city feeling like exposed thieves.

Joab, who had borne the main brunt of the actual battle against Absalom, had no patience for David's orgy of grief over a son who had not only rebelled against him but had almost killed him. Joab berated the king for "loving your enemies and hating those who love you" (v 7). Joab threatened David with a far worse rebellion if he refused to pull out of his mourning and pacify the people. David acceded and held his peace against his ever-more assertive commander-in-chief, but already had in mind to replace him and immediately prior to his own death ordered Solomon to take vengeance on Joab (I Kings 2:5-16).

With the collapse of Absalom's rebellion, the tribes of Israel and the tribe of Judah - neither of which had exactly given their support to David - now began bickering over who should have the honor of restoring him to the kingship. The people were returning to their senses, realizing that David had been the national savior while Absalom had contributed nothing and was now dead (v 10). Nevertheless, as we will soon see, these new-found feelings of loyalty to David were to prove short-lived, showing the people's great fickleness.

David sent Tzadok and Eviatar, (who had been serving as High Priests concurrently after Eviatar's failure to elicit an answer from the Urim Ve-Tumim) to sue for reconciliation with his own tribe of Judah after their having gone after Absalom. True to character, David particularly sought reconciliation with Amasa, despite his having served Absalom as commander-in-chief (ch 17 v 25). David now wanted to appoint him as his own commander-in-chief in place of Joab.

As the tribe of Judah accompanied David back across the Jordan into the Land of Israel proper, he was greeted with a succession of delegations. First came Shimi ben Gera, the Benjaminite who had cursed and stoned David on his flight from Jerusalem (ch 16 vv 5ff) and who now wanted to apologize in order to save his own skin. Joab's brother Avishai wanted to kill Shimi ben Gera, but once again David dissociated himself from the "trigger-happy" sons of Tzeruyah and forgave Shimi - though he later instructed Solomon to take vengeance on him (I Kings 2:8-9). The Midrash states that David saved Shimi because he saw with holy spirit that Mordechai was destined to come forth from Shimi's loins and save Israel from extermination. From Esther 2:5 we see that Mordechai was descended from Shimi! (Yalkut Shimoni).

Following Shimi came Tzeeva, the servant of the House of Saul whom David had appointed executor/manager of Saul's estates for the benefit of his grandson Mephiboshet, and who had slandered Mephiboshet to David claiming that he failed to join David in his flight because he was hoping to seize the throne for himself (ch 16 vv 1-4). The lame Mephiboshet now came to greet David literally disheveled because of his consternation over David's plight, and claiming that Tzeeva had deceived him. When David ordered that the estate be divided between Tzeeva and Mephiboshet, a heavenly voice declared that his own kingdom would therefore be torn apart and divided between his grandson Rehaboam and the rebel king of the Ten Tribes, Jeraboam (Talmud Yoma 22b).

Barzilai the Gil'adite who escorted David across the Jordan had no need to make any apologies to David, having been one of his chief supporters when he fled to Machanayim (ch 14 v 27). Yet when David invited Barzilai to accompany him back to Jerusalem and live in the court, Barzilai argued that he was too old to enjoy the life of the court because he no longer felt any taste in his food and couldn't hear the singing properly. The Talmud cites Barzilai as the exemplar of senility but states that senility jumped on him prematurely owing to excessive self-indulgence (he mentioned the female singers) yet is not inevitable in old age, citing the case of an old maid in the house of R. Judah the Prince who even at the age of 92 still regularly checked the taste of the food as it cooked in the pot (Talmud Shabbat 152a).

Having crossed the Jordan into the Land of Israel proper, David arrived in Gilgal, where arguments broke out between the men of Israel (the Ten Tribes) and the men of Judah over whether the latter had been justified in being the first to escort David back. Considering that neither side had given David their support against Absalom, their arguments seem somewhat fatuous: each side was hurt and ruffled over being upstaged by the other, and the Israelites' protestations of loyalty to David soon proved disingenuous when they angrily went after Sheva ben Bichri instead, as narrated immediately afterwards.

CHAPTER 20

"And all the men of Israel went up from going after David and went after Sheva ben Bichri" (v 2). Although the rebellion of Sheva ben Bichri, who was a relative of King Saul, takes up far less of the narrative than that of Absalom, David considered it to be potentially far more serious (v 6).

There is some evidence of cracks in the unity of David's supporters. Having sent his new candidate for commander-in-chief, Amasa, to muster the tribe of Judah, David soon discovered that Amasa had no intention of rushing into action because he failed to bring troops within the three-day time-limit he had been given. David immediately dispatched Joab's brother Avishai against Sheva ben Bichri. Joab saw this as a further step towards his own displacement and personally went out with the troops after the rebels, intending to take matters into his own hands. Meeting the unsuspecting Amasa on the way, Joab once again demonstrated his "trigger-happy" attitudes and killed him in vengeance for his having supported Absalom and in order to secure his own position.

With David's men in pursuit, Sheva ben Bichri advanced towards the north of Israel, arousing all the tribes against David as he went. The town of Aveil Beit Ma'achah where Joab caught up with him (v 14) is near the northern border of present-day Israel between Metullah and Kfar Giladi, while the "Beirim" whom he recruited to his cause (ibid.) are thought to have lived in the town of Biryiah immediately north of Safed.

THE WISE WOMAN OF AVEIL BEIT MA'ACHAH

Once again, a mysterious wise woman suddenly appeared just in time to save Israel from needless bloodshed by calling to Joab from the walls of Aveil Beit Ma'achah as he laid siege to the town in order to capture Sheva ben Bichri. The sages identified this wise woman with Serah, daughter of Asher the son of Jacob, who is credited with having sung to Jacob that Joseph was still alive and with having helped Moses discover where Joseph's coffin had been hidden in the Nile when the time came to take it up out of Egypt. Serah, daughter of Asher was among those who entered the Land with Joshua, and would now have been very many hundreds of years old. Those who find their belief being stretched beyond limits may rationalize that the ancient **spirit** of the wise Serah spoke through the lips of the mysterious wise woman of Aveil Beit Ma'achah. "**Anokhi sh'loomey emooney Yisrael**" - "I am from among the complete believers of Israel" (v 19). This woman was the inner soul of the long-suffering people, appealing to Joab for an end to the cycle of bloodshed. She wanted him to understand that the inhabitants of the town harbored no traitorous feelings against David. In her words to Joab in v 18 - "Let them surely ask in Aveil and they would certainly make peace" - she alluded to the Torah law that when an Israelite army makes war against a gentile city, they should first offer them peace (Deut. 20:10). How much more so, then, should Joab invite the Israelite inhabitants of Aveil to make peace!

The wise woman persuaded the inhabitants to deliver Sheva ben Bichri to Joab because otherwise the entire town would be killed. Normally if someone threatens to kill all the members of a group unless they hand over one of their number, it is forbidden to do so, because "we do not cast off one soul in order to save another". However, "if the designated individual deserves the death penalty like Sheva ben Bichri, they should give him over, though we do not issue such a ruling from the outset. However, if he does not deserve the death penalty they should all die rather than hand over a single Israelite soul" (Rambam, Yesodei HaTorah 5:5).

With the delivery of Sheva ben Bichri's head to Joab, the revolt was at an end and now that David's kingship was reestablished, our text concludes by enumerating his principal officers.

CHAPTER 21

Our present chapter is highly opaque allegory which can be unraveled only partially with the help of the Midrash of the Rabbis.

"And there was famine in the days of David for three years..." (v 1). As the narrative draws towards the conclusion of the history of David, it shows how he settled all outstanding accounts in his lifetime. David understood that the cause of the famine lay in some national moral flaw and sought out God to show him what it was.

According to the rabbinic interpretation of v 1 as brought by Rashi, the flaw related to Saul but had two somewhat different sides to it. On the one hand, Saul had never been properly buried and eulogized because of the national panic that followed his defeat by the Philistines. This was a flaw in the honor due to the kingship. On the other hand, Saul himself had caused a flaw through his "killing" of the Gibeonites. The Gibeonites were the Canaanite inhabitants of the town of Gibeon, who had tricked Joshua and the princes of the Tribes into making an oath to protect them even though they were forbidden to make a covenant with the Canaanites (Joshua ch 9). On discovering the trick, Joshua turned the Gibeonites into a caste of Temple wood-hewers and water-drawers, but he was unable to nullify the oath of protection because of the desecration of God's Name that would be caused by Israel's failure to keep an oath even if extracted by trickery.

Some rabbis held that when Saul slaughtered the Kohanim (priests) of Nov for aiding David (I Samuel ch 22), this cut off the livelihood they provided to the Gibeonites, which was considered tantamount to killing them. Other rabbis held that during the massacre in Nov, Saul actually did kill two Gibeonite hewers of wood, two drawers of water, an attendant, a manager and a scribe (Rashi on v 1). Either way, this was considered a breach of Israel's oath of protection of the Gibeonites, and now the Gibeonites demanded justice. They were in the position of **Go'el Ha-Dam** ("redeemer of the blood") of their fallen compatriots - and they were implacable. They demanded to be given seven members of Saul's household to kill in vengeance for the seven dead Gibeonites, and because of their cruel insistence, verse 2 says that "the Gibeonites were not from the Children of Israel" - implying that they lacked the three defining characteristics of Israel: compassion, bashfulness and kindness (Talmud Yevamot 79a).

David agreed to give over seven members of Saul's house in order that justice should not only be done but should also be seen to have been done. Although our text states that five of the seven were the sons of Michal, Saul's younger daughter, our rabbis taught that they were actually the sons of his older daughter Meirav, since it was she and not Michal who was married to Adri-el (v 8, see I Samuel 18:19). However, since Michal foster-mothered these children after the death of Meirav, they were accounted as Michal's children, teaching the great merit of fostering orphans (Talmud Sanhedrin 19b).

The Torah forbids leaving the bodies of hanged criminals overnight, let alone for six months (Deut. 21:23), but in this case a great **Kiddush HaShem** ("Sanctification of God's Name") came about when gentile passers-by saw the bodies and asked why they were there. When they were told that they had been hanged to make amends for Saul's breach of the Israelite covenant with the Gibeonites, the gentiles were so impressed by the Israelite respect for their oath that 150,000 converted (1 Kings 5:29, Talmud Yevamot 79a).

Through the righteousness of Saul's concubine Ritzpah daughter of Ayah in camping out by the bodies and driving away the predatory vultures, the bodies were preserved intact for over six months from the time of the barley harvest (Nissan) until the rains came (Cheshvan). The downfall of rain after three years of famine showed that the flaw had been rectified (Metzudat David on v 10), and the bones of the seven members of Saul's house were taken for burial together with the bones of Saul and Jonathan. The state funeral that was now held for the latter rectified the affront to their honor in not having been properly buried and mourned immediately after their death on the battlefield.

We may thus infer that although Saul fell because he failed to extirpate Amalek, this did not make him a "bad" king. On the contrary, Saul had been an outstanding Tzaddik, a mighty warrior and a savior of his people, and the establishment of David's kingship was only complete when the proper respect was shown to Saul and any remaining flaws were rectified. As for the Gibeonites, while Joshua had banned them from marrying into the Assembly of Israel only when the Temple stood, David added to the ban and forbade them to marry into the Assembly even when there was no Temple (RaDaK on v 1). Because of their display of cruelty, they were thus permanently excluded from the Assembly of Israel.

"And there was more war with the Philistines…" (v 15). "And it was afterwards that there was more war in Gov with the Philistines…" (v 18). "There is no before and afterwards in the Torah": these wars with the Philistines had taken place earlier in David's reign (Rashi on v 18) and are mentioned here in order to complete the story of the killing of the four giant sons of "Harafa" (="the giantess"), whom the rabbis identified with Orpah, daughter-in-law of Naomi and sister-in-law of David's great-grandmother, Ruth (Talmud Sotah 42b; see commentary on I Samuel ch 17). These four giants allude to impure kelipot ("husks") which Mashiach has to crush.

"…and David was faint. And Yishbi in Nov..." (vv 15-16). Some rabbis said that the actual name of this giant was Yishbi BeNov, while others said that David had to face Yishbi **because of Nov** - i.e. because he himself had been responsible for Saul's slaughter of the priests of Nov since he had fled to the Sanctuary there, causing the priests to be accused of treason. The Talmud (Sanhedrin 95) has a lengthy and very colorful aggadah about David's mysterious encounter with Yishbi, in which he was very nearly killed. Through a kind of telepathic message, Avishai realized that David was in extreme danger and went rushing off to save him. On the way, he succeeded in killing Orpah, which devastated Yisbhi, and Avishai then rescued David through the invocation of God's name.

Although verse 19 attributes the killing of Goliath to "Elchanan ben Ya'arei Orgim", the Rabbis identify the latter with David himself, who was said to be "son of the forests of the weavers" because his family wove curtains for the Temple, which is called a "forest" (Rashi on v 19). Since we know from I Samuel ch 17 that it was David who killed Goliath, the use of another name for him in our present passage is an indication that cryptic verses such as this were included in the text for the sake of the midrashic teachings that derive from them.

CHAPTER 22

"And David spoke the words of this song on the day God saved him from the hand of all his enemies and from the hand of Saul" (v 1). David had enemies all around him throughout his life, but none of them was more formidable than Saul, because of his very saintliness. Nevertheless, God saved David from all his enemies, and at the end of his days he sang this paean of praise over his complete delivery.

Our present text is virtually identical with Psalm 18 except for a number of very minor differences in phraseology. This is the song of the soul of Mashiach, which endures the most terrible protracted danger and darkness, being subjected to the breaking waves of death itself and the terrifying floods of wickedness (v 5). Nevertheless, God is his "rock, fortress, refuge, mountain, shield, horn of salvation, high place, place of succor and savior from **hamas**" (v 3) [**hamas**=violent injustice, as in the case of present-day **Hamas**]. David fortifies himself with expression after expression signifying his unshakable faith in the rock-solid saving power of God.

Out of his pain, Mashiach **cries out** to God, and God **hears** and **responds**. All of the elements of creation surge forth to protect Mashiach: the **earth** rages and foams with volcanic fury (v 8). The skies rage with smoke and **fire** (v 9). God rides and swoops on the wings of the **wind=air** (v 11) and swathes Himself with thick clouds of **water** (v 12). All creation fights on behalf of the soul of Mashiach, for whom the very Red Sea had split (v 16, see Rashi).

David testifies that God saved him because of his great purity and righteousness. He has the attributes of the three patriarchs, Abraham, Isaac and Jacob, who are alluded to in verse 26. God himself teaches David how to fight and conquer all his enemies. This is because "I hate those who hate You" (Psalms 139:21). David hated falsehood and loved God's Torah (Psalms 119:163). It is this that brings David victory until all the world will come to serve him - for to serve Mashiach is to work for the glory of God.

This song is David's, but it is said for every one of us, giving expression to the Messianic "point" contained within each one of us, which prompts us to pursue justice and righteousness for the sake of God and for the repair of the entire world.

* * * II Samuel 22:1-54 is read as the Haftarah of Parshat **Ha'azinu**, Deuteronomy 32:1-52, and also as the Haftarah on the Seventh Day of Pesach * * *

CHAPTER 23

"AND THESE ARE THE LAST WORDS OF DAVID..." (v 1)

This verse is rendered by the Targum as: "These are the words of the prophecy of David that he prophesied about the end of the world and the days of comfort that are destined to come." David testified that his words came not through his own wisdom and intelligence but through "prophecy" - holy spirit. This final prophecy of David (vv 1-7) is very dense and highly allusive. In effect, it is David's own self-composed "epitaph" summarizing his status and achievements. In the same breath, he calls himself "David son of Yishai" and "the anointed one of the God of Jacob" (v 1), as if to say that prophecy never left him from the time that he was David the lowly shepherd until he became God's anointed Mashiach (Metzudat David).

"Says the man that was raised up (**hookam'al**)" (v 1). The Talmud darshens that David raised (**heikim**) the yoke (**'ol**) of repentance, because having repented even after his serious sin with Batsheva, he showed the wicked that anyone can repent no matter how serious his sins (Avodah Zarah 5a, Yalkut Shimoni). The word **'al** in the verse has the numerical value of 100 (Ayin 70 + Lamed 30), corresponding to David's institution of the requirement to recite 100 blessings every day. (These include all the daily morning blessings, the blessings over Psukey DeZimra and over the morning and evening

Shema, the thrice-repeated Shmonah Esray, the blessings before and after eating, etc.) David instituted these blessings in order to rectify the ignorance of the people of his generation about the Temple that had to be built (Bamidbar Rabbah 18) - for the Temple is "built" out of prayers and blessings. This ignorance was the root cause of the terrible plague described in the next chapter. David's whole concern was to prepare for the Temple, and he merited being the "sweet singer of Israel" (v 1): it was the songs of David that were sung ever after in the Temple services.

As ruler over his people, David was unique, because the purpose of his rule was to instill in everyone the fear of God (v 2). God made an eternal Covenant with David because David based his own life and that of his household only upon the Torah (Rashi on v 3).

"THESE ARE THE NAMES OF THE MIGHTY WARRIORS OF DAVID..." (v 8)

Our text's registry of David's mighty warriors and some of their outstanding exploits is also extremely dense and highly allusive. These were not merely sword-wielding fighters in the literal sense: they were mighty warriors of the Torah, forerunners of the Tannaim and Amoraim of the Mishnah and Talmud. Verse 8 which speaks of "Adino Ha-Etzni" is interpreted as alluding to David himself, who would sit with the utmost wisdom in the Sanhedrin and was **Rosh HaShaloshi** (lit.="leader of the three") in the sense that he was first in beauty, wisdom and might (Rashi) as well as being head of the chain (**shalshelet**) of the three patriarchs (RaDaK), i.e. David is the fourth "leg" of the throne. The name Adino Ha-Etzni alludes to the way David would "delight himself" (**me-aden**) like a worm whilst studying the Torah yet harden himself like a mighty tree (**etz**) when going out to fight in war.

The leading mighty warriors of David are listed in sets of three. In verses 9, 13, 18, 19, 22, 23 and 24, the words **sheloshah** (=3), **sheloshim** (=30) and **Shalishim** (="captains", as in Ex. 15:4) keep recurring. While "the text does not depart from its simple meaning", the arrangement of David's warriors in sets of three also alludes to the way in which the attribute of Malchut, the "receiving vessel", is built through receiving a balance of the influence descending to it from the hierarchy of triads of attributes above it.

The mysterious exploits of Shamah ben Ogei in the field full of lentils (v 11) are midrashically connected with the three captains who came to David during his wars against the Philistines and who, in response to his craving for water from the wells of Bethlehem, risked their lives to bring him the water despite the presence of the Philistine garrisons there. The midrash teaches that what David wanted was Torah (=water) from the Torah wellsprings at the gate (=Sanhedrin) of Bethlehem. The Philistines were hiding behind sheaves of lentils in the field, and David wanted to know if he was permitted to destroy sheaves that belonged to Israelites in order to "flush out" the enemy. Even though, as king, he was permitted to do so without asking, "he did not want to drink from the waters" - he did not want to have any benefit from his fellow Israelites if there was even a question about its legality (see RaDaK on v 16).

Benayah son of Yehoyadah (v 20) was later to become Solomon's commander-in-chief. His smiting of the "two mighty lions of Moab" is explained allegorically to mean that he was so outstanding in Torah wisdom that he had no equal in either the first or second Temples. (Ariel is an allusion to the Temple, which was built through the efforts of David, who was descended from Ruth the Moabite - Berachot 18b).

There is merit in simply reading the names of David's warriors as listed in this chapter, since these were the outstanding Tzaddikim of his generation, who prepared the way for the building of the Temple.

This very mysterious chapter is a fitting climax to the story of David, because it describes the chain of events that led him to discover the site of the Temple, to the preparation for whose building his entire life had been devoted.

Rashi on I Kings 3:7 provides a detailed chronology of the last twelve years of David's life from the birth of Solomon onwards. Solomon had been born immediately prior to Amnon's rape of Tamar, two years after which Absalom held the sheep-shearing celebration at which he had Amnon assassinated. Thereafter, Absalom spent three years in exile in Geshur before returning to Jerusalem for two years before his rebellion. This was followed by the three years of famine that were rectified through the reburial of Saul's bones together with those of his 7 grandchildren slain by the Gibeonites (II Sam. ch 21:1). This was in the tenth year after the birth of Solomon.

It was thus in the eleventh year after Solomon's birth that David ordered his count of the population, while in the twelfth year - which was the last year of David's life - he reorganized the priestly Temple duty-rota, after which he died. (Solomon was 12 years old when he came to the throne.)

David's census was apparently carried out for "military" purposes since the numbers given in verse 9 are of "sword-wielding men", but this also alludes to the "sword" of prayer. It is not clear exactly what David had in mind when he insisted on holding a census despite the fact that the Torah expressly teaches that Israel must not be counted directly in order not to suffer a plague (Exodus 30:12). From David's later contrition for having sinned (v 10) it is clear that he knew very well that it was wrong to count the people. The fact that he was able to persuade himself to do so indicates that he allowed himself to fall prey to some kind of rationalization that justified the census. The mind can play tricks on even the greatest of people. It was evidently through this rationalization which God planted in his mind that He "incited" David to sin (v 1). It is said that He did so in retribution for David's having introduced the same concept when he much earlier said that God had "incited" Saul against him (I Samuel 26:19). The paradox is that despite the fact that the census was a mistake and led to a terrible plague, it did, nevertheless, lead indirectly to David's discovery of the site of the Temple in Jerusalem.

Joab was opposed to the census, arguing eloquently that Israel can be greatly blessed numerically by God without having to count them - Joab's blessings for Israelite population growth are compared favorably with those of Moses (Deut. 1:11). Joab's opposition to the king here is noteworthy since he actually rebelled against him at the very end of David's life one year later. Yet in spite of his reservations, Joab journeyed around the entire Israelite settlement east and west of the River Jordan. From Jerusalem, he crossed over to the east bank of the Jordan and started his mission in the city of Aro'er, the southernmost settlement of the Reubenites. There "he camped" (v 5) - i.e. he took his time, hoping all along that the king would relent. Then he worked his way up northwards through the territories of Gad and Menasheh in Gil'ad, before going up to Dan (in the north of present-day Israel), further north to the "new" settlements in Syria and the **Bik'ah** (valley) of Lebanon, and then westwards to the Mediterranean coast, where he counted the Israelite populations in Sidon, Tyre and all the settlements further south, returning thereafter to Jerusalem. We thus have biblical evidence of Israelite settlements in Syria and Lebanon back in the time of David.

As soon as Joab returned with his report, David was smitten with remorse and contrition for having counted Israel - because Israel are beyond the concept of number, which is finite. Putting a "number" on Israel puts finite limits on the people and their ability to receive blessing. Souls cannot be counted, because each one is totally unique and has infinite potential. Counting the people lays them open to the Evil Eye, which views abundant blessing with mean-eyed hostility.

It was the prophet Gad who brought God's grim decree to David: until the very end of his life, David conducted himself in all his affairs in accordance with the prophets, unlike Saul, who had disobeyed them. Gad offered David three alternatives in order to expiate his sin: seven years of famine, three months of defeat in war or three days of plague. (Similarly, David had said that Saul would die in one of three ways, I Samuel 26:10). In a famous verse that is part of the Tachanun supplications in the daily prayers (v 14), David threw himself upon God's mercy - reasoning that famine would hurt the poor more than the rich and war would hurt the weak more than the mighty, while a plague would strike indiscriminately, thus spreading the suffering more fairly (RaDaK on v 14).

"Through the very wound, God sends the medicine". The plague was mercifully short - less than the three days originally announced by the prophet (v 15, RaDaK), and when David saw the angel with his sword drawn over Jerusalem, he prayed for compassion. According to the midrash on v 16 (**ba'am rav**, lit. "with many people"), the dead included Avishai son of Tzeruyah (Joab's heroic brother): the loss of a sage who was the equivalent of more than half (rov) of the Sanhedrin brought atonement (Berachot 62b). With this, the Angel stopped the slaughter - and David saw that the Angel was standing by the side of the Threshing-floor of Aravnah (RaDaK on v 16). Aravnah was the "Jebusite" Prince of Jerusalem - though not one of the Canaanite Jebusites, but a Philistine descendant of Avimelech in the time of Abraham. According to Metzudat David (v 16), he was a righteous convert.

Since it is prayers in the Temple that save Israel from plagues and other evils, David knew that the site at which he prayed successfully for the cessation of the plague was none other than the location of the Temple, which God had promised He would choose from among the territories of the tribes (Deut. 12:14).

Aravnah was willing to **give** David the site to build his altar together with the ox for the sacrifice and the wood to burn it (v 22) but David protested, "I shall surely **acquire** them from you for a price and I will not offer up to the Lord my God burnt offerings that cost nothing" (v 24). There is a discrepancy between the fifty shekels of **silver** mentioned as the price here and the sum of **six hundred** shekels of **gold** mentioned in I Chronicles 21:25. This is resolved through the fact that David collected fifty golden shekels from each of the twelve tribes to buy the site of the Temple ("from all your tribes" Deut. 12:4; 50 x 12 = 600) while he paid for the ox and wood for his altar with fifty silver shekels (Talmud Zevachim 116b).

Just as Abraham had **purchased** the Cave of Machpelah as the burial place of the patriarchs with **good money**, similarly David purchased the site of the Temple with good money, which means that all those who claim that Hebron and the Temple Mount do not belong to the people of Israel are guilty of blatant slander.

"The rabbis taught that all the thousands who fell from the plague in the days of David, died because they did not demand the building of the Temple. If people who had never had a Temple built or destroyed in their lifetimes fell in the plague because they had failed to demand the Temple, how much more are we, who have already had a Temple and had it destroyed, obligated to demand the rebuilding of the Temple. Therefore, the elders and prophets instituted the planting of prayers three times daily in the mouths of Israel for the return of the Divine Presence and Kingship to Zion and the order of Your service to Jerusalem, Amen" (Radak on v 25).

מלכים

KINGS

Although the Book of Kings is divided for convenience into I Kings and II Kings, it is really all one book spanning a period of over four hundred years from the last days of David and the golden age of Solomon's glory through the split of his kingdom into two and the succeeding eras of decline, revival and further decline leading eventually to the exile of the Ten Tribes, the destruction of the First Temple and the exile of the tribes of Judah and Benjamin to Babylon. The simple moral of the Book of Kings is that only through faithful obedience to the Torah of Moses can the people of Israel survive and flourish in their Land.

DAVID'S LAST DAYS

David never had a moment of rest and tranquility from the beginning of his career until the very end of his life, when new troubles broke out with the attempted seizure of the throne by Adoniyahu. Old age had jumped upon David - he was only seventy years old - because of the long series of exhausting wars he endured. The coldness from which he suffered is said to have resulted from his having been chilled by the specter of the sword-wielding angel he had seen in Jerusalem at the time of the plague, while his inability to be warmed even when covered with garments is attributed to his having shown disrespect for clothes when he tore the corner of King Saul's garment (I Chronicles 21:30; Talmud Berachot 62b). David's "coldness" also signifies his ascent to a supreme level of contemplative understanding, for "Cold of spirit is the man of understanding" (Proverbs 14:27).

Our text attributes Adoniyahu's rebellion to a pedagogical failure by David, who never properly disciplined his handsome, personable son, who went in the ways of Absalom (v 6). David's commander-in-chief Joab supported Adoniyahu's bid for the throne because he knew that David was angry with him for having killed Avner, Amasa and Absalom and would make sure that Solomon took revenge on him if he ever came to the throne. Eviatar the Priest had taken refuge with David when Saul killed the priests of Nov and had served as High Priest thereafter until the time of Absalom's rebellion, when he failed to elicit an answer from the Urim Ve-Tumim and was deposed in favor of Tzadok. Eviatar was from the ill-fated house of Eli the Priest who had been rejected from serving in the Temple that Solomon was to build, and thus Eviatar had an interest in siding with Adoniyahu.

The reason why Nathan the Prophet rather than Gad intervened on behalf of Solomon was because Nathan himself had prophesied to David that Solomon would reign (II Samuel 7:12; I Chronicles 22:9). It is said that when Batsheva's first child from David died, she refused to agree to any further relations with David unless he swore to her that her child would reign - in order to dispel the aura of scandal that surrounded David's marriage with her (II Samuel 12:24; I Kings 1:17).

Batsheva concluded her demand to David to fulfill his oath to her by pointing out that if he failed to assert Solomon's rights to the throne and Adoniyahu reigned, "I and my son Solomon will be **lacking**". The use here of the Hebrew word **chata'im**, which in other contexts is translated as "sinning", throws considerable light on the Torah concept of **cheit**, "sin". The root **chata** is explained by Rashi (on v 21) as "missing the mark", as when an archer misses his target. In other words, if we "sin", we **fall short** of what we could and should have attained.

THE ANOINTMENT OF SOLOMON

God had given the kingship over Israel to David **and his seed** forever, and according to the Torah law of kings, a son who succeeds his father as king is not normally anointed because the kingship is his by inheritance (Talmud Shekalim 16a). However, David saw that it was necessary to have Solomon ceremonially anointed in the presence of the High Priest together with the Urim Ve-Tumim as well as the prophet Nathan and David's new Commander-in-Chief Benayahu ben Yehoyada in order to publicly reject Adoniyahu's counterclaim to the kingship.

Riding on David's own mule was itself a sign that Solomon was king, since nobody but a new king is permitted to use any of the appurtenances of the previous king. (Since a mule is a hybrid of a horse and donkey, it would normally be forbidden to ride on one because of the prohibition of **Kil'ayim**, "forbidden mixed species", but there is a tradition that David's **pered** was a unique animal dating from the six days of creation, Yerushalmi Kil'ayim 8:2). Solomon was anointed with the anointing oil prepared by Moses in the Wilderness. The ceremony took place at the spring of Shilo'ah, which is also called Ha-Gihon from the Hebrew root **gi-ah** meaning "to flow, be drawn", signifying that Solomon's kingship would continue forever. Benayahu was not afraid even in David's presence to bless Solomon that he should be even greater than his father, because Benayahu knew that "a man is not jealous of his son's success" (Rashi on v 37). Thus, David gave over the throne to Solomon in his own lifetime with great joy (compare the opening section of Rabbi Nachman's Story of the Seven Beggars), and Adoniyahu was put under house arrest.

* * * The passage in I Kings vv. 1-31 is read as the
Haftarah Parshat **Chayey Sarah** Gen. 23:1-25:18 * * *

CHAPTER 2

DAVID'S LAST WILL AND TESTAMENT

David called Solomon and reminded him of the inevitability of death: "I am going the way of all the earth..." (v 2). In his final will and testament to his son, David instructed him to follow the essential formula for all Israelite success: to go in the ways of God and guard His statutes and commandments "as written in the Torah of Moses" (v 3).

SETTLING OLD SCORES

Joab had been David's loyal commander-in-chief almost to the very end, staying with him even during the supreme challenge of Absalom's rebellion (though it is said that Joab very nearly went after Absalom). Nevertheless, David was unable to forgive Joab for having assassinated Saul's commander-in-chief Avner precisely when David wanted to bring an end to the civil war with the House of Saul, and also for having killed his own beloved son Absalom contrary to his specific orders as well as assassinating Absalom's commander-in-chief Amasa. Yet despite the fact that Joab had wielded the sword of Judgment even more implacably than David, he was head of the Sanhedrin and a most formidable Torah sage as well as a man of kindness who made his home like a wilderness in that it was constantly open to all the poor people (see Rashi on v 34). Thus, David did not want to wreak vengeance on Joab forever. When he told Solomon, "Do not bring his hoary old age down to She'ol=Hell", what he meant was that Solomon should ensure that Joab would not die a natural death in order that his being killed in this world should atone for him, save him from hell and bring him to the life of the world to come (Rashi on v 6).

While Barzilai the Giladite and his sons had supported David when he fled from Absalom and were to be rewarded, Shimi ben Gera - head of the Sanhedrin and a leading member of the tribe of Benjamin - had come out cursing and stoning David in his flight. His curse is described as **nimretzet** ("extremely strong"): the letters that make up this Hebrew word are the initial letters of all the unpleasant names that Shimi ben Gera called David: **No'ef** ("adulterer"), **Moavi** ("Moabite", i.e. a "sheigitz"),

Rotze'ach ("murderer"), **Tzorer** ("persecutor"), **To'eyva** ("abomination"). David said to Solomon that Shimi is **"with you"** (v 8), because - paradoxically - Shimi, an outstanding Torah sage, was actually Solomon's **teacher** (Talmud Berachot 8a).

ADONIYAHU'S PLOT

It is said that David never had relations with Avishag the Shunemite (I Kings 1:4), and accordingly she was not technically forbidden to Adoniyahu as his father's concubine. Nevertheless, it was seditious of Adoniyahu to ask Batsheva to intercede with her son Solomon to give him Avishag, because "a private individual is forbidden to have any benefit from the scepter of the king". By requesting Avishag, Adoniyahu was plotting to get his foot inside the door of the kingship.

Solomon displayed all the proper **kavod** ("honor") to his mother Batsheva when she innocently went in to put this request to him (v 19). The Midrash states that when Solomon "placed a chair for the mother of the king", this was actually for "the mother of the kingship", i.e. David's great-grandmother Ruth who was still alive (Bava Batra 91b; Rashi on v 19). Yet with all his show of maternal respect, the young Solomon (who was only 12 years old at the time, Rashi on I Kings 3:7) was far from being a tender softie and understood much more clearly than his own mother the real implications of Adoniyahu's little request, sending his commander-in-chief Benayahu to dispatch him as a traitor.

EVIATAR

As indicated in the commentary on the previous chapter, Eviatar the former High Priest was "sent home" by Solomon (v 26) not only because he had joined Adoniyahu's rebellion but also because the time had come to build God's eternal House in Jerusalem, while the line of priests descending from Eli (who traced their lineage to Aaron's fourth son Itamar), had because of their corruption been deposed from serving in the Temple in favor of the priests who came from the line of Aaron's third son, Elazar, and his son Pinchas.

JOAB'S FLIGHT TO THE ALTAR

On hearing the reports of how Solomon was settling scores with those who had fallen foul of his father David, Joab fled to the Sanctuary Altar, whose power to give succor to unwitting killers is learned from the verse in Exodus 21:14: "When a man intentionally plots against his neighbor to kill him craftily, even from My altar shall you take him to die". This verse indicates that the Altar has the same power as the Cities of Refuge to give succor to unwitting killers.

Joab's killing of Avner, Amasa and Absalom had in fact been intentional and Solomon would have been permitted to have him taken from the Altar and killed. The rabbis discussed at length what Joab had to gain from being killed at the Altar rather than being executed after due trial as a traitor. They answered that while those executed by the court are buried in a special "criminals" section of the cemetery, by being killed at the Altar, Joab could be buried in his family plot together with his ancestors. Although the text states that he was buried in his home "in the wilderness", it would be ridiculous to take this literally, and the phrase is darshened as explained above - that Joab's house was open to the poor like a wilderness - and also as indicating that after his death Israel was left like a barren wilderness (RaDaK on v 34).

By putting Shimi ben Gera under permanent house arrest and making him swear to remain there, Solomon craftily contrived to ensure that Shimi would be responsible for his own death when circumstances would arise - as they surely would - to induce him to leave his home. Despite Solomon's having sent Benayahu to perform yet another in his series of bloody executions of David's foes, the text states that "the kingship was established in the hand of Solomon" (v 46) in order to indicate that he was not punished for this and that his kingship was ordained by God.

* * * I Kings 2:1-12 is read as the Haftarah of **Parshat Vayechi**, Genesis 47:28-50:26 * * *

CHAPTER 3

SOLOMON'S MARRIAGE TO PHARAOH'S DAUGHTER

Our chapter opens with the very surprising news that Solomon married the daughter of the king of the very nation that had ignominiously enslaved and been forced to release Israel hundreds of years earlier. Rashi (on v 3) notes that the verses in this chapter are not in historical sequence, for Solomon's dream in Giv'on (vv 5ff) took place at the very beginning of his reign, whereas it was not until three years afterwards that he made his marriage alliance with Pharoah. This was directly after the death of Solomon's teacher, Shimi ben Gera (narrated out of sequence at the end of the preceding chapter in order to complete the account of Solomon's settling David's outstanding scores). From the proximity of verse 1 of our present chapter to the last verses of the previous chapter, our rabbis taught that as long as his teacher was alive, Solomon did not make this questionable move of intermarriage, deducing that a person should always live close to his teacher in order to stay on the right track (Rashi on v 1).

Solomon's move was questionable because the Torah states that "you shall not intermarry with them [i.e. the other nations]" (Deut. 7:3). Some rabbis held that intermarriage would only be forbidden if the non-Israelite party to the marriage does not convert, but others held that converting them in order to marry is also forbidden. Another factor raising questions about Solomon's move is the tradition that no converts were accepted in the times of David and Solomon because the prestige of Israel was so great that potential converts would all have had ulterior motives. However, the Talmud explicitly states that this did not apply to the daughter of Pharaoh, who had enough wealth not to need to marry Solomon for money (Talmud Yevamot 76a).

A further question is how Solomon could have converted and then married an Egyptian woman when the Torah states that an Egyptian convert may not enter the Assembly until the third generation (Deut. 23:9). However, this objection is countered by a tradition (not accepted halachically) that the referenced verse applies only to an Egyptian male but not to a female (which would make the law of the Egyptian parallel to the law forbidding a Moabite but not a Moabitess from ever entering the Assembly.

Despite the many questions that surround it, we do not find Solomon's marriage to Pharaoh's daughter criticized in our text as being intrinsically sinful: verse 3 **does** implicitly criticize Solomon for sacrificing at many high altars but does **not** criticize him for marrying Pharaoh's daughter. It was only in his old age, when Solomon took many wives, that he was criticized for allowing them to turn his heart aside from God.

It stands to reason that the exact intent of the supremely wise Solomon in marrying the daughter of Israel's former persecutors would be beyond the ability of simple people like ourselves to grasp. Since **Pharaoh** represents the **oreph** ("back of the neck", same Hebrew letters as Pharaoh) of creation as opposed to its inner face, the conversion of his daughter by Solomon and her integration into the holy edifice that he was building was a "coup" similar to the conversion of Batya, the daughter of Pharaoh who drew Moses out of the water. The "daughter of Pharaoh" represents the source of all the different kinds of worldly wisdom (which are her "handmaidens"). By "converting" and "marrying" her, Solomon was perhaps very daringly and ambitiously striving to deepen and enhance the revelation of

God's unity on all levels of creation. If so, it was apparently still over-ambitious, because Solomon proved unable to hold his "catch" within the bounds of holiness, and indeed he himself strayed beyond them. In retribution, said the rabbis, at the very moment when Solomon married Pharaoh's daughter, the angel Gabriel (**Gevurah**, "might", withholding and concealing) descended and drove the first stake into the sea in the very place where more and more sediment eventually collected to form the foundation of what was to become Israel's nemesis: the city of Rome (Talmud Shabbat 56b).

"AND SOLOMON LOVED GOD..." (v 3)

Prior to his heart-enticing marriages with foreign women, Solomon passionately followed the Torah of his father David. If he was criticized, it was only for "sacrificing in the high places". This was actually permitted as long as the Temple was not built in Jerusalem. Since the sacking of the Sanctuary of Shilo by the Philistines in the time of Eli and the slaughter of the priests of Nov by Saul, the Sanctuary with the vessels of Moses had been in Giv'on, except for the Ark of the Covenant, which David had taken to Jerusalem. Whereas David had sacrificed only at the "great" Altar in Giv'on (this was the copper Altar made by Moses) or at an altar that he erected before the Ark in Jerusalem, Solomon also sacrificed in other high places (until the building of the Temple), and while this was still permitted, it was seen as a deviation from David's path and as needlessly delaying the building of the Temple in Jerusalem (Rashi and RaDaK on v 3).

THE WISDOM OF SOLOMON

Whereas David's kingship was founded on the sword of prayer and faith - he had to fight throughout his life - Solomon's kingship was founded on the very **wisdom** and **understanding** which he had the good sense to request when God offered him anything he wanted. At the tender age of 12 (Rashi and RaDaK on v 7), when many intelligent youngsters tend to be highly arrogant, the wise young King Solomon had the humility to understand he would need divine help in judging the busy, quarrelsome Israelites - for kingship (**Malchut**) is founded on Judgment (**Mishpat=Tiferet**, the center column, balance) and the repair of Judgment depends upon **Binah**, "understanding". Solomon thus asked God to "give Your servant a **listening** heart" (v 9) in order to **hear** and **understand**, while God responded even more generously by giving him a heart that was **wise** as well as **understanding** (v 12). **Chokhmah**, "wisdom", is the ability to grasp, know and remember what one learns, while **Binah**, "understanding", is the ability to **analyze** what one knows in order to make new inferences, "understanding one thing from another" (RaDaK on v 12).

When Solomon awoke from his dream he knew that his request had been granted, because "he heard a bird chirping and understood its language, and he heard a dog barking and he understood what it was saying" (Rashi on v 15).

COT DEATH: WHOSE IS THE LIVING CHILD?

Solomon's first dramatic demonstration of his divinely-granted powers of judgment came with the arrival of the two "whores" who were quarreling about which of their two babies died and to whom the surviving child belonged.

The Talmudic teacher Rav held that these two "whores" were actually spirits. Rabbi Simon in the name of R. Yehoshua ben Levi said they were literally prostitutes. A third opinion, offered by unnamed sages, is that they were actually a mother-in-law and her daughter-in-law (Shir HaShirim Rabbah 1:10).

This third opinion immeasurably sharpens the dispute between them on the assumption that the aggrieved mother who started pleading before the king saying that she had been the first to give birth (vv 17-18) was the mother-in-law. If the second woman - her daughter-in-law, who gave birth three days later - lost her husband **after** the birth of her mother-in-law's baby and subsequently lost her own baby (an only child), it would mean that according to the law of the levirate marriage she would have to marry her mother-in-law's baby, the brother of her dead husband, her **Yavam**, since with the death of her own baby her dead husband left no living issue. In any event she would have to wait thirteen years until her mother-in-law's baby became a legal adult in order to either carry out the mitzvah of **Yibum** by marrying his dead brother's widow or release her from their bond through **Chalitzah**, "removal of the brother-in-law's sandal" (see Deut. 25:5ff).

Having to wait for thirteen years as a stranded **Agunah** before she could regularize her status would give the daughter-in-law a very strong incentive to take her mother-in-law's baby as her own, because if she could make it appear that her dead husband did have surviving issue this would release her from the bond of **Yibum** with any of his brothers. Likewise, it would not bother her in the least if the king sliced the living child in half, because if he was indeed the sole surviving brother of her dead husband, his death would automatically release her from any bond of **Yibum** in the absence of any **Yavam**, leaving her free to marry anyone she wanted.

Before Solomon delivered his judgment, he first made sure to repeat the claims of each woman in his own words (v 23) to make it clear that he had understood exactly what they were saying. In this he provided a model for every good **Dayan** ("judge"), who must review the claims made by the rival claimants before delivering judgment.

Solomon's brilliant bluff ordering a sword to be brought immediately elicited the natural motherly compassion of the true mother and exposed the lying baby-thief for what she was. "And all Israel heard the judgment that the king decided and they were in awe before the king, for they saw that the wisdom of God was in him to do judgment" (v 28).

> * * * The passage in I Kings 3:15-28 and 4:1 is read as the Haftarah of Parshat **Miketz**,
> Genesis 41:1-44:17 unless this parshah is read on Shabbat Chanukah * * *

CHAPTER 4

"AND SOLOMON WAS KING OVER ALL ISRAEL" (v 1)

David had been king over Judah in Hebron before he was accepted as king over all Israel. It is a tribute to David's lifelong struggle that the entire nation was now able to unite in accepting one king. They did so because they saw Solomon's divinely-bestowed wisdom, and everyone rejoiced in his kingship (Rashi on v 1).

Listed first and foremost among Solomon's officers is the Priest - because the entire national agenda was now focused on building a functioning Temple. Solomon had scribes to write down his governmental decisions and dispatch them for execution; he had a **Mazkir** (lit. "one who makes you remember") i.e. a "secretary" to make records of events and archive them. Like Saul and David, Solomon had his commander-in-chief. Listed among his officers is also "the king's friend" - presumably one who was likewise very wise indeed and with whom Solomon doubtless loved to fathom the depths of wisdom.

THE TWELVE PROVIDING OFFICERS

Solomon's kingship is portrayed as a model of good order, in which twelve **Netzivim**, "appointed officers", were in charge of collecting all the provisions, materials and other needs of the royal household and army from twelve regions into which the Land of Israel was divided. These regions did **not** correspond to the territorial portions of the Twelve Tribes, which were uneven both in area and in the kind of land they comprised. Rather, these twelve regions represented a fair division of the entire land into portions each one of which could sustain the royal household for one of the twelve months of the year (Radak on v 8).

The twelve months of the year correspond to the twelve possible permutations of the holy "essential" name of God, "HaVaYaH" (YKVK). These are discussed at length in **Sefer Yetzirah**, the earliest kabbalistic text, attributed to our father Abraham. This was certainly known to Solomon (whose Proverbs contain certain allusions to the wisdom of Sefer Yetzirah).

Just as the "sun" of the Name of HaVaYaH (=Zeir Anpin) shines month by month with different permutations to the "moon" of **Malchut**, "kingship" (=Nukva), so King Solomon (**Malchut**, the receiving vessel of Zeir Anpin=Chochmah) received his **parnassah** ("livelihood") from **twelve** different regions of Eretz Israel, which itself corresponds to the Partzuf of Malchut.

"Judah and Israel multiplied like the sand of the sea in multitude, eating and drinking and rejoicing" (v 20). "In the time of Solomon, they were blessed with the fruit of the womb and they multiplied, as did the fruits of their animals and their land, and they ate and drank and rejoiced, for they had no fear of any enemy" (RaDaK on v 20).

May a new golden age even greater than that of Solomon speedily be inaugurated by the building of the Holy Temple that we now await!

CHAPTER 5

SOLOMON'S EMPIRE

Abraham had been a truly international figure, having traveled throughout the "Fertile Crescent" from Babylon to Aram Naharayim, throughout the Land of Israel and down into Egypt. Jacob too traveled to Aram and to Egypt. However, since the time of the entry of the Israelites into their Land, their main preoccupation had been to battle against their immediate neighbors - the Canaanites, Philistines, Moabites and Ammonites - in order to maintain their hold over the Promised Land.

It was through the victories of David over all Israel's enemies that an entirely new international vista opened up in the time of Solomon, whose "empire" or "sphere of influence" extended over the entire swathe of territory promised to Abraham "from the river of Egypt to the Great river, the Euphrates" (Genesis 15:18; cf. I Kings 5:1 & 3).

Our text evokes Solomon's opulent royal lifestyle (vv 2-3) including his ownership of multiple thousands of horses (v 6), which despite being prohibited to the king by the Torah (Deut. 17:16) remain a mark of royalty until today. While the various nations that comprised Solomon's empire paid taxes and gifts, this was not an exploitative colonial empire or one that kept its grip through military force alone. For "he had **peace** on all sides around" (v 4) - a situation that modern Israel can only envy, having experienced no peace for a single moment since the inception of the state and for years and years before it.

Our text testifies that the very key to Solomon's influence over this great area of territory as well as over the neighboring foreign powers lay in his unique, God-given **wisdom**, which "exceeded the wisdom of all the children of the east and all the wisdom of Egypt. And he was wiser than every man (**adam**), than Eitan the Ezrachi and Heyman and Khulkol and Darda the sons of Mahol." While the simple explanation is that these last names are those of the leading Levite Temple singers of the time, the Midrash identifies "every man" with **Adam**, Eitan with Abraham, Heyman with Moses, Khulkol with Joseph and Darda with the Generation of the Wilderness (**Dor De'ah**, "generation of **knowledge**), who were "children of forgiveness" (**Mechilah**).

Most of the narrative in the book of Kings portrays Solomon and his achievements from the outside, but his true wisdom shines forth in his surviving literary creations alluded to in verse 12: Proverbs, Song of Songs and Kohelet (=Ecclesiastes). Most translations render **alaphim** and **eleph** in this verse as "thousand(s)", but Rashi relates them to the same root as in **ulpan** meaning "education": the verse thus speaks of three **educational orders** of Proverbs (the expression **Mishley Shlomo** appears three times in the book of Proverbs); these, together with Song of Songs and Kohelet constitute the **five** orders of Solomon's "song". According to the simple meaning of **eleph** as 1,000, Rashi brings the Midrash that Solomon taught three thousand parables on every single verse of the Torah and gave 1,005 explanations of each parable (see Rashi on vv 11-12). "He spoke about the trees from the cedar in Lebanon to the hyssop that comes out of the wall" (before God, the highest and the lowest are equal, Bamidbar Rabbah 13). According to Rashi this verse means that not only did Solomon understand the healing properties of all the different trees and plants and exactly how to cultivate them, but that he also explained why the purification of the leper involves the cedar and the hyssop (Lev. 14:4). "He spoke about the animals and birds and creeping creatures and fish." (v 13): not only did he understand all their different qualities, but also why the **Shechitah** of animals requires the cutting of both the windpipe and the gullet, while that of birds requires the cutting of only one, and why locusts and fish do not require **Shechitah** at all. (Rashi on v 14).

HIRAM, KING OF TYRE

The tragic history of modern Lebanon has overshadowed the one-time greatness of this very beautiful country with its once very extensive forests. While Sidon was established by the firstborn son of Canaan (Gen. 10:15), the city of Tyre to its south was an immensely powerful city state built up by the Phoenicians, whose prosperity was founded on the magnificent tall trees out of which they built the ships they used to develop a trade empire throughout the Mediterranean area and beyond.

While Hiram king of Tyre is a legendary figure (particularly in the lore of freemasonry, where he is seen as the "father" of the Temple), Ibn Ezra (on Genesis 41:10) views Hiram as the generic name of all the kings of Tyre just as Pharaoh was the generic name of all the kings of Egypt. In later Biblical times Tyre saw Jerusalem as a dangerous rival and hoped to benefit from its destruction (cf. Ezekiel 26:2, "I shall be filled from her destruction"), but the Hiram who befriended King David and King Solomon was - from the testimony of our text - a believer in the One God who (unlike the nations of today) **rejoiced** when he heard that Solomon wanted to build Him a Temple in Jerusalem (v 20).

Hiram struck a Covenant with Solomon (v 26) inaugurating the first ever venture in international cooperation to build God's Temple. Hiram provided the timber and stone that were the building materials for the Temple in return for very ample supplies of choice wheat and olive oil that were the specialty of Israel. The lumber was tied up to form rafts that were floated down the Mediterranean from the coast of Lebanon to the point nearest to Jerusalem on the Israeli coast. From there it was transported by land to the site of the Temple. The 70,000 "porters" and 80,000 "excavators" who extracted and transported the massive stones for the Temple were **Gerim Gerurim** - would-be converts who were not admitted into the Assembly of Israel (as no full converts were accepted in the time of Solomon, see commentary on I Kings ch 3) but were nevertheless allowed to participate in the enterprise of building of God's House of Prayer for all the Nations.

CHAPTER 6

The building of the Temple commenced in the fourth year of Solomon's reign, 480 years after the Exodus from Egypt and 440 years after the people's entry into the Land. The actualization of this project to join Heaven and Earth took a total of seven years (vv 37-8).

In his work on the "Secrets of the Future Temple" (Mishkeney Elyon) the outstanding 18th century Kabbalistic sage R. Moshe Chayim Luzzatto (Ramchal) explains that creation has two roots: the "revealed root" of **Chokhmah** ("wisdom") and the "concealed" root of **Keter** ("the crown"). The two roots are alluded to in the first letter of the first word of the Torah, the Beit (=2) of Bereishit, "In the beginning".

"Know too that the sin of Adam spoiled everything and caused all perfection to become concealed, with the result that the world was not even able to return to its previous state [i.e. the level of Wisdom] except in the days of Solomon, when the Temple was first built. Thus it is written: 'And God gave wisdom to Solomon' (I Kings 5:26). For then Wisdom was revealed in all its beauty and radiant glory, enabling all the lights to shine with great strength and joy. In those days, on every level in all the worlds there was only holy power and delight the like of which had never been seen. Even so, because everything was based only on Wisdom and did not reach the ultimate goal [of Keter], this peace and tranquility came to an end and the Temple was destroyed. But in time to come, when the hidden beginning I mentioned [Keter] is revealed, the happiness will be far, far greater, and it will never cease" (Ramchal, Secrets of the Future Temple).

Although Ramchal's work - which explains in detail the "sacred geometry" that underlies the design of the Temple - is primarily concerned with the **Future** Temple as depicted by Ezekiel (chs 40ff), the principles on which it is based apply also to the Temple of Solomon, all of whose chambers, walls, gates and courtyards in all their various dimensions allude to and **embody in stone** the various divine attributes as they relate to one another.

Besides the information about Solomon's Temple contained in our text, we have detailed supplementary information in Masechet **Middot**, the Mishnaic Tractate of "Measurements", which deals with the design of the Second Temple, which was mostly modeled on the first. The rabbinic commentators wrote entire treatises about the structure of the Temple.

The Temple had very distinctive features, such as its windows, which were "wide open from the outside but closed and narrow on the inside" (v 4). This was because the Temple had no need for the light from the outside, since it was lit from within (both by the Candelabra and by the spiritual light that shined in it): on the contrary, light emanated **from** the Temple windows **outwards**.

Another distinctive feature was that as the very center of world peace, the Temple was a place where it was not fitting for the sound of metal hammers and axes to be heard (v 7) since metal is the material of weapons of war. All the stones were cut and dressed outside the Temple, and Solomon also miraculously found the Shamir worm, which would silently eat its way across a stone so as to split it just as it had cut the stones of the gems in the High Priest's breastplate in the days of Moses. (This is not a worm that is easy to find; Sotah 48b, Gittin 68a).

Most distinctive of all was that the survival of the Temple was entirely conditional upon Israel's keeping the Torah, as God promised to Solomon (vv 11-13): "If you go in My statutes and carry out My laws. I shall dwell amongst the Children of Israel and I will not abandon My people Israel."

The main Temple building, a structure of 60 x 20 cubits (on the inside) was divided into two unequal parts: the **Heikhal** (40 x 20) containing the Menorahs (Candelabra) Show-bread Tables and Incense Altar, and within, the Holy of Holies (20 x 20) containing the Ark of the Covenant with the wooden figures of two Cherubs overlaid with gold standing with their wings outstretched over it and filling the entire inner chamber. Across the entire front of the **Heikhal** stood the **Oulam** ("Vestibule").

Around the walls surrounding the Heikhal and Holy of Holies on three sides were a series of cells banked up in three stories one on top of the other. These cells may have been used to store the Temple treasures. Esoterically, they allowed the **Shefa** (divine influence) emanating from within the Temple to be concentrated intensely prior to its flowing outwards to nourish the outside world.

The ceiling and roof of the Temple were made of wood, and its stone walls were entirely paneled with wood from top to bottom. The wood (which alludes to the **Tree** of Life) was carved with the forms of cherubs, palms, garlands and flowers. All the walls and all the carvings were overlaid with gold, as was the ceiling and the floor, the effect of which must have been absolutely stunning.

Through God's providence, we have reached the description of the building of Solomon's Temple. Just as we celebrate the festival of Chanukah in commemoration of God's miracles for Israel in the Second Temple, so too, in the merit of our studies, may He quickly bring peace to our troubled world and speedily build the Temple we are now awaiting, from which the love and fear of God will spread forth to all the world.

*** The passage in I Kings 5:26-32 and 6:1-13 is read as
the Haftarah of Parshat **Terumah**, Exodus 25:1-27:19 ***

CHAPTER 7

The account of the building of the Temple is interrupted briefly at the beginning of our present chapter in order to describe the building of Solomon's royal palace, which took thirteen years. According to most opinions Solomon did not build his own palace until **after** the completion of the Temple, which took only seven years: Solomon displayed commendably greater alacrity in building for God's glory than he did for his own, yet his palace too was clearly very magnificent. The "House of the Forest of Lebanon" (v 2) was a cool, airy, most elegantly proportioned summer house with rows upon rows of windows. It was the many wooden columns that made it seem like a forest [which was perhaps conducive to Hitbodedut]. In the same complex was the king's throne-room where he sat in judgment (v 7) as well as his own private apartments (v 8). From verse 12 we see that the walls of Solomon's palace were built in the same style as those of the Temple (see Metzudat David on this verse), indicating that great thought was lavished on the harmonious appearance of the Holy City of Jerusalem.

HIRAM THE CRAFTSMAN

Some Bible readers have assumed that the Hiram mentioned in our present chapter (v 13) is identical with Hiram king of Tyre mentioned in ch 5 vv 15ff, but this is highly unlikely. Hiram the craftsman was an Israelite whose father was from the tribe of Naftali while his mother was from the tribe of Dan (see II Chronicles 2:13). He was living in the prosperous city of Tyre, where perhaps the opportunities to apply his expertise had been greater than they were in his native tribal areas before the time of Solomon.

Hiram the craftsman is compared with Betzalel, who constructed the Sanctuary in the Wilderness - prototype of the Temple in Jerusalem. One of the reasons why Hiram's tribal origins are specifically mentioned is to show that Rachel was answered when she prayed, "With great wrestlings (**naftulei**) have I wrestled with my sister" (Genesis 30:8). Betzalel, builder of the wilderness Sanctuary, was from the tribe of Judah (Leah's son) - yet he could not build it alone and had to have help from Oholiav, who was from the tribe of Dan (son of Bilhah, **Rachel**'s handmaiden). Likewise, Solomon (Judah-Leah) required the help of Hiram, who was from the tribe of Naftali, also Rachel's foster-son through Bilhah. Thus, the Partzufim of Rachel and Leah were both involved in the construction of the Sanctuary and the Temple.

Chapter 6 described the construction of the Temple buildings themselves out of stone (Malchut), wood (Tiferet) and gold (Binah). Our present chapter describes the ornaments and vessels of the Temple, which were made out of copper/bronze (Nechoshet), corresponding to Netzach and Hod, the "legs" (cf. Daniel 2:32).

Thus, the account of Hiram's work begins with the two great columns named Yachin ("He will establish") and Bo'az ("in Him is strength") that stood on the two sides of the entrance to the **Oolam** ("Vestibule") of the Temple building. These columns, with their very beautiful ornate "crowns", are the "legs" supporting the Temple, channeling its light downwards.

The copper "Sea" of Solomon was an enormous circular copper pool supported by twelve copper oxen and containing sufficient water to fill 150 Mikvehs ("purificatory ritual pools"). The Cohanim-priests would immerse here before beginning their service in the Temple. As our text states, the pool had a diameter of ten cubits, and "a line of thirty cubits would go around it" (v 23). In various Talmudic discussions involving the ratio of the diameter of a circle to its circumference, this verse is cited, although the commentators do point out that the figure of thirty cubits given here is only approximate, since the actual ratio is "Pi" - 3.14 (Eiruvin 14a, Succah 8a etc.).

The **Mechonot** and **Keerayim** described in vv. 27ff were respectively the bases and lavers from which the priests drew water to ritually wash their hands and feet prior to Temple service (Ex. 30:17-21).Verse 36 describes how the **Mechonot** - the bases on which the lavers stood and could be wheeled around - were engraved with cherubs, lions and palms **ke-ma'ar-eesh ve-loyot saviv**. The standard biblical translations do little justice to the mystery of this verse, where **ma'ar** has the connotation of attachment, as does the word **loyot**. Rashi commenting on the same word **loyot** in v 29 states that they were "a kind of male and female attached one to the other". This clearly relates to the basic mystery of the Temple, which is the attachment of the Holy One blessed be He with His Indwelling Presence - the Shekhinah. This gives special point to the Gemara (Yoma 54a), which tells that "when the alien foreigners entered the Sanctuary and saw the Cherubs embracing one another, they took them out into the market place and said 'Is this what these Israelites, whose blessing is a blessing and whose curse is a curse, keep busy with?' Immediately they despised them, as it is written, 'All those who honored her despised her because they saw her nakedness (**ervatah**, from same root as **ma'ar**)' (Lam. 1:8)."

As our text narrates, all these copper vessels were cast in the Jordan valley, where the earth was particularly suitable for making the earthenware moulds into which the molten metal was poured (RaDaK on v 46). There was so much copper that it was simply impossible to calculate the exact quantity (v 47).

Verse 49 tells us that Solomon made **ten** golden Menorahs (Candelabras). He did not put away the Menorah made by Moses in the Wilderness, but arranged five of his new ones on each side of that of Moses, which stood to the south of the Sanctuary. Although they are not mentioned in our present text, we learn from II Chronicles 4:8 that Solomon also made **ten** Showbread Tables, which were likewise arranged on each side of Moses' Showbread Table, which stood to the north of the Sanctuary (see RaDaK on I Kings 8:6).

All Solomon's innovations in the Temple were based on specific instructions which he received from his father David, "everything in writing from the hand of HaShem upon me" (II Chronicles 4:8): everything in the Temple was based upon prophecy.

"And all the labor was complete (**va-ti-shlam**)" v 51. "**Va-tehi-shalom** - 'it was all **peace**': Not one of the craftsmen that built the Temple died or became sick during the work and none of their tools ever broke" (P'sikta Rabati 6).

* * * The custom of the Sephardim is to read I Kings 7:13-26 as
the Haftarah of Parshat **Vayakhe**l, Exodus 35:1-38:20 * * *

* * * The custom of the Ashkenazim is to read I Kings 7:40-50 as
the Haftarah of Parshat **Vayakhel**, Exodus 35:1-38:20 * * *

* * * In years when the first and last days of Chanukah fall on Shabbat,
I Kings 7:40-50 is read as the Haftarah on the second Shabbat of Chanukah * * *

CHAPTER 8

With the completion of all the work it was time to inaugurate the new Temple. Solomon brought up the Ark from where David had taken it to rest temporarily on Mount Zion, and he brought up the Sanctuary from where it had been in Giv'on ever since the destruction of Shilo and Nov. Some of the Sanctuary items that would no longer be in use were now honorably hidden away in a **Genizah**, presumably under the Temple Mount, which Solomon apparently designed with an intricate secret subterranean network.

A new stage had arrived in the revelation of God's glory with the completion of the Temple rooted in **Chokhmah**, "wisdom". Now that everything was complete and in place, the Glory of God, His Indwelling Presence, "came down", as it were, into the building.

It was then that Solomon, who was then 23 years old, addressed the entire nation of Israel assembled at the Temple, after which he turned to the Altar, got down on his knees and raised his arms to the heavens to offer his most eloquent prayer for God to bless His House and fulfill its intent. Many phrases from this prayer are incorporated into the prayers and supplications in the Siddur and Selichot etc.

Having erected the building, Solomon now came to teach its true function and purpose - to reveal how God governs the whole of creation with direct providence over every detail (**Hashgachah Pratit**). It is a revelation of the complete unity of God when people pray in the Temple or even "through" it from a great distance away, because embodied in the actual courtyards and buildings and vessels of the Temple are attributes of God, attached to one another in unity **ke-ma'ar-eesh ve-loyot saviv**.

Thus Solomon details the many different needs for which people must pray. Verses 31-2 speak of people's prayers for justice in the face of wrong-doing they have suffered from others (including adultery, which can take a man's wife from him or vice versa and destroys the sanctity of the family, and is specifically alluded to here, see Rashi).

Verse 33 teaches that it is our own sins that cause our enemies to strike us, and that we must repent and pray for salvation. Verse 35 deals with drought; verse 37 with famine, which may be caused by bad winds, crop failure, locusts etc., and with illness. Verse 38 teaches that each person must pray about the afflictions he feels in his own heart and that he must understand that "You give to a man according to all his ways". This implies that if we are unworthy, we cannot expect God to answer our prayers (though in His mercy, He may!)

From vv 41ff we learn that God will also listen to the prayers of the **Nachri**, the non-Israelite, who hears of His great Name and comes to pray at the Temple. Indeed, Solomon asks God to "do according to all that the **Nachri** cries out to You in order that all the peoples of the earth should know Your Name to fear You..." (v 43). The **Nachri** may not understand that God does not always answer the undeserving - he may not even realize that he is undeserving, and if he receives no answer from God at the Temple he may not blame it on himself but on the Temple. This is why Solomon asks God to answer the **Nachri** for the sake of His great Name (Rashi on v 43).

From verses 46-50 we learn that even when Israel are in exile and captivity far from their Land, their prayers to God are efficacious when they pray to God "by way of their Land that You gave to their fathers, the city that You chose and the House that You have built for Your Name" (v 48). This implies that everyone should direct his or her prayers to God through the Temple in Jerusalem, no matter where in the world they are. (This is why Jews turn in the direction of the Temple to pray the daily **Amidah** prayer.)

According to the Rabbis, the inauguration of the new Temple took place in the month of Tishri from the 8th to the 14th of the month and was followed immediately by the celebration of the festival of Succot. This was such an important event that according to most opinions, fasting was suspended that year on Yom Kippur in order for the people to partake of the **Shelamim** (peace offerings) - see RaDaK on v 65.

May we very soon know what it is to celebrate **Chanukat HaBayit**,
the inauguration of the new Temple that we are eagerly awaiting.

* * * I Kings 7:51 and 8:1-21 are read as the Haftarah of Parshat **Pekudey**, Exodus 38:21-40:38 * * *

* * * In Diaspora communities, II Kings 8:2-21 is read as the Haftarah on the Second Day of Succot, and I Kings 8:54-9:1 is read as the Haftarah on the Festival of Shemini Atzeret * * *

CHAPTER 9

"MY EYES AND MY HEART WILL BE THERE..." (v 3)

The entire face of Israel was changed with the completion of Solomon's Temple and his other magnificent building projects in Jerusalem together with the development of a network of international diplomatic and trading links that brought a flood of gold, silver, exotic woods, spices and other luxuries into the Land.

Solomon took the first twenty-four years of his reign to build the Temple and his palace, while David had previously reigned for forty years. This means that it was little more than sixty-five years since Saul had become king at a time when the Israelites were so poor and technologically dependent on the

Philistines that they didn't even have blacksmiths of their own to repair their farm implements (I Samuel 13:19-22).

For almost five centuries since their entry into the Land, the Israelites had been a nation of small farmers living a very simple life. Now suddenly, through the genius of Solomon the peace-maker and bridge-builder, Israel and its glorious capital of Jerusalem were at the very center of the economic and cultural life of the entire Fertile Crescent and way beyond. The nation that once slaved to build store cities for Pharaoh (Exodus 1:11) now had helot slave nations of their own to build them "store cities, cities of chariots and cities of horse riders and whatever fancy that Solomon fancied to build in Jerusalem and Lebanon and in all the land of his rule" (I Kings 9:9). In a sense Solomon's marriage with Pharaoh's daughter can be seen as his attempt to wed and subordinate the material grandeur represented by Egypt to the Torah of Israel.

The question was whether he could succeed - or would the pull of materialism turn Israel aside from their adherence to the Torah. Therefore, God's message to Solomon when He appeared to him for the second time following the completion of his building projects (v 1) was strictly conditional: "**If** you will go before Me. I shall establish the throne of your kingship over Israel forever" (vv 4-5). At the very moment when the Temple had just been consecrated, God was already threatening that it would be destroyed if Israel were to go astray and that the people would then become an international byword for the terrible consequences of sin (vv 7-8, cf. Deut. 29:17-27).

In certain ways the test faced by Solomon and the Israel of his times was similar to the test faced by modern Israel since the reestablishment of the Jewish settlement in the Holy Land within the last few hundred years and particularly since the establishment of the State. At the time of the War of Independence in 1948 the Israeli army was a makeshift affair that was victorious not because of superior weaponry but through a combination of heroism and divine miracles, as in the times of Saul and Jonathan. Less than 20 years later in June 1967 the Israeli army saw stunning successes in the space of only six days, extending the tiny country by many times its original size. Since then Israel has attained a prosperity and technological sophistication unimaginable only sixty years ago, and is at the center of an international nexus of diplomatic and commercial relations. However in the eyes of many, this very material success has been accompanied by a tragic decline into decadence, corruption and loss of national vision. Can Israel reverse this decline and return to the Torah ideals that give meaning and purpose to its existence?

The way to reverse this decline is given in our text: "My eyes and My heart will be there..." (v 3). Targum Yonatan renders this verse: "My Indwelling Presence (=eyes) will dwell in it **if** My will (=heart) is done". "My will" is the Torah: the moral of the Prophet is the same as the moral of the Torah in whose voice he speaks: "And it shall be if you will surely listen to My commandments..." (Deut. 11:13; second paragraph of Shema).

SOLOMON'S COVENANT WITH HIRAM

Solomon's treaty of peace, cooperation and reciprocal trading with Hiram of Tyre is emblematic of the international diplomatic policy through which Solomon laid the foundations for Israel's prosperity.

It is therefore somewhat strange to discover that Solomon "gave" Hiram twenty cities in the Galilee which found no favor with the latter, who contemptuously dismissed the region as being "barren" or "fruitless" (vv 11-13; **kavul** literally means "chained", implying that the land was full of bogs from which it was hard to pull up one's feet when trying to walk there). How Solomon could have "given" even a small part of Israel's God-given inheritance to a foreign king is explained by some commentators with reference to a parallel passage in I Chronicles 8:2, which says that it was Hiram who gave Solomon a number of cities that were then populated with Israelites. This would indicate either that Hiram returned the cities given by Solomon, or that each country's making some of its land available to the other was some kind of reciprocal leasing arrangement. Some say that Solomon intentionally gave Hiram inferior land so that he would not be able to make use of it. Despite the "diplomatic rumpus" caused by Solomon's unattractive gift, Hiram continued lavishing friendship upon his wise Israelite ally, sending him huge amounts of gold (v 14) and cooperating in ambitious naval ventures that brought even more gold and exotic treasures into Israel (vv 26ff; cf. ch 10 vv 11 etc.).

SEEDS OF LATER TROUBLES

The very account of Solomon's glory includes references to factors that were later to prove disastrous. Verse 20-21 describe how the remaining Canaanites "whom the Children of Israel were unable to drive out" were effectively transformed into disenfranchised serf helots who performed menial labors for their masters, while the Israelites were a free elite manning the king's army and government. While our present text voices no explicit criticism of this arrangement, it is clear from elsewhere that it was the Israelite failure to drive out the Canaanites that was the root cause of their later exile, because they adopted the Canaanite idolatries.

Similarly, Solomon's building of the **Millo** in Jerusalem for the daughter of Pharaoh (v 24) was one of the root causes of the later rebellion of the Ten Tribes under Jerabo'am. The **Millo** was a large area by the city which David had left vacant in order to provide space for the pilgrims who came up for the foot festivals to pitch their tents. Solomon **filled in** (Heb. **mila**) this area with earth in order to build homes for Pharaoh's daughter's servants and attendants, causing great popular resentment among the home-born Israelites over the requisitioning of land left for their benefit for the sake of a foreign princess. It was precisely over this that Jeraboa'm reproved Solomon (ch 11 v 27).

CHAPTER 10

THE VISIT OF THE QUEEN OF SHEBA

Many beautiful legends have been woven around the visit of the Queen of Sheba to Jerusalem as described in our present chapter. Solomon's development of the ports of Etzion-Gever by **Eilot** (=present day Eilat) and his joint naval ventures with the sea-faring experts of Hiram's Tyre opened up not only the Red Sea and surrounding coastal regions of present-day Somalia, Ethiopia, Arabia and Yemen but also gave access to the Indian Ocean and many far-off, exotic sources of luxury goods.

Some commentators identify Sheba with India (cf. Gen. 10:7), but rabbinic tradition identifies it with present-day Ethiopia, which would agree with Ethiopian folklore.

The Talmud states: "Whoever says that the Queen of Sheba was a woman is simply mistaken; what is **Malkhat** Sheba? It is the kingdom (**mamlekhet**) of Sheba!" (Bava Batra 15b). Some people have taken this to mean that the Biblical account of the visit of the Queen of Sheba is nothing but an allegory about some kind of cultural exchange between King Solomon and some far-off nation. However, this misconception is dispelled by the comment of Maharsha (ad loc.) that all the Talmud means here is that the Queen of Sheba was not merely the wife-consort of a King of Sheba but that she was actually a Queen in her own right.

The riddles posed to Solomon by the Queen of Sheba as elaborated in the Midrashim have exercised many minds throughout the generations. "And King Solomon gave to the Queen of Sheba all her desire that she asked..." (v 13). Rashi (ad loc.) comments that what Solomon gave her was nothing but a lesson in wisdom, adding that to satisfy her desire, he had relations with her and she conceived a child whose descendant was Nebuchadnezzar, who was to destroy Solomon's Temple four hundred and ten years after it was built. Once again Solomon's ambitious ventures in trying to join the holy with the unholy sowed the seeds of later destruction.

SIX HUNDRED AND SIXTY-SIX TALENTS OF GOLD

The information that the total sum of Solomon's annual income of gold was six hundred and sixty-six talents of gold (v 14) is likely to be somewhat chilling to those who have been exposed to the various occult teachings that associate 666 with great evil. Rashi (ad loc.) explains that this sum was made up of 120 talents given by Hiram, another 120 talents given by the Queen of Sheba, and a further 420 talents brought by the ships of Tarshish from Ophir. "And as for the other six, I don't know where they were from" (Rashi). Other commentators point out that it was this very wealth that proved to be Solomon's undoing, and that 666 is the sum of the numerical value of the Hebrew letters in the word **tassur** (Tav 400, Samach 60, Vav 6, Reish 200), "turn aside", as in the verse, "And you shall not **turn aside (tassur)** from all the things that I am commanding you today" (Deut. 28:14, cf. Deut. 17:11).

SOLOMON'S THRONE

Another theme around which many fabulous legends have been woven is Solomon's amazing throne (vv 18ff). One of the main sources for more details about this throne is the Second Targum on Esther 1:2, which provides a complete description of the many different figures of animals that adorned this throne and their various ways of dealing with intruders, false witnesses who came to testify before Solomon, etc. Among the various kings who were said to have later unsuccessfully tried to sit on this throne were Pharaoh Necho, Nebuchadnezzar, Achashverosh and Alexander the Great. Rabbi Elazar the son of Rabbi Yossi said that he had seen the shattered remnants of this throne in Rome. (See also Rabbi Nachman's tale of the Exchanged Children, which alludes to this throne at the climax of the story.)

The six steps of the throne mentioned in our present text correspond to the Six Orders of the Mishnah - for despite his excesses, Solomon based his kingly authority only on the Torah as handed down through the oral tradition. Solomon's throne was the earthly representation of the heavenly Throne of Glory, and according to tradition was adorned with a wolf side by side with a lamb, a leopard with a kid goat and a calf with a lion (cf. Isaiah 11:6) indicating that through faithful adherence to the wisdom and judgments of the Torah, perfect Messianic peace can reign.

CHAPTER 11

"AND KING SOLOMON LOVED MANY FOREIGN WOMEN..." (v 1)

Foreign "women" - in the form of the religions, worldviews, philosophies, arts, sciences, cultures and lifestyles of the other nations - have had an irresistible allure for many Israelites in generation after generation despite the solemn Torah injunctions against their pursuit. It is surely impossible for ordinary people to understand precisely what the wisest man that ever lived really intended in going after so many foreign women, but Rabbi Nachman of Breslov - who also attained supreme heights of wisdom - teaches that reliance on wisdom alone is intrinsically dangerous:

"When a person follows his own mind and clever ideas, he can fall into many pitfalls and errors and come to great evil. Tremendous damage has been caused by such people, like the infamous great villains who, through their intelligence and cunning, have led the entire world astray" (Likutey Moharan

II, 12). For Rabbi Nachman, the very essence of Judaism is simplicity: "Throw aside all wisdom and clever ideas and serve God with simplicity. Make sure that your deeds are greater than your wisdom, because the main thing is not study but its practical application. This obviously applies to most ordinary people's clever ideas, which are mere folly, but it even applies to genuine wisdom. When it comes to serving God, even a person whose head is filled with genuine wisdom should set it all aside and serve God simply and innocently" (ibid. II, 5).

The Talmud indicates that Solomon did not necessarily actually marry the "many foreign women" that he "loved": he is considered to have done so only because he permitted himself to become entranced by them (Yevamot 76b). "Everyone who says Solomon sinned is simply mistaken, as the verse says, 'His heart was not perfect with HaShem his God like the heart of his father David' (v 4): this means that he was not wholehearted with God like David, but **he did not sin**. Then, how are we to understand the verse that says, 'In the time of Solomon's old age his wives inclined his heart after other gods' (ibid.)? They inclined his heart, but he did not actually follow after" (Shabbat 56b).

The Torah forbids the king from marrying too many wives "lest his heart turn astray" (Deut. 17:17). According to the Talmud, Solomon's flaw lay in believing that he was so saintly that he had the power to flout the Torah and multiply wives while remaining immune to their allurements (Sanhedrin 21b). The rabbis said that Solomon himself did not actually build the idolatrous temples listed in vv 7-8, but is only credited with having done so because he did not protest when his wives built them (Shabbat 56b). Perhaps his multi-cultural enthusiasm was so great that he **imagined** he had brought these foreign women under the wings of the Shechinah while willfully blinding himself to the fact that they never truly emerged from the idolatrous attitudes from which he hoped to wean them.

"And God spoke to Solomon..." (v 11). According to RaDaK, God spoke to Solomon through the same prophet who enters the narrative later in our present chapter (vv 29ff) – Achiyah HaShiloni. According to tradition, Achiyah was a Levite and had been a boy at the time of the Exodus from Egypt. He had heard Torah from Moses and later received Torah from David and his court (Rambam, Introduction to Mishneh Torah). Not only was Achiyah the teacher of Elijah the Prophet (ibid.); his soul also came regularly to teach Rabbi Israel, the Baal Shem Tov, founder of the Chassidic movement (Shevachey HaBesht).

The prophet's grim message to Solomon was that because he was divided in his own heart, the very kingdom itself would be divided and torn into two so soon after the establishment of the House of David and the building of God's Temple in Jerusalem. The glorious age of Solomon's international empire and Israelite cultural hegemony proved to be very short-lived indeed. Yet the House of David's loss of their rule over all the tribes of Israel was different from the collapse of the House of Saul, for while the latter disappeared completely, the House of David always retained the loyalty of Judah and Benjamin, and is destined to regain its rule over all Israel in the end of days. Indeed, Achiyah's prophecy to Jerabo'am that God would afflict the seed of David "**but not for all the days**" (v 39) is taken as a promise that eventually Judah will once again be reunited with Ephraim and the Ten Tribes (RaDaK).

Serious trouble did not break out until after the death of Solomon, but already in the twilight years of his reign God's providence was at work preparing the adversaries who would come to test and try the House of David. Isaac had long before told Esau that whenever Jacob would fall from his level and give Esau cause to resent his having received the blessings, "you shall break his yoke from upon your neck" (Genesis 27:40). Thus, the very first "satan" against Solomon was the Edomite prince Hadad, who had escaped to Egypt during David's campaign against Edom and who was willing to give up a life of royal splendor in Egypt in order to stir up his remaining people against the Israelite "occupiers" (vv 14-22).

At the same time Razon was at work in the Syrian provinces of Aram to undo their subjugation by David (v 23f).

Most serious of all was the rupture between the Kingdom of Judah and the Ten Tribes under the leadership of Ephraim, the consequences of which are with us until today and the first premonition of which also came in Solomon's lifetime. Unlike the prophet Samuel, who physically anointed David as king during the lifetime of Saul, Achiyah HaShiloni did not actually anoint Jerabo'am son of Nevat as king over the Ten Tribes. His dramatic ripping of the "new garment" (v 29 - whether it belonged to Achiyah or Jerabo'am is unclear, RaDaK) and giving ten of the twelve shreds to Jeraboam was intended to indicate that Jerabo'am had the power to lead the Ten Tribes but not that he necessarily had to rebel.

Although Jerabo'am later became the archetype of those who lead others into sin, he started off as "a mighty man of valor" (v 28): he was one of the outstanding Torah sages of all time. "Jerabo'am's Torah had no flaw" (Sanhedrin 102a). The reason why he and Achiyah are described as having been "alone in the field" is because "all the other Torah scholars were like the grass of the field in comparison with them" (ibid.). As the officer in charge of tax collection from the tribe of Ephraim, Jerabo'am was energetic and efficient. According to the sages, his main flaw was his pride. "God said to Jerabo'am: 'If you will only repent, I, you and the son of Jesse will stroll in the Garden of Eden.' Jerabo'am asked, 'Who will be at the head?' When God said, 'The son of Jesse will be at the head,' Jerabo'am replied, 'I don't want to'." (Sanhedrin ibid.)

CHAPTER 12

The rumblings that began to be felt in the last years of Solomon's life broke out into the open as soon as he died. Evidently, knowledge of Achiyah's appointment of Jerabo'am as leader of the Ten Tribes had become public, and he was seen as the one person who could redress the people's grievances over the heavy yoke of the monarchy. Jeraboa'm's public criticism of Solomon over requisitioning parts of Jerusalem for Pharaoh's daughter's household (ch 11 v 27) put him in the status of a **Moreid BeMalchut** ("state traitor") whom the king sought to kill, but Jerabo'am escaped to Egypt, where the new king Shishak was probably only too happy to give protection to a potential counterweight to the expansionist House of David (ibid. v 40). With the death of Solomon, the people recalled Jerabo'am from Egypt, indicating that their resentment was already seething.

Solomon's successor Rehabo'am showed the same kind of inexperience as many new rulers heady with their first taste of power: he thought the best way to suppress popular resentment would be through a resolute display of heavy-handedness. One wonders if the yoke about which the Israelites were complaining was purely economic - they were being taxed heavily, but it was to pay for the army to maintain the peace - or was it perhaps the yoke of halachic stringency represented by the House of David? (Solomon and his court had introduced a number of new "rabbinic" enactments to safeguard Torah law, such as **Eiruvey Chaterot** on Shabbat etc.) If so, one might see a parallel between Rehabo'am's response to the hankering for greater laxity on the part of the Israelites and the response to the laxity of many of their coreligionists by those sectors of the Torah community who seem to be taking refuge in a fortress of ever greater stringencies, which often merely increase the rebelliousness of those outside the fortress.

When Rehabo'am told the very people who were hoping for greater laxity that "my father chastised you with whips but I will chastise you with scorpions" (v 14) he surely did not realize that he was with his own mouth sealing the decree against the House of David. It was under the sign of the Scorpion that Jerabo'am began the rebellion of the Ten Tribes: "And Jerabo'am made a festival in the **eighth** month on the 15th day of the month". The eighth month is Marcheshvan, coinciding with the astrological sign of Scorpio (Heb. **Akrav**). Ever since, the month of Marcheshvan has been a period when the sting of exile has often been particularly painful. This month is also especially associated with Rachel, mother of Joseph (Ephraim): Rachel's **Yahrtzeit** ("death anniversary") is on the 11th of Marcheshvan. Rachel was Jacob's favorite wife, his **Ikar Bayit** ("essential house"): the Hebrew letters IKaR Bayit are the same as **akrav**.

The two golden calves that Jerabo'am set up in Beit El and Dan in order to discourage people from going up to the Temple in Jerusalem "became a sin" (v 30) but they were not set up as idols from the very outset. If they had been, it is highly unlikely that the super-intelligent Israelites would all of a sudden have simply bent the knee to the very kind of idols the Torah loudly proscribes. RaDaK explains that in order to "compensate" people for not being able to go up to Jerusalem to experience the Shechinah in the Temple, Jeraboa'm set up these golden calves much in the same way as Aaron the Priest made the Golden Calf in the wilderness as a kind of visible sign of the Shechinah in the absence of Moses (RaDaK on vv 28-29).

Rabbi Nachman of Breslov taught that the idolatry surrounding these golden calves was not something simple and primitive but was supported by theoretical underpinnings and rationalizations that were so deep as to be totally overwhelming and convincing to most ordinary people. Out of mercy for the world, God has arranged it so that the literature justifying this idolatry has been totally erased in order to save people from its allure (Likutey Moharan II:32). The ox is one of the animals of the divine chariot, and by representing in gold the perpetrators of this idolatry were separating it from the divine unity, making it as if a power in itself. Moreover, the root of the word **egel** is also related to the root **igul**, a "circle" or "cycle", alluding to the great cycle of creation (cf. the comparison of an angel to an "ox", **egla**, in Ta'anit 25b) as if this angel was an independent domain.

CHAPTER 13

David and Solomon had been the spiritual as well as temporal leaders of the people, but with the split in the kingdom the spiritual authority of the kings was undermined, and from now on the voice of truth and reproof came from the prophets.

The "man of God" who came from Judah to Beit El was Ido the Prophet (Sanhedrin 89b; cf. II Chronicles 9:29). At the very beginning of the rebellion of the Ten Tribes, Ido already prophesied that a king of Judah would later arise who would destroy the idolatrous altars of Israel (verse 2). This was the saintly King Josiah, who lived three hundred years later and came to the throne at the tender age of eight years old, bringing the people of Judah to one final flowering of repentance and national revival a generation before the destruction of the First Temple. Josiah was one of six who were given their name before they were even born (the others being Ishmael, Isaac, Moses, Solomon and Melech HaMashiach – Yalkut Shimoni #200). Josiah was mourned by the prophet Jeremiah as "the breath of our nostrils, HaShem's anointed Mashiach" (Lam. 4:20; II Chron. 35:25).

The length of the time between Jerabo'am's building of his idolatrous altar and its final destruction by King Josiah 300 years later shows God's great patience. This is also illustrated by the fact that even as Jerabo'am served at his idolatrous altar in defiance of Heaven, nothing whatever happened to him until the moment when he tried to seize Ido the Prophet. This was when Jerabo'am's hand "dried up" (v 4), showing that God avenged the honor of the Tzaddik more than He avenged the affront to His own honor (Rashi ad loc.).

Ido had been instructed not to eat or drink in Beit El because it is forbidden to enter a city of idolaters except for the purpose of giving them a warning: it would have created the wrong impression if people had seen the prophet enjoying himself in the course of his mission, and if he had left the city by the same route he had taken to get there, it would have given unnecessary prestige to the road leading to the city.

"And a certain old prophet dwelled in Beit El" (v 11). Some rabbis identify this prophet with Michah or Jonathan son of Gershom the son of Moses (Judges 17-18; RaDaK on I Kings 13:11). Those who find it hard to believe that Michah and/or Jonathan could have lived so long may prefer to think that perhaps the soul or spirit of Michah/Jonathan was somehow incarnated again in this old prophet. Targum Yonatan (onv 11) states explicitly that he was a **false** prophet, yet our text indicates that he was a sociable fellow. Despite the fact that he lied (v 18) when he told Ido that he had been prophetically instructed to feed him bread and water, he momentarily attained true prophecy in the merit of having showed hospitality: "We see the greatness of giving someone a little refreshment from the fact that it caused the Divine Presence to rest even on the prophets of Baal" (Sanhedrin 104a).

For eating this bread and water in defiance of his own prophetic instructions, Ido was punished with death at the hands of Heaven (i.e. by the lion), because the Torah states that "whoever will not listen to the words of the prophet who speaks in My name, I shall require it of him" (Deut. 18:19). If this applies to one who hears true prophecy from another, how much more does it apply to the one who receives the prophecy himself (RaDaK on v 18; see Rambam, Hilchot Yesodey HaTorah 9:3).

The lion killed Ido yet did not eat him or even his donkey (v 24), showing that God exacts retribution with the utmost accuracy and fairness. The prophet had defied His word and had to pay with his life, yet since he was a Tzaddik in all other respects his body was left intact, as was the donkey he had ridden upon in his lifetime. Ido's body was laid to rest in the grave which the old prophet of Beit El had prepared for himself, and when he died he too was buried there at his side. This gave the false prophet protection three hundred years later when King Josiah had all the graves of the prophets of Baal dug up (II Kings 23:17-18).

Even though Jerabo'am had directly witnessed God's providence when his hand dried up on his altar, and he doubtless heard how Ido was killed by the lion, this did not deter him from his rebellious path. He now established his own alternative priesthood, "and this thing became a sin to the house of Jerabo'am, even to cut it off and to destroy it from off the face of the earth" (v 34). Jerabo'am was "cut off" in this world and "destroyed" in the world to come: this verse is the foundation of the rabbinic teaching that Jerabo'am was one of those who had no share in the world to come (Sanhedrin 101b).

CHAPTER 14

Jerabo'am originally had the soul of Joseph, but it left him when he sinned, as it is written, "And he sinned with the Baal and he **died**" (Hosea 13:1; ARI, Sefer HaLikutim on I Kings ch 11). Despite his dogged obstinacy, Jerabo'am was so distressed by the illness of his son (ch 14 v 1) that he sent his wife to Achiyah the Shiloni, who had been the one who originally told him that he would reign over Israel. The rabbis said that Achiyah had become blind on account of having raised a wicked disciple (Bereishit Rabbah 65). This blindness did not prevent Achiyah from seeing the terrible decree that was hanging over the house of Jerabo'am and which initiated the bloody history of violent regime change that afflicted the kings of Israel ever after.

"AND RECHAV'AM THE SON OF SOLOMON RULED IN JUDAH..." (v 21)

For the whole of the remainder of the book of Kings (Parts I and II) until the exile of the Ten Tribes a few generations prior to the destruction of the First Temple, the narrative swings back and forth repeatedly from the exploits of the kings of Judah to those of the kings of Israel and back again in order to give a full account of what happened in each generation during those tumultuous times.

According to the time-frame of the rabbinic Midrash **Seder Olam** ("Order of the World"), which is based on a combination of tradition and acute analysis of all the years enumerated in the biblical texts, Solomon came to the throne in the year 2924 (= -837 B.C.E.). He started building the Temple in the fourth year of his reign, and the 410 years that it stood are counted from the year in which the building commenced, 2928 (-833 B.C.E.). The First Temple thus stood until the year 3338 (-423 B.C.E.). Solomon's son Rechav'am came to the throne in 2964 (-797 B.C.E.) and reigned until 2981 (-780 B.C.E.), initiating the period in which even Judah strayed ever deeper into idolatry (vv 22-3) and sexual immorality (v 24).

When Joseph had been ruler of Egypt, he sucked all the wealth of Egypt and the surrounding countries into the coffers of the Egyptian kings (Gen. 41:57 and 47:14). When the Children of Israel came up out of Egypt, they took all this wealth with them (Exodus 12:36). It remained in Israel's hands until the time of Rechav'am, when "Shishak king of Egypt went up to Jerusalem and took the treasures of the House of God and the treasures of the House of the king." (v 26). According to the rabbis, this wealth was subsequently seized by Zerach king of Kush, from whom it was taken back by King Asa who sent it as a bribe to the king of Aram. It was taken back again by King Jehoshaphat, and remained in the hands of Israel until the time of King Ahaz, from whom it was taken by Sennacherib, from whom it was taken in turn by the Babylonians, the Persians and the Greeks, from whom it was seized by the Romans, who took it to Rome, where it remains until today (Pesachim 119a).

CHAPTER 15

With the death of Solomon's son Rechav'am, the latter's son Aviyam (also called Aviyah - II Chronicles 13:1) became king of Judah. Our text states that Aviyah followed in the sinful ways of his father Rechav'am, who "did evil for he did not prepare his heart to seek out HaShem" (II Chron. 12:14). Yet despite the recurrent failings of the kings of Judah, David's line was never extirpated: this was his reward for his outstanding and unwavering loyalty to God. Although there were many ups and downs in the history of the House of David, all were part of the long-drawn out process of **Birur** ("sifting and selection") that is to lead eventually to the final ascendancy of **Melekh HaMashiach**.

The exact nature of the evil for which the various kings are criticized in the Bible is often hard to pin down definitively and can sometimes only be inferred from the most subtle of hints in the text, some of which are elaborated in the Talmud and Midrashim. Our most important source for a wider perspective on many of the laconic comments contained in our present text lies in the parallel account of the exploits of the kings of Judah and Israel in the Book of Chronicles, which often provides crucial supplementary details.

Thus our present text passes over Aviyah's war against Jerabo'am in complete silence, but it is described in great detail in II Chronicles ch 13, which records Aviyah's public call to the tribes of the northern kingdom to submit themselves again to the hegemony of Judah on the grounds that Judah alone had remained faithful to the Torah tradition under which only the Levites and the Cohen-priests descended from Aaron were authorized to minister to God in Jerusalem and nowhere else. On the face of it Aviyah's speech seems impeccably righteous, yet the Midrash Seder Olam points out that he scathingly denounced the prophet Achiyah HaShiloni as one of the "worthless people" who supported Jerabo'am (II Chron. 13:7); he also publicly castigated the tribes of Israel for keeping the golden calves (ibid. v 8) - yet after all his criticisms, the Midrash says that when he came to Beit El and saw them, he almost joined in worshiping them, which is why he was "hit" by Jerabo'am's armies even though he eventually subdued them (ibid. v. 20, see Rashi ad loc.)

"AND ASA DID RIGHT...LIKE DAVID HIS FATHER" (v 11)

King Asa is the first example of the various righteous descendants of King David (such as Hezekiah and Josiah etc.) who succeeded in bringing about a greater or lesser spiritual revival during their reigns. Although our text (v 10) states that Asa's mother was Maachah daughter of Avshalom, the commentators agree that she was actually his grandmother, the wife of Rechav'am and mother of Asa's father Aviyah (see v 2). It is unclear whether she was actually the daughter of David's rebellious son Absalom, but this is quite possible as she bore the name of Absalom's mother. In the time of Asa she was the Queen Mother, and she had evidently played a prominent role in spreading idolatry in Judah (v 13), having set up a **Mifletzet**. Until today this Hebrew word literally means a "monster", but the sages (Avodah Zarah 44a) darshened it as a compound of **maphlia** ("wondrous", "astonishing") and **leitzanuta** ("mockery"). According to Rashi (on v 13) she attached a large phallus to her idol and made daily use of it.

Despite the fact that she was the Queen Mother and Asa's own grandmother, the king displayed his Davidic righteousness in showing no compunction about removing her from her royal position and grinding up her monster and casting it into a valley where nobody would have any benefit from the dust.

Our text notes that in spite of Asa's whole-heartedness with God, he did not remove the **Bamot** ("high places"). It is necessary to bear in mind that throughout almost the entire turbulent 410 year history of the Kingdom of Judah, the Holy Temple actually functioned every day and remained the main focus of the people's spiritual life. Ever since the inauguration of the Temple in Jerusalem, it had been forbidden to offer sacrifices to HaShem anywhere else: this is an explicit Torah prohibition that carries the penalty of **Karet** (early death and spiritual excision, see Lev. 17:3ff). The sages associated the practice of sacrificing at a **Bamah** with pride and arrogance, as if the celebrant was reluctant to submit to the authority of the Cohen-priests and wanted to be his own priest. The fact that for most of the period of the kings of Judah the **Bamot** were not eliminated indicates that the blemish of pride and arrogance persisted behind this outer display of religiosity and devotion.

Our present text does not mention the invasion of Judah by Zerach HaKushi ("Zerach the black man") during the reign of Asa (II Chron. 14:8ff). This was apparently an invasion from the south west by hordes of Nubians and Libyans, which Asa heroically repelled with the same faith and trust in God displayed by the Judges (ibid. v 10). Unfortunately, Asa failed to display similar faith and trust when confronted by a serious blockade on Judah by Ba'sha king of Israel (our present chapter v 17). Asa took the Temple and royal treasures and sent them to the king of Aram as a bribe to make trouble for Ba'sha on his northern flank in order to force him to dismantle his blockade against Judah (vv 18-21). The ploy worked, but Asa was severely castigated for paying a foreign king to attack his Israelite brothers. According to Seder Olam this war took place thirty-six years after the death of Solomon. Solomon had married Pharaoh's daughter in the fourth year of his reign and lived for another thirty-six years. The decree of the division of his kingdom was originally intended to last only thirty-six years after his death, and had Asa trusted in God alone to save him from Ba'sha's blockade, the rabbis said that he would have been able to restore his hegemony over all the tribes of Israel. His bribing of the king of Aram was a lapse of faith that lost him the opportunity to restore David's united kingdom, which will not return until the coming of Mashiach (see II Chronicles 16:7ff, Seder Olam).

Asa sought to build a strong Judah, and even called bridegrooms from their marriage celebrations and Torah scholars from their study halls in order to fortify its cities (I Kings 15:22; see RaDaK). For the sin of interrupting the studies of the scholars - the supporting "legs" of the Torah - Asa was punished with illness in his legs (this is said to have been an extremely painful "podagra" or gout, which felt like needles pricking into raw flesh, Sota 10b), but instead of going to the prophets to find out what he needed to correct, Asa went to the doctors instead - and found no cure (II Chron. 16:12).

CHAPTER 16

The concluding section of Chapter 15 turned from the history of Judah to that of the northern kingdom, summarizing the brief two-year reign of Jerabo'am's son Nadav, who in fulfillment of Achiyah's prophecy was overthrown in a bloody coup while campaigning against the Philistines (who despite having been routed by David were now able to raise their heads again as God's staff of chastisement on account of the Israelite idolatry).

The Biblical narrative about the succession of bloody military coups and regime changes that characterizes the history of the northern kingdom may make the leading actors seem like nothing more than a bunch of brutal gangsters. In order to correct this impression, we would do well to note the comment of our rabbis that the wicked king Jerabo'am was able to expound the book of Leviticus in one hundred and three different ways, while Ahab - who prostrated to the Baal in Sidon and built Temples for Baal and Ashera worship in Shomron (vv 31-3 in our present chapter) - could expound Leviticus in eighty-five different ways (Sanhedrin 103b). It would appear that these wickedly wise leaders must have had the power to totally entrance their Israelite constituencies with the profoundest kabbalistic theorization, despite the fact that the Israelites had always shown themselves to be exceptionally sharp and critical people.

Ba'sha had destroyed Nadav and with him the entire house of Jerabo'am. Ba'sha was succeeded by his son Eylah, but this inept drunkard was killed in another coup after only two years (v 9), and the coup leader, Zimri - an army general - went on to wipe out the whole house of Ba'sha. Zimri's rule lasted no more than seven days (v 15) as it did not find favor with the people, who preferred another general -- Omri - who was busy fighting the Philistines ("security is everything"). Omri left off fighting the Philistines and laid siege to Tirzah - a town about 10 kilometers north of Shechem (Nablus) that had served as the capital of the northern kingdom since the days of Jerabo'am (see I Kings 14:17). After an initial division among the people as to whether to go after Omri or his rival Tivni son of Ginat (v 21), the Omri faction gained sway and after the death of Tivni, Omri ruled over all the Ten Tribes.

"Why did Omri attain the kingship? Because he added one great city in the Land of Israel" (Sanhedrin 102b). This was Shomron (verse 24 in our present chapter), which was about 15 kilometers north east of Shechem and which subsequently became the royal capital of the northern kingdom. Archeological remains found at the site of Shomron attest to the very great magnificence and cultural sophistication of this capital city of the kings of Israel.

Omri continued in the path of Jerabo'am, refusing to allow the Israelites to go up to the Temple in Jerusalem (until just before the exile of the Ten Tribes, heavily armed police were posted on all the paths leading to Jerusalem with instructions to break the bones of anyone who tried to go up). Yet even the evil of Jerabo'am was exceeded by Omri's son Achav, who added to the existing worship of

Jerabo'am's golden calves the new element of Baal worship imported from the Canaanite city-state of Sidon, the daughter of whose king - the accursed Jezebel - Ahab took as his wife.

If Achav "did evil **in the eyes of God** more than all that were before him" his evil was apparently not seen at the time by most of the human Israelites: this paradoxical figure, who was like a brother (**ach**) and a father (**av**) to all his people, was a lover of the Torah - he could darshen Leviticus in 85 ways - and a supporter of Torah scholars. He knew and spoke with Elijah the Prophet, and no less than Jehoshaphat king of Judah entered into a marriage alliance with him, marrying his sister. Yet despite all this, "he wrote on the gates of Shomron, 'Ahab denies the God of Israel'" (Sanhedrin 102b) - "and he therefore has no share in the God of Israel" (ibid.).

The ultra-sophisticated spiritual decadence into which Israel had sunk by the time of Ahab was epitomized by the rebuilding of Jericho despite Joshua's severe curse against anyone who would dare to do so (Joshua 6:26). Jericho was in the territory of Benjamin, who had remained faithful to the House of Judah - which indicates that Ahab himself was not necessarily the initiator of this despicable project; rather, it was Ahab's influence that created the climate in which it could come about. It is said that after Hi-el of Beit El, who rebuilt Jericho, lost all his sons one by one because of Joshua's curse, King Ahab and Elijah the Prophet went to visit him as he sat in mourning, and it was there that they had the conversation in which Elijah delivered the grim prophecy with which the following chapter opens (Rashi on I Kings 17:1).

CHAPTER 17

To raise the people from the deep spiritual decline into which they had fallen in the time of Ahab required a figure of outstanding stature. Opinions differ as to which tribe Elijah came from: some rabbis said he was from the tribe of Gad, which inherited Gil'ad. Others darshened from I Chron. 8:27 that he was from the tribe of Benjamin, while others identified him (or his soul) with Pinchas son of Elazar the Cohen (pointing to Elijah's request in v 13 to the widow of Tzarphat to give him the first portion of her dough, corresponding to the priestly Challah, Numbers 15:20-21).

Elijah received the Torah tradition from Achiyah HaShiloni and gave it over to Yehoyada HaKohen, as well as being master of all the subsequent great prophets of Israel (Rambam, Mishneh Torah, Introduction). After Elijah's ascent alive to Heaven in a chariot of fire, he became a legendary figure, making repeated miraculous appearances at moments of dire crisis.

"And through a prophet [Moses] God brought Israel up from Egypt, and through a prophet [Elijah] they were protected" (Hosea 12:14). While Moses was the agent of God's redemption of Israel from Egypt, Elijah will be His agent to redeem them in time to come (Malachi 3:23). There are numerous parallels between Moses and Elijah. Both are called "the man of God"; both ascended to Heaven; Moses killed the Egyptian while Elijah killed Hi-el (who built Jericho, Midrash on Hosea 13:1). Moses was sustained in exile by a woman (Tzipporah) while Elijah was sustained by the widow of Tzarphat. Moses fled from Pharaoh while Elijah fled from Jezebel. Both fled to a well (Ex. 2:I5; Kings 19:3). Moses brought about supernatural miracles (Numbers 16:29) and so did Elijah by stopping and starting the rains. God passed by both (Ex. 34:6; I Kings 19:11) and both heard "the voice" (Numb. 7:89; I Kings 19:13). Both came to Horeb (Ex. 3:1; I Kings 19:8) and both were hidden in a cave (Ex.33:22; I Kings 19:9). Moses assembled Israel at Mount Sinai, while Elijah assembled them at Mount Carmel. Moses uprooted idolatry (Ex.32:27) while Elijah killed the prophets of Baal (I Kings 18:40) and so on (Midrash Pesikta Rabbati).

"AND HE SHALL SHUT UP THE HEAVENS AND THERE WILL NOT BE RAIN"
(Deut. 11:17)

The rabbis darshened from the **semichut** ("immediate proximity") of Elijah's stopping of the rains (ch 17 v 1) to the account of the death of the sons of Hi-el, who rebuilt Jericho, that Elijah and Ahab both went to visit Hi-el in his mourning. When Elijah said that Hi-el's sons had died because he had defied Joshua's curse in rebuilding Jericho, Ahab asked how it was possible that God would uphold the curse of the student (Joshua) while not fulfilling the curse of the master (Moses) who had said that if Israel turned aside to serve idols, God's anger would burn and He would shut up the heavens - yet idolatry was rampant in the time of Ahab and it still rained regularly (see Rashi on v 1).

It was as a rejoinder to this insinuation that everything is governed by chance and that there is no divine judgment or providence that Elijah brought about a drought through the power of his own words, showing that God gives over the very keys of creation into the hands of His prophets. Elijah hoped that drought and famine would chastise the hearts of the arrogant idolaters of the time and bring them to humble themselves before God.

Immediately after making his decree, Elijah had to flee - the wicked Jezebel, who obviously called the shots in Shomron, had instigated a reign of complete terror, killing all true prophets, in an effort to efface the Torah from the hearts of Israel.

When God commanded the ravens - the cruelest of birds - to nonetheless bring bread and meat to Elijah (which they are said to have taken either from the kitchen of Ahab, or more likely from that of Jehoshaphat king of Judah, which was more kosher), it was a hint that it was time for Elijah to have mercy on the people and soften his harsh decree. Rabbi Nachman teaches that the radical change the ravens made in their normally cruel attitudes is emblematic of the change every Jew must make in his normally selfish ways in order to force himself to give charity. When a person gives charity because he is naturally generous-hearted, this is not a real act of service. Charity is only service when we break our instinctive cruelty and selfishness in order to help others - and such charity opens up all the gates of holiness (Likutey Moharan Part. II Discourse 4).

The widow of Tzarphat who courageously gave Elijah her last remaining food even at the height of a famine is symbolic of Knesset Israel - the Assembly of Israel - who had descended to the very bottom in the time of Ahab, yet were restored through the spiritual power of the prophet. Thus, the widow's son (identified with the prophet Jonah) was if not actually clinically dead at the very least no longer breathing (v 17) when Elijah performed his miraculous resuscitation. The prophet's ability to revive the lifeless lad is a sign that God's Redeemer will save Israel from even the worst decline.

CHAPTER 18

Out of compassion for His suffering people God sent Elijah to bring down the rains. The dire famine forced the very king himself to go out in search of forage for the animals (v 5), which shows the tenderness of Ahab's Israelite heart compared to that of his foreign wife, who had instigated a murderous rampage against God's prophets.

Even more surprising than this compassionate trait of Ahab's is the fact that as officer over his royal household he had appointed none other than the saintly prophet Obadiah, whom the Biblical text praises even more than Abraham since of the latter God said, "I know you fear God" (Gen. 22:12) while Obadiah is described as having "feared God **very much**" (I Kings 18:3; Sanhedrin 39b). Obadiah was a righteous proselyte who originated from Edom, and he was so great that he alone of all the prophets was allowed to prophesy the downfall of Edom in the end of days. "Why did Obadiah attain prophecy? Because he hid one hundred prophets in a cave" (Sanhedrin ibid.)

When Obadiah encountered his master Elijah, he told him, "There is not a nation or kingdom to which my lord [Ahab] has not sent to seek you out. and he made the kingdom and the nation swear that they could not find you" (v 10). From the fact that Ahab had enough leverage over all the kingdoms and nations that he could force them to take an oath, the rabbis learned that Ahab presided over a global empire or sphere of influence. "Three kings ruled over the whole dome of the globe: Ahab son of Omri, Nebuchadnezzar and Ahashverosh" (Megillah 11a). The mere fact that later historians have turned a blind eye to if not intentionally tried to efface the fact that there was an extensive Israelite sphere of influence in Biblical times should not deceive us into underestimating its greatness.

"How long will you go limping between the two opinions?..." Elijah asked the people (I Kings 18:21). To raise the people from their spiritual collapse, a **Kiddush HaShem** (Sanctification of God's Name) of the greatest magnitude was required. As discussed in the commentary on I Kings 16, since the building of the Temple in Jerusalem it was forbidden to sacrifice on any outside **Bamah** ("altar") on pain of **Karet** (early death and spiritual excision). Elijah's decision to sacrifice on Mount Carmel was **hora'at sha'ah**, a one-time legal ruling necessitated by the spiritual peril facing the nation. Elijah was not entirely uprooting the prohibition against sacrificing outside the Temple from the Torah (which would have been a sign of false prophecy) but simply suspending it for one time (Rambam, Hilchot Yesodey HaTorah 9:3) for the very purpose of **healing the Altar** (v 30). "He built an altar in order to remind Israel that God's Altar should have their foremost attention in their hearts and should constantly be mentioned on their lips, because it had been destroyed

Initially Elijah told the prophets of Baal to **choose** (v 25) one of the oxen (both were twins from the same mother that since birth had been together constantly in the same manger), but when it came to it, the false prophets "took the ox **which he gave them**" (v 26). Why did he have to **give** it to them? The Midrash tells that after Elijah and the false prophets cast lots for their oxen, the ox that fell to the lot of the false prophets ran to Elijah and took shelter under his cloak, refusing to move because his twin brother was going to sanctify heaven while he himself would be sacrificed to an idol. Only when Elijah assured this ox that God's name would be sanctified equally by both of them did it agree to go to the false prophets, and this is why it says, "**which he gave them**". It is said that the false prophets hid Hi-el (builder of Jericho) under their altar with instructions to secretly light a fire at the requisite moment, but he was bitten by a snake and died before he could do so.

The great miracle that all the people witnessed when fire came down from heaven to consume Elijah's sacrifice caused them to fall on their faces declaring, "**HaShem** - He is God! "**HaShem** - He is God!" (v 39). This phrase is solemnly repeated at the very climax of the concluding Yom Kippur **Ne'ilah** service and on other occasions when we wish to affirm and accept upon ourselves the yoke of the Kingdom of Heaven.

* * * I Kings ch 18 vv 1-39 is the Haftarah to Parshat **Ki Tisa**
(Exodus 30:11-34:35) read around Purim time. * * *

CHAPTER 19

* * * I Kings 18:46 and 19:1-21 is read as the Haftarah of Parshat **Pinchas**, Numbers 25:10-30:1 * * *

With the rout of the prophets of Baal on Mount Carmel, Elijah had brought about a tremendous **Kiddush HaShem** ("Sanctification of God's Name"). Even Ahab was impressed, but the implacable

Jezebel was unshaken and intended to use repressive terror to undo the results of Elijah's feat, swearing by her gods to kill him (v 2).

Elijah understood that now was not the time to "press the hour" and insist that God should overthrow the regime immediately, for "whoever tries to press the hour, the hour presses him" (P'sikta Zuta Gen. 27). Instead Elijah fled, just as Jacob had fled from Esau and Moses from Pharaoh. Elijah had tried to use drought and famine followed by the miracle on Mount Carmel to bring Israel to repent, but now he was overwhelmed with a terrible sense of failure and he wanted to "resign" from his ministry and leave it to God to redeem His people. Elijah went out into the wilderness without any food or water, and crouching under a solitary broom-tree that afforded scarcely any shade, he begged God to take his life.

God miraculously provided Elijah with sufficient refreshment to sustain him for forty days and nights - parallel to the forty days and nights that Moses did not eat when he ascended to Heaven to receive the Torah - and Elijah retraced the steps of the Master of the Prophets in reaching "the Mountain of God in Horeb", i.e. Mount Sinai, where Elijah entered into the same cleft in the rock from which Moses had seen God's glory (Ex. 33:22).

"And he said, I have been very zealous for the Lord God of hosts..." (v 10). Elijah's zeal for God was like that of Pinchas, whose soul he bore, and of whom God had testified that "he turned My wrath away from the Children of Israel in that he was **zealous** for My sake" (Numbers 22:11). Feeling that he had failed in his mission, Elijah was now asking God Himself to avenge the breach of His Covenant and the destruction of His Altar and the killing of His priests.

Without yet giving Elijah any answer, God told him to stand at the opening of the cave where, as a reward for his zeal, God "passed before Him" to let him see His glory. Targum Yonatan explains that the "great and mighty wind", "earthquake" and "fire" (vv 11-12) were successive revelations of great "camps" of angels - the agents through whom God controls the creation. (**ru'ach** and **esh** are respectively the air and fire elements, while **ra'ash** is not necessarily only an earthquake but also alludes to the water element: Targum renders **ra'ash** as **ziyah**, which also has the connotation of sweating: from the sweat of the Chayot comes the River Dinoor.)

In a lesson to all spiritual seekers at all times, our text teaches that the true glory of God was not in these sensational pyrotechnics but in the tranquil silence of the "still, small voice" that came afterwards (v 12). When we search for God, we must listen with the utmost attentiveness to the almost imperceptible voice of truth that speaks so softly deep down in the heart and soul.

Metzudat David explains that God took Elijah through this "performance" to show him that He wants to show kindness rather than arousing all His anger and coming against His creatures with hurricanes, earthquakes and fire. In asking him again, "What are you doing here Elijah?" (v 13) God was saying "Are you still here to ask for vengeance?" It was when Elijah repeated his complaint about the breach of the Covenant and his implicit request for vengeance (v 14, cf. v 10) that God told him to anoint another prophet in his place (v 15), in effect saying, "I can't take your prophecy since you are making accusations against My children" (Rashi ad loc.).

It is said that for having accused the Children of Israel of abandoning the Covenant (i.e. ceasing to practice circumcision) while seven thousand still remained faithful (v 18), Elijah was penalized by having to attend every **Brit Milah** ("circumcision") ceremony performed ever after by those who go by the name of Israel. For this reason, it is customary to prepare the "Chair of Elijah" at every circumcision and to place the baby upon it for a moment immediately prior to the performance of the operation, invoking the spirit of Elijah to inspire the child and everyone else present with his spirit of purity and zeal.

In accepting Elijah's request to resign his ministry, God told him to anoint (1) Haza-el as king of Aram, (2) Jehu son of Nimshi as king over Israel, and (3) Elisha son of Shaphat as successor to himself (vv 15-16). To appreciate the significance of these prophecies, it is necessary to understand that Elijah himself did **not** personally anoint either Haza-el or Jehu. It was Elijah's disciple Elisha who anointed both of them (II Kings 8:9ff and 9:2ff). Since on Elijah's return from the wilderness he immediately encountered and anointed Elisha (our chapter v 19), he realized that the third element in God's message was fulfilled before the first and second and thereby inferred that Elisha would be the one to anoint Haza-el and Jehu later on as his "agent" (RaDaK). Haza-el proved to be a far crueler adversary against Israel than the kings of Aram who preceded him, while after the death of Ahab Jehu overthrew and massacred his entire house in a bloody coup, taking Israel deeper into sin and idolatry.

In this way God relieved Elijah of his public ministry (though he continues to serve God and intervene, visibly or invisibly, at all kinds of junctures) and He took back the providence into His own hands, as it were, while appointing Elisha to succeed Elijah. It was not that Elijah had never seen Elisha before: according to tradition, it was Elisha who poured the water into the trough when Elijah called for fire from Heaven to consume his sacrifice (I Kings 18:34-5). However, Elijah now placed his mantle over Elisha for a moment (v 19) as an invitation to full ordination as his successor. Elisha was already presiding over twelve pairs of plowing oxen - a sign that he was to be appointed as prophet and reproof-giver to the Twelve Tribes of Israel (RaDaK). Delaying only to bid his parents and friends farewell, Elisha went after Elijah "and ministered to him" (v 21) - for "ministering to Torah scholars is even greater than learning the Torah itself" (Eliyahu Rabbah 5).

CHAPTER 20

The wars of Aram against Israel narrated in our present chapter are **not** the war that God foretold to Elijah (ch 19 vv 15 &17), which came a generation later. Nevertheless, ever since the end of King Solomon's reign the Arameans had been organizing to throw off the yoke of subjugation that King David had laid upon them. The endemic Aramean envy and hatred of Israel dated back to Laban and Bilaam, who epitomize the use of crafty intelligence and wisdom to **hide** Godliness. Behind the account of their war against Israel as told in this chapter lie allusions to the way in which the **Kelipah** (husk) of Aram (corresponding to the vernacular language - "Aramaic" - and mundane intelligence) seeks to "hijack" the holy wisdom of the Torah for its own purposes.

Thus Ben-Hadad king of Aram came against Israel with **thirty-two** kings (corresponding to the thirty-two pathways of wisdom rooted in the twenty-two letters and ten vowels of Hebrew).

The rabbinic interpretation of Ben-Hadad's provocative ultimatum to King Ahab (vv 3; 6, see Sanhedrin 102b) is that he did not only want Ahab's silver and gold and wives and children but "all the **machmad** - delight - of your eyes". This is an allusion to the Torah, whose teachings are "more delightful - **nechmadim** - than purest gold" (Psalms 19:11). Ben-Hadad wanted to have the Torah surrendered into his own hands in order to reinterpret and falsify it in any way he chose. The amazing thing is that Ahab - the Baal and Ashera-worshipper - was perfectly willing to give up everything else but **balked** at the idea of giving up the Torah to the point that he was ready to go to war rather than submit. Ahab called all the elders of Israel (v 7), who certainly included the seven thousand who were still faithful, and the entire nation agreed to flout Aram, which shows that they were far from being crude idolaters who were in flight from their whole tradition. "For what reason did Ahab merit to rule for 22 years? Because he gave honor to the Torah, which was given with 22 letters" (Sanhedrin 102b). Verse 9 contains 22 Hebrew words.

It was surely in the merit of the Israelite zeal burning in King Ahab that a true prophet informed him that God would deliver the Arameans into his hand (v 13). The prophet told him that instead of sending out his entire army to fight them, the king should dispatch only the "young men of the princes of the provinces"(v 14). These were the children of the princes of Ahab's subject states, whom they were forced to send to his capital as "collateral" to ensure that they would not rebel. The fact that there were 232 of these children again points to the great extent of Ahab's sphere of influence, which the Arameans were now trying to undermine. In addition, 232 is significant as the sum of the gematrias of the four chief **milu'im** ("fillings") of the name of HaVaYaH - 72, 63, 45 and 52. Moreover, this figure encompasses all the 231 "Gates" through which the 22 letters of the Hebrew alphabet are permuted with one another to make up the words of the Hebrew language (see Sefer Yetzirah and commentaries).

Through a series of miraculous deliveries, God proved that Aramean military might was nothing in the face of Torah spirit. To disabuse the Arameans of their illusion that the God of Israel had power only in the hills, He lured them out to the valleys, where Israel smote 100,000 of them in one day (alluding to the destruction of a complete array of the Ten Sefirot of impurity, each consisting of sub-arrays and sub-sub-arrays). After the survivors fled to Aphek (which is a few kilometers east of the southern tongue of the Kinneret, Lake Tiberias), collapsing fortifications killed another 27,000 (corresponding to the 22 basic letters of the Hebrew alphabet together with the five "final" letters, a total of 27, each of which contains its own arrays and sub-arrays of the Ten Sefirot).

Ben-Hadad fled but he knew as well as Israel's Arab adversaries know until today that the Israelite heart is tender, merciful and forgiving and that he would only have to say a few soothing words to the king against whom he had just unleashed two major wars in order to be able to enter into a "peace process" with him (vv 31-34). God had maneuvered Ben-Hadad into His trap (v 42) but Ahab let the Aramean king get away, much as recent Israeli governments have almost never lost an opportunity to allow the country's enemies to get away with their endless aggressions and provocations. God's prophet told Ahab that his misplaced kindheartedness would cost him his life and cause enormous national suffering, but Ahab did not want to listen and rushed off home in a furious temper.

CHAPTER 21

The sorry story of the murderous expropriation of Nabot's vineyard by King Ahab put the final seal on his fate and that of his dynasty. Many people permit themselves to believe in what they please while claiming themselves to be quite as moral, if not more so, than those who seek to uphold the law of God's Torah. Ahab first allowed himself to go after the gods of the other nations. Now we see how his willingness to violate what may seem to be the least serious of all of the Ten Commandments - coveting the property of others (Exodus 20:14) - drew him into a spiral of sin that led him to violate at least half of them.

What could be wrong with gazing at something belonging to somebody else and merely wishing it was mine?

In the words of Rambam: "The appetite for wealth brings one to desire the property of others, and this brings a person to robbery. If the owners refuse to sell their property even after being offered much money and put under heavy pressure, if they seek to prevent the covetous person from robbing them, it can bring him to actual bloodshed. Go out and learn from the story of Ahab and Nabot" (Laws of Robbery 1:11).

The Torah law of kings does permit the king to expropriate the private property of his subjects for certain purposes (I Samuel 8:14), but most rabbinic opinions hold that Ahab had no legal right to take Nabot's vineyard, which is why he had to resort to framing Nabot in order to grab it.

The text makes it seem that Ahab himself only sulked when Nabot refused to give over his ancestral portion to the king, while it was really the wicked Jezebel who egged Ahab into taking action to have Nabot killed in order to get the vineyard. Nevertheless, kings are not allowed to let their wives rule over them - that had been the cause of Solomon's undoing - and they certainly cannot be forgiven when they carry out crimes at their wives' behest. As a result of his covetousness (contrary to the Tenth Commandment), Ahab allowed false witnesses to stand up and accuse a righteous man of blasphemy and high treason (contrary to the Ninth Commandment). Through this false testimony, Nabot was murdered (contrary to the Sixth Commandment) and Ahab stole his vineyard (contrary to the Eighth Commandment. And by also killing Nabot's children (II Kings 9:26, cf. Likutey Moharan I, 69) it was as if Ahab had stolen his very wife (contrary to the Seventh Commandment). In this way Ahab violated all of the five commandments between man and man on the second of the Two Tablets.

It is noteworthy how as Jezebel sets up the framing of Nabot she does so with the utmost piety, calling on the elders of Nabot's city to call a public fast (v 9) as an opportunity for soul-searching and the investigation of the sins of the people. She takes care to have Nabot framed not only for high treason against the king (for which, most conveniently, his property is by Torah law confiscated by the crown) but also for blasphemy!

What is clear from this chapter is that the Ten Tribes had not merely fled the Torah in some simple sense so as to sink totally into some completely alien idolatry. With all their dalliance with the gods of the nations, they still saw themselves as following the Torah path: Torah observance and Torah violation were most subtly intermingled. Only through the clear vision and judgment of the true prophet is it possible to try to disentangle them and see things the way they really are.

"Have you murdered and also inherited?..." Elijah asked Ahab (v 19) in words that could with justice be repeated to numerous "kings" and leaders of our own times. Elijah prophesies the bloody destruction of the house of Ahab and Jezebel - after which, in yet another twist to the story of this very complex, subtle character, we see that Ahab is truly chastised and repents, putting on sackcloth, fasting and going barefoot!

CHAPTER 22

"And they stopped for three years: there was no war between Aram and Israel" (v 1). It was symptomatic of the times that there was no longer such a thing as peace, but only a temporary cessation of war - very similar to the way things are today.

Another of the surprises in our story is that Yehoshaphat king of Judah was actually in alliance with the idolatrous Ahab. Yehoshaphat was indeed married to Ahab's sister in an alliance forged by their respective parents, Asa king of Judah and Omri king of Israel.

Whereas the earlier kings of Judah had tried to regain their hegemony over the rebellious Ten Tribes through force, the policy of Asa and Yehoshaphat was to stretch out the arm of friendship - what in modern terms is called "outreach". In certain respects, the alliance of the Kingdom of Judah and that of Israel in the times of Ahab and Yehoshaphat bears comparison with the alliance between the secular Zionists who established the State of Israel and the mainstream of Torah observant Jews without whose support it would probably have collapsed long ago.

Another factor that has a contemporary ring is that the bone of contention between Israel and Aram (= Syria) was "Ramot Gilead" (v 4) - none other than the Golan Heights!

In the tradition of David his father, Yehoshaphat wanted to consult prophets before going out to war. When Ahab assembled four hundred of his own prophets, all of whom foretold victory using exactly the same words, Yehoshaphat felt extremely uneasy, but he was too polite to tell Ahab directly that he thought they were a bunch of false prophets: he merely asked if there was no true prophet present. Ahab's prophets remind one of the kinds of present day think tank experts and news commentators who act as soothsayers to the general public while the world falls apart all around us.

The true prophet Michayahu son of Yimlah who was now called upon to prophesy has already appeared without being named in Chapter 20 vv 13, 28 and 35ff, where he previously prophesied to Ahab. In ch 20 vv 42 he had prophesied that Ahab's soul would be taken in payment for his having freed Ben-Hadad king of Aram, and this was why Ahab hated him.

In a prophecy of Ahab's coming death, Michayahu told of his vision of Israel "scattered on the mountains like a flock that has no shepherd" (v 17) - a vision that seems to apply until today!!! Michayah depicts the heavenly court in judgment over Ahab. The "spirit" that steps forward in v 21 offering to trick Ahab into going to war is said to have been the spirit of Nabot. The rabbis say that despite Ahab's idolatry, his fate was hanging in the balance because he was generous with his money and gave support to Torah scholars. What tipped the balance was his sin of taking Nabot's vineyard, which sealed Ahab's fate.

Through the spirit of falsehood that spoke on the lips of his soothsaying prophets, Ahab was drawn out to war against Aram, in which an innocent archer (said to be Na'aman, the king of Aram's commander-in-chief, II Kings ch 5) shot the arrow that killed him. Despite being mortally wounded Ahab ordered his chariot driver to prop his body up in the chariot so that the Israelites should not see that he was dying and lose heart, and Ahab was praised for this final act of heroism.

The Book of Kings is conventionally divided in printed Bibles into Parts I and II for the sake of convenience, but in handwritten parchment scrolls of Sefer Melakhim, it is all one continuous book. The division in the printed Bible at this point is relatively arbitrary since it happens to come near the middle of the book (and it actually comes in the middle of a parshah=paragraph of the Hebrew text). However, the subject matter at the beginning of II Kings is a direct continuation of the narrative at the end of I Kings telling how Ahab's son Ahaziyahu came to the throne of Israel and continued in exactly the path of his father and mother.

"And Moab rebelled against Israel after the death of Ahab" (v 1). After their subjugation by King David, the Moabites had been a client state within the Israelite sphere of influence and paid Ahab 100,000 sheep annually in tribute (II Kings 3:4). When the Moabites rebelled, the new king literally **fell through the floor** - i.e. through a thin wooden lattice-work screen that covered an aperture in the floor of his upper storey chamber (Metzudat David) through which one could presumably look down unseen at what was going on below. Apparently, the king tripped over it and fell through - showing further how weak were the foundations of Ahab's dynasty!

The king must have been seriously injured. True to form, he sent not to an Israelite prophet to find out his prognosis (he probably feared the answer he would receive) but to priests of the cult of **Zvuv**, the "fly" god of the Philistine city of Ekron. (Similarly, in recent generations many alienated Jews have been searching for spiritual meaning in every tradition except their own.)

For an Israelite king to do such a thing was a serious affront to the honor of the God of Israel and His prophets, and this itself sealed the sick king's fate. In what was to be the last public mission of his ministry, Elijah the Prophet was sent to intercept the king's envoys and tell them to tell him he was going to die.

When the king heard the news, and asked his envoys to describe the man who told them this, they said he was "a man of much hair with a belt of leather girded around his loins" (v 8). The abundant hair alludes to the exalted heights of Elijah's perceptions of God (each **se'ar**, "hair", is a **sha'ar**, "gateway" of apprehension). His "girded loins" indicate his supreme moral purity and sanctity: the "leather" was said to have come from the ram of Isaac (Gen. 22:13). On hearing these signs, the king immediately knew the prophet's identity and sent a captain with a squadron of fifty soldiers to order him to come down from his mountain to the palace in Shomron.

The captain brusquely ordered the prophet to go down, as if the honor due to his king was greater than the honor due to God's prophet. God Himself sent fire to burn up the captain and his fifty men in order to avenge the insult to the prophet, and lest the king should interpret this as a mere coincidence, He did the same to his second captain and squadron of fifty. Only the more respectful attitude of the third captain mollified Heaven sufficiently to send prophecy to Elijah to appear before the king and castigate him directly. For "Those who honor Me shall I honor, but those who despise Me shall be despised" (I Sam. 2:30). Now that the kings of Israel had gone astray, their moral authority was discredited, while God himself would vindicate the authority of His true prophets.

With his fate sealed, Ahaziahu died, and, having no children, was succeeded by his brother Yehoram son of Ahab. This initiated a period in which the kings of Israel and Judah both had the same name, since Yehoshaphat king of Judah had also called his son Yehoram.

Elijah had already asked to be relieved of his ministry of zeal and fire (I Kings 19:4), and now he was taken up to heaven in a chariot of fire. The narrative of Elijah's ascent in our present chapter contains many teachings about the nature of prophecy. Elijah tried to persuade his disciple Elisha not to follow him, but Elisha knew prophetically that his master was to be taken from him (vv 3, 5) and refused to leave his side. The other prophets who came out to meet them also knew that Elijah was about to ascend to heaven (ibid.) - for the departure from earth of **Tzaddik HaDor**, the "righteous leader of the generation", was an event of the greatest significance even though ordinary mortals may have been quite unaware of it.

Elijah's journey with Elisha took them to some of the key spiritual sites in the Land, including the first Israelite encampment after their original entry, Gilgal (also having the connotation of **gilgul**, reincarnation) and Beit El, where Abraham and Jacob had prayed long before Jerabo'am made his golden calves.

The "sons" of the prophets who came out of Beit El and Jericho (vv 3, 5) were not necessarily their biological offspring but rather the students of the prophets, "and from here we learn that students are called children, and likewise it says, 'And you shall diligently teach them to your children' (Deut. 6:7), and just as students are called children, so the teacher is called a father, as it says, And Elisha watched and he called, 'My father, my father'" (II Kings 2:12; Sifrey,Va-etchanan 6).

The fact that there were bands of students of prophecy in Beit El and Jericho "teaches you that there was not a city in Israel that did not have prophets - and the reason why their prophecies were not recorded is because only those prophecies that were required by subsequent generations were written down while those that were not required by subsequent generations were not written down" (Yalkut Shimoni). The fact that the prophets of Jericho, speaking to Elisha about Elijah, called the latter "**your** master" and not **ours** indicates that they were as wise as Elijah (Tosefta to Sotah).

Going in the reverse direction from the Israelites on their entry into the Land, Elijah went from Jericho to the River Jordan, which he split miraculously with his "mantle". "It would appear that Elijah had been informed through prophecy that he would be taken on the east bank of the Jordan - perhaps he was taken in the very place where Moses our Teacher was gathered in to the place of His glory, for the level of Elijah was very close to the level of Moses" (RaDaK on v 1).

If the students of the prophets are their "sons", Elisha asked of Elijah as his parting gift to be given "a double portion of your spirit upon me", alluding to the "double portion" of the firstborn son (Deut. 21:17). We do indeed see in the ensuing narratives about Elisha that he performed double the miracles of Elijah. Everything that Elisha did, he did in the power of his master, and this power came into him precisely because he was present when Elijah ascended the chariot of fire drawn by horses of fire.

RaDaK (on v 1) explains (on the level of **p'shat**, the simple meaning of the text) that the "storm wind of Heaven" with which God raised Elijah (v 1) was an invisible **Ru'ach** which lifted the prophet up into the air taking him up through the will of God to the "sphere of fire" where all his garments except for his mantle were burned up and where his flesh and bones were consumed, while his spirit ascended to God who gave it. According to this explanation, the Chariot of Fire that appeared to Elisha came to teach him that with the ascent of Elijah the "chariot of Israel and its riders" had gone up from upon Israel. However, despite this literal interpretation of the text, RaDaK continues: "The opinion of the masses and the opinion of our sages is that God took him alive into the Garden of Eden together with his body just as Adam had been before his sin."

On the level of **sod** (mystery) Rabbi Nachman teaches that while only the lower soul of the Tzaddik is revealed through his life and works in this world, the higher soul exists concurrently in the upper world. When the time comes for the Tzaddik to leave this world, his upper soul "descends" into this world in the form of the "chariot of fire", and because of the close bond between the upper and lower soul, the latter leaps out to join and reunite with the upper soul which then ascends back to the upper world. The descent of the upper soul is accompanied with an enormous revelation of wisdom and knowledge which the Tzaddik pours forth on his last day. Those of his students who are present at the time of his ascent receive a great share of this light because their souls have the same root as the Tzaddik. But whereas the Tzaddik's time has come to leave the world and he ascends, the students' time has not yet come, and they therefore remain in this world but with the greater wisdom - the "double share" - they received from their master at the moment of his ascent, as in the case of Elisha (Likutey Moharan I, 66).

Back again to the level of **p'shat**, Elisha's rending of his garment on the departure of his teacher is the foundation of the law that any student must rend his garment in two and never repair it when he loses his outstanding Torah teacher, and the same applies to all the community on the death of the Head of the Sanhedrin (Rambam, Laws of Mourning 9:2).

Having inherited his master's mantle, Elisha was now the leader of the generation, and the new spirit that had entered into him was immediately visible when he too used Elijah's mantle to split the Jordan and return to the Land of Israel. On seeing this, the other prophets immediately prostrated and submitted to his authority. Their asking Elisha to send out a search party to find Elijah (vv 16-17) after having previously prophesied that he was going to be taken away (vv 3, 5) was understood by the rabbis to indicate that from the moment Elijah ascended, holy spirit increasingly departed from the prophets and there was no longer much holy spirit in Israel (Rashi on v 16).

Elisha also inherited the passionate zeal of Elijah, and while he miraculously healed the waters of Jericho for the prophets, he showed no compassion on the "small lads" who came out from Beit El mocking his "baldness" (they were complaining that he had left the land bald by taking away their livelihood since previously they earned money by importing water from elsewhere). The commentators teach that they were called **na'arim** ("lads") because they were **me-nuar-im** ("stripped bare") of Mitzvot! Elisha saw that these were souls that would never produce any good even in the generations to come and this was why he cursed them (Rashi on v 23; Sotah 46b). For "Those who honor Me shall I honor, but those who despise Me shall be despised" (I Sam. 2:30).

CHAPTER 3

"And Jehoram son of Ahab ruled over Israel... in the **eighteenth year of Jehoshaphat** king of Judah" (v 1). This verse appears to contradict the verse in II Kings 1:17 which says that Jehoram son of Ahab came to the throne in the **second year** of the reign of **Jehoram** son of Jehoshaphat. A further problem is that the death of King Jehoshaphat has already been recorded at the end of I Kings 22:51, while our present chapter relates how Jehoshaphat joined Jehoram in his war against the rebellious Moabites.

The apparent inconsistencies are resolved through the rabbinic teaching that when Jehoshaphat agreed to join Ahab in his war against Aram at Ramot Gilead (I Kings 22:4-5), it was decreed that Jehoshaphat should die in the battle as did Ahab. However, just as the Aramean forces were about to kill him, Jehoshaphat screamed out in prayer to God and was miraculously saved (ibid. vv 32-3) and in virtue of his repentance, he was granted another seven years of life. Jehoshaphat was greatly humbled, and gave over the throne to his son Jehoram in his lifetime (II Chronicles 21:3).

The narrative of the war of the kings of Judah, Israel and Edom against Moab is positioned here in order to continue the cycle of stories of the miracles performed by Elisha. A careful count of these miracles reveals that they number a total of sixteen - double the eight miracles performed by Elijah, in fulfillment of Elisha's request to receive a "double portion" of his master's spirit (ch 2 v 9; see Rashi on ch 3 v 1).

Elisha had given up his livelihood and abandoned his family in order to follow Elijah (I Kings 19:20). Elisha's ministry continued through the reigns of five kings of Israel until his death in the time of Jeho'ash son of Jeho'ahaz ben Jehu (II Kings 13:14ff), and according to the Midrash Seder Olam, it lasted for more than sixty years - longer than that of any other of the prophets of Israel. Unlike his master Elijah, who was somewhat of a "loner" spending much of his time secreted away in Hitbodedut, Elisha not only traveled from place to place but also dwelled for extended periods in a variety of locations, where he taught the "sons of the prophets" and spread Torah - we find Elisha visiting Gilgal, Jericho, Mount Carmel, Shunem and Dotan in the Land of Israel as well as the wilderness of Edom and Damascus outside the Land. From ch 4 v 23 we learn that it was customary for Elisha's disciples to join him for Sabbaths and New Moons, somewhat like the way the latter-day Chassidim travel to their Rebbes for Sabbaths and festivals.

The rebellion of the Moabites has already been recorded at the beginning of II Kings 1:1 but only now in Chapter 3 do we hear of the campaign by Jehoram king of Israel to subdue them. He was joined not only by Jehoshaphat king of Judah (who was still trying to cooperate with the kingdom of Israel as a means of "Torah outreach") but also by the king of Edom, which was still subject to Judah and rebelled only after the death of Jehoshaphat.

Campaigning in the arid wilderness areas east of the Dead Sea, these three kings almost lost their entire armies because they found no water. The situation was critical and was saved only by Elisha, who went with them not to join the battle but because he had been ordered to do so prophetically in order to perform a miracle for Jehoram in the hope that it would bring him to repent (RaDaK on v 11). At the height of the crisis, when Jehoshaphat king of Judah characteristically asked to consult a prophet, the servant of the king of Israel who pointed to Elisha described him as "having poured out water over the hands of Elijah" (v 11). According to the Midrash, it was Elisha who had poured the water all around Elijah's altar on Mount Carmel in his contest with the prophets of Baal (I Kings 18:34-5), and "his ten fingers became like fountains filling the entire trench with water" (Rashi and RaDaK on II Kings 3:11).

The true prophet thus flows with the waters of Torah, and in Elisha's merit, God miraculously filled the dry valley in the wilderness of Edom with wells brimming with water. Initially, Elisha did not want to even look at the sinful king of Israel, and in his anger the spirit of prophecy left him, for wisdom and prophecy cannot dwell side by side with anger (Pesachim 66b). It was only when Elisha called for musicians to play joyous music that the spirit of prophecy dwelled with him again (v 15), teaching that "the Shechinah does not dwell through sadness and lethargy but only through the joy of a mitzvah, as it is written, Take for me a musician." (Shabbat 30b).

Confronted with miracle after miracle performed by God in favor of the Israelites, the king of Moab turned to his astrologers and asked them what was the secret of the Israelites' success. When they told him that their first patriarch Abraham had been willing to sacrifice his very son to God, the Moabite king took his own firstborn son and offered him up **al hachomah** (v 27). This is literally translated as "on the wall", but since the word **chomah** is spelled here without the letter Vav and can be read as **Chamah**, "the sun", we learn that this sacrifice was to the sun-god whom the Moabites worshiped (Rashi and RaDaK ad loc., Sanhedrin 39b). The king of Moab 's sacrifice caused "great anger" against Israel (v 27) because they too had taken to worshiping idols and no longer showed the same willingness to sacrifice all for God as Abraham.

Some have compared the Moabite king's willingness to slaughter his first-born son for the sake of victory to the Jihadi willingness to send out suicide bombers in all directions. However, the comparison is not quite accurate as research indicates that the typical profile of the suicide bomber is one of a chronic depressive social reject who has very little to lose by giving up his life for the sake of 72 virgins in "paradise". Nevertheless, the lesson Israel should learn from the suicide bombers is that the way to dissipate God's "great anger" is not by throwing away our lives in an orgy of destruction but by heroically offering all our strength and vitality on the altar of God's service every day.

CHAPTER 4

The first part of this chapter (vv 1-37) is familiar as the Haftarah of Parshat Vayeira (Genesis 18:1-22:24) telling of the announcement of the birth of Isaac, which is paralleled by Elisha's promise to the woman of Shunem that she would bear a son (II Kings 4:17).

The miracle of the oil performed by Elisha for "a certain woman" as narrated in the opening section of this chapter (vv 1-7) is, like the ensuing story of the birth, death and revival of the son of the Shunemite woman (vv 8-37), a very heavily veiled allegory that is explained at length by ARI (Sefer HaLikutim on Kings 2:4) in terms that are incomprehensible without an extensive knowledge of the Kabbalah and the Hebrew language. While the rabbis of the Midrash identify this "certain woman" as the widow of the prophet Obadiah, who was unable to repay to Jehoram son of Ahab the debts and very heavy **ribbit** ("interest") incurred by her late husband in supporting the persecuted prophets of God (I Kings 18:4), ARI explains that she represents Rachel/Shechinah, whose vessels are empty owing to the sins of Israel, which make it impossible to elevate the scattered sparks and "pay back the debts".

In the case of Elisha's miracle for the woman of Shunem, ARI explains that his purpose was likewise to release and redeem the souls of Israel from sin. "And it was on **that day**"(v 8): this refers to Rosh Hashanah, the Day of Judgment. This was when Elisha "passed over to **Shunem**", which literally refers to a town in the Jezreel Valley, but which, according to ARI, is emblematic of the treasury of all the souls - for on Rosh Hashanah it is decreed who will die and who will come to life. The purpose of the Shunemite woman was to bring a very elevated soul into the world - according to Zohar her son was the prophet Habakuk (cf. v 16, "you will embrace - **choveket** - a son").

Returning to the level of **p'shat**, the "simple meaning", we see that the Shunemite woman excelled in the virtue of **hospitality** to a Torah scholar, and "everyone who hosts a Torah scholar in his home and gives him benefit from his possessions is accounted as if he had offered the daily Temple **continual offering**" (=**Tamid**, the last Hebrew word in v 9; see Talmud Berachot 10b). The Shunemite woman created a miniature Sanctuary in her own home (v 10). The "bed" corresponds to the Ark of the Covenant, the "table" to the Showbread Table, the "chair" to the Incense Altar and the "lamp" is the Menorah. Through her hospitality to Elisha, the Shunemite woman gave birth to one of the great prophets of Israel, demonstrating that even when it is difficult or impossible to go up to the Temple, through creating a sanctuary in our very homes and our private lives, we can draw holy spirit and prophecy back into the world.

CHAPTER 5

The last few verses of the previous chapter (I Kings 4:42-44) together with the first 18 verses of the present chapter are the Haftarah of Parshat Tazria (Lev. 12:1-13:59), most of which deals with the laws of **tzara'at** ("leprosy").

The salvation that God had given to Aram through Na'aman was that he had been the archer who innocently shot King Ahab at the battle of Ramot Gil'ad (I Kings 22:34; Rashi ad loc.). As a result of his military distinction, Na'aman became arrogant (Bamidbar Rabbah 7) and was afflicted with **tzara'at**, a skin and hair affliction that is a manifestation on the surface of the body of the inner flaws of the soul. An Israelite girl taken captive by a band of Aramean marauders was telling her mistress that her husband could surely be cured by visiting the wonder-Rebbe miracle worker, Elisha the Prophet. (His name, **El yisha**, means "God will save").

The king of Aram now sends to Jehoram king of Israel saying "Heal my captain" - which is somewhat as if a present-day Iranian leader were to send a message to the Israeli prime minister saying, "We will nuclear bombard your country unless you heal Mr X". King Jehoram - a complex character - rent his very garments in despair: how could he personally turn to Elisha, even though he knew God did miracles for him? Jehoram was too ashamed to ask the prophet to pray, knowing that he himself would not listen to him and stop worshiping Jerabo'am's golden calves (RaDaK on v 7).

Elisha now sanctified the Name of Heaven through the miraculous healing of Na'aman. The latter was expecting Elisha to come out like a white-robed guru and wave his hand to heal him. However, the way the Tzaddik actually healed him was by giving him a simple piece of advice - to bathe seven times in the River Jordan. The advice of the Tzaddik is so easy but yet so hard!!! Na'aman was insulted, considering the Amanah and Parpar rivers much better. RaDaK (on v 12), cites a comment in the name of his father that Na'aman was saying he already washed every day. In modern terms, he felt he was scrupulously hygienic and couldn't understand how merely washing in the River Jordan had the power to remove the inner moral filth that lay behind the deceptive appearance of his impeccable exterior bodily cleanliness.

After the miracle, Na'aman wanted to "pay", but Elisha adamantly refused: to have accepted "payment" for God's miracle would have been a terrible **Chillul HaShem**, "Desecration of the Name", which would have undermined the entire **Kiddush HaShem** Elisha had brought about. Na'aman asked to be given two mule-loads of holy earth from the Land of Israel in order to build an altar to God in his home city. (Although it is forbidden for an Israelite to sacrifice anywhere except on the Temple Altar in Jerusalem, it is permitted for a Noahide to offer animal sacrifice to God elsewhere if it is performed in the correct way according to Torah law.)

The negative side of Elisha's **na'ar** - his "attendant" or, in modern terms, his **Gabbai** - has already appeared in ch 4 v 27, when he tried to push the Shunemite woman away from Elisha when she came to beg him to intercede on behalf of her son. It is said that when Elisha told him to hurry on ahead without talking to anyone in order to lay the prophet's staff on the boy, Gehazi showed the staff to all passers-by, cynically asking if it really had the power to resurrect the child.

Now the appetite for wealth overcame him, which unfortunately tends to happen among certain Gabba'im whose eyes pop out at the vast wealth they see in many pockets of the world outside of the Torah kingdom - wealth that owing to the selfishness of many of its owners rarely percolates within the Torah community to ease the economic plight of its Torah scholars. Taking money from Na'aman for Elisha's miracle under false pretences (v 22) and then hiding it away for himself (v 24) was an outrageous **Chillul HaShem**, which was the very opposite of what Elisha wanted, and this is why through the mystery of exchanges and payment for everything, he "transferred" the **tzara'at** of Na'aman on to Gehazi so that he would no longer be able to keep the blemishes of his soul hidden.

Chapter 6 continues narrating the miracles of Elisha. The occasion for the first one told here - making metal float on water (vv 1-7) - was the planned expansion of Elisha's Beit Midrash ("study hall"), which was necessary because Gehazi's way had been to drive students away, while after his rejection by Elisha many students arrived making the classroom cramped (Rashi on v 1). Some students had gone to the Jordan to cut down wood for the expansion project when the metal head of the borrowed axe of one of them fell off its handle into the water. This was a disaster for the impecunious student, who did not have the money to pay. Asking to see the place where it happened, Elisha cut a piece of wood and with supernatural ingenuity cast it under the water, where it entered into the hole in the axe-head where the handle fitted and thereafter floated up to the surface bringing the axe-head with it. The reason why Elisha could not use the existing wooden handle is that for miracles to happen, there has to be something new (RaDaK on v 6).

The next miracle (vv 8ff) took place when Elisha repeatedly gave King Jehoram advance information about planned Aramean marauder incursions into his territory without the use of satellite pictures, phone tapping, listening devices etc. but purely through prophetic clairvoyance to the point where, as one of his servants (Na'aman?) told the king of Aram, "Elisha the prophet that is in Israel will tell the king of Israel the things you say in your bedroom" (v 12). Examples of similar kinds of **Ru'ach HaKodesh**, "holy spirit", are told in the case of outstanding Tzaddikim like Rabbi Shimon bar Yochai (in Zohar), the ARI (in Shevachey HaAri), the Baal Shem Tov (in Shevachey HaBesht) and Rabbi Nachman of Breslov (in Chayey Moharan/Tzaddik) etc. In our own generations, many stories about the Lubavitcher Rebbe, Baba Sali and other great Tzaddikim attest to their foreknowledge of dangers to individuals and communities as well as their ability to see things in other parts of this world and in many other worlds.

Elisha's "leaks" so infuriated the king of Aram that he sent troops to capture him. Seeing the Aramean forces surrounding the town of Dotan, where Elisha was visiting, terrified his attendant - until the prophet assured him that "more are they who are with us than those who are with them" (v 16). As in the case of stories of how the Baal Shem Tov and other Tzaddikim would sometimes open the eyes of some of those around them to the worlds they themselves could apprehend, Elisha asked God to open the attendant's eyes so that he could see the "horses and chariots of fire all around Elisha" (v 17).

Rather than praying that the Aramean squadron should just drop dead, Elisha asked that they should be struck with a "blindness" which enabled him to hypnotically direct them away from himself in the small town of Dotan until they came bang into the center of the capital city, Shomron, where they were naturally greatly outnumbered by the Israelite forces on their home territory. Seeing the captured Aramean squadron in his capital city, King Jehoram was ready to kill them, but Elisha would not allow this, telling him instead to feed and water the captives and send them home - so that they could tell everyone about the miracle.

This brought the period of mere Aramean marauding to a close (v 23), convincing them that more serious measures were called for against the stubborn Israelites. "And Ben-Hadad king of Aram gathered all his camp" - this was a major mobilization - "and laid siege to Shomron" (v 24). The terrible famine that ensued in Shomron brought things to the stage where the curses Moses had called down upon those who rebel against the Torah (Deut. 28:53) were actually fulfilled when the most refined of women were reduced to eating their own children (our chapter vv 28-9). Hearing this greatly shocked King Jehoram, who rent his garments and put on sackcloth (v 30) - and went on, like today's **Chilonim** ("the secular"), to blame all his problems on the Torah community as embodied in its leader, Elisha son of Shaphat (="he judged").

The furious king now sends a squadron to go and put a quick end to the prophet, but Elisha - who has perfect foreknowledge of the advancing contingent - tells his students to block their way, leaving us at the end of Chapter 6 with a "cliff-hanger" wondering what is going to happen next.

CHAPTER 7

At the height of the murderous famine in Shomron, with the king of Israel's envoy standing at Elisha's door with instructions to kill him as if he was responsible, the prophet announces that by the same time tomorrow there will be a complete turnabout, with cheap flour in abundance for the people and even cheaper barley for their animals. On hearing this, the king's foremost aide cynically expresses total disbelief, at which Elisha prophecies that the aide will see it with his eyes but not eat (v 2). This is how God pays "measure for measure": since the king's officer did not believe that God had the power to send a miracle, he would not have any benefit from it, and indeed, as we learn at the end of the chapter, he was trampled to death by a stampede of starving people surging forward to get food (vv 17-20).

"And there were four men - lepers - at the entrance of the gate" (v 3). According to tradition, these were Gehazi, who had been cursed with leprosy by Elisha, together with his three sons, who were afflicted because they had complicity in their father's embezzlement since they knew about it (RaDaK on II Kings 5:27). They were at the gate, just outside the city, as it is written, "he [the leper] shall sit alone outside the camp" (Lev. 13:46; Rashi on v 3).

They realized that if they were to stay there by the besieged city they would die of starvation, whereas if they were to go over to the camp of the Aramean besiegers there was a chance they might survive. From this the rabbis learned that a person living in a city struck by famine should get up and leave even if it is not certain that he will survive elsewhere (Bava Kama 60b). When Gehazi and his sons came to the Aramean camp, they discovered that all the Aramean forces had fled, abandoning their tents, horses, donkeys and all their food and wealth. This was because God had "played with their minds", making them hear sounds of a great army, which they imagined must be Hittites and Egyptians hired by the Israelites against them.

King Jehoram could not believe that the Arameans had simply fled and feared that they wanted to lure his forces out of the city into an ambush. However, he was persuaded to send a small force to check, because even if the force were to be killed by the Arameans, they would be no worse off than those left in Shomron, who would in any case die of famine. The reconnaissance party discovered that the Arameans had indeed fled east of the Jordan in total disarray. The starving inhabitants were able to come out of Shomron to the Aramean camp and take food for themselves and their animals in unbelievable abundance, just as Elisha had prophesied, while the king's aide, who had expressed his disbelief, witnessed the miracle but lost his life in the rush for food.

Verses 3-20 of this chapter are the Haftarah of Parshat **Metzora** (Lev. 14:1-15:33) dealing with the laws of purification from leprosy.

CHAPTER 8

Even miracles of such an order did not persuade King Jehoram of Israel to change his path, and Elisha now prophesied that God had called for seven years of famine to chastise the hearts of the Israelites. Elisha sent the righteous Shunemite woman, whose son he had revived, together with her entire household to dwell in the territory of the Philistines. According to the rabbis, in the first year of the famine, the Israelites who remained in their own territories ate everything they had left in their homes. In the second year they ate everything left in their fields. In the third year, they ate the meat of their kosher animals, in the fourth year, they ate the meat of their unkosher animals. In the fifth year, they ate the meat of mice and rats and such like; in the sixth year, they ate their sons and daughters, and in the seventh year they ate the flesh of their own arms (Ta'anit 5a).

These chastisements obviously moved something in Jehoram's heart since after the seven years we find him asking Gehazi to tell him about the miracles performed by his master Elisha (v 4). Just as Gehazi started talking about how Elisha had revived the Shunemite woman's son, there she was with her son! She had come to the king to complain that in her absence, robbers had taken over her house and fields. The rabbis commented that her sudden appearance just as Gehazi started talking about her came to prevent him from saying any more, because God does not like to hear praise from the mouths of the wicked (Vayikra Rabbah). Gehazi was punished because he referred to Elisha by name (v 5) instead of respectfully saying "my master" (Sanhedrin 100a).

King Jehoram restored the woman's property, showing that he was fair-minded. But fair-mindedness alone was not sufficient for a king of Israel, who was supposed to lead his people to faith in the One God. This was why Elisha immediately went to Damascus, where his mission was to anoint a king over Aram who would be far more cruel to Israel than the present king, Ben Hadad. The rabbis say that another reason for Elisha's visit to Damascus was to try to bring Gehazi to repent. Gehazi had gone there to seek out Na'aman and ask him for some big favor in return for having taken on his leprosy. Far worse, Gehazi had "dropped out" of Torah, using the occult arts he must have learned in the school of Elisha to make Jeraboa'm's golden calf appear to hang in mid-air (through the use of some kind of magnet effect), and carving a sacred name in its mouth to make it say the first two of the Ten Commandments: "I am..." and "You shall have no other gods besides Me..." (Exodus 20:2-3). Gehazi told Elisha that he had heard from him that one who sins and makes others sin is not given the possibility of repenting, and he therefore declined his overtures (Sotah 47a).

It was because of such stubbornness on the part of the Israelites that Elisha had to appoint a new king over Aram who would be a far harsher "rod of chastisement". This was Haza-el, and his anointment by Elisha was in fulfillment of the prophecy sent to his master Elijah years earlier when the latter had begged God to revoke his ministry (I Kings 19:15). The present king of Aram, Ben-Hadad, was seriously ill, and on hearing of Elisha's presence in his capital, sent Haza-el to "consult the oracle" - Ben-Haddad well knew of Elisha's outstanding prophetic powers. In his cryptic prophecy to Haza-el, Elisha hinted that he himself would kill his master and take over the throne (RaDaK on v 10). Elisha wept over the evil that Haza-el would later perpetrate against Israel as their rod of chastisement. When Haza-el returned to the sick Ben Hadad, it would appear (although the text is somewhat ambiguous) that it was he who took a thick blanket steeped in cold water and placed it over the king's face - ostensibly to cool his fever but actually to chill him or suffocate him to death (RaDaK on v 15).

The war that Haza-el stirred up against Israel (v 28) was to prove the undoing not only of the House of Ahab but also of the king of Judah, as we shall see in the ensuing chapters. Thus, our text now moves back to the House of Judah, telling of the reign of Jehoram son of Jehoshaphat (vv 16-24) and that of his son Ahaziahu (vv 25-29). Both of these two kings of Judah were literally married into the House of Ahab: Jehoshaphat had been married to the daughter of Omri king of Israel, Ahab's sister. Jehoshaphat had married his son Jehoram off to Ahab's wicked daughter Ataliah (who is described in v 26 as the daughter of Omri but was actually his grand-daughter), and thus Ahaziahu king of Judah was Ahab's son-in-law and brother-in-law of Jehoram king of Israel.

The marriage alliance of the kings of Judah with the House of Ahab was originally intended as a form of "outreach" to bring the kingdom of the Ten Tribes back under the hegemony of the House of David, but it did not in fact bring the kings of Israel to repentance. [Similarly the "alliance" of the establishment rabbinate of Israel and the religious political parties with the secular Zionists who control the country has not brought the latter nearer to the Torah but if anything has served only to give them legitimacy without actually changing them.]

Judah was sliding deeper into sin, yet God did not want to destroy them for the sake of David, His servant (v 19). Nevertheless, more and more troubles were breaking out on every side. It was in the reign of Jehoram king of Judah that the Edomites rebelled after eight reigns in which they had remained subject to Judah (v 20, see Rashi). Jehoram's son King Ahaziahu together with his brother-in-law Jehoram king of Israel went out to war against the Arameans (v 28) and they got a heavy beating (v 29). It was Ahaziahu's sick visit to his wounded brother-in-law King Jehoram that led to his downfall together with the downfall of the House of Ahab, as we will read in the following chapters.

CHAPTER 9

When the prophet Elijah had asked to be relieved of his ministry, God had told him to do three things: anoint Elisha as his successor, appoint Haza-el as king of Aram and anoint Jehu son of Nimshi as king of Israel (I Kings 19:16). In the previous chapter, we saw how Elisha carried out Elijah's instructions to appoint Haza-el as king of Aram. Now the time had come for him to fulfill the third part of Elijah's prophecy and anoint Jehu as king of Israel in order to take vengeance on the House of Ahab for their idolatry and criminality.

Jehu ben Nimshi was in fact the son of a man called Jehoshaphat (not to be confused with Jehoshaphat king of Judah) and Nimshi was Jehu's grandfather, but he is usually known as Jehu ben Nimshi. He was one of the leading military officers of Jehoram king of Israel, who had been campaigning against the Arameans in Ramot Gil'ad (in the Golan Heights) and who had gone to Jezreel to recuperate from wounds he had sustained in the war. Jehu and his fellow officers were still in Ramot Gil'ad when the young prophet sent by Elisha - according to tradition, the prophet Jonah (Rashi on v 1) - arrived to carry out his secret mission, which was highly dangerous as he was appointing Jehu to instigate a mutiny against the king. Taking Jehu into an inner chamber, Jonah delivered his prophecy and fled.

"THE DRIVING IS LIKE THE DRIVING OF JEHU BEN NIMSHI..." (v 20)

Jehu was evidently a man of great strength with his own brand of zeal for God, and with the new power that came from his anointment by the prophet, he soon won over his fellow officers and quickly master-minded a surprise assault on King Jehoram as he lay recuperating in Jezreel. As Jehu rode with his band of men towards Jezreel, the city watchman saw them in the distance. Before the watchman could identify them, the king sent out successive horsemen to find out who they were and what they wanted. But instead of coming back, they joined the advancing party. Reporting this, the watchman said, "The driving (**minhag**) looks like the driving of Jehu ben Nimshi, for he drives (**yinhag**) with madness" (v 20).

Not only does this phrase graphically depict the kind of man Jehu was. It might also fairly be applied to certain crazy customs (**minhag**=custom) that various people practice with religious fervor as if they were Torah from Sinai when in fact they have nothing to do with true **Minhag Yisrael** as recorded in the Shulchan Arukh and other authoritative compilations. Since the Bible is telling us that there is a kind of driving (**minhag**) that is crazy, this should prompt us to examine our own religious **minhagim** ("customs") with great care to check that we are not diverging from the authentic **Minhag Avoteinu** ("practice of our ancestors").

When King Jehoram himself came out towards Jehu together with his brother-in-law, Ahaziah king of Judah, who had been "visiting the sick", Jehu's arrow struck Jehoram between the arms and through his heart. The sages said that this was **middah keneged middah**, "measure for measure", because he had hardened his heart and stretched out his hands to receive **ribbit** ("interest") on loans which Ahab's righteous chamberlain Obadiah had taken in order to support the true prophets (II Kings 4:1; Shemot Rabbah 31). Jehoram's body was thrown out from his chariot into the Jezreel field that had been the ancestral portion of Nabot, whom Jehoram's father Ahab had had killed in order to seize his vineyard (I Kings ch 21).

After killing Jehoram, Jehu now went on to "cleanse" Israel of the sinful House of Ahab. First, he killed Jehoram's brother-in-law and ally, Ahaziah king of Judah (vv27-8), who had also followed the path of Ahab and is said to have scratched out divine names from the Torah and replaced them with the names of idols (Rashi on v 27; Sanhedrin 102b).

Next Jehu turned his attention to the queen mother, Jehoram's mother and Ahab's widow, the accursed Jezebel, who was in Jezreel. When she heard that Jehu was on his way, she slapped on her make-up, did up her hair and called to him from her window, hoping to allure the man who had just killed her son into marrying her. However, Jehu had sufficient zeal not to pay attention to her enticements and had her pushed out of the window - following the method of the Sanhedrin in casting those condemned to **sekilah** ("stoning") from an upper storey. In accordance with Elijah's prophecy, which Jehu had heard from Jonah (v 10), the dogs ate up Jezebel's body, leaving only her skull, feet and hands. It is said that these were saved because when a wedding party would pass by her house, she used to take ten steps out into the street to greet them, waving her hands and legs and shaking her head (Rashi on v 35; Pirkey d'Rabbi Eliezer 17). Knowing that a woman as wicked as Jezebel nevertheless received a reward for some slight gestures she made to carry out the mitzvah of making a bride and groom happy should encourage us to throw ourselves body and soul into the performance of God's commandments.

CHAPTER 10

In order to complete his "cleansing" of Israel, Jehu ben Nimshi now went on to destroy all vestiges of the House of Ahab. He persuaded the leading denizens of Shomron to slaughter the seventy sons of Ahab (which is somewhat reminiscent of Avimelech in the time of the Judges having the seventy sons of Gideon killed, Judges 9:5). By cleverly thereby implicating the denizens of Shomron in his own coup (v 9) Jehu widened his support base and began seeking out remaining members of the House of Ahab's power-base.

On his way from Jezreel to Shomron, Jehu encountered a large band consisting of forty-two brothers of Ahaziah king of Judah, all of whom were caught up in the Ahab network into which their brother Ahaziah was intermarried. These too Jehu slaughtered, and then advanced into Shomron itself.

"AHAB SERVED BAAL A LITTLE; JEHU WILL SERVE HIM A LOT" (v 18)

Gathering all the people together, Jehu declared: "Ahab served Baal a little; Jehu will serve him a lot" (v 18). The introduction of Baal worship had been Ahab's own innovation (I Kings 16:30-33) - previously the kings of Israel had only encouraged the worship of Jerabo'am's golden calves. Jehu himself did not intend his words literally. He was putting on a front in the hope of pulling off a brilliant coup. By making all the Baal worshipers of Shomron think the new king was on their side and that they had nothing to fear, he intended to lure them all out of the woodwork and bring them together for what was billed as the Baal celebration of all time in order to be able to destroy them all in one great massacre.

Jehu did indeed succeed in his immediate objective, but nevertheless his words proved to be a snare that led to his downfall. He had been anointed to be king over Israel. Had he gone all the way in eliminating idolatry from Israel, he could have brought them back to the Torah and under the hegemony of the House of David, which could have brought Mashiach. But having said, "Jehu will serve [the idol] a lot", he was ensnared by the words of his own lips.

In the words of Rabbi Nachman: "Never let a word of wickedness leave your mouth. Don't ever say you will be wicked or commit a sin, even if you mean it as a joke and have no intention of carrying out your words. The words themselves can be very damaging. They can compel you to fulfill them even though you did not mean them seriously. This was what caused King Jehu's downfall, because he said, "Ahab served Baal a little, but Jehu will serve him very much" (II Kings 10:18). When King Jehu said these words, he had no intention of committing idolatry. He said them only to trick the Baal worshipers, as explained in the following verse. Yet these words were his downfall, because he later came to commit idolatry. From this the Talmud learns that "a covenant is made with the lips" (Sanhedrin 102a). You should therefore be very careful about what you say" (Sichot Haran #237).

In spite of his great display of strength in eradicating the Baal worship that had plagued Israel for two generations, Jehu could not bring himself to uproot the worship of Jerabo'am's golden calves. This was "out of anxiety that the kingship would revert to the House of David, which is what Jerabo'am had been afraid of" (Rashi on v 29, I Kings 12:26). For without the golden calves, Israel would have turned their hearts back towards God's chosen House in Jerusalem.

In the merit of Jehu's mighty deeds, he earned the kingship for himself and his offspring to the fourth generation (verse 30), but because he did not repent, God chastised Israel by sending Haza-el king of Aram to create an "intifada" which was initially focused particularly on all the Israelite territories east of the River Jordan (v 33). This was the beginning of the end of the hold of the Ten Tribes on their ancestral portions, leading eventually to their exile.

CHAPTER 11

Ataliah - the wife of King Jehoram of Judah and the mother of King Ahaziah of Judah, whom Jehu ben Nimshi had slain when he came to Jezreel - was the daughter of King Ahab of Israel. She had brought the plague of Ahab into the Holy City of Jerusalem itself in the form of a functioning temple to Baal complete with a high priest bearing the pleasant-sounding name of Matan, "giving". Ataliah ruined part of the structure of Solomon's Temple and pillaged its treasures to bring them to her own temple of Baal (II Chron. 24:7). RaDaK (on II Kings 12:5) states that through her influence there was an overall weakening in public support for Solomon's Temple to the point where the income from the people's half-shekel contributions was insufficient to cover the daily sacrifices, which were suspended for a time. [Ataliah's conception of Jerusalem would probably correspond to that of the contemporary secularists who take pride in its shopping malls, sports stadiums, theaters and multi-religious character, while the Temple of God lies in ruins.]

When Ataliah realized the implications of the death of her son Ahaziah king of Judah at the hands of Jehu ben Nimshi, she made a bloody attempt to assert the supremacy of the House of Ahab over Jerusalem itself by wiping out all descendants of King David (v 1) with the goal of ruling all by herself, which she did for six years.

At this fateful moment, the entire future of the House of David until Mashiach hung in the balance, and his line would have been wiped out completely but for the heroism of Yehosheva daughter of Jehoram king of Judah and paternal sister of the slain King Ahaziah. Taking his one remaining son, the infant prince Yo'ash, she hid him and brought him up in **Hadar Ha-Mitot**, the "chamber of the beds" (v 2). This was certainly with the cooperation of the High Priest, for according to tradition, **Hadar Ha-Mitot** was none other than an upper storey above the Temple Holy of Holies (Rashi, RaDaK on v 2). The Holy of Holies is called by this allusive name in accordance with the verses in Songs 1:13, "He lies between my breasts" and ibid. 1:16, "also our couch is green". (See Rambam, Hilchot Beit HaBechirah 4:3 on the place of this upper storey in the Temple structure.) This would indeed have been an ideal place for concealing the baby prince from the tyrannical Ataliah since it was strictly off bounds to all - the High Priest entered the Holy of Holies only once a year on Yom Kippur, while the upper storey was checked for maintenance purposes only at very long intervals, and in any case from the following chapter it would appear that the Temple was not maintained at all during the time of Ataliah.

It was for the boy prince Joash hidden away above the Holy of Holies that King David had prayed in Psalms 27:5: "For He will hide me away in his Tabernacle, He will conceal me in the secrecy of His Tent" (Rashi on v 2).

When Joash was seven years old, the initiative to restore the kingship of the House of David came from Yehoyada the High Priest, an outstanding Tzaddik who showed the zeal of a Pinchas in extirpating the plague of Ataliah. (The long-established bond between the priesthood and the royal tribe of Judah dated back to the marriage of Aaron the High Priest to the sister of Nachshon ben Aminadav, the prince of Judah, Exodus 6:23.) In a daring coup against a woman who had certainly greatly strengthened her power-base in six years of tyranny, Yehoyada mobilized all the priests in Jerusalem, using the classic stratagem employed by many of the Judges in dividing his "forces" into three, this time to surround and protect the new boy king at his surprise "unveiling" and coronation in the Temple. The creative boldness of Yehoyada in overthrowing Ataliah equaled that of Jehu seven years earlier in destroying the priests of Baal in Shomron (see previous chapter), but because Yehoyada was a true Tzaddik, his enterprise (unlike that of Jehu) did not backfire. "And he brought out the king's son and put upon him the crown and the testimony" (v 12) - the "testimony" is the Torah scroll, which the king "must read all the days of his life" (Deut. 17:19). After Ataliah was put to death, Yehoyada renewed the Covenant that bound the king and the people together in the service of God.

It is clear from the present chapter that there was a very sizeable "grass roots" of **Am Ha'Aretz** (v 14) - "ordinary" members of the tribe of Judah - who were faithful to the House of David and everything it stood for and who were only too happy to support the High Priest's initiative against Ataliah and her idol-based regime. They all came up to destroy the temple of Baal and its priest (v 18), after which the new king was conducted to the royal palace, the people rejoiced, and the city became calm (v 20).

CHAPTER 12

King Joash ruled for forty years, and he "did right in the eyes of God all his days as Yehoyada the priest instructed him" (v 2). This verse must be understood in the light of II Chronicles 24:17, from which we learn that after the death of Yehoyada (at the ripe old age of 130), "the leaders of Judah came and prostrated to the king; then [**az**] the king listened to them". The leaders of Judah reasoned that if this man had survived being brought up in the Holy of Holies, of which it is said that "the stranger who draws near shall die" (Numbers 18:7), he must be divine - and they began to worship him like a god. Not only did Joash stray into idolatry; he became so enraged by criticism that he had Yehoyada's son, the prophet Zechariah, who stood up in the Temple to castigate him, murdered on the spot (II Chron. 24:21) - for generations his blood boiled in the Temple courtyard where it had been shed, refusing to subside, until Nebuchadnezzar came and destroyed the Temple.

Despite the negativity of these later developments, they followed a most important period while Yehoyada was still alive in which the king and the priests not only renovated the Temple but also made important innovations in its management, some of which endured for a long time thereafter. These innovations were centered on the reorganization of the financing of the Temple maintenance and its day-to-day running through the annual half-shekel contributions of the people and their other dedications.

Thus, the closing verses of the previous chapter (II Kings 11:17-20) together with the better part of our present chapter (vv 1-17) are the Haftarah of Shabbat Shekalim, the first of the four special Shabbatot during the six weeks leading up to Pesach, when in addition to the usual weekly parshah we also read **Maftir** from Exodus 30:11-16 on the half-shekel Temple "poll tax" on the population. (Shabbat Shekalim comes either immediately before or on Rosh Chodesh Adar, late Feb./early March.)

King Joash came to the throne only 155 years after the building of Solomon's Temple, which in the days before the kinds of emissions and pollutants in the atmosphere today was not long enough to cause a marked deterioration in the stone and timber building. It was largely the ravages of Ataliah (II Chron. 24:7) that had caused damage to the Temple structure, giving rise to the urgent need for **Bedek Ha-Bayit**, "checking" of the Temple to see what was required to restore it to its rightful glory. Besides the need for maintenance of the building, there was also a need for funds to cover the expenses of the regular sacrifices each day, on Sabbaths, New Moons and festivals etc. As discussed in the commentary on the previous chapter, it appears that for a time during the rule of Ataliah, the regular sacrifices may have been suspended as the system for collecting the funds to pay for it had fallen into disuse.

Initially, Yo'ash called on the priests to collect all the income from the annual half-shekel contributions and other dedications for use on the Temple renovation project. Since each priest had his own circle of Israelites who would give him their tithes, the initial idea was that the priests themselves should collect the funds for the renovation work from their regular supporters (v 6). However, by the twenty-third year of Yo'ash's reign the work had still not been done and the king apparently suspected that the priests were filching off the money for themselves (v 8). This was not so - the priests had been saving the contributions until there was a large enough sum to complete the work (RaDaK on v 8) - but to avoid all suspicion, the priests were perfectly content to agree to a new system in which the public made their contributions directly to the Temple, placing their coins in a chest placed conveniently in the Temple courtyard (v 10). This new system became the basis for the system of half-shekel collection that is described at length in the Talmudic Tractate Shekalim.

The money collected in the time of Joash was used initially to restore the Temple building (vv 12-13). According to v 14 the money was **not** used for Temple vessels and musical instruments etc. but this contradicts II Chron. 24:14, from which we can infer that these were purchased **after** the building restoration was complete (Ketubot 106a; RaDaK on v 14).

From verse 16 we learn that the financial affairs of the Temple were all based on trust (which makes a refreshing change from today, when almost nobody can or will trust anyone else).

From verse 17 the rabbis teach that Yehoyada darshened that the **Kohanim** priests were allowed to have personal benefit from the skins of animals sacrificed on the Temple Altar as **Olah** (burnt) offerings (Temurah 23b, see Rashi on v 17).

"THEN HAZA-EL, KING OF ARAM ROSE UP..." (v 18)

"Then - **Az** - Haza'el rose up..." This happened because "then (**az**) the king listened to them" (II Chron. 24:17) - i.e. to the leaders of Judah who wanted to worship him as an idol. This is what gave strength to Haza'el as God's rod to chastise the House of David after his many years of chastising Israel. Now he took the Philistine town of Gat, which King David had taken for himself more than a hundred and fifty years earlier.

Haza-el wanted to advance on Jerusalem itself, but Yo'ash bought him off using the Temple treasures (v 19) thereby undoing much of what had been achieved during the lifetime of Yehoyada the High Priest.

In II Chron. 24:24 we learn that Haza-el made a second attack on Jerusalem, in which he succeeded in doing considerable damage, "and they carried out judgments on Yo'ash", who was severely wounded. He was killed in a conspiracy by two of his servants whose mothers - according to II Chron. 24:26 -- were respectively a Moabitess and an Ammonitess. The Moabites and Ammonites were descended from Lot, and showed great ingratitude to Abraham, who had rescued Lot, when they hired Bil'am to curse his descendants. It was thus **middah ke-neged middah**, "measure for measure", that two servants from Moab and Ammon should take vengeance on Yo'ash, who failed to show gratitude to Yehoyada the High Priest for saving his own life as a child when he went on to kill his son Zechariah.

CHAPTER 13

After completing the account of the reign of Yo'ash, king of Judah at the end of the last chapter, the narrative now moves back to the kings of Israel who followed Jehu ben Nimshi. In the merit of his uprooting of the house of Ahab (from the tribe of Ephraim), Jehu (from Menasheh) earned the kingship for himself and his offspring to the fourth generation, while the Ten Tribes remained under the leadership of the descendants of Joseph.

Jehu was succeeded by his son Jeho'ahaz, who continued in the path of Jerabo'am. This led to the continuing chastisement of Israel by Aram to the point that Jeho'ahaz was left with a greatly depleted army (v 7). The pressure from Aram brought even the idolatrous Jeho'ahaz to entreat God for help (v 4). "And God gave Israel a savior, and they went out from under the hand of Aram (v 5). As Rashi (ad loc.) points out, this "savior" was in fact Jeho'ahaz's son and successor, King Yo'ash of Israel, about whose exploits we hear later in the present chapter and in the next.

To those who are already feeling somewhat dizzy from the confusing succession of names of the kings of Judah and Israel, the present chapter is likely to be even more disorienting, because after its brief account of the exploits of Jeho'ahaz king of Israel (vv 1-9) it moves on to those of his son Yo'ash and appears to conclude the account of Yo'ash's life (vv 12-13) - yet immediately afterwards Yo'ash reappears in the narrative (vv 14-19) and remains a central figure in the narrative in the next chapter which speaks about the exploits of Amatziah king of Judah (ch 14 vv 1-16). Indeed verses 15-16 in the next chapter (ch 14) retell the death of Yo'ash king of Israel in words almost identical to those in our present chapter vv 12-13.

Rashi (on v 13) offers an explanation for the apparent interpolation in our present chapter of verses 12-13 speaking of the death of Yo'ash in between the verses that speak about his idolatry and those that speak about the final illness of the prophet Elisha: "I say that these verses were written only for the sake of making a break so that the account of the death of Elisha should not follow on immediately after the verse speaking about Yo'ash's idolatry".

"AND ELISHA WAS SICK WITH THE SICKNESS FROM WHICH HE WOULD DIE" (v 14)

We may infer from this verse that Elisha also suffered previous illnesses, from which he recovered. This in itself was a miracle - we should not take healing even from colds and chills for granted! "Until the time of Elisha there was no such thing as someone who was sick being healed - until Elisha came and begged for mercy and was healed" (Bava Kama 87a). "Elisha suffered three illnesses: one after setting the bears on the "young children" (II Kings 2:23-4); one after he rejected Gehazi with both hands, and the one from which he died" (Sotah 47a).

It is striking that Yo'ash king of Israel, despite his involvement in idolatry, not only visited Elisha on his deathbed but cried out to him in the very same words that Elisha himself had used to his master Elijah: "My father, my father, chariot of Israel and its riders" (v 14, cf. II Kings 2:12).

The prophet told the king to take arrows, open the eastern window (facing Aram) and shoot arrows. The prophet cried: "An arrow of salvation for God and an arrow of salvation against Aram." (v 17). Elisha was teaching the king of Israel to shoot **arrows of prayer**. It was up to Yo'ash to decide how many he would shoot. He shot three - perhaps he thought this would be a sufficient gesture - but he did not understand that in order to accomplish decisive results, our prayers must be repeated persistently time after time after time after time.

Elisha's death was followed immediately by incursions into the Land of Israel by the Moabites - showing that it was the Tzaddik who had been protecting the land during his lifetime.

When an Israelite funeral procession was disrupted by a Moabite incursion, the startled coffin-bearers hurriedly threw the corpse into the cave in which Elisha was buried. "And the man touched the bones of Elisha and came to life and stood on his feet" (v 21). This was Elisha's second revival of the dead (his first was the resuscitation of the son of the Shunemite woman, II Kings ch 4), showing that he truly received a "double portion" of Elijah's spirit since the latter revived only one dead person (I Kings ch 17; Sanhedrin 47a). Some rabbis said that the man who was revived through touching Elisha's bones lived only briefly, walking away only to drop again so that he was buried elsewhere (for "a wicked person should not be buried next to a Tzaddik", Sanhedrin 47a). Others identified him as the father of Shalom ben Tikvah, who was one of the great Tzaddikim of his generation, who would sit at the gates of his city giving water to weary wayfarers, in the merit of which holy spirit came into his wife, who was Hulda the Prophetess (II Kings 22:14; see RaDaK on our present chapter v 21).

Yo'ash king of Israel was a mighty warrior, and through God's mercy on His people for the sake of His Covenant with the patriarchs, Yo'ash succeeded in recapturing cities taken by the Arameans, and he inflicted three major defeats on Aram corresponding to the three arrows he had shot from Elisha's window.

CHAPTER 14

The narrative now moves back from the kings of Israel to those of Judah, telling the story of Amatziah son of Yo'ash king of Judah. During his reign, there were signs of regeneration in Judah somewhat parallel to the revival seen in the same period in the kingdom of Israel under Yo'ash, who, as we saw at the end of the last chapter, took back cities that had been captured by Aram. After a period in which Amatziah consolidated his own position in Judah following the assassination of his father (vv 5-6), he went on to campaign against the Edomites whose territories were to the south east of the Dead Sea, and who had rebelled against Judah in the time of his grandfather Jehoram king of Judah (II Kings 8:20). These territories included some highly fertile areas with good supplies of water.

Commenting on the name Yokt-el given by Amatziah to the conquered Edomite stronghold, Rashi (on v 7) states that it merely caused him grating (**kihuy**) of the teeth, because "after Amatziah came from striking the Edomites he brought the gods of the children of Se'ir...and prostrated before them" (II Chronicles 25:14). The worst god of all is pride and arrogance - and the over-confidence engendered in Amatziah as a result of his victory over Edom led to his downfall when he "overplayed his hand" against Yo'ash king of Israel (who ruled over **ten** tribes). When Amatziah began his campaign against Edom, he hired one hundred thousand Israelite warriors to go with him (II Chronicles 25:6) but on the instructions of a prophet he told them to go home, and in anger they started despoiling the cities of Judah. Amatziah took this as a casus belli and challenged Yo'ash king of Israel to fight. Refusing to heed Yo'ash's warnings to stand down, Amatziah was badly beaten in the battle of Beit Shemesh (vv 9-12) and Yo'ash entered Jerusalem, tore down a major section of the city walls (v 13) and pillaged the treasures of the Temple and the royal palace etc. (v 14).

Amatziah lived another fifteen years after this, but he no longer ruled in Jerusalem. The people took his son Azariah=Uzziah as king, while Amatziah retreated to the southern city of Lachish, where he was eventually assassinated.

Yo'ash king of Israel died soon after his attack on Jerusalem, and was succeeded by his son Jerabo'am, who was third in the line of kings of the dynasty of Jehu ben Nimshi. He is known as Jerabo'am II to distinguish him from Jerabo'am son of Nevat who started the rebellion of the Ten Tribes against the House of David during the reign of Solomon's son Rechav'am.

Jerabo'am II was a powerful warrior who restored Israelite hegemony over all the ancestral territories east of the River Jordan and recaptured Aram "according to the word of HaShem the God of Israel that He spoke by the hand of His servant Jonah son of Amitai the prophet." (v 25). This prophecy is nowhere recorded, but according to tradition it was Jonah who had anointed Jehu (Rashi on II Kings 9:1). Just as Jonah's prophecy of doom against Nineveh was overturned when the people of that city repented (Jonah ch 3), so was the evil decree against Israel overturned in the days of Jerabo'am II, and from having been like "dust for grinding up" under the feet of Aram (ch 13 v 7) they were saved by Jeraboa'm II, who retook all the territories they had lost to Aram in the previous generations.

CHAPTER 15

AZARIAH (=UZZIAH) KING OF JUDAH

After Amatziah king of Judah was trounced by Yo'ash king of Israel and fled to Lachish, the people of Judah appointed Amatziah's son Azariah as king, and he ruled for fifteen years in his father's life-time. In II Chronicles 26 and in the prophecies of Isaiah, Azariah is called Uzziah.

Our present text passes over in almost complete silence the great achievements of Uzziah in his reign of over half a century (52 years). Just as Jerabo'am II of Israel subjugated the territories that had rebelled against the kings of Shomron who preceded him, so Uzziah restored the lowlands, coastal areas and south of the country to Judah as they had been in the times of David and Solomon. He established Judean sovereignty over the shores of the Red Sea, building Eilat as a naval stronghold. At the same time as restoring Judah's boundaries, Uzziah worked harder than any other king with the exception of David to develop and populate settlements throughout his territories, as is attested by numerous archaeological finds in the coastal plains and the Negev.

Just as our text passes over Uzziah's positive achievements in silence, so it does not explain the reason for the sudden visitation of leprosy that afflicted him for the rest of his life (v 5). This is explained in full in the parallel history in II Chronicles 26:16. It was perhaps his very success that led to a pride that brought him - with the most righteous intentions - to offer incense in the Temple Sanctuary in defiance of the strict Torah prohibition against any **Zar** (non-priest) officiating as a priest at any offering. As Uzziah stood in the Sanctuary burning incense, leprosy broke out on his forehead and spread to his whole body.

It was on the very day that Uzziah offered incense in the Temple that Isaiah began to prophesy (Isaiah 1:6 - the "death" of King Uzziah mentioned in that verse is a reference to his leprosy). The stormy period of Uzziah's reign and those that followed it until the destruction of the Temple (end of II Kings) is thus one whose inner soul is opened up to us in the books of Isaiah and the great prophets who followed him - Jeremiah and Ezekiel. Rambam (Introduction to Mishneh Torah) traces the chain of transmission of the Torah from Elijah as follows: Elijah handed the tradition to Elisha, who taught Yehoyada the High Priest (II Kings 11-12), who taught his son Zechariah, who taught Hosea, who taught Amos, who taught Isaiah.

In our present chapter, we learn that the leprosy-stricken Uzziah dwelled in **Ha-Beit Ha-Chophshit**, "the House of Immunity". The Hebrew root **chophesh** means freedom. This is because Uzziah was now freed from the duties and obligations of kingship, and also because he built himself a house in the cemetery (for a leper is forbidden to come into the camp - the city), and it is written, **be-meitim chophshi**, "I am free among the dead" (Psalms 88:6; see RaDaK on our present chapter v 5).

THE LAST RULERS OF THE NORTHERN KINGDOM

Jehu ben Nimshi, who overthrew the House of Ahab, secured the kingship for himself until the fourth generation. The bloody coup against his great-grandson Zechariah in full view of the public (v 10) was followed by a whole series of coups, most, though not all of which were very short-lived, as we learn in verses 8-32.

The single most important geopolitical factor in this period was the rise of Ashur ("Assyria") as the major regional player in the Fertile Crescent. Ashur was situated in the upper Tigris valley in the north of Iraq near its borders with present-day Syria, Turkey, Kurdistan and Iran. What began as a small, aggressive, predatory power turned into a major land empire that stretched southwards along the Euphrates and westwards into northern Syria. The Assyrian rulers annexed many lands and turned others into tributary states. They were particularly noted for their use of the method of population transfer and exchange to uproot people from their own ancestral territories and turn them into landless migrants with no real attachment to the earth. This was precisely what the Assyrians did to the Ten Tribes, sending them into an Exile the redemption from which is only beginning to take place in our days.

There is some evidence that back in the days of King Ahab, when the Assyrians were beginning their westward push into Syria, the three major powers in the region - Aram, Hamat and Ahab's Israel - formed a military alliance to repel them, and succeeded for the time being. But by the time of Menachem ben Gadi, who ruled over Israel during the last ten years of the reign of Uzziah king of Judah, the Assyrians under their king **Phool** were again pushing westwards (v 19), and Menachem had to buy them off with a huge bribe that could be raised only through a heavy tax on all his able-bodied men (v 20).

However, the merit of the Israelites was no longer sufficient to permanently stem the Assyrian tide, and by the time of Pekah ben Remalliah, the Assyrian king Tiglat Pilesser captured Gil'ad and the Galilee, sending their Israelite inhabitants into exile. Until today historians debate where they went and where their descendants are to be found today.

YOTAM, KING OF JUDAH

Yotam, son of Uzziah "did right in the eyes of God according to all that Uzziah his father did" (verse 34). Commenting on the almost identical verse in II Chronicles 27:2, Rashi states that Yotam followed only in his father's good ways, which explains the statement by Rabbi Shimon bar Yochai (Succah 45b): "If Abraham our father would take on himself all the sins of the generations up until his time, I would take upon myself the sins of the generations from Abraham until myself, and if Yotam, son of Uzziah was with me, we could take on ourselves the sins from Abraham until the end of the generations". As Rashi explains, out of all the kings before and after him, Yotam is the only one to whom the text does not attribute any sin whatever (making a most refreshing change from the rest of the story of all the kings!) This is signified in his very name: **Yo** (God), **tam** ("pure, complete").

Despite Yotam's purity, in his days Judah began suffering from new aggressions by Aram and the kingdom of Israel, and in the time of his son, Ahaz king of Judah, these developed into a major scourge.

CHAPTER 16

One of the great ironies and very deep mysteries that we find in the Bible is that often the most righteous of fathers beget the most wicked of sons. In the ensuing stories of the kings of Judah, we find that a Tzaddik - Yotam - had a son who was a major Rasha ("villain") - Ahaz, while Ahaz had Hezekiah, who was a major Tzaddik. Then Hezekiah had Menasheh, who was a major Rasha, though he repented, and after the reign of Menasheh's son Amon, who was a Rasha, came Amon's son Josiah, who was a major Tzaddik.

At precisely the time that the kingdom of Israel was tottering as a result of its devotion to foreign idolatry, Ahaz king of Judah felt compelled to introduce foreign idolatry into his own kingdom and into the very Temple itself. As we learn in verse 3, "he also passed his son through the fire": in other words, he gave his son over to the priests of Molech, which was considered the most serious of all the abominations of Canaan and is severely prohibited in the Torah (Lev. 20:1-5). It is said that it was Hezekiah who was passed by Ahaz through the fire.

The ensuing invasion of Judah by Aram in alliance with Israel is the subject of the dramatic prophecy in Isaiah chapter 7.

Verse 6 in our present chapter is of great interest because it describes how the Arameans recaptured Eilat at the southernmost tip of Judah's sphere of influence and drove the **Yehudim** out. For one thing, this is the first appearance of this term in the Bible. Secondly, where the text **(kri)** says "and Edomites came to Eilat", the **ktiv** - the word as written in the parchment scroll - is **Aromim**, which not only includes the Arameans but also seems to allude to the Romans. This would provide support for interpreting the numerous Biblical and rabbinic texts that speak of Aram and its role at the end of days as alluding to Edom and their latter-day descendants.

In order to ward off the Aramean and Israelite forces attacking him from the north and in the south, Ahaz turned to Tiglat Pilesser of Ashur and submitted himself to him as a subject nation (v 7), bribing him to attack Aram and Israel. That a king of Judah felt forced to resort to this showed how dire things were on all levels.

Ahaz's ploy had two serious negative consequences. One was that when Ashur knocked down Aram, it simply brought the Assyrians nearer to the Israelite territories whose inhabitants they would shortly be taking into exile. Secondly, Ahaz himself went out to pay his respects to Tiglat Pilesser king of Ashur in Damascus - and discovered a new kind of (idolatrous) altar that so took his fancy that he instructed his High Priest to make a copy of it in the Holy Temple in Jerusalem itself. The remainder of our chapter describes the changes Ahaz made in the Temple in order to accommodate his idolatry.

CHAPTER 17

Hoshe'a ben Elah, the last king of Israel, had, like his predecessors, come to power through a violent coup (II Kings 15:25), but "he was not like the kings of Israel that were before him" (our chapter v 2). This was because for the first time since the days of Jerabo'am ben Nevat, Hoshe'a ben Elah removed the armed guards that had been posted on all the borders to prevent the Ten Tribes from going up to the Temple in Jerusalem. (According to tradition, this happened on the 15th of Av, a day of salvation and holiness, see commentary on Judges ch 21; Ta'anit 30b.) However, now that there was no impediment to their going up to Jerusalem, the Israelites could no longer hang the blame for their not doing so on their kings. Despite the removal of the guards they still did not go up to Jerusalem - and this was what finally sealed the decree of exile against the Ten Tribes in the days of Hoshe'a ben Elah (Gittin 88a; Rashi and RaDaK on v 2).

The exile of the Ten Tribes took place in three stages (see Rashi on v 1). The first was when Pilesser king of Ashur sent the inhabitants of the Galilee (Naftali) to Ashur (ch 15 v 29). The second came eight years later, when he exiled the tribes of Reuven and Gad. This prompted Hoshe'a ben Elah to plot with Sou king of Egypt in the hope of changing the map of the entire Middle East by overthrowing Ashur, to whom he ceased paying tribute. This brought Shalmanesser king of Ashur to arrest and imprison him (v 4) eight years after the exile of Reuven and Gad, but the remaining leadership of Shomron continued their resistance against the Assyrians, leading Shalmanesser to lay siege to the city for three years (v 5). After the fall of Shomron, the inhabitants were sent into exile by Sargon II of Ashur. The date of the final exile of the Ten Tribes (according to the dating system of Midrash Seder Olam) was in the year 3205 (-555 B.C.E.): this was 133 years before the destruction of the First Temple and the exile of the tribes of Judah and Benjamin to Babylon.

The Ten Tribes were exiled to a variety of locations, some in Mesopotamia and others east of the River Tigris in the mountainous areas of Medea (located in the great mountain chain of western Iran between Hamadan and Shiraz). What happened to them afterwards and where, if anywhere, they wandered are mysteries to which no conclusive solution has been found until today.

The major part of our present chapter is in effect the "indictment" against Israel, expressing the essential "moral" of the entire history contained in the Nevi'im (Prophetic writings): Israel's possession of the Land of Israel is conditional on their observance of the commandments of God's Torah, and it was their sins - in particular their lapse into idolatry - that caused their exile from the Land.

"And the Children of Israel fabricated things that were not right against HaShem their God" (v 9). Metzudat David (ad loc.) explains that "in secrecy they said things about HaShem that are not fit to repeat, for they denied His knowledge of what goes on in the world and His providential government". "For they said, HaShem does not see us, for HaShem has abandoned the earth" (Ezekiel 8:12).

RaDaK in a lengthy comment on v 27 explains that the Israelites did indeed continue to believe in HaShem even though they made the golden calves. They made them only to serve as an intermediary between themselves and HaShem. Thus we see that even the most wicked of the Israelites also sought out HaShem, such as when Jerabo'am begged the prophets to intercede on account of his paralyzed arm and sick baby (I Kings 13:6; 14:2), or when Ahab agreed with Elijah about the prophets of Baal (cf. also I Kings 20:42; 21:27), or when his son Yehoram saw the hand of HaShem behind the danger hanging over his mission with the kings of Judah and Edom against Moab (II Kings 3:10). It was not that they did not believe in HaShem. Their flaw was to serve intermediaries.

THE SAMARITANS

"And the king of Ashur brought [people] from Babylon and from Kutah... and settled them in the cities of Shomron instead of the Children of Israel..." (v 24). This was part of the Assyrian policy of population exchange. However the new inhabitants of these areas of the Holy Land did not yet know the "Law of the God of the Land" (v 26), which is God's Torah, and indeed, having seen the Israelite population expelled from their land, they apparently thought that He had been unable to protect them against the Assyrians - until they found themselves being terrorized by lions, and the King of Ashur was compelled to send an Israelite priest back from exile in order to teach them Torah. This priest allowed them to continue worshiping the gods they had brought with them from their old homelands, while instructing them in the most serious prohibitions of the Torah, such as those against incest (see RaDaK on v 27).

It seems like **middah ke-neged middah**, "measure for measure", that people who mixed in fear of HaShem together with idolatry came to replace the Israelites of Shomron, who had done the same. The section in vv 24-25 on the practices of the new residents of Shomron - the Samaritans - is important for our understanding of the roots of the deep suspicion with which the rabbis viewed them, so that even though they were **Gerim** ("proselytes") there were many rabbinic ordinances limiting Jewish interaction with them, until after the discovery of an idol in the image of a dove on Mount Gerizim, after which they were ruled to be **Akum**, idolaters, and cast outside the boundaries of **Am Yisrael**.

CHAPTER 18

It was at this moment of extreme national crisis - when the link of Israel with their Land and their very survival as a people were hanging in the balance following the exile of the Ten Tribes and their assimilation into the surrounding peoples - that Hezekiah succeeded his father Ahaz as king of Judah.

"In HaShem the God of Israel did he trust, and after him there was none like him among all the kings of Judah or among those that were before him" (v 5).

The wicked, idolatrous Ahaz had left his son a kingdom torn apart and largely wasted as a result of the incursions of the neighboring Philistines, Edomites and Arameans etc. Hezekiah dealt a heavy blow to the Philistines (v 8) but in the fourth year of his reign Shalmanesser king of Ashur laid siege to Shomron, and its capture and the subsequent exile of the Ten Tribes made the looming threat of Ashur against Jerusalem even more palpable and fearsome.

With the courage of a David, Hezekiah made a complete turnabout from the path of his father, going so far as to drag Ahaz's very bones through the streets (Pesachim 56a). For the first time since the reign of Solomon, Hezekiah finally removed the **Bamot**, the "private altars" that had been forbidden ever since the inauguration of the Temple in Jerusalem, and he cut down the Ashera tree-idol and even ground up the bronze serpent made by Moses in the wilderness (Numbers 21:8-9), which by his time had turned into the focus of a healing cult. This, together with his "hiding away the book of remedies" (Pesachim ibid.), shows that he was determined to take away the intermediaries people had relied upon (idols, medicines) and lead them on the path of pure faith in HaShem.

"In the fourteenth year of King Hezekiah, Sennacherib king of Ashur came up against all the fortified cities of Judah and captured them" (v 14). Tens of thousands of inhabitants of Judah were then exiled to Ashur. With Sennacherib bearing down on him in Lachish to the south of Jerusalem, Hezekiah was in such danger that at first, he tried to buy him off (v 14).

But Hezekiah was a rebel, who wanted a free, independent Judah that would serve God. His courage in defying the Assyrian superpower should serve as an example for the true Israelites of today when they see how successive governments of the state of Israel have turned it into little more than a client state of foreign powers whose dictates are followed consistently even when they are clearly against the interest of the Jews and contrary to the purpose and destiny of the Holy Land.

"And the king of Ashur sent Tartan and Rav Saris and Ravshakeh from Lachish to King Hezekiah with a heavy force to Jerusalem..." (v 17). This was a major act of psychological warfare intended to frighten and demoralize the inhabitants of Jerusalem, who were effectively under siege, and to encourage them to capitulate and agree to "transfer", i.e. exile. According to tradition, Ravshakeh was himself a **Meshumad**, a "lapsed Jew" (see RaDaK on v 17, Rashi on v 22 and Sanhedrin 60a).

Standing at the walls of the city dramatically calling to Hezekiah's chief ministers to capitulate, Ravshakeh intentionally addressed them in the Judaic vernacular so that all the people could hear him as he emphasized the great might of Ashur and mocked the flimsiness of Judah's remaining army, their trust in Egypt and their very trust in HaShem.

A significant faction in Jerusalem were far from trusting that Hezekiah's courageous stand against Ashur was going to be successful, and one of the three royal ministers who stood on the ramparts of Jerusalem listening to Ravshakeh - Shevna the Scribe - was in fact a fifth-columnist who later tried to open the gates of Jerusalem to the Assyrians (RaDaK on v 18; see Isaiah 22:15ff).

Ravshakeh promised that if the people would give in willingly, the king of Ashur would take them "to a land like your land" (v 32) - he could not say "to a better land" because everybody listening would have known he was lying since there was no better land than Judah - not even the "land of grain and wine" he mentioned, namely N. Africa (Rashi on v 32). However, if the people were stubborn and refused his offer, Ravshakeh threatened the full might of Assyria against them, and we are left at the end of the chapter wondering how King Hezekiah will respond.

CHAPTER 19

On hearing from his ministers about Ravshakeh's blasphemy, King Hezekiah rent his garments over the desecration of God's Name (Rambam, Laws of Idolatry 2:10). As King David's worthy successor, Hezekiah's response to the Assyrian taunts was to turn only to God - through his own prayers and through sending a message to Isaiah, the prophet of the generation. Hezekiah's main plea in both his prayers and his message to the prophet was that God should avenge the affront to His Name.

In response, Isaiah prophesied of Sennacheriv: "Behold I shall put a spirit in him and he will hear a rumor and return to his land and I shall cause him to fall by the sword in his land" (v 7). As Rashi (ad loc.) explains, this prophecy was fulfilled in stages. The "rumor" that took Sennacheriv from Lachish near Jerusalem down to Egypt and North Africa was that Tirhakah king of Kush had decided to stand up to Ashur's sole world superpower aspirations. Sennacheriv went to fight against Kush and its allies, Phut and Egypt, and he was victorious, taking all their treasures. (RaDaK on v 7 explains that this was so that Judah would be greatly enriched with booty when the angel finally struck Sennacheriv's army.) The next stage of the prophecy - "he will return to his land" - was fulfilled after Sennacheriv lost his entire army in one night (v 35) and fled, and the last stage - "I shall cause him to fall by the sword in his land" -- took place when his own sons killed him (v 37).

Meanwhile Sennacheriv was still riding on the crest of his wave of success. From the battlefields of North Africa, Sennacheriv - swelled with pride - sent more emissaries to Jerusalem in order to intensify his psychological warfare against the tiny city under siege. The letters they brought were full of more ranting blasphemy as Sennacheriv paraded his many victories, unaware that they had come only because God had taken him as His rod and scourge against the nations for His own holy purpose. Through Sennacheriv's policy of exiling people from their own ancestral lands and moving them to areas with which they had no connection, he "mixed up all the nations" (Berachot 28a; Yoma 54a etc.). This in itself was in preparation for the eventual exile of Judah, just as "Joseph moved people from city to city as a reminder that they had no more share in the earth, and he sent the people of one city to another. His intention was to remove the disgrace from his brothers so that people would not be able to call them exiles" (Rashi on Genesis 47:21).

Hezekiah took the letters from the hands of Sennacheriv's emissaries and after reading them, went up to the Temple, where he "spread them out before God" (v 14). Of course, God knows everything, but when Hezekiah spread out the letters, he was teaching that when we pray, we should talk out everything that is on our minds and weighing in our hearts. Setting everything out before God in detail is an essential part of personal prayer.

Hezekiah's prayer vv 15-19 was a request to God to sanctify His name by thwarting Sennacheriv now despite all his earlier successes over idolatrous peoples in order to show that God alone rules and not idols of wood and stone. Hezekiah's argument is somewhat comparable to that of Moses when he interceded for Israel after the sin of the Golden Calf begging God not to destroy them so that the Egyptians should not be able to say that He was unable to save them in the wilderness (Ex. 32:12).

Isaiah's prophecy (20-34) is an eloquent affirmation that everything is in God's hands and that He raised up Sennacheriv and He will destroy him for the sake of David and Jerusalem.

But Sennacheriv was still riding high. Having completed his successful campaign against Kush and its allies, he again set his sights on Jerusalem and marched to Nov (whose priests had been killed by Saul), where he was poised ready to attack the nearby capital (Rashi on v 35). The outstanding miracle whereby his overwhelming forces were simply struck down in one night by God's angel is celebrated in the songs of the Pesach Seder night, on which it took place. The sages commented that while Pharaoh had uttered his blasphemies himself so that his armies were struck down at the Red Sea by God Himself, Sennacheriv's armies were destroyed by God's angel (**Mal'ach**) because Sennacheriv's blasphemies were delivered by an emissary (**Mal'ach**; Sanhedrin 94b-95a). It is said that his forces' bodies were burned up from the inside but their garments were left intact around them because they were from the descendants of Noah's son Shem, as it says, "The children of Shem, Eilam and Ashur" (Gen. 1:22), and Shem together with his brother Yaphet covered the nakedness of their father with a garment (Gen. 9:23). For this reason, God said to the Angel Michael, "Leave their garments and burn their souls" (Gen. 9:23; Shemot Rabbah 18:5).

Sennacheriv's ignominious end was his just desserts for his overweening pride and arrogance.

CHAPTER 20

"In those days, Hezekiah became mortally sick..." (v 1). Rashi (ad loc.) states that this took place three days before the destruction of Sennacheriv's army: it greatly adds to the drama of the mortally stricken king and his "great weeping" (v 3) when we understand that it took place precisely as the overwhelming hordes of Assyrian troops were encamped outside Jerusalem poised for their final attack. It looked like the very end for Judah, the House of David and the entire enterprise that started when Israel received the Torah at Sinai. There was an influential fifth column in Jerusalem ready to open the gates to Sennacheriv. Everything depended on the king - and the prophet was telling him "you are going to die..." - "in this world" - "...and you will not live" - "in the world to come" (Rashi).

A lesser person might have resigned himself to his terrible fate, but not Hezekiah, who said, "I have a tradition from the house of my father's father (=David) that even if a sharp sword is resting on a man's neck, he should not hold back from prayer" (Berachot 10a). "And he turned his face to the wall and prayed..." (v 2). Rabbi Nachman explains that the "face" is the person's inner spiritual and intellectual powers, while the "wall" is inside the stony heart, and that if our hearts are dulled and insensitive, we must turn our minds and intellectual powers and shine them into the heart (Rabbi Nachman's Wisdom #39).

Hezekiah prayed, "...please remember... that I did good in Your eyes" (v 3). From here we learn the power of arousing our good points in our personal prayers and Hitbodedut. The rabbis commented that Hezekiah was specifically alluding to his having put away the Book of Remedies in order to take away material means of healing so that people would have no other option but to pray, believe and trust in God for healing. Now Hezekiah himself was faced with the challenge of life-threatening illness - and his response was to repent completely and weep with all his heart.

Hezekiah's miraculous healing through the power of complete repentance is the archetype of Torah healing, and is discussed in detail in "Wings of the Sun: The Torah Healing Tradition".

The Talmud (Berachot 10a) teaches that the "sin" that led to the terrible decree against Hezekiah was that, having seen with holy spirit that he was destined to have a wicked son - his successor Menasheh - he refused to marry. The prophet castigated him for delving into Torah mysteries instead of carrying out the Torah commandment to procreate. Hezekiah asked if Isaiah would agree to give him his daughter in marriage so that they might produce righteous children, but Isaiah answered that the decree had already been made, and Hezekiah undertook to have children. In the merit of his complete repentance Hezekiah was granted healing and another fifteen years were added to his life (v 5).

TURNING THE CLOCK BACK

While still mortally sick but having heard the prophecy that he was to live, Hezekiah asked for a sign that he would indeed be healed and ascend to the House of God on the third day (v 9). Isaiah offered him his choice of a sign: either the sun would go forward by ten degrees on the special steps that were carefully positioned to serve as a natural clock like the sundial, or else it would go backwards. Hezekiah requested the harder option: that time should go backwards so as to have a ten-hour longer day (v 11) and the prophet called out to God, who sent the sign. It is said that on the day Hezekiah's idolatrous father Ahaz had died, the sun set ten hours early to leave no time for any eulogies, and now, to compensate, it set ten hours later.

Perhaps the miracle of time stopping still to make a longer day was a sign of the extra time Hezekiah was given to live and strengthen Judah in preparation for the decree of the destruction of the Temple and the exile to Babylon, which came about as the end result of his son Menasheh's idolatry in Jerusalem. The decree was irrevocable, but in Hezekiah's fifteen years of grace he was able to "stop the clock" for the time being, as it were, in order to continue with his spiritual revival in Judah.

ENTER BABYLON

Babylon, the very cradle of "civilization" in the era after Noah's flood (Genesis ch 11), was among the cities subject to Ashur at the height of its power (II Kings 14:24). The destruction of Sennacheriv's army at the gates of Jerusalem brought about the downfall of the Assyrian empire, enabling Babylon to advance to the center of the world stage. Babylon was destined to be the rod of chastisement that would complete the moralistic story of the Prophets with the destruction of Jerusalem and the exile of Judah. Everything had started in Babylon. Abraham had gone out from Babylon and the "furnace of the Kasdim" in search of the Promised Land, and it was to Babylon that Judah would have to return in order to prove that it is possible to observe and study the Torah even in exile.

Hezekiah's miraculous recovery was major news in the world of his time - it is said that on the day that time stopped still, the king of Babylon got up from his long post-breakfast/lunch sleep to find that it was morning. He thought it was already the next morning and was furious with his attendants for having let him sleep for so long, until they told him that the sun had gone backwards through the will of the God of Hezekiah (P'sikta 14; Rashi on v 12). It was on hearing this that the Babylonian king B'rodach Baladan ben Baladan sent greetings to Hezekiah (v 12).

In the latter's great exhilaration in the aftermath of his own miraculous healing and the sensational downfall of Sennacheriv's army, both of which took place on the same day, he very injudiciously took his exotic Babylonian visitors on a detailed tour of all his treasure-houses and inside the Temple itself, where he even opened up the Ark of the Covenant and showed them the Tablets of Stone (Rashi on v 13). It is most unwise to show all one's treasures to unknown strangers, and Hezekiah's indiscretion planted the seeds of the Babylonian appetite for the Temple treasures that resulted in their being looted when it was destroyed.

CHAPTER 21

KING MENASHEH

The account of King Menasheh and his 55 year reign as presented in our present chapter is one of unmitigated negativity, making it appear that he undid everything accomplished by his father King Hezekiah in the latter's whole-hearted return to the authentic Davidic pathway.

Menasheh is portrayed as a voracious idolater who introduced every possible kind of foreign idolatry into Jerusalem and into the very Temple itself, including not only the Baal and Asherah worship followed by Ahab but all the "abominations of Canaan", including Molech-worship and all the different kinds of forbidden divination (v 6).

The divine warnings to Menasheh that the consequent fate of Jerusalem would be one that would make the ears of all who heard it tingle (v 12) were delivered by the prophets Nahum and Habakuk (Rashi on v 10), but the voice of Isaiah was silenced, because Menasheh had him killed (Sanhedrin 103b). Thus, among Menasheh's crimes was that "he spilled very much innocent blood until it filled Jerusalem from one end to the other (=**peh la-peh**, lit. 'mouth to mouth'" (v 16). In the words of Yerushalmi Sanhedrin 10:2): "But how could any mortal fill Jerusalem with innocent blood from one end to the other? What this verse means is that he killed Isaiah, who was the equivalent to Moses, of whom it is said 'Mouth to mouth (**peh el peh**) shall speak with him' (Numbers 12:8)".

Yet in spite of the unmitigated negativity of our present chapter, we should avoid jumping to hasty conclusions about Menasheh. We should take a lesson from Rav Ashi, the Babylonian Amora who was the redactor of the Talmud Bavli. One day he was teaching his students the Mishnaic chapter "**chelek**" (Sanhedrin ch 10) discussing those who do and do not have a share in the world to come. Leaving off the day's class just before Mishnah 2, which lists the three kings who have no share in the world to come (Jeraboa'm, Ahab, and, according to one opinion, King Menasheh), Rav Ashi concluded by saying, "And tomorrow we'll start off with our friends (**chaverim**)" referring to the kings as if they were the same kind of people as Rav Ashi and his fellow scholars. That night King Menasheh appeared to Rav Ashi in a dream and said: "So you call us your friends and the friends of your father? Let me ask you where on the loaf should one cut when making **Ha-Motzi** (the blessing over bread)?" "I don't know," replied Rav Ashi. "You never learned where to cut the bread when you make **Ha-Motzi** and you call us your friends? You cut it where the crust is baked the most..." "Then why did you worship idols" asked Rav Ashi. "If you had been there," replied King Menasheh, "you would have taken hold of the bottom of your robe and come running after me" (Sanhedrin 102b).

In that mishnah, Rabbi Yehudah dissents from the opinion that King Menasheh had no world to come on the grounds that the more detailed account of his reign in II Chronicles chapter 33 tells us that he repented. Menasheh was undoubtedly taught Torah by his father Hezekiah, and he heard the dire warnings of the prophets of his day, yet nothing influenced him to repent except suffering. The remaining Assyrian armies came to Jerusalem and captured him, taking him to Babylon where they put him in a copper pot full of holes and lit an enormous furnace underneath. Targum on II Chronicles 33:12-13 tells how after calling out to all his idolatrous gods in vain, Menasheh finally cried out in pain to HaShem, and despite the protests of the angels, God then cut a tunnel beneath the throne of glory to hear and accept his repentance and prayer.

The remaining narrative in Chronicles tells how Menasheh was restored to the kingship in Jerusalem, where he repented, removed his idols from the Temple, and told the inhabitants of Judah to serve HaShem the God of Israel. "And Menasheh knew that HaShem is the God" (II Chronicles 33:13).

However, Menasheh's son King Amon, with the story of whose two-year reign our chapter concludes, reverted to the ways of the old Menasheh and not only worshipped all his idols but also burned the Torah and committed incest with his own mother (Sanhedrin 103:6).

CHAPTER 22

After the evil of Menasheh and Amon, the reign of King Josiah comes as the last burst of shining light before the inhabitants of Judah followed the Ten Tribes into exile and the Temple of Solomon was destroyed.

The reign and the very name of the saintly Josiah had been prophesied at the very beginning of the split between Judah and the Ten Tribes, when Jeraboa'm was sacrificing on his idolatrous altar and God's prophet called to the altar saying, "Behold a son is born to the house of David, Josiah is his name..." (I Kings 13:2).

How the eight-year old Josiah was able to turn from the corrupt ways of his evil father and grandfather is unknown. Perhaps the penitent Menasheh (who died when Josiah was six) saw his wayward son Amon and tried to do everything he could to inculcate in his little grandchild, third in line to the throne, the truth of HaShem as Menasheh now knew it.

Josiah's restoration of the Temple structure is reminiscent of that of his ancestor, King Joash (II Kings ch 12), the Hebrew letters of whose name are contained in the letters of the name **Yoshiahu** (="Joash"). Joash's restoration of the Temple had taken place 224 years earlier (RaDaK on v 4 of our present chapter). Since that time the evil kings (such as Joash's son Ahaz and Menasheh) had seriously modified and damaged the original Temple structure for idolatrous purposes, and even the saintly Hezekiah cut down the golden doors of the Sanctuary to pay off Sennacherib (II Kings 18:16). This was why the Temple was badly in need of repair, and its restoration was emblematic of the tremendous spiritual revival that occurred under Josiah, exemplified by the great national Passover celebration he held in Jerusalem, as described in II Kings:21ff and II Chronicles ch 35.

Our present chapter describes how, in the course of the Temple renovations the High Priest Hilkiah told the king's scribe, "I have found the scroll of the Torah in the House of HaShem." The "discovery" of this scroll has provided grist for the mills of Bible commentators of all colors, not least those who have set themselves up as the "Bible Critics", who gleefully point to this chapter in support of their claims that the Five Books of Moses were (**chas ve-shalom**) composed by a variety of later writers to support their own interests, and that the scroll of Deuteronomy with its dire warnings of destruction and exile which the priests now sent to the naïve young king was in fact a scam because the priests were simply interested in keeping the Temple going for their own sake.

To lovers of the Torah who revere and caress every letter of the sacred text in their search for God's truth, these claims are patently absurd, as well as being negated by the very text of the Book of Kings, where when King Amatziah killed the assassins of his father Joash, he specifically did not kill their children "as is written in the book of the Torah of Moses that HaShem commanded saying, fathers shall not die because of their children and children shall not die because of their fathers." (II Kings 14:6). The words of Moses quoted here appear precisely in the book of Deuteronomy (24:16), which was in the possession of King Amatziah two hundred years before its "discovery" in the time of Josiah.

The authentic Torah commentators explain that because Ahaz and some of the later wicked kings actually burned Torah scrolls, the priests were concerned that they might try to seize the Torah scroll that lay by the side of the Ark of the Covenant, which Moses had written from the mouth of God, and for this reason they hid it away. Later generations no longer knew where it was until it was discovered during the Temple renovations under Josiah (Metzudat David on v 8; cf. RaDaK at length ad loc.).

Our sages had the tradition that the scroll found now in the Temple was rolled up so that it opened at the curse in Deuteronomy 28:36: "HaShem will take you and the king that you shall set up over you to a people that you did not know..." (Yoma 52b).

Hearing the reading of the curses of Deuteronomy so moved the tender young Josiah that he sent to Huldah the Prophetess. The question is asked why he sent to her since the Tzaddik of the Generation was now the prophet Jeremiah, who began to prophesy in the thirteenth year of Josiah's reign, five years before the discovery of the scroll (see v 3). According to some opinions, Jeremiah was then absent from Jerusalem on his mission to try to restore the Ten Tribes, some of whom he did indeed succeed in bringing home to the Land of Israel. Others say that Josiah sent to Huldah because women are more compassionate (Megillah 14b).

Huldah was one of the descendants of Rahab the harlot (Joshua ch 2ff). The "second quarter" where Huldah sat in Jerusalem – **ba-Mishneh** (v 14 of our present chapter) - was outside the gate of the Temple courtyard that was called after her (Middot 1:3), where she taught the **Mishnah** (Oral Law) to the elders of the generation (Rashi on v 14). Until today the bricked-up gate in the southern wall of the Temple Mount is called Huldah's Gate, and those who meditate near this holy spot may feel something of the spirit of the ancient prophetess.

With all her compassion, Huldah could not hide the decree of doom and destruction hanging over Judah and Jerusalem, but could only assure the king that it would not be fulfilled in his days. The wise, saintly king took her message to heart. Although it is not recorded here, he took the precaution of hiding away the Ark of the Covenant and the Torah scroll of Moses that lay with it (together with the flask of the Manna and Aaron's rod) in the underground channels that Solomon had ingeniously built into the structure of the Temple Mount (see II Chronicles 35:3 and Yoma 52b).

CHAPTER 23

*** II Kings 23:1-9 and 21-25 are read as the Haftarah in
Diaspora communities on the Second Day of Pesach ***

The great cleansing performed by Josiah in the Temple, Jerusalem and its environs shows the extent of the proliferation of idolatry in Judah in the previous generations. As discussed in a number of earlier commentaries, the idolatries involved were not just a matter of prostrating to some piece of wood or stone: they were backed up by elaborate theologies and sophisticated astrology, divination, occult arts etc. We get a picture of Jerusalem in the period just before Josiah as a kind of international center of pantheistic multiculturalism. Our present chapter enumerates virtually every kind of idolatry and divination proscribed in Torah sources. From v 13 we see that the cult centers built around Jerusalem by Solomon's wives were still there. Thus, the flaw of idolatry that led to the destruction of the Temple had its roots in the foreign marriages of the very king who built it, even if his original intention was to bring the realm of the unholy under the dominion of the holy.

All these idolatrous cult centers were destroyed by Josiah in a mission of national cleansing that even took him to Beit El and Shomron, the main idolatrous centers of the fallen kingdom of Israel. Josiah's destruction of the altar of Beit El and its priests was in fulfillment of the prophecy of Ido when Jerabo'am first sacrificed there (I Kings 13:2) and the false prophet who detained Ido after his mission was wise to ask to be buried next to him, as his bones were thus saved from being dug up and burned in the merit of Ido (ibid. vv 31-2; our chapter vv 17-18).

After all this cleansing, King Josiah held a jubilant Pesach in Jerusalem the like of which had not been seen since the days of Samuel prior to the division of the kingdom. Josiah struck a Covenant with the people to serve God faithfully and follow His commandments (v 3).

Yet after all this: "But HaShem did not turn from the burning of His great anger against Judah, over all the provocations with which Menasheh provoked Him" (v 26). Why did He not, when under Josiah the people renewed the Covenant with God? In the words of Metzudat David (ad loc): "Although Josiah repented with all his heart and taught the people the ways of HaShem, secretly the people still held to the provocations of Menasheh, wanting to serve idols just like him."

JOSIAH AGAINST PHARAOH NECHO

The campaign against Pharaoh Necho by Josiah was a literally fatal error which had the same effect as the various schemes based on mistaken calculations that were employed by the last kings of Judah who succeeded him, all of which simply brought the destined exile closer.

By the closing years of Josiah's reign, the empire of Ashur was crumbling, and initially the king of Judah showed great skill in taking advantage of the situation, expanding the boundaries of his kingdom until in his eighteenth year he was able to take his campaign of cleansing from idolatry up to Shomron itself, which had previously been an Assyrian client state, and he ruled over all of the Land of Israel (see II Chronicles 34:33). He may also have held sway over territories east of the River Jordan, as had Hezekiah in his time.

The decline of Ashur also filled Josiah's powerful southern neighbor Egypt with renewed imperial aspirations. Egypt hoped that by lending a hand to the embattled Assyrians against the rising star of Babylon, she herself would be able to establish her own supremacy over the entire swathe of territory west of the Euphrates all the way to Egypt (see ch 24 v 7). Pharaoh Necho wanted to strike down the Babylonians at Kharkhemish (today called Jerablus), a strategic stronghold in the upper valley of the Euphrates near the present-day Syrian-Turkish border about 100 km north east of Aleppo. In order to advance to Kharkhemish, Pharaoh Necho had to march his troops all the way along the coastal plain of the Land of Israel before turning east some way south of Haifa in order to make his way inland and up into Syria.

The rabbis stated that the reason why the saintly King Josiah went out to try to stop him was because he sought to bring the Land of Israel to a messianic state of peace where the promise would be fulfilled: "…And no sword shall pass through your Land" (Leviticus 26:6). Josiah interpreted this verse to mean not only that no enemy would come up against Israel but also that no foreign army would pass through the Land even if they were only on their way elsewhere (see RaDaK on v 29).

In order to intercept Pharaoh Necho as he made his push from Israel's coastal strip inland, Josiah went up to Megiddo, which is in the hills running along the south side of Emek Yizre'el (by Route 65 about halfway between Umm Al-Fahm and Afula). There Josiah met his death, which was a disaster for Judah as he had no worthy, righteous successor. Josiah's death was mourned in a special elegy composed by the prophet Jeremiah (II Chron. 35:25; Lamentations ch 3).

Initially the people of Judah chose Yeho-ahaz to succeed Josiah even though he was not his oldest son. The reason they **anointed** him (v 30) was precisely because he had at least one rival with stronger claims to the throne: it may be that the leaders of Judah hoped that Yeho-ahaz would be a more assertive leader on the international stage than his older brother.

Pharaoh Necho meanwhile had been temporarily successful at Kharkhemish and came back to Egypt via Israel, where he installed Yeho-ahaz's older brother El-yakim as king, renaming him Yeho-yakim. However, Egypt retained her influence for no more than four years, after which Nebuchadnezzar struck Pharaoh, who thereafter did not any more go out of his land, as we read in the following chapter.

CHAPTER 24

The last kings of Judah appear to have been divinely inspired to misread the new geopolitical reality that was taking shape with the decline of Assyria, believing that they could defy the rising star of Babylon by depending on Egypt, which also wanted to thwart Babylon. In this way, they deafened their ears to the message of Jeremiah and the other prophets, who were consistently warning not to depend on the "broken reed" of Egypt and not to meddle in international politics but rather to accept the divine decree of exile and submit to Babylon (see Jeremiah ch 25). The prophets also emphasized that if the king swore allegiance to a foreign power with an oath in God's Name, he was obliged to keep his oath and forbidden to scheme and rebel, which would be a desecration of the Name.

"But by the mouth of God it was against Judah, to remove him from before Him..." (v 3). Pharaoh Necho was struck by Nebuchadnezzar and could not help Judah even if he had ever wanted to. Yeho-yakim plotted against Nebuchadnezzar, who captured him to take him to Babylon. During the journey Yeho-yakim was tortured and died. He was succeeded by his son Yeho-yachin, but the latter ruled no more than three months in Jerusalem before being taken into exile by the Babylonians together with a total of ten thousand "mighty warriors" (v 14) consisting of three thousand of the choicest members of the tribe of Judah (including the greatest sages and scholars, see Rashi ad loc.) and seven thousand members of Benjamin and the other Ten Tribes who had returned from exile under Sennacheriv.

The exile of King Yeho-yachin, also known as Yechoniah, is the exile mentioned in Megillat Esther (2:6) which eventually brought Mordechai and Esther to Shushan. This was eighteen years before the destruction of the Temple. Those who accepted the divine decree and moved to Babylon did so with dignity and soon succeeded in establishing thriving communities devoted to Torah and prayer in their place of exile.

As king over those who remained in Judah (where the Temple still stood for the moment) Nebuchadnezzar now appointed Yeho-yachin's uncle **Mataniyah**, who was the son of Josiah and a brother of the late king Yeho-ahaz (see RaDaK at length on II Kings 23:29). The Babylonian king hoped that the new king would remain loyal, changing his name to **Tzidkiyahu** as if to say, "God will justifiably exact judgment against you if you rebel against me". The new king swore allegiance, but even as he did so he was already plotting to rebel.

CHAPTER 25

The grim closing chapter of the Book of Kings laconically records stage by stage the destruction of the Temple and Jerusalem, the cruel fate of Tzidkiyahu king of Judah and other leading figures of the priesthood and royal court, the exile of most of the remaining population of Judea to Babylon and the final collapse of the last vestiges of Judean independence with the assassination of Gedaliah son of Achikam.

Our present text is supplemented by the parallel account in II Chronicles ch 36 and in particular by the detailed narrative in Jeremiah chs 37-44 & 52, as well as in various passages in Ezekiel, who prophesied in Babylon during the period of the destruction of the First Temple. The full horror of the siege and capture of Jerusalem and the subsequent exile is graphically expressed in Lamentations and its accompanying midrashim as well as in many passages in the **Kinot** ("mourning dirges") recited on the anniversary of the destruction of the Temple on Tisha Be-Av (the 9th of the month of Av, July-August).

Nebuchadnezzar began his siege of Jerusalem "in the tenth month on the tenth of the month" (v 1). This is commemorated by the Fast of the 10th of Tevet (December-January), the tenth month counting from Nissan.

In verse 4 we learn that the city walls were breached "on the ninth of the month", and in Jeremiah 52:6 we learn that this was in the fourth month (=Tammuz, July). The Jerusalem Talmud (Ta'anit 4) brings an opinion that as a result of the great distress and confusion at that time, the actual date was confused, and that the breach in the city walls in fact took place on the 17th of Tammuz, the same date as the breach in the walls of Jerusalem by the Romans in the time of the destruction of the Second Temple. These events are thus commemorated in the fast of the 17th of Tammuz.

Rashi on v 4 tells us that King Tzidkiyahu had a secret tunnel that led from his house to the plains of Jericho through which he tried to flee. However, the Holy One blessed be He arranged that a deer passed by over the opening of the cave outside the city, and when some Babylonian troops chased after the deer they saw the king and captured him, fulfilling the prophecy of Ezekiel, "And I shall spread My net upon him and he will be caught in My trap" (Ezekiel 12:13).

Although we read in the previous chapter that Tzidkiyahu "did evil in the eyes of HaShem" (II Kings 24:19), the rabbis said that in fact Tzidkiyahu was the saving grace of his generation: "The Holy One blessed be He wanted to return the whole world to formlessness and void on account of the generation of Tzidkiyahu, but when he looked at Tzidkiyahu He calmed down. Then why does it say that 'he did evil in God's eyes'? Because he had the power to protest against what the people of his generation were doing but he failed to do so" (Sanhedrin 103a).

"And in the fifth month on the seventh of the month. he burned the House of God." (vv 8-9). The fifth month is Av. The parallel account in Jeremiah (52:12) states that the burning of the Temple took place on the **tenth** of the month of Av. The rabbis resolved the discrepancy by explaining that the Babylonians entered the Sanctuary on the 7th of Av and then ate, drank and desecrated and damaged the Temple until the late afternoon of the 9th, when they set it on fire, and it kept on burning until it was completely destroyed on the 10th (Ta'anit 29a). Since the moment when the Temple was actually set on fire was the most serious, the fast commemorating its destruction was fixed on the 9th of Av.

"And every **great** house he burned with fire" (v 9): this refers to the study halls and synagogues of Jerusalem, which were destroyed together with everything else (Rashi ad loc.)

Many of the Temple treasures had already been looted in earlier raids (II Kings 24:13), including the gold with which Solomon had overlaid the carved wood paneling that covered the Temple walls on the interior. The account of the bronze vessels that were now looted, including Solomon's pool and the massive pillars with their ornate capitals that flanked the entrance to the Sanctuary Vestibule (**Oolam**) echoes the account of how these glorious adornments were originally made by Hiram four centuries earlier (I Kings ch 7) in order to enhance our understanding of the magnitude of the disaster that now struck.

Unlike the Assyrians, the Babylonians did not go in for population **exchange**, but simply exiled most of the Judean population to Babylon without importing other peoples to occupy their former lands. Thus, Judea was mostly left barren and empty, except for "the poor of the land" who were left to be "vine-dressers and field-workers" (v 12). According to the rabbis, these "vine-dressers" were in fact left to collect the luxury balsam oil from Eyn Gedi and the surrounding areas, while the "field-workers" continued to harvest the **chilazon** snails whose blood was used in the manufacture of **techeilet** blue-dye from the coastal strip from Tyre to Haifa (Shabbat 26a).

The Babylonians left Gedaliah son of Achikam as governor over the remaining Jewish population in Judea. Gedaliah, who was a Tzaddik, followed the policy endorsed by the prophets of accepting the decree of subjugation to Babylon and collaborating with the occupying power. Because of this he was assassinated by those who stubbornly persisted in the belief that they could still fight for Judean independence. His assassination, which is described in greater detail in Jeremiah and which led to the final collapse of the last vestige of Jewish semi-independence in Judah, is commemorated annually by the Fast of Gedaliah on the 3rd of Tishri, immediately following the two-day Rosh HaShanah festival.

Our present chapter thus enumerates all the events that are commemorated in the four annual fasts relating to the destruction of the Temple: the 17th of Tammuz, 9th of Av, 3rd of Tishri and 10th of Tevet.

Only in the closing verses of this chapter (vv 27-30) is there any relief from the overall gloom with the account of how immediately after the death of Nebuchadnezzar, his son and successor Eveel Merodakh released Yeho-yachin (who had been exiled and deposed from the throne of Judah in favor of Tzidkiyahu) from prison. The Babylonian king gave Yeho-yachin food from his table. Thus, the very curse that King David had put on his commander-in-chief Joab - that his descendants would be lacking in bread - was fulfilled on David's own descendant, who depended for bread on the king of Babylon (Sanhedrin 48b).

May we speedily see the fulfillment of the prophecy of Zechariah that "the fast of the fourth and the fast of the fifth and the fast of the seventh and the fast of the tenth (months) will be for rejoicing and happiness for the House of Judah" (Zechariah 8:19).

9 780995 656062